Object-Oriented ActionScript for Flash 8

Peter Elst and Todd Yard
with Sas Jacobs and William Drol

friendsof

DESIGNER TO DESIGNER™

an Apress® company

Object-Oriented ActionScript for Flash 8

ISBN-13 (pbk): 978-1-59059-619-7

ISBN-10 (pbk): 1-59059-619-6

Printed and bound in the United States of America 9 8 7 6 5 4 3

Distributed to the book trade worldwide by Springer-Verlag New York, Inc., 233 Spring Street, 6th Floor, New York, NY 10013. Phone 1-800-SPRINGER, fax 201-348-4505, e-mail orders-ny@springer-sbm.com, or visit www.springeronline.com.

For information on translations, please contact Apress directly at 2560 Ninth Street, Suite 219, Berkeley, CA 94710. Phone 510-549-5930, fax 510-549-5939, e-mail info@apress.com, or visit www.apress.com.

The information in this book is distributed on an "as is" basis, without warranty. Although every precaution has been taken in the preparation of this work, neither the author(s) nor Apress shall have any liability to any person or entity with respect to any loss or damage caused or alleged to be caused directly or indirectly by the information contained in this work.

The source code for this book is freely available to readers at www.friendsofed.com in the Downloads section.

Credits

Lead Editor Chris Mills	**Assistant Production Director** Kari Brooks-Copony
Technical Reviewers Jared Tarbell, Stephen Downs	**Production Editor** Katie Stence
	Compositor Dina Quan
Editorial Board Steve Anglin, Dan Appleman, Ewan Buckingham, Gary Cornell, Jason Gilmore, Jonathan Hassell, James Huddleston, Chris Mills, Matthew Moodie, Dominic Shakeshaft, Jim Sumser, Matt Wade	**Proofreader** April Eddy
	Indexer Michael Brinkman
Project Manager Sofia Marchant	**Artist** April Milne
Copy Edit Manager Nicole LeClerc	**Interior and Cover Designer** Kurt Krames
Copy Editor Ami Knox	**Manufacturing Director** Tom Debolski

*Dedicated to everyone at Macromedia, now Adobe, for their years
of unceasing commitment to the Flash community.
—Peter Elst*

*Dedicated to my wife, Lydian, who loves me despite the fact that after
all the hours I spent on this book she only gets this sentence.
—Todd Yard*

CONTENTS AT A GLANCE

Foreword xv

About the Authors xvi

About the Technical Reviewer xvii

Acknowledgments xviii

PART ONE: OOP AND ACTIONSCRIPT xx

Chapter 1: Introduction to OOP 1

Chapter 2: Programming Concepts 11

Chapter 3: ActionScript 2.0 Programming 19

PART TWO: FLASH OOP GUIDELINES 32

Chapter 4: Planning 33

Chapter 5: Project Workflow 49

Chapter 6: Best Practices 65

PART THREE: CORE OOP CONCEPTS 82

Chapter 7: Encapsulation 83

Chapter 8: Classes 103

Chapter 9: Inheritance **121**

Chapter 10: Polymorphism **135**

Chapter 11: Interfaces **145**

Chapter 12: Design Patterns **157**

Chapter 13: Case Study: An OOP Media Player **201**

PART FOUR: BUILDING AND EXTENDING A DYNAMIC FRAMEWORK **240**

Chapter 14: Framework Overview **241**

Chapter 15: Manager Classes **259**

Chapter 16: UI Widgets **279**

Chapter 17: OOP Animation and Effects **333**

PART FIVE: DATA INTEGRATION **382**

Chapter 18: Interrelationships and Interactions Between Components **383**

Chapter 19: Communication Between Flash and the Browser **417**

Chapter 20: Server Communication (XML and Web Services) **439**

Chapter 21: Case Study: Time Sheet Application **483**

Index **521**

CONTENTS

Foreword . . . . **xv**

About the Authors . . . . **xvi**

About the Technical Reviewer . . . . **xvii**

Acknowledgments . . . . **xviii**

PART ONE: OOP AND ACTIONSCRIPT . . . . **xx**

Chapter 1: Introduction to OOP **1**

The scoop with OOP? 2
Understanding the object-oriented approach 2
    Classes and objects 3
    Properties 3
    Encapsulation: Hiding the details 4
    Polymorphism: Exhibiting similar features 7
    Inheritance: Avoid rebuilding the wheel 8
What's next? 9

Chapter 2: Programming Concepts **11**

About programming slang 12
Building blocks of programming 13
    Variables 13
        About variable data 14
    Arrays 14

Functions 15
    About calling functions 15
    About function parameters 15
Loops 16
Conditionals 16
OOP concepts 16
What's next? 17

Chapter 3: ActionScript 2.0 Programming **19**

ActionScript 1.0 vs. ActionScript 2.0 20
    Declaring variables 20
    Classes vs. prototypes 21
    Public and private scope 25
Strong typing and code hints 27
ActionScript trouble spots 29
    Case sensitivity 29
    Declaring variables 30
    Use of the this keyword 30
What's next? 31

PART TWO: FLASH OOP GUIDELINES **32**

Chapter 4: Planning **33**

The importance of planning 34
    Initial phase: Planning reusability! 35
    Planning encapsulation 35
    Planning inheritance 36

Analyzing a Flash ActionScript project 39
    Flash files run on the client 39
    Securing data sent to the server 39
    Parsing data in Flash 40
Introduction to UML modeling 40
    Why use UML? 41
        UML offers standardized notation and has a language-neutral syntax 41
        UML can be used to model anything 42
    Class diagram 42
    Association and generalization 43
    Aggregation and composition 44
What's next? 46

Chapter 5: Project Workflow **49**

Introducing version control 50
    About Concurrent Versions System 50
    Using TortoiseCVS 52
Approaches to programming 58
    Rapid Application Development 59
    Extreme Programming 60
Usability testing 62
What's next? 63

Chapter 6: Best Practices **65**

External ActionScript 66
About commenting 68
Naming conventions 70
    Variables 70
    Constants 71
    Functions 71
    Classes 71
    Methods 72
    Properties 72
    Packages 72
Programming styles 73
Alternative programming styles 77
    Coding practices: Todd Yard 77
    Coding practices: Sas Jacobs 79
        Commenting code 79
        Naming conventions 80
What's next? 81

PART THREE: CORE OOP CONCEPTS ... 82

Chapter 7: Encapsulation ... 83

Setting up encapsulation ... 84
   Creating new layers ... 85
   Drawing a background ... 87
   Aligning and locking the background ... 87
   Drawing a ball ... 88
   Converting the ball into a Library symbol ... 89
   Content summary ... 90
Writing the code ... 91
   Creating an event handler ... 91
   What about encapsulation? ... 93
   Testing the event handler ... 94
   Updating the Ball ... 95
Improving the code ... 96
   Enhancing behavior with properties ... 96
   Narrowing the focus with functions ... 97
Encapsulation summary ... 99
What's next? ... 101

Chapter 8: Classes ... 103

Classes vs. prototypes ... 104
   Constructors ... 106
   About this ... 109
   Methods ... 112
   Anonymous functions ... 113
Implementing a class ... 116
   The Mover class ... 116
What's next? ... 118

Chapter 9: Inheritance ... 121

About class hierarchy ... 122
A quick inheritance test ... 122
   About inheritance syntax ... 125
The Bouncer class ... 126
The Gravity class ... 129
Inheritance summary ... 133
What's next? ... 133

Chapter 10: Polymorphism 135

Building a polymorphism example 136
Implementing polymorphism for application reuse 138
    Basic concept of polymorphism 138
    Functional polymorphism at work 139
What's next? 142

Chapter 11: Interfaces 145

Interfaces overview 146
    Interface use-cases 147
    What an interface looks like 147
Implementing an interface 148
What's next? 155

Chapter 12: Design Patterns 157

Understanding design patterns 158
Implementing design patterns 160
    Observer pattern 160
        Basic implementation 160
        Practical implementation 167
        Extending the practical implementation 169
    Singleton pattern 171
        Basic implementation 172
        Practical implementation 177
        Building an interface 181
    Decorator pattern 183
        Basic implementation 183
        Practical implementation 184
        Applying the Decorator pattern 186
    Model-View-Controller pattern 191
        Basic implementation 192
        Practical implementation 193
        Bringing together the Model, View, and Controller 196
Design patterns summary 197
What's next? 198

Chapter 13: Case Study: An OOP Media Player 201

Planning the player 202
    Picking a pattern 202
    Guaranteeing methods and datatypes with an interface 203
    Examining class structure 204

Building the media player 206
   IntervalManager 207
   Defining the interfaces 209
   Dispatching events 209
      Media interfaces 214
   Controlling media 215
      Defining properties 215
      Private methods 216
      Public methods 218
   Controlling FLVs 222
   Building a video view 228
   Controlling SWFs 229
   Building a SWF view 236
   Controlling MP3s 238
Summary 239
What's next? 239

**PART FOUR: BUILDING AND EXTENDING A
DYNAMIC FRAMEWORK** **240**

Chapter 14: Framework Overview **241**

Introducing the framework 242
Understanding the MovieClip class 246
Understanding the UIObject class (mx.core.UIObject) 253
Understanding the UIComponent class (mx.core.UIComponent) 255
Understanding the View class (mx.core.View) 256
Framework summary 257
What's next? 257

Chapter 15: Manager Classes **259**

Planning the framework 260
   What to manage 260
   Diagramming the classes 261
Building managers 263
   StyleFormat 263
   StyleManager 266
   Adding style 269
   SoundManager 272
   Sounding off 275
Summary 277
What's next? 277

Chapter 16: UI Widgets 279

Diagramming the classes 280
    UIObject 280
    Block 283
    SimpleButton 284
Making the foundation 285
Basic building block 292
Building a component 294
Skinning a widget 303
Changing state 307
Adding some style 308
More ways to skin a cat 313
Attaching from scratch 316
Tying in events 320
Pulling it all together 325
Summary 329
What's next? 330

Chapter 17: OOP Animation and Effects 333

Preparing for animation 334
    Animator 335
Tweening properties and values 336
    Tweener 336
    Easer 341
    Testing the Tweener 344
    Enhancing Tweener 347
    Mover 354
    Motion blur 357
Transitioning views 360
    Transition 360
    FadeTransition 363
    Testing transitions 364
    ColorTransition 369
    BlurTransition 371
    NoiseTransition 374
    DissolveTransition and WaterTransition 376
Summary 381
What's next? 381

PART FIVE: DATA INTEGRATION **382**

**Chapter 18: Interrelationships and Interactions
Between Components** **383**

    Data binding 384
        The mx.data.binding package 385
        Creating a simple binding 386
            Creating EndPoints 386
            Specifying a location 387
            Creating the binding 388
            Using the execute method 388
    Working through a simple binding example 389
    Using formatters 395
        Using built-in formatters 396
            Using the Boolean formatter 396
            Using the Compose String formatter 396
            Using the Date formatter 397
            Using the Rearrange Fields formatter 397
            Using the Number formatter 397
        Working through a simple formatting example 398
        Understanding custom formatters 404
    Including validators 406
        Working with built-in validators 407
        Working with a custom validator 413
    Summary 415
    What's next? 415

**Chapter 19: Communication Between Flash and
the Browser** **417**

    Communication with Flash Player 7 and below 419
        Sending variables into Flash 419
        Calling JavaScript from Flash 419
        Using the Flash/JS Integration Kit 421
    Understanding the ExternalInterface class 423
        Understanding Flash Player 8 security 424
        Using the call method 424
        Using the addCallback method 429
        ActionScript communication with other languages 434
            Calling a non-JavaScript method 434
            Calling an ActionScript method from an application 435
    Summary 435
    What's next? 436

Chapter 20: Server Communication (XML and Web Services) 439

Understanding XML 440
   XML declarations 442
Using XML in Flash 443
   XMLConnector component 443
   XML class 447
What are web services? 454
Understanding SOAP 454
Talking to web services 456
   WebServiceConnector component 456
   WebService class 464
Flash Player security sandbox 478
   System.security.allow.Domain() 478
   Cross-domain policy files 478
   Using a server-side proxy script 480
Summary 480
What's next? 481

Chapter 21: Case Study: Time Sheet Application 483

Planning the application 484
Structuring the application 485
Writing stub code 487
   Model-View-Controller classes 487
      TimeSheetModel class (Model) 487
      TimeSheetView class (View) 488
      TimeSheetController class (Controller) 490
   Project and Task classes 491
      Project class 491
      Task class 492
   Bringing it all together 493
   Initializing the layout 493
   Adding a project 495
   Displaying projects 498
   Adding a task 501
   Project and task details 506
   Running a task timer 510
   Persisting time sheet data 512
   Summary 517
   Conclusion 518

Index 521

FOREWORD

If there's one thing I've learned as a developer, it's this: Complexity happens; simplicity, you have to consistently strive for. Nowhere is this truer than in education. Our role as teachers, by definition, is to simplify subjects so that they can be easily understood. A good teacher dispels trepidation with anecdote, abstraction with analogy, superstition and magic with knowledge.

Simplicity, however, is not easily attained. In order to simplify, you must first gain an encompassing understanding of the complex. It is a rare person who can simultaneously exist in both the simple and complex plains of a problem domain and communicate effectively at both levels. It is, however, these rare people who make the best teachers.

Object-oriented programming (OOP) is a subject that many Flash developers do not approach due to a widespread erroneous perception of its enormous scope and complexity. Nothing could be further from the truth.

The core concepts behind OOP are simple enough for a primary school student with a particularly nasty case of Hynerian flu to understand in a single sitting.

It must be because OOP is essentially such a simple concept that we sometimes feel the need to protect ourselves with important-sounding words the length of major rivers in order to explain it. Because, hey, if we said that OOP involves the interaction of objects, each of which is an instance of a certain blueprint and has certain traits and behaviors—well, that would just be too simple. Who'd respect our geeky prowess then? Instead, we lock ourselves in our ivory towers, hiding behind unscalable walls of inheritance, composition, polymorphism, and encapsulation, and hope that the FlashKit masses will tend to their tweens and leave us to meditate on the path to programming nirvana.

Unfortunately, OOP is so often presented in such pretentious prose so as to be illegible to all but a handful of PhDs. If grandiose, self-important passages of academic rambling are what you're after, then you should put this book down and walk away now. I'm sure you'll find an 800-page hardback elsewhere to satisfy your thirst for confusion. If, however, you are looking for a pragmatic guide to OOP and ActionScript 2 (AS2) that is simply written and easy to understand, you could do far worse than to look through these pages more closely.

Aral Balkan
2 January 2006
Famagusta, Cyprus

ABOUT THE AUTHORS

Peter Elst is a Flash-certified professional and former Team Macromedia volunteer, and he runs his own company, named MindStudio, doing mostly freelance Flash and Flex consultancy, development, and training. As a valued contributor to the online Flash community, Peter has presented at numerous international events and conferences and has had his work published in leading magazines and websites.

Over the years, the focus of his work changed from interactive animations to multimedia applications, e-learning, and content management systems. Peter is user group manager for the MMUG Belgium and blogs on his personal website: www.peterelst.com.

Sas Jacobs is a web developer who loves working with Flash. She set up her business, Anything Is Possible, in 1994, working in the areas of web development, IT training, and technical writing. The business works with large and small clients building web applications with ASP.NET, Flash, XML, and databases.

Sas has spoken at such conferences as Flash Forward, MXDU, and FlashKit on topics relating to XML and dynamic content in Flash. In her spare time, Sas is passionate about traveling, photography, running, and enjoying life. You can find out more about her at www.sasjacobs.com.

Todd Yard is currently a Flash developer at Brightcove in Cambridge, Massachusetts, where he moved early in 2005 in the middle of a blizzard. Previously, he was in New York City, where he initially moved in 1996 in the middle of a blizzard, working with EGO7 on their Flash content management system and community software while freelancing with agencies developing web applications for clients such as GE and IBM. Todd originally hails from Phoenix, where there are no blizzards, and has written for a number of friends of ED books, of which his favorites are *Flash MX Studio* and *Flash MX Application and Interface Design*, though he feels *Extending Flash MX 2004: Complete Guide and Reference to JavaScript Flash* is probably the most useful. His personal site, which he used to update all the time, he fondly remembers, is www.27Bobs.com.

William Drol entered Macromedia Flash development with a varied background in object-oriented programming and graphic design. His first experience with Macromedia was the admittedly quirky but OOP-based Macromedia Director and Lingo. Today, there are many reasons to be excited about Flash MX and the hugely improved ActionScript. Drol looks forward to integrating Flash MX with web services, and he pursues other technologies such as XML, XSLT, and his current favorite, Microsoft C#. Learn more about the author at http://www.billdrol.com.

ABOUT THE TECHNICAL REVIEWERS

Tink, a.k.a. **Stephen Downs**, has been a freelance Flash designer/developer for the past four years, and he has a background in art, design, and photography. Based in London, England, he works on a wide range of projects, both for other companies and his own clients.

He has worked on projects with various agencies for brands such as MTV, Xbox, AMD Athlon, PG Tips, AGCO, Interflora, Motorola, Shockwave.com, UK Government, French Music Bureau, and many more. The growth in his workload has recently lead to the startup of Tink LTD.

His primary focus is user interaction and interactive motion, integrating design, and development using best practice methodologies.

www.tink.ws
www.tink.ws/blog

Jared Tarbell was born in 1973 to William and Suzon Davis Tarbell in the high-altitude desert city of Albuquerque, New Mexico. First introduced to personal computers in 1987, Jared's interest in computation has grown in direct proportion to the processing power of these machines. Jared holds a Bachelor of Science degree in Computer Science from New Mexico State University. He sits on the Board of the Austin Museum of Digital Art where he helps promote and encourage appreciation of the arts within the global community. Jared is most interested in the visualization of large data sets, and the emergent, life-like properties of complex computational systems. Jared has recently returned to Albuquerque to work closer to friends and family while enjoying the unique aspects of desert living.

Additional work from Jared Tarbell can be found at levitated.net and complexification.net.

ACKNOWLEDGMENTS

Special thanks to Jared Tarbell and Tink for their thorough technical review; to Chris, Sofia, and the rest of the friends of ED/Apress team for their help and patience in getting this book written; and to coauthors Todd and Sas for their excellent chapters!

Peter Elst

PART ONE **OOP AND ACTIONSCRIPT**

1 INTRODUCTION TO OOP

Object-oriented programming (OOP) sounds much scarier than it actually is. Essentially OOP is nothing more than a way of looking at a particular problem and breaking it down into smaller pieces called *objects*. These objects form the building blocks of object-oriented applications, and when designed properly they help form a solid framework on which to build your project.

The scoop with OOP?

Before OOP became commonplace, we had something called *procedural programming*, which often required developers to write very complex and highly interdependent code. A minor change to any part of the code could spell disaster for the entire application. Debugging that type of application was a terribly painful and time-consuming task that often resulted in the need to completely rebuild large pieces of code.

When more and more user interaction got introduced in applications, it became apparent that procedural programming wouldn't cut it. Object-oriented programming was born as an attempt to solve these very problems. Although it certainly isn't the be-all and end-all of successful programming, OOP does give developers a great tool for handling any kind of application development.

The wonderful thing about object-oriented thinking is that you can look at practically any item in terms of a collection of objects. Let's look at a car for example. To the average Joe, a car is simply a vehicle (or object) that gets you places. If you ask a mechanic about a car, he'll most likely tell you about the engine, the exhaust, and all sorts of other parts. All these car parts can also be thought of as individual objects that work together to form a larger object, "the car." None of these parts actually know the inner workings of the other parts, and yet they work (or should work) together seamlessly.

Understanding the object-oriented approach

> *"'See that bird?' he says. 'It's a Spencer's warbler. (I knew he didn't know the real name.) Well, in Italian, it's a Chutto Lapittida. In Portuguese, it's a Bom da Peida. In Chinese, it's a Chung-long-tah, and in Japanese, it's a Katano Tekeda. You can know the name of that bird in all the languages of the world, but when you're finished, you'll know absolutely nothing whatever about the bird. You'll only know about humans in different places, and what they call the bird. So let's look at the bird and see what it's doing, that's what counts.'"*
>
> —*Richard Feynman*

When studying OOP you'll come across a *plethora* of big words like *encapsulation, polymorphism, and inheritance*. Truth be told the ideas behind them are often quite simple, and there's no real need to memorize those terms unless you'd like to use them for showing off at your next family get-together.

Knowing the theory behind this terminology is, however, essential, and that's just what we'll be discussing next.

Classes and objects

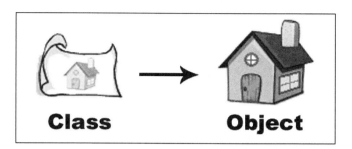

When studying OOP, you cannot ignore classes and objects, as those are the fundamental building blocks of any project. A good understanding of what classes and objects are and the roles they play will help you get on track to understanding OOP.

There's a subtle difference between a class and an object. A *class* is a self-contained description for a set of related services and data. Classes list the services they provide without revealing how they work internally. Classes aren't generally able to work on their own; they need to instantiate at least one object that is then able to act on the services and data described in the class.

Suppose you want to build a house. Unless you build it yourself, you need an architect and a builder. The architect drafts a blueprint, and the builder uses it to construct your house. Software developers are architects, and classes are their blueprints. You cannot use a class directly, any more than you could move your family into a blueprint. Classes only describe the final product. To actually do something you need an *object*.

If a class is a blueprint, then an object is a house. Builders create houses from blueprints; OOP creates objects from classes. OOP is efficient. You write the class once and create as many objects as needed.

Because classes can be used to *create* multiple objects, objects are often referred to as *class instances*.

Properties

Properties give individual objects unique qualities. Without properties, each house (from the previous example) would remain identical to its neighbors (all constructed from the same blueprint). With properties, each house is unique, from its exterior color to the style of its windows.

Let's look at a Ball class for example. From that one class you can create multiple ball instances; however, not all balls look identical to one another. By providing your Ball class with properties such as color, weight, and shape, you can create instances that describe balls as diverse as a basketball, bowling ball, or rugby ball just by assigning different values to properties in each instance of the class.

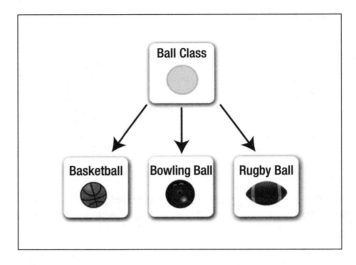

In OOP, you write classes to offer predefined behaviors and maybe hold some data. Next, you create one or more objects from a class. Finally, you endow objects with their own individual property values. The progression from classes to objects to objects with unique properties is the essence of OOP.

Encapsulation: Hiding the details

When you get into your car, you turn the key, the car starts, and off you go. You don't need to understand how the car parts work to find yourself in rush-hour traffic. The car starts when you turn the key. Car designers hide the messy internal details so you can concentrate on important things like finding another radio station. OOP calls this concept encapsulation.

Analogies like the preceding car example are very useful to explain concepts such as encapsulation, but it is no doubt more appealing to take an in-depth look at potential real-world scenarios like, for example, an accounting office.

Accountants love details (all the numbers, receipts, and invoices). The accountant's boss, however, is interested in the bottom line. If the bottom line is zero, the company is debt-free. If the bottom line is positive, the company is profitable. She is happy to ignore all the messy details and focus on other things. Encapsulation is about ignoring or hiding internal details. In business, this is delegation. Without it, the boss may need to deal with accounting, tax law, and international trading at a level beyond her ability.

OOP loves encapsulation. With encapsulation, classes hide their own internal details. Users of a class (yourself, other developers, or other applications) are not required to know or care why it works. Class users just need the available service names and what to provide to use them. Building classes is an abstraction process; you start with a complex problem, and then reduce it down (abstracting it) to a list of related services. Encapsulation simplifies software development and increases the potential for code reuse.

To demonstrate, I'll present some pseudo-code (false code). You can't enter pseudo-code into a computer, but it's great for previewing ideas. First, you need an Accounting class:

```
Start Of Accounting Class
End Of Accounting Class
```

Everything between the start and end line is the Accounting class. A useless class so far, because it's empty. Let's give the Accounting class something to do:

```
Start Of Accounting Class
    Start Of Bottom Line Service
        (Internal Details Of Bottom Line Service)
    End Of Bottom Line Service
End Of Accounting Class
```

Now the Accounting class has a Bottom Line service. How does that service work? Well, I know (because I wrote the code), but you (as a user of my class) have no idea. That's exactly how it should be. You don't know or care how my class works. You just use the Bottom Line service to see if the company is profitable. As long as my class is accurate and dependable, you can go about your business. You want to see the details anyway? Okay, here they are:

```
Start Of Accounting Class
    Start Of Bottom Line Service
        Do Invoice Service
        Do Display Answer Service
    End Of Bottom Line Service
End Of Accounting Class
```

Where did the Invoice and Display Answer services come from? They're part of the class too, but encapsulation is hiding them. Here they are:

```
Start Of Accounting Class
    Start Of Bottom Line Service
        Do Invoice Service
        Do Display Answer Service
    End Of Bottom Line Service
```

```
Start Of Invoice Service
    (Internal Details Of Invoice Service)
End Of Invoice Service

Start Of Display Answer Service
    (Internal Details Of Display Answer Service)
End Of Display Answer Service
End Of Accounting Class
```

The Bottom Line service has no idea how the Invoice service works, nor does it care. You don't know the details, and neither does the Bottom Line service. This type of simplification is the primary benefit of encapsulation. Finally, how do you request an answer from the Bottom Line service? Easy, just do this:

```
Do Bottom Line Service
```

That's all. You're happy, because you only need to deal with a single line of code. The Bottom Line service (and encapsulation) handles the details for you.

When I speak of hiding code details, I'm speaking conceptually. I don't mean to mislead you. This is just a mental tool to help you understand the importance of abstracting the details. With encapsulation, you're not actually hiding code (physically). If you were to view the full Accounting class, you'd see the same code that I see.

```
Start Of Accounting Class
    Start Of Bottom Line Service
        Do Invoice Service
        Do Display Answer Service
    End Of Bottom Line Service

    Start Of Invoice Service
        Gather Invoices
        Return Sum
    End Of Invoice Service

    Start Of Display Answer Service
        Display Sum
    End Of Display Answer Service
End Of Accounting Class
```

If you're wondering why some of the lines are indented, this is standard practice (that is not followed often enough). It shows, at a glance, the natural hierarchy of the code (of what belongs to what). Please adopt this practice when you write computer code.

Polymorphism: Exhibiting similar features

Are you old enough to remember fuel stations before the self-service era? You could drive into these places and somebody else would fill up your tank. The station attendant knew about OOP long before you did. He put the fuel nozzle into the tank (any tank) and pumped the fuel! It didn't matter if you drove a Ford, a Chrysler, or a Datsun. All cars have fuel tanks, so this behavior is easy to repeat for any car. OOP calls this concept polymorphism.

Much like cars need fuel to run, I take my daily dose of vitamins by drinking a glass of orange juice at breakfast. This incidentally brings me to a great example showing the concept of polymorphism.

Oranges have pulp. Lemons have pulp. Grapefruits have pulp. Cut any of these fruit open, I dare you, and try to scoop out the fruit with a spoon. Chances are, you'll get a squirt of citrus juice in your eye. Citrus fruits know exactly where your eye is, but you don't have to spoon them out to know they share this talent (they're all acid-based juice-squirters). Look at the following Citrus class:

```
Start Of Citrus Class
    Start Of Taste Service
        (Internal Details Of Taste Service)
    End Of Taste Service

    Start Of Squirt Service
        (Internal Details Of Squirt Service)
    End Of Squirt Service
End Of Citrus Class
```

You can use the Citrus class as a base to define other classes:

```
Start Of Orange Class
    Using Citrus Class
    Property Named Juice
End Of Orange Class

Start Of Lemon Class
    Using Citrus Class
    Property Named Juice
End Of Lemon Class
```

```
Start Of Grapefruit Class
    Using Citrus Class
    Property Named Juice
End Of Grapefruit Class
```

Besides demonstrating inheritance again, the Orange, Lemon, and Grapefruit classes also exhibit similar behaviors. This is polymorphism. You know that the Orange, Lemon, and Grapefruit classes have the ability to squirt (inherited from the Citrus class), but each class has a Juice property. So the orange can squirt orange juice, the lemon can squirt lemon juice, and the grapefruit can squirt grapefruit juice. You don't have to know in advance which type of fruit, because they all squirt. In fact, you could taste the juice (inherited from the Citrus class) to know which fruit you're dealing with. That's polymorphism: multiple objects exhibiting similar features in different ways.

Inheritance: Avoid rebuilding the wheel

Grog roll wheel. Wheel good. Grog doesn't like rebuilding wheels. They're heavy, made of stone, and tend to crush feet when they fall over. Grog likes the wheel that his stone-age neighbor built last week. Sneaky Grog. Maybe he'll carve some holes into the wheel to store rocks, twigs, or a tasty snack. If Grog does this, he'll have added something new to the existing wheel (demonstrating inheritance long before the existence of computers).

Inheritance in OOP is a real timesaver. You don't need to modify your neighbor's wheel. You only need to tell the computer, "Build a replica of my neighbor's wheel, and then add this, and this, and this." The result is a custom wheel, but you didn't modify the original. Now you have two wheels, each unique. To clarify, here's some more pseudo-code:

```
Start Of Wheel Class
    Start Of Roll Service
        (Internal Details Of Roll Service)
    End Of Roll Service
End Of Wheel Class
```

The Wheel class provides a single service named Roll. That's a good start, but what if you want to make a tire? Do you build a new Tire class from scratch? No, you just use inheritance to build a Tire class, like this:

```
Start Of Tire Class
    Using Wheel Class
End Of Tire Class
```

By using the Wheel class as a starting point, the Tire class already knows how to roll (the tire is a type of wheel). Here's the next logical step:

```
Start Of Tire Class
    Using Wheel Class
    Property Named Size
End Of Tire Class
```

Now the Tire class has a property named size. That means you could create many unique Tire objects. All of the tires can roll (behavior inherited from the Wheel class), but each tire has its own unique size. You could add other properties to the Tire class too. With very little work, you could have small car tires that roll, big truck tires that roll, and bigger bus tires that roll.

What's next?

Now that wasn't too difficult, was it? In this chapter I covered the basic idea of OOP as well as an introduction so some of its key features including encapsulation, polymorphism, and inheritance. I'll explain those ideas in much greater detail in Part Three of this book.

Coming up next, I will focus on the general programming concepts common to modern high-level computer languages.

2 PROGRAMMING CONCEPTS

In this chapter, I'll introduce you to some common programming concepts you'll want to know about before starting to program with ActionScript 2.0.

When working closely with computer programmers, you no doubt get slapped round the head with acronyms and techno-babble at regular intervals. If you are new to the game, don't fear, I'll soon have you joining in with this typical bonding ritual, thus affirming your newly acquired position in the office tribe.

In all seriousness, though, learning some basic terminology is really very useful. You'll come across many of the terms discussed in this chapter when reading articles, tutorials, or talking to fellow developers. Let's get started by looking at common programming slang.

About programming slang

Slang	Meaning
IDE	Integrated Development Environment, the software in which you develop an application
The code	The entire body of source code found in a computer application
Writing code	The process of creating the computer program (entering the code)
Run, running	Starting, using, or testing an application or self-contained piece of code
Runtime	When the application runs, and the things that occur during the run
Execution	The process of running a certain piece of code during runtime
Compile, compilation	The process of assembling code into a format usable for executing the code
Design time	When the application is developed (writing the code and so on)

In general, application development shifts continuously between design time and runtime (between creating and testing) until the computer application is "finished." Some computer languages (such as ActionScript) may require compilation before the code can be previewed, run, or deployed to another machine.

Building blocks of programming

Computer languages consist of certain building blocks that store data and determine the way an application needs to run. These building blocks are very similar across different languages, but the way in which they are implemented may differ. Certain languages are better equipped to deal with certain tasks, but there's no single one that's perfect for all types of applications. The following table lists the major building blocks of programming:

Building Block	Purpose
Variables	For storing temporary data
Arrays	For storing lists of temporary data
Functions	For grouping and reusing instructions
Loops	For repeating instructions
Conditionals	For making decisions

Let's consider variables first.

Variables

When you write down what a typical application needs to do, you immediately think of storing and retrieving data. The role of data in an application is temporary; you need to have a placeholder for information you get from the keyboard and mouse, a database, the Web, on a network drive, etc.

These placeholders in your application are called *variables*. For every single piece of data you'll want to work with in your application, you'll declare a variable, give it a name, and assign a value to it. Any time you want to retrieve, modify, or delete a variable, you'll just use that very name you gave it. To write this in English, I might use the following:

    The number of paper clips in the box is 500.

To write this in ActionScript 2.0, I might use this:

    var paperClipsPerBox:Number = 500;

The name of the variable is paperClipsPerBox. It holds numeric data, specifically 500. Variables can hold many kinds of data (more than just numbers). The different values that can be assigned to a variable are called *data types*, and we'll discuss those next.

About variable data

What kind of data may variables hold? It depends upon the computer language, but in practice, most languages accommodate a similar set of data types (numbers, text, true/false values, and more). Some computer languages handle variables with a strict set of rules, while others do not. The strict languages demand that a single variable stores one type of data, so numeric variables can store numbers, but nothing else.

The not-so-strict languages (such as ActionScript 1.0) allow variables to hold any type of data, even to the point that a single variable may hold a number first and then maybe a sentence of text later. If you think this is good, think again. When the developer makes a mistake, the computer has far less power to help spot the error.

Luckily, with ActionScript 2.0 you can use strong typing, which greatly increases the ease of debugging Flash applications. You are however still free to choose if you like to use that strict approach to programming. Even when using the latest ActionScript version you can choose to code in a way that does not enforce a particular data type for each variable— the power is in your hands. You'll learn all about programming ActionScript 2.0 in the next chapter.

Arrays

Arrays are like variables, but they're a little different. Other variables store a single piece of data per variable, like a number in this case:

```
var paperClipsPerBox:Number = 500;
```

The variable paperClipsPerBox can only hold one value at a given time; that value may change while the application is running, but at no point will you be able to assign two values to that single variable.

Arrays on the other hand allow you to store multiple values in a single instance. This is great for storing related items, such as a list of personal phone numbers. To write this in English, I might use the following:

```
1. Jenny (555) 867-5309
2. Pauly (555) 422-4281
3. Ricky (555) 383-9287
...
25. Benny (555) 954-2921
```

To write this in ActionScript 2.0, I might use this:

```
myPhoneList[0] = "Jenny (555) 867-5309";
myPhoneList[1] = "Pauly (555) 422-4281";
myPhoneList[2] = "Ricky (555) 383-9287";
...
myPhoneList[24] = "Benny (555) 954-2921";
```

With arrays, you have a single variable named `myPhoneList` and you access the data by number. If you need the third phone number in the list, you ask for `myPhoneList[2]` and the computer answers

```
Ricky (555) 383-9287
```

Arrays combine the convenience of simple variables with the power to access data in an ordered list. Arrays are dynamic objects in most computer languages, which means you can insert or remove array items as often as needed. It is even possible to add arrays inside arrays to create more complex data structures called *multidimensional arrays*. Building on the previous example, we could, instead of simply storing a phone number, create an array for each item in `myPhoneList` that holds their additional information such as e-mail address, location, date of birth, etc.

Functions

Functions provide a means to call a specific set of instructions that achieve a single, specific task in your application. When first starting to program you might be tempted to put too much into a function. Just remember: one (and only one) task per function. The function may include 10, 20, 30, or more separate instructions to achieve its task. That's fine, as long as the whole group maintains a single and focused purpose. While this practice is by no means enforced by OOP, it is strongly recommended, and I believe it will help you build reusable and more effective code.

About calling functions

Calling a function means *using* a function. Once you declare a function, you may call its name from elsewhere in the application. Once called, the application carries out the instructions defined by the function. You declare a function once, but call it as needed.

Suppose you have an application to convert distances. You don't have to retype the conversion instructions every time you need them. Instead, you can create a single function named `milesToKilometers` and call it from elsewhere in the application. The `milesToKilometer` function returns the resulting data once it has finished its calculation. The resulting data from a function is typically stored in a variable that you can use later on in your application.

About function parameters

Functions can accept additional (agreed upon) information called *function parameters*. Using function parameters, the `milesToKilometers` function can accept a variable for miles. That way, the function can calculate an answer for 15 miles, 500 miles, 600 miles, and so on. Function parameters make functions reusable and flexible.

As with variables, in some computer languages these function parameters are assigned a particular data type and only allow that particular type of value to be used when a function is called.

Loops

Loops repeat a specific set of instructions. The number of times a loop may repeat depends on the situation. The loop may repeat a fixed number of times, or perhaps a condition determines when it expires.

A good example of where you'd use a loop is when working with arrays. Doing this allows you to easily go through each and every item stored in the array and retrieve those values for use in your application.

Conditionals

Conditionals are a major building block of any type of programming. Conditional instructions let applications make decisions; they're the actual logic and control the flow of your code.

Think of the last time you used a vending machine. You put some money in and choose your particular flavor of soft drink. The machine then uses some programming logic to determine if you put in an exact amount, too little, or too much cash. If you use exact change the vending machine will immediately give you your soft drink, if you put in too little, it won't give you the drink and will wait for you to put more money in or press the refund button. Finally, if you put in too much money (and the machine detects that it has enough spare change), you'll get the drink and the remaining money.

Computer languages call this conditional structure an *if-then-else* statement. You can read it like this: "if a condition is met, *then* do this, otherwise (*else*) do this instead." You'll find if-then-else logic in every piece of software you can imagine.

OOP concepts

OOP really is a methodology, a way of using the building blocks of programming to create dynamic, flexible, and reusable applications. Here's a brief review of what I discussed:

Classes. From a code-centric view, a class is a collection of functions and variables working together to support a common goal. When you get to the heart of it, though, classes handle custom data. The variables in a class store the data and functions manipulate the data. Classes provide a powerful and self-contained way of organizing and processing every type of custom data you can possibly think of.

Objects. Classes cannot do any real work themselves—for that they need to be instantiated as objects. Classes are merely templates that provide a blueprint for multiple objects. Every object automatically contains the data (variables) and behaviors (functions) described by the class. Just remember: one class can have very many objects.

Properties. Properties allow objects to be customized. Suppose you use a class named House to build 25 House objects. All houses based on the House class will look identical because they are built from the same master plan. However, House objects can individually change their own properties they got from the House class and make themselves unique from their neighbors.

What's next?

Now that we've covered the basic programming concepts, let's get started with the real work. I will discuss ActionScript 2.0, the latest incarnation of the Flash scripting language, and run you through its new class-based syntax. Before you know it, you'll be coding your own very first object-oriented projects.

3 ACTIONSCRIPT 2.0 PROGRAMMING

In this chapter I'll introduce you to programming with ActionScript 2.0, the latest version of the language that comes with Flash 8.

If you were already familiar with programming in ActionScript prior to this release, it's worth noting that the syntax used in previous versions of Flash is now dubbed ActionScript 1.0. Don't worry, you won't have to start from scratch. Much of the ActionScript 1.0 syntax has remained the same in version 2.0; the bulk of the learning curve will be learning about the new features and how to apply those to your code.

Let's get started by looking at the key differences between ActionScript 1.0 and Action-Script 2.0 and familiarize ourselves with some new concepts.

ActionScript 1.0 vs. ActionScript 2.0

You've probably been wondering how ActionScript 1.0 differs from ActionScript 2.0 and whether you should really be bothering to learn it. I always answer that this latest release of ActionScript is a great tool to have if you're building any type of application in Flash, and learning it is well worth the effort.

The biggest problem usually is that developers (not in the least including myself) are inherently lazy: we don't like to type longer code, we don't like to comment every function—heck, we don't even like to get out of our chairs to get a cup of coffee. Important to realize is that the process of building an application often consists of about 20% writing code, 10% tweaking that code, and 70% debugging. By using ActionScript 2.0 you can greatly reduce that time needed for debugging because of a concept called *strong typing*, which helps you signal type mismatch bugs and gives you far more descriptive error messages (more about this later on in this chapter).

Another thing to note is that ActionScript 2.0 compiles down to ActionScript 1.0 syntax. This is a great feature that makes your project compatible with both the Flash 6 and Flash 7 player. There is an exception to this rule when using Flash 7 specific-code such as when using the new try-catch-finally feature, which can't be made available for the Flash 6 player.

Not every project will need to make use of ActionScript 2.0, so don't feel you must build everything in the new syntax. If you're on a strict deadline and need to put a simple Flash-based form online, don't waste your time writing an ActionScript 2.0 class for handling your data. If, however, you're building any type of application or some code that will likely need some further tweaking or additional features added later on, spend that extra hour getting your code strongly typed and set up as ActionScript 2.0—it will save you some serious headaches down the line.

Declaring variables

If you were already using ActionScript 1.0, you know that declaring a variable was very easy indeed, and it's not that much different from this latest version.

```
foo = "Object Oriented Flash 8"; // ActionScript 1.0
```

The only time you'd use a var keyword was when you wanted to declare a variable to be of a local scope inside a function, which ensured it was removed from memory after the function had finished its task. *Scope* is the range of visibility for a particular variable; not all variables are available throughout an entire project. You'll learn more about this later on in this chapter. When declaring a variable using ActionScript 2.0, however, you'll always want to use that var keyword.

```
var foo = "Object Oriented Flash 8"; // ActionScript 2.0
```

The preceding example shows you how a basic variable is declared in ActionScript 2.0. Good to know is that this variable is not strongly typed. Just like in ActionScript 1.0 you can assign any data type to it without an error being thrown:

```
var foo = true; // ActionScript 2.0
```

Important to know is that you only use the var keyword the first time you declare your variable; from then on you just assign values to it by referring to its name.

```
foo = "ActionScript 2.0"; // ActionScript 2.0
```

ActionScript 2.0 now automatically handles assigning the correct scope to a variable. If you declare a new variable inside a function, it will automatically be given a local scope; otherwise it will be given a timeline scope.

Classes vs. prototypes

ActionScript, like several other languages (including JavaScript), is based on ECMA-script standards. These standards are taken very seriously as is pointed out by the company becoming a member of the ECMA consortium.

ActionScript 1.0 made use of a prototype-based syntax for building classes. Using a so-called prototype chain, you could modify or extend classes as well as simulate a form of inheritance that is a crucial aspect of OOP. There was no clear-cut way to see if you were dealing with a simple function or an actual class apart from the this keyword and the prototype keyword.

ActionScript 1.0

```
function Ball(color, weight, shape) {
  this.color = color;
  this.size = size;
  this.weight = weight;
}
basketBall = new Ball("orange","light","round");
bowlingBall = new Ball("blue","heavy","round");
rugbyBall = new Ball("brown","light","oval");
```

Extending built-in classes using a prototype object became very popular in ActionScript 1.0; you can find an example of this in the following code:

```
MovieClip.prototype.setPosition = function(x,y) {
  this._x = x;
  this._y = y;
}
```

The preceding code extends the blueprint of the MovieClip class, which makes the setPosition function available to all instances of MovieClip in your project. The setPosition function allows you to set both the x and y position of a movie clip on stage using a single function call. Let's say you've got two movie clips in your project with instance names mc1 and mc2; you could use the following function calls to position them:

```
mc1.setPosition(10,50);
mc2.setPosition(50,70);
```

Now let's look at building classes in ActionScript 2.0. The most obvious new requirement is that you need to use external files for each of your classes. If you build a class named Ball, you are required to save that in a file named Ball.as. You can save that file in either the folder where the Flash FLA sourcefile is stored or in the First Run/Classes directory of your Flash 8 installation.

ActionScript 2.0 also supports something called *packages*, which are a way to call classes by their folder structure. Let's say you save the Ball.as file in a subfolder called sports; you can instantiate that Ball class by using its fully qualified classpath: sport.Ball. Using class packages has a number of advantages; first, it prevents any possible name conflicts and also allows for easy importing of a series of classes. The import keyword can be used to include all classes in the sports package for use in your project:

```
import sports.*;
```

If you had more classes than just Ball placed in that directory, you'd have those all included for use inside your project.

By default Flash 8 looks for classes in the install directory, and if not found there moves on to the folder in which you saved the FLA. If you want, you can also add your own locations for Flash to look for classes. This could be handy if you'd like to store your ActionScript classes in a central custom location.

To add a custom classpath location, you go to Edit ➤ Preferences, select the ActionScript tab, and click the ActionScript 2.0 Settings button in the Flash IDE.

When the ActionScript Settings dialog box pops up (see Figure 3-1), you can use the plus button to manually add a new location, the minus button to remove one, or the target button to browse for a location. The up and down arrow buttons can be used to set the priority for each of the locations, the topmost being the first place Flash looks.

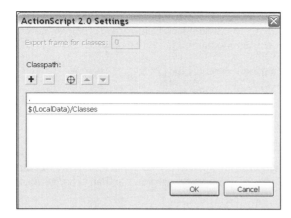

Figure 3-1.
ActionScript 2.0 Settings

3

ActionScript 2.0

Ball.as

```
class sports.Ball {
  function Ball(color,size,weight) {
    trace("Ball created");
    color = color;
    size = size;
    weight = weight;
  }
}
```

The preceding code should be saved as a file called Ball.as and in a subfolder called sports. (Note that both the class filename and package name are case sensitive!) In that same folder where you created the subfolder, you save a new FLA that contains the following lines of code on Frame 1 of the main timeline:

```
basketBall = new sports.Ball("orange","light","round");
bowlingBall = new sports.Ball("blue","heavy","round");
rugbyBall = new sports.Ball("brown","light","oval");
```

The preceding example declares class instances by referring to the full classpath. Another approach is shown here:

```
import sports.Ball;
basketBall = new Ball("orange","light","round");
bowlingBall = new Ball("blue","heavy","round");
rugbyBall = new Ball("brown","light","oval");
```

By using the import keyword, we can simply instantiate the class by using its class name and not giving its full path. Both examples do exactly the same thing, and if you test the project you'll see "Ball created" listed three times in the output panel.

Just like I showed you with ActionScript 1.0, this version of ActionScript allows you to add your own custom functionality to a class. Instead of using prototype, we now use the extends keyword in an external class .as file named CustomMovieClip.as.

```
class CustomMovieClip extends MovieClip {
  function setPosition(x,y) {
    _x = x;
    _y = y;
  }
}
```

Now, unlike we saw before with ActionScript 1.0, the setPosition function is not automatically available to all instances of MovieClip because we didn't actually change anything to the MovieClip class itself.

What we did was create our own subclass that inherits all functionality from the MovieClip class and adds its own. To have this all work, we need to associate a movie clip with our new ActionScript 2.0 class. The way you handle that in Flash 8 is quite easy. In the Library panel of the Flash IDE, you choose the movie clip object you'd like to associate this class with. You then right-click that particular movie clip and choose Linkage, which pops up a dialog box (see Figure 3-2).

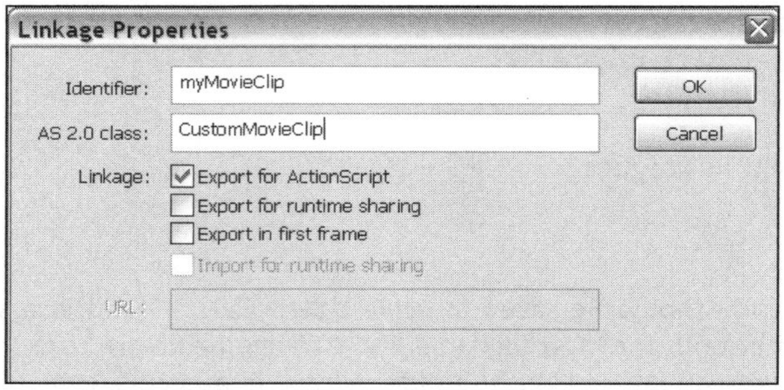

Figure 3-2. Linkage Properties dialog box

In this dialog box you check the Export for ActionScript checkbox and type CustomMovieClip in the AS 2.0 Class text field. The other options in the dialog box are not important to us in this case, so you can leave those set to the defaults for now.

When you click OK to close the dialog box, you've just associated that MovieClip object with the custom class. You can now start using the setPosition function with all instances of that object. Drag two instances of the MovieClip on stage and name them mc1 and mc2. Just like with the ActionScript 1.0 example, you can now use the following code:

```
mc1.setPosition(10,50);
mc2.setPosition(50,70);
```

Those of you familiar with component development in ActionScript 1.0 might remember `Object.registerClass`, which was used to associate an object with a class just like we did in this dialog box.

Public and private scope

ActionScript 1.0 had no real means of enforcing private scope, that is to say, all functions of a class could be called outside the scope of that class. What would usually happen is that developers used either the $ or _ sign to prefix a private class function so as to indicate that it is not supposed to be used as a publicly available function.

3

ActionScript 1.0

```
function CountSheep(maxSheep) {
  this.currentSheep = 0;
  this.maxSheep = maxSheep;
}
CountSheep.prototype.startCounting = function() {
  this.countInterval = setInterval(this,"$incrementSheep",1000);
}
CountSheep.prototype.$incrementSheep = function() {
  if(this.currentSheep < this.maxSheep) {
    this.currentSheep++;
    trace(this.currentSheep+" sheep counted");
  } else {
    trace("Sleeping ...");
    clearInterval(this.countInterval);
  }
}
mySleep = new CountSheep(5);
mySleep.startCounting();
```

In the preceding example, you can see a simple ActionScript 1.0 class that helps you count sheep to fall asleep. The constructor takes one parameter, which is the amount of sheep you want to count. I personally am an easy sleeper, so I've just specified to count five sheep.

If you look at the way the code is structured, you'll notice that there really is only one function that you'll want to have called outside the scope of this class and that is `startCounting`. The `incrementSheep` function is only useful inside the class and would be a good candidate to give a private scope. Having the function called outside the class scope might in fact even break our code. You can see I prefixed the code with a $ sign to indicate that it shouldn't be considered a public function. As I explained before, no enforcement occurs there whatsoever. In ActionScript 1.0, you can only indicate private scope by naming convention.

ActionScript 2.0

CountSheep.as

```
class CountSheep {
  var currentSheep;
  var maxSheep;
  var countInterval;
  function CountSheep(maxSheep) {
    this.currentSheep = 0;
    this.maxSheep = maxSheep;
  }
  public function startCounting() {
    countInterval = setInterval(this,"incrementSheep",1000);
  }
  private function incrementSheep() {
    if(this.currentSheep < this.maxSheep) {
      this.currentSheep++;
      trace(this.currentSheep+" sheep counted");
    } else {
      trace("Sleeping ...");
      clearInterval(this.countInterval);
    }
  }
}
```

As you can see, this is largely the same as any other ActionScript 2.0 class, with the only difference that we've got a public and private keyword in front of the class functions. It's pretty obvious what those keywords will do for you, so you'd expect the following code to work in an FLA that you've saved in the same location as this class:

```
var mySleep = new CountSheep(5);
mySleep.startCounting();
```

Hoorah, it works! But wait a minute, let's see if our private function really is private:

```
var mySleep = new CountSheep(5);
mySleep.incrementSheep();
```

Oh dear, one of the few times you'd want the compiler to spit out an error and it doesn't. The private function is called and behaves just like a public function would. That's not what we want, is it?

The key to this problem is that the variable we used for our countSheep class instance isn't typed as countSheep. When you want ActionScript 2.0 to enforce private scope, you'll need to use the following code:

```
var mySleep:countSheep = new CountSheep(5);
mySleep.incrementSheep();
```

If you test these lines of code we get the long awaited error message:

```
**Error** Scene=Scene 1, layer=Layer 1, frame=1:Line 2:
The member is private and cannot be accessed.
    mySleep.incrementSheep();


Total ActionScript Errors: 1     Reported Errors: 1
```

This about wraps up my comparison between ActionScript 1.0 and ActionScript 2.0. Important to note is that all examples in this section until now have not used any form of strong typing. I'll soon set that right and discuss strong typing and its benefits in ActionScript 2.0 next.

Strong typing and code hints

Strong typing is a very useful feature and not that difficult to implement. I discussed declaring variables in ActionScript 2.0 earlier in this chapter; the only difference when it comes to strong typing is you add a colon and then type the class you want it to be an instance of.

Flash 8 automatically pops up a list of all available built-in classes as soon as you type a colon when declaring a variable (see Figure 3-3).

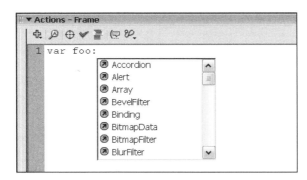

Figure 3-3.
Class code hints

In this example we'll declare our variable as a String type and give it the value "Object-Oriented Flash 8".

```
var foo:String = "Object-Oriented Flash 8";
```

Now any time we use this particular variable, we automatically get context-sensitive code hints listing all available functions for variables of that type. In this example, we get all functions available for the String data type (see Figure 3-4).

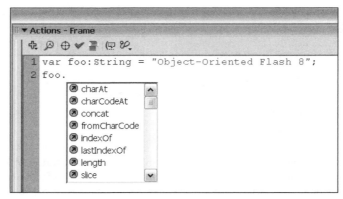

Figure 3-4. Context-sensitive code hints

Code hints are all well and good, but the most important advantage of using strong typing is that it allows for easy debugging.

If you declare a variable of type String and try to assign another data type to it, the compiler will send out an error warning you of a type mismatch:

```
var foo:String = "Object-Oriented Flash 8";
foo = true;

**Error** Scene=Scene 1, layer=Layer 1, frame=1:Line 2:
Type mismatch in assignment statement: found Boolean
where String is required.
        foo = true;

Total ActionScript Errors: 1    Reported Errors: 1
```

You can see that, when using strong typing with ActionScript 2.0, you get much more detailed and descriptive error messages. In this case the output panel states that we have a type mismatch and we used a Boolean where a String is required.

Apart from using strong typing to enforce data types on variables, it also allows us to assign types to both function parameters and function return values.

```
function milesToKilometers(miles:Number):Number {
  var ratio:Number = 1.609344;
  return miles*ratio;
}

trace(milesToKilometers(200)); // outputs 321.8688
```

The preceding example shows a function that accepts a single parameter Number data type and also returns a value of a Number data type.

Just as you would expect, calling the function as follows will have the compiler throw an error:

```
trace(milesToKilometers("Flash"));

**Error** Scene=Scene 1, layer=Layer 1, frame=1:Line 7: Type mismatch.
    trace(milesToKilometers("Flash"));

Total ActionScript Errors: 1    Reported Errors: 1
```

Equally changing the function return type to String results in an error because the value the function returns is of a Number type:

```
function milesToKilometers(miles:Number):String {
  var ratio:Number = 1.609344;
  return miles*ratio;
}
trace(milesToKilometers(200));


**Error** Scene=Scene 1, layer=Layer 1, frame=1:Line 3:
The expression returned must match the function's return
type.
        return miles*ratio;

Total ActionScript Errors: 1    Reported Errors: 1
```

As you can see, strong typing and code hints are very useful features when you want to do any application development in Flash 8 and ActionScript 2.0. In the end it is well worth the effort of applying it to your variables, function parameters, and return types. This small additional effort will help you out when it comes to debugging the application in the long run.

ActionScript trouble spots

ActionScript 2.0 does have some weaknesses and things you will want to watch out for. In this section I'll discuss some common trouble spots.

Case sensitivity

Unlike in the previous release, ActionScript 2.0 is case sensitive as the following example shows:

```
var myVariable:String = "Object-Oriented Flash 8";
trace(myvariable); // outputs undefined
trace(myVariable); // outputs Object-Oriented Flash 8
```

Declaring variables

When you initially declare a variable, you use the var keyword. You do need to watch out you don't use that keyword later on in the application when referring to the variable. Doing that would overwrite any data type that you applied to it using strong typing.

```
var myVariable:String = "Object-Oriented Flash 8";
var myVariable = true;
```

If you use a var keyword on that second line that assigns a Boolean true value to the variable, you don't get a type mismatch error message when compiling.

Use of the this keyword

When building classes in ActionScript 2.0, there is no need to use the this keyword to refer to variables of the class scope.

```
class MyClass {
  var myString:String;
  function MyClass(param:String):Void {
    myString = param;
    outputString();
  }
  function outputString() {
    trace(myString);
  }
}
```

As you can see in the preceding example, there is a variable named myString that is of a class scope, and we can refer to it without use of the this keyword. The same thing can be seen when the outputString function is called.

Although you can safely remove the this keyword, I would advise you to keep using it to make the distinction between variables of a class scope (myString) and a local scope (param). The same code with the this keyword looks like this:

```
class MyClass {
  var myString:String;
  function MyClass(param:String):Void {
    this.myString = param;
    this.outputString();
  }
  function outputString() {
    trace(this.myString);
  }
}
```

What's next?

I covered a great deal of information in this chapter, and you'll have learned the differences between ActionScript 1.0 and ActionScript 2.0 and the benefits of using strong typing.

This chapter closes Part One of this book. We now move on to discuss OOP guidelines, best practices, and planning. Even if you are already familiar with programming concepts, I'd highly recommend that you read the following chapters to start off on the right foot before we get to the in-depth OOP concepts and put theory into practice.

3

PART TWO **FLASH OOP GUIDELINES**

4 PLANNING

Ah, the magic word "planning," where would we all be without it? Most likely out of a job, that's for sure!

When you think of it, planning is nothing more than an object-oriented way of scheduling a project. You divide the project up into tasks, look at the task dependencies, and try to get those pieces to fit together within a predefined deadline.

Your initial impulse might be to skip this chapter and go right for the information on in-depth OOP, but I'd like to convince you to do otherwise. In this chapter I'll discuss the importance of planning as an integral part of object-oriented projects and run you through the process of analyzing and modeling your application.

The importance of planning

If you've ever been in a situation where your entire project lacks any form of planning, you're working in a team with both remote and local developers, and the client keeps calling you every 10 minutes with an ever increasingly loud voice warning you that the deadline is coming ever closer—you'll soon know what you're missing.

Of course, not all projects are like the one just described, and there are numerous situations in which you could think the planning stage is obsolete. Let's look at some of these possible scenarios and see why it is not:

We don't have time for planning (deadline is next month).

The time you'll spend planning a project will greatly decrease development time and time needed for debugging. In that sense, you'll notice that the planning stage will help you better manage projects with a tight deadline.

We don't have a budget for planning (we need to begin today).

Planning will enable you to save money on development costs. At the end of the day, what's the cost of a few pieces of paper compared to possibly rebuilding your application from scratch because nobody thought of taking that one critical parameter into consideration?

We don't need planning (this is just a quick little project).

Planning is useful for any type of application. What if a few months down the line the client figures out that the application doesn't quite fit in with their existing data infrastructure? Wouldn't you be frustrated to rebuild from scratch what a few simple notes could have avoided?

The preceding situations are some of the most common reasons why people tend to think that planning is not necessary. These examples show that even in these circumstances planning is a very important part of the development process.

As I briefly discussed in the introduction to this chapter, you can look at planning as an object-oriented process. The different sections of your planning can be handled just like objects in OOP, and each have their own particular role to play in the bigger whole. The tasks of the project can be considered as self-contained objects, project dependencies are comparable to interaction between classes, etc.—in that sense planning should not be handled much differently than writing actual code. This object-oriented nature of planning makes it very suitable to be written down in a structural model, which is what we'll do later on in this chapter. Next, I'll discuss the various steps involved with the process of planning and walk you through various examples.

Initial phase: Planning reusability!

Long-term reusability for your applications doesn't just happen by accident; it needs to be carefully planned. A first step in this planning process is getting the various tasks of your application down on paper.

Doing initial planning on paper is usually best because it allows you to *focus* on the issues at hand without getting distracted by details like what font and color scheme to use, which line style to use, etc. It's often a good thing to turn off your computer at this stage as it helps you to stay focused on the bigger scheme of things rather than get involved with exactly how you want the presentation and layout to look like.

The first question you'll need to ask yourself is *what* the application needs to do, not *how* it does it. We'll look at the ways in which the necessary tasks will be achieved at a later stage, but to start with you need to be clear on what exactly it is you need.

Suppose you need to build a car. In itself that is a rather generic term; you could come up with various solutions that cover the load. You could build something resembling a car with a whole bunch of clay. You could build a car from a kit. If you have way too much money, you could commission BMW to build a prototype car for you. As you can see, just knowing a car is what you want to build isn't really enough information to know enough about *what* you need.

In the initial phases of planning, you repeatedly ask what until it is extremely clear what the final product should be (but you can still leave most of the difficult, technical how-to questions for later).

Planning encapsulation

After reading through Chapter 1, you know that encapsulation is a key feature in OOP and serves to *hide the internal workings of a class*. I'll run you through planning encapsulation for your project with the following example:

Let's say we're faced with a ball and want to have it bounce. If we abstract this in object-oriented terms, we come up with a Ball class and a Bounce or, in more general terms, Mover class.

If you're not that familiar with OO concepts, you might not have considered creating that Mover class, instead adding the functionality directly to the Ball class. Think about it, what would be the benefit of making it a separate class? The answer is quite simple: you want to avoid duplicate code and increase reusability.

> *The Ball class is a special case in our example; it is in fact a movie clip instance of the MovieClip class. No need to worry about this just now, it'll be explained in more detail in Chapters 7 through 10.*

Now, how does this work in Flash? If you've worked with ActionScript before, you know that there are quite a few events that the built-in objects broadcast. One very important event is onEnterFrame, which runs once every frame. Let's say we've got a frame rate of 30 frames per second that would have the onEnterFrame event, and thus the *event handler* we attached to that event, broadcast 30 times every second. You can see that using this event you can quite easily simulate movement using ActionScript.

An event handler is a function that you apply to an event; how exactly that event handler code looks is not important in this example—we'll just focus on how it is set up.

Figure 4-1.
Mover class diagram

Figure 4-1 shows the class diagram for Mover.

The Ball class calls the startMoving function in the Mover class. This startMoving function then sets the onEnterFrame event that calls the updatePosition function. The internal details of the Mover class and the updatePosition function aren't important from the event handler's point of view (encapsulation).

That completes the circle any time the onEnterFrame event is broadcast and the updatePosition function is executed, which results in the simulated motion we wanted.

Planning inheritance

Let's expand on that encapsulation plan; without knowing exactly how the Mover class works, we want to add additional functionality. To achieve just that we'll be using inheritance.

Inheritance allows you to extend or enhance classes that already exist, without altering existing behavior. Inheritance allows new classes to *inherit* the services of some other existing class. When you use the new class, you get the features of the existing class too (as if they were both merged into a single bigger class).

Inheritance is more than simply an organized way to add new features—it also prevents you from breaking applications that already use existing classes (because you're not modifying the existing classes one single bit).

Let's build on our example. This time I'm adding another new class named Bouncer. The Bouncer class will inherit from the Mover class, and will consequently be able to do everything the Mover class can do, but add its own additional functionality. In particular, I want the class to bounce the ball whenever it hits a border.

Just like before, we're not concerned with the details of how the ball will bounce or how the borders are determined. Right now, I only need to invent the proper function names to cover the behavior I want to provide.

Figure 4-2 shows the class diagram for Bouncer.

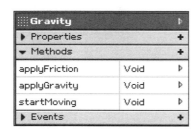

Bouncer		▷
▶ Properties		+
▼ Methods		+
bounceAtBorder	Void	▷
startMoving	Void	▷
▶ Events		+

Figure 4-2.
Bouncer class diagram

1. The startMoving function in the Bouncer class sets the onEnterFrame event handler that calls the updatePosition function in the Mover class. The internal details of the Bouncer class aren't important from the event handler's point of view (encapsulation).

2. The Mover class doesn't know it, but the Bouncer class has an additional behavior (the bounceAtBorder function). The Bouncer class can use this behavior without revealing it to the Mover class.

3. The Ball class doesn't know it, but the Bouncer class has inherited the Mover class. Indeed, the Ball class has no idea that the Mover class even exists. The Bouncer class initiated the request to inherit; it doesn't need permission from the Ball class to do so. The Ball class has no idea that any of this is happening, and that's just the way it should be. The Bouncer class can do anything the Mover class can do, plus it contains a bounceAtBorder function.

This completes another code sequence that *somehow* (we haven't looked at a single line of code yet) moves the ball instance and bounces it back any time it hits a border.

While we're at it, let's go one step further and add a class that simulates friction and gravity to give our ball some more natural movement. I'll name this class Gravity and have it inherit from the Bouncer class so it can use all functionality that is already defined in there.

Remember, the Bouncer class itself inherits from the Mover class so we've really got a great inheritance chain going on here. One thing to note is that a class can inherit functions from many classes down but can only interact directly with its parent class (for the Gravity class that is the Bouncer class).

We're still not bothered about the workings of our new Gravity class but simply add two functions called applyFriction and applyGravity. Let's look at the setup of this new class. Figure 4-3 shows the class diagram for Gravity.

Gravity		▷
▶ Properties		+
▼ Methods		+
applyFriction	Void	▷
applyGravity	Void	▷
startMoving	Void	▷
▶ Events		+

Figure 4-3.
Gravity class diagram

37

1. The startMoving function in the Gravity class sets the onEnterFrame event handler that calls the updatePosition function in the Bouncer class (which in turn calls the updatePosition function in the Mover class). The internal details of the Gravity class aren't important from the event handler's point of view (encapsulation).

2. The Ball class doesn't know it, but the Gravity class has inherited from the Bouncer class. The Gravity class can do anything that the Bouncer class can do, plus it provides its own unique functions named applyFriction and applyGravity.

3. The Bouncer class inherits from the Mover class. This implies that the Gravity class has also inherited (be it indirectly) the functionality of the Mover class (without it even knowing that the Mover class exists).

This wraps up another sequence that is still just triggered by the Ball class calling the startMoving function. The entire series of events that we added from the Mover class, through the Bouncer class, down to the Gravity class is executed every time the onEnterFrame event triggers the updatePosition function and any additional functions the class provides.

I've covered a lot of information in this example that will have helped you get an idea of how to model your project with encapsulation and inheritance in place. You might not have noticed, but we've also implemented the concept of polymorphism by using the same startMoving function in all our classes. We're not bothered what particular class is used to move the ball (Mover, Bouncer, or Gravity) because we just need to trigger that same startMoving function to have it start moving.

If you've lost your way in the class setup, take a look at Figure 4-4.

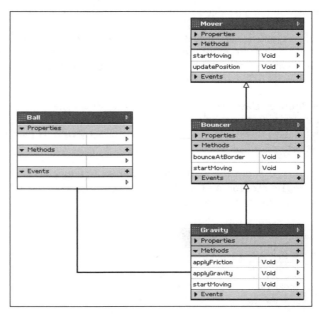

Figure 4-4. Mover class inheritance diagram

Next, I'll walk you through the specifics of applying the planning techniques we just discussed on a Flash ActionScript project.

Analyzing a Flash ActionScript project

For a long time serious developers have shied away from using Flash and ActionScript, not because they weren't impressed by its functionality but mostly because of its *unconventional timeline metaphor* and cluttered coding practices. Up until quite recently, Flash was mainly classified as a tool for the creative and the odd few experimental developers. Luckily this is all changing rapidly; they are putting their money on building a framework that allows the creation of **R**ich **I**nternet **A**pplications (RIA) and more and more developers are venturing into this field.

When analyzing projects that are to be built in Flash and ActionScript, it is important to take certain things into consideration. I'll discuss some of these trouble spots here and offer you some ideas on how to approach those when planning your application.

Flash files run on the client

When you deploy your Flash file on the web, the SWF file is not run on the server but is cached and displayed in the browser using the Flash player plug-in. This brings up certain risks with what you include in your project file. There are several SWF decompilers available on the Web these days, and it is very easy for anyone to decompile your file and extract sensitive information (password information, high score submission URL, etc.).

There is no foolproof way of protecting your SWF content, but one thing you should always do is move all your database connection details, SQL queries, and anything else that you don't want to be public knowledge on the server.

Securing data sent to the server

Building on the previous point, you wouldn't do password verification on the client side but rather send it to a server-side script that checks this for you and returns whether or not the user was validated.

There are a couple of difficulties with doing something like that, the first one being that the login information sent from Flash to the server is not encrypted in any way. Anyone using a packet sniffer could pick up the login information and use it to get access illegally.

How this is typically handled is the data entered into Flash is concatenated to the user's IP and encrypted using an ActionScript implementation of either MD5 or SHA1, which are algorithms that allow you to create an irreversibly encrypted string from whatever data you pass to it. This encrypted password data is then sent to the server along with the username and a randomly generated string in plain text. The server-side script now does exactly the same as our ActionScript did. It detects the user's IP and encrypts that with the password in the database associated with the login that was sent. Finally, it returns a true or false value along with the same randomly generated string to Flash.

You can see that this is a useful way to secure login information but doesn't really help you out with data you can't compare on the server. Other types of data transfer are harder to secure with Flash; in most cases the best bet there is to use a Secure Socket Layer (SSL) connection.

Parsing data in Flash

Despite some serious increases in Flash player performance with parsing XML and text data, it isn't equipped to handle large data loads very well. The key is to organize your data transfers as efficiently as possible; you want to avoid long waits when the application initializes and don't want to trigger too many calls to the server to make the user experience as fluent as possible.

Let's take a train schedule for example. If you were to write a Flash application that allows users to look up train schedule information, you obviously wouldn't load all the departure times, trains, and platform number information in at the same time. Yet at the same time just loading information for one particular train might not be the best thing to do. You could predict that a user might want to know about the previous and next train and returning this information from your call to the server makes the whole experience much more enjoyable. Balancing out data load with task workflow is what you'll have to bear in mind.

For applications like the one discussed previously, you might want to consider using Flash Remoting technology, which uses binary AMF files to communicate directly with Flash from the server. Using this technology allows your server-side data to keep its datatype intact when loaded into Flash so that it doesn't require any further parsing (see Chapter 18 for more information).

As you'll have noticed, most concerns you'll have to deal with when planning a Flash project are related to data security and performance issues. Now, how does this affect the planning process?

From my own experience I've seen that back-end development and Flash applications are often designed and modeled as totally different processes. The consequence there is that it brings all the stress of your application to the middle scripting layer, which is forced to do extensive data manipulation to get it molded into shape for use with the Flash application. It's not easy to have a square peg fit into a round hole.

Ideally the scripting layer should simply act as a *gateway* for presenting the back-end data to the Flash client. To achieve that it is important to look at the data flow between the server and the client and model in a way that allows for easy integration.

Introduction to UML modeling

The Unified Modeling Language (UML) is an incredibly useful for tool for modeling applications. The language was first introduced in 1997 as a way to visually represent object-oriented projects and has become the de facto means to visually represent object-oriented structures and processes.

When building a model of your application, you typically have multiple views that are mapped in diagrams. UML supports nine different diagrams that can be applied to create different views: class, object, use case, sequence, collaboration, statechart, activity, component, and deployment diagrams. You can find a short overview with a description of the different diagrams in the following table:

Diagram	Description
Class	Describes the static class structure of an application
Object	Describes the static structure of class instances at a certain point in time
Use case	Describes application functionality using actors and use cases
Sequence	Describes data interaction between individual classes
Collaboration	Describes class interaction in the application as a whole
Statechart	Describes class behavior in response to external data
Activity	Describes the flow between different tasks of the application
Component	Describes dependencies between components of the application
Deployment	Describes physical resources used for deploying the application

In the scope of this book, I'm not able to provide you a full and in-depth reference for UML modeling but will introduce you to the concepts that will help you get started modeling Flash ActionScript projects.

I'll first run you through the reasons for choosing UML and then move on to discussing building a class diagram, which is without doubt the most essential diagram to have from a code-centric point of view.

Why use UML?

Why would you use UML to model your application? There are several reasons why UML is the way to go and I'll discuss a couple of those right now.

UML offers standardized notation and has a language-neutral syntax

Standards are very important when modeling an application; you want to have something that everyone can understand. If you model an application using UML and a different developer is assigned to its development, that developer should easily be able to take over the project.

UML can be used to model anything

You can model anything from a business process down to a software class structure. The various diagrams that are supported by UML allow you to visually represent just about anything you might need.

Aside from the advantages discussed previously, you'll soon notice that using UML helps you out tremendously in the planning process. Being able to visualize concepts and application structure helps you to easily point out any possible weaknesses or imperfections unlike any other method you might have used before. I personally find that using UML in the planning process improves the overall development workflow and decreases the amount of time you'll need to spend on debugging and tweaking the application.

> Any ActionScript developer wanting to get involved with UML for Action-Script 2.0 will do well to give Grant Skinner's free gModeler tool a try (www.gskinner.com/gmodeler/). Not only does this award-winning Flash application allow you to build UML models of your ActionScript project, it also exports ActionScript 2.0 stub code, which is a real time-saver!

Class diagram

The UML class diagram is without doubt the most important diagram you'll be using when planning your Flash ActionScript project. Class diagrams describe the static structure of your application, the classes with their attributes and methods and relationships between them.

Let's look at some basic notation you'll need when creating a class diagram. The first thing you'll notice is that classes are shown as a rectangle that contains its name. Note that the Ball class I'll use as an example in Figure 4-5 is not related to the Ball class discussed earlier in this chapter when looking at planning your project.

Figure 4-5. UML class notation

All classes in your project will be shown in such a rectangle; this is the minimal state in which they need to appear in the class diagram. More often though you'll want to have the attributes (variables) and methods (functions) of that class showing as well. To do this the UML notation extends the class rectangle symbol with two other areas: the top-most is used for attributes and the bottom one for methods (see Figure 4-6).

You might have noticed that the attributes and methods in the Ball class have plus or minus signs before their names. Those signs indicate whether the attribute or method is of a public (+) or private (−) scope. Attribute and method scopes aren't always provided when drawing a UML class diagram, but I find it very useful to do so as it helps with visualizing class interaction.

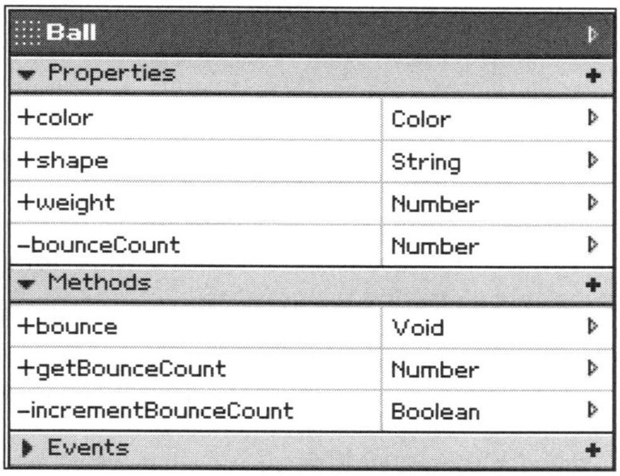

Ball		▷
▼ Properties		+
+color	Color	▷
+shape	String	▷
+weight	Number	▷
−bounceCount	Number	▷
▼ Methods		+
+bounce	Void	▷
+getBounceCount	Number	▷
−incrementBounceCount	Boolean	▷
▶ Events		+

Figure 4-6. UML class attributes and methods

In the preceding example we see three public attributes: shape, weight, and color, which means those values are available outside the class. There also is a bounceCount attribute that is set to private; it cannot be accessed outside the class, but if you look closely there is a public getBounceCount method that returns this value. I'll discuss getter and setter methods in greater detail in later chapters, but its important to note how this helps you achieve encapsulation and prevent attributes from being altered outside the class, which could cause problems with the internal workings. You can also notice that the attributes and methods are followed by a datatype written after their names; this shows you the particular datatype of the attribute, or in the case of methods the datatype of the value it returns.

> At the time of writing this chapter, the gModeler tool does not support public or private scope using the + and - characters when exporting to ActionScript 2.0 stub code. This is, however, easy enough to manually tweak and it will likely be supported in the not-too-distant future.

When you've drawn all classes for your project, you're all set to define their relationships to each other. I'll discuss the most important relationships you'll be needing when working on a Flash ActionScript project next.

Association and generalization

Association is the simplest link you can have between two classes; it describes two classes working together on a conceptual level (see Figure 4-7).

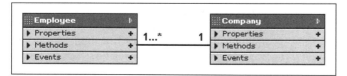

Figure 4-7. UML association relationship

This example shows an association between an Employee class and a Company class. You can clearly see that those two classes are separate entities, and yet there is a link between the two concepts.

In UML notation we show this by connecting the classes with a line; you can optionally write a description of the relationship above the line, in this example "works in." There are situations in which associations will deal with a concept called *multiplicity*. Multiplicity determines the type of association the classes are dealing with. Some types of multiplicity are one to one, one to many, one to one or more, etc.

In the example of our Employee and Company classes, the Company has a one-to-one-or-more association. A company can have one or more employees; that sounds about right.

Generalization is nothing more than a UML term for what we've been calling class inheritance. Using generalization in a class diagram shows what classes inherit from other classes. Let's look at the example shown in Figure 4-8.

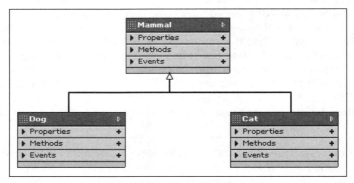

Figure 4-8. UML generalization relationship

As you can see, we've got a Dog and Cat class that both inherit from a Mammal superclass. A superclass or base class is the class that you use to base your new class on. You'll learn more about this in Chapter 9. The notation is not that much different from a class association apart from the fact that the line that connects the classes has an open-ended arrow facing the class from which it inherits. Both the Dog and Cat class will inherit everything that was defined in the Mammal class.

If you look at a UML class diagram and trace the class back in the direction the empty arrows are pointing, you automatically arrive at one or more base classes for the application from which it all started.

Aggregation and composition

There will quite often be situations in which you need to model a class that consists of multiple components. The way UML handles this is by relationships called *aggregation* and *composition*.

Let's take a PC for example. As shown in Figure 4-9, the way you would visualize that is by creating class elements for each of the components and a class that represents the whole. The components are connected to the whole with a solid line, and an empty diamond shape is added at the end to represent an aggregation-type relationship.

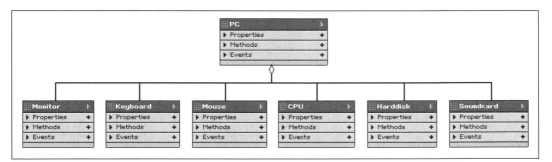

Figure 4-9. UML aggregation relationship

The model shown in Figure 4-9 is a limited representation of a PC that consists of components like a monitor, keyboard, mouse, etc. Now, what exactly is the difference between aggregation and composition? It's not always an easy distinction to make but a good rule of thumb is the following:

> *In aggregation the whole cannot exist without its components, while in a composition the components cannot exist without the whole.*

A good example of composition is a human being. If the human dies, its parts die with it. If we look at our PC aggregation example, while the PC might not continue working, the monitor, keyboard, and mouse components will all remain functional as stand-alone parts and can be used in another PC.

UML notation for composition is very similar to that of aggregation except for the fact that it uses a filled diamond shape at the connection between the component and the whole, as you can see in Figure 4-10.

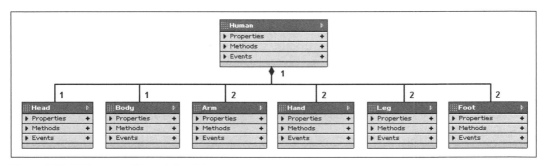

Figure 4-10. UML composition relationship

The difference between aggregation and composition is mostly conceptual for Flash ActionScript projects; it just shows you whether or not the components need to be destroyed when the whole is destroyed.

This concludes my short introduction to UML. This is by no means a complete overview but has taught you some basic skills that will enable you to start modeling most Flash ActionScript applications. For more information on the topic, you might want to look at the book *Fast Track UML 2.0* by Kendall Scott (Apress, 2004), which is dedicated to the subject and goes far beyond just the class diagram.

What's next?

Be sure not to underestimate the importance of this chapter; I've covered some essential information here that will help you work more efficiently and productively. The introduction to UML is a must-read if you're interested in pursuing application development in Flash ActionScript.

Coming up in the next chapter, I'll discuss project workflow, versioning control, and usability testing, which are all very important topics to read up on before embarking on actual application development.

5 PROJECT WORKFLOW

We've certainly covered quite a number of topics by now; you've learned about programming concepts, using ActionScript 2.0, and how to plan and model your applications. Now it's time to look at how you can take all those things and integrate them in your project workflow.

Project workflow describes the process by which you most efficiently handle applications from start to finish. In Chapter 6 I'll discuss best practices for coding in ActionScript 2.0, but first I want to introduce you to some topics that are essential to painlessly completing your projects. One of those topics is version control, which has no doubt saved many developers from chronic insanity. Be sure to read up on this, if you're not already using it!

After covering the basics of version control, I'll move on to discussing some important approaches to programming that will help you be more productive in the way you work.

Introducing version control

Version control is a system that allows you to keep track of multiple versions of source code. It provides you with a history of your development process and supports some advanced features that simple backup files just can't match.

You might think that it is all well and good to track the history of your code, but wouldn't that take an enormous amount of disk space storing all those copies of the project? No it won't; version control is smart enough to store only the actual changes that were made to files, not the entire files themselves. Which is, when you think about it, much more efficient than the way we usually back up our code.

Whether you're working in a team or as a single developer, it is imperative that you use a form of version control to prevent any loss of code or wasted hours of coding trying to revert to a version you might have created days earlier. Not using version control is probably the single biggest risk you can take when developing an application.

I'll be discussing the benefits of using a version control system as well as running you through the basics of setting up and managing a local *Concurrent Versions System* repository for your project in the following few sections of this chapter.

About Concurrent Versions System

Concurrent Versions System (CVS) is without doubt the most well-known open source implementation of version control. Using CVS, your source code gets maintained in a code *repository* where it generates a branched tree structure based on the different versions of a file you (or colleagues) submitted. The reason why CVS uses a tree structure is because that allows developers not just to work in a linear sequence, but also build out different branches of code based on a particular revision of a file.

The application uses a client/server model that hosts your code repositories. It also uses a nonexclusive process whereby multiple developers can simultaneously work on the same file without breaking each others' code—isn't that just brilliant!

When I look back at my early web developer days, there were many a occasions when there needed to be some very last-minute changes made to a website before it could be pushed live. This resulted in the entire team (often project manager included) frantically typing code to get all the tweaks done on time. About half an hour before deadline, we usually managed to get it all finished up only to realize that some of us were working on the very same page and had overwritten each others' work, resulting in a lot of shouting, finger pointing, and even more frantic typing.

Those days are luckily in the past. Using CVS, you can now have developers working on the same file by *checking out* that file from the code repository and *committing* changes back to repository when they've finished. If another developer made changes to the file and committed it to the repository before you did, you'll be asked to *update* your file, which automatically *merges* your changes with the latest copy from the repository. If by any chance multiple developers were working on the same line of code, CVS will not be able to merge the files, and you'll be prompted to manually correct that line before it gets merged.

Getting confused? You shouldn't be; let's recapitulate and look at some basic CVS terminology in the following table:

Repository	Directory in which all CVS files are stored.
Module	Files in the repository are grouped in modules.
Add	Add a local file to a module in the CVS repository.
Remove	Remove a file from a module in the CVS repository.
Check out	Get a local copy of a file from the CVS repository.
Update	Merge the latest version of the file in the CVS repository with your local copy.
Commit	Add or merge the local copy of a file with the CVS repository.
Release	Remove the local copy of a file retrieved from the CVS repository.
Revision	Number indicating the version of particular file.
Tag	Give a common version name to all files in a module.
Diff	Retrieve the difference between a local file and the one in the CVS repository.
History	Retrieve the revision history for a file in the CVS repository.

The commands as listed in the preceding table are those you'll most commonly use. This by no means attempts to be a full and comprehensive list, but it should give you a good idea of what to expect.

The way you would usually work with CVS is walk through the following steps for each file you want to make changes to:

1. Check out a file from the CVS repository.
2. Make the necessary changes to that file.
3. Execute an update command on that file.
4. Commit your changes to that file back to the CVS repository.

Now what does that mean in plain English? Well, it's not very difficult: you get a file from the CVS server, make changes to it, and before submitting your changes back to the CVS server, you check whether there is a more recent version available on the server (someone might have submitted a newer version while you were working). If there is a newer version available on the CVS server, it will merge with your file, which you can then safely submit back to the server.

All those goodies do come at a price. A CVS server can be quite hard to install and configure and has a small but relatively steep learning curve. Luckily for us, there is software out there that makes this all much easier for us. My personal favorite is the *TortoiseCVS* client, which actually gives you CVS control at the click of a mouse right from within Windows Explorer.

> *TortoiseCVS is unfortunately not available for Mac. The following section discusses how the software can be used on the PC platform. There is, however, a great open source Mac CVS client available called MacCVS, which is based on the WinCVS client, the source code which in turn TortoiseCVS was originally based on. You can find more information about this on* www.wincvs.org.

Using TortoiseCVS

TortoiseCVS is an easy-to-use CVS client that supports common CVS tasks. It allows you to check out, update, and commit files right from within your familiar Windows Explorer interface. More importantly, it won't cost you a cent; the client software is open source and available as a free download at www.tortoiseCVS.org.

One of the key benefits of TortoiseCVS is that it supports local repositories, which is perfect if you're a single developer working on a project and don't want to go to the trouble of installing a CVS server. It's complete enough for most enterprise projects and basic enough for your basic programming needs.

Charlie Vernon Smythe (CVS for short) is the lovable mascot for TortoiseCVS (see Figure 5-1) and, despite the reputation of its species, will have your local repository set up by the time you're back from the bathroom. OK, well that's not entirely true . . . you will have to do some actual work yourself. Not to worry, though, I'll walk you through it in a couple of easy steps.

Figure 5-1.
Charlie the TortoiseCVS mascot

First, the obvious: you download a copy of TortoiseCVS from the website (www.tortoiseCVS) and install it on your PC. You'll be prompted to restart your system; be sure to do that to make sure the icons in Windows Explorer will work properly.

The next thing you'll want to do is create a repository for your code. Open up Windows Explorer and browse to the folder you'd like to have act as your repository. You right-click that folder and choose CVS ➤ Make New Module, which brings up the dialog box shown in Figure 5-2.

Figure 5-2.
Make New Module dialog box

In this dialog box you set the protocol to Locally Mounted Folder and specify the full path to the folder (including the folder name itself) in the Repository folder field. Next, you click the OK button, which brings up the import dialog box. Wait for another dialog box to pop up telling you no repository was found and asking you whether or not you want to initialize one (see Figure 5-3). You select that checkbox and again click OK to continue.

Figure 5-3. TortoiseCVS initialize repository dialog box

Now that the repository is initialized, wait for the module dialog box to finish and click OK to close it (see Figure 5-4).

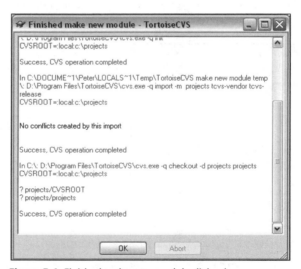

Figure 5-4. Finished make new module dialog box

That's not bad, is it? It probably took you longer to read this than to actually do it. Well this is it, you've got yourself a local CVS repository and module to work in. You'll notice that the folder now has a green overlay indicating that it is controlled by CVS.

Now, let's go one step further and add some actual source code to this local repository. Create a new file in that folder and name it SomeClass.as. As soon as you've created that file, you'll notice that you see a big question mark sign on top of the normal icon associated with an ActionScript file. The question mark shows you that the file is not yet added to the repository; to do this you right-click the file and choose CVS add, which brings up the dialog box you see in Figure 5-5.

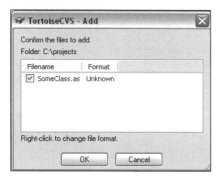

Figure 5-5.
TortoiseCVS Add dialog box

You notice that the dialog box shows your SomeClass.as file but isn't able to determine the filetype format. You just right-click the file and choose Text/ASCII. Good to note is that TortoiseCVS also supports binary files, which allows you to keep a version history for images or even your FLA source files. When you click the OK button, you get a dialog box confirming that your file has been added to the module in your repository (see Figure 5-6). The overlay icon for the file now changes from a question mark to a red mesh.

Figure 5-6. TortoiseCVS Finished add dialog box

Now that your file is added to the repository, you can add some initial code to it. Open up SomeClass.as and insert the following code:

```
class SomeClass {
  function SomeClass() {
  }
}
```

You've just added a basic class structure to the file and can now save it. What you do now is commit the file to the local *repository*. Because you are working in a local repository, you only deal with one developer and do not have to worry about *updating* your code first. Back in Windows Explorer, right-click the file SomeClass.as and choose CVS commit, which brings up the dialog box in Figure 5-7.

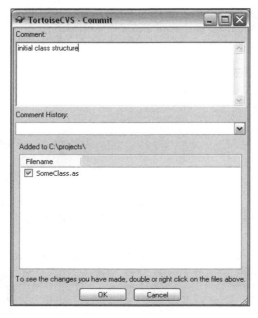

Figure 5-7.
TortoiseCVS Commit dialog box

In the Commit dialog box you notice a Comment field; I'd advise you always to include something in this field. Doing so allows you to easily see what particular review you made; a time and date doesn't do as much to refresh your memory. Add "initial class structure" as the comment for your first SomeClass.as revision. After clicking the OK button, a dialog box pops up telling you that the file has been committed to the repository (see Figure 5-8).

Figure 5-8.
TortoiseCVS Finished commit dialog box

After you close the Finished commit dialog box the overlay icon for SomeClass.as will change from a red to a green mesh, confirming that the revision has been posted to the repository.

Let's do one more basic revision to the file to show you how the version history works and how to revert to an earlier version. Make the following changes to SomeClass.as:

```
class SomeClass {
  function SomeClass() {
    trace("constructor called");
  }
```

```
    function someMethod() {
    }
}
```

In a real-world situation, you would obviously not commit a file back to the repository for such a minor revision. Save the file and again right-click the file in Windows Explorer, choose CVS commit, follow the steps as described earlier, and set the comment field to "added someMethod method". You will have noticed that once you saved your changes, the icon overlay changed back from green to red, indicating that there were changes that have not yet been committed to the repository.

Now that you've got two revisions to your file, you can look at the version history. To do this you right-click SomeClass.as and choose CVS ➤ History, which brings up a dialog box showing you all revisions (see Figure 5-9).

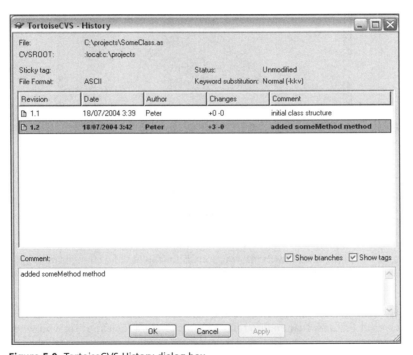

Figure 5-9. TortoiseCVS History dialog box

You'll notice that the History dialog box shows you the revision number, date and time, and author for that specific file. It also shows you how many lines of code were added and how many removed. In this case it shows you that three lines of code were added and none removed between revision 1.1 and 1.2 and the comments you added for those revisions.

To revert to an earlier version of a file, you just right-click that revision in the History dialog box and choose Get this revision (sticky). When you close the History panel, that particular revision will be saved back to your local file. Don't worry about losing any changes you made later on, those are still tracked in the History panel and you can always get that revision should you need it.

Another very nice feature in TortoiseCVS is the ability to get a graph showing your revisions. You do this by right-clicking the file and choosing CVS ➤ Revision graph (see Figure 5-10).

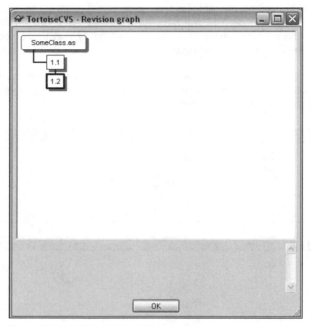

Figure 5-10. TortoiseCVS revision graph

The revision graph gives you a nice overview of the history of a file. By clicking any of the revisions, you'll be presented with information about the author, changes made, and comments. This is a very handy feature to use if you want to look back at the development path of your files.

This concludes my brief introduction to the TortoiseCVS client. I'm sure it has shown you some powerful features that will undoubtedly make life a lot easier for you when doing object-oriented programming with ActionScript 2.0.

Approaches to programming

Over the last few years we've heard a lot about various approaches to programming. No, these aren't just buzzwords for cunning marketeers. Both the client and yourself can actually benefit from choosing an effective and complementary way to work on a particular project.

Whatever acronym you decide to call it is of little importance, but more importantly you need to have the rules for your way of working clearly outlined and consistently used. I'll briefly be discussing two programming concepts that have become quite popular recently, especially for projects that use Flash and ActionScript: Rapid Application Development and Extreme Programming.

Rapid Application Development

Rapid Application Development (RAD) is a popular programming methodology that allows applications to be built under a tight deadline and often limited budget. It lends itself well to applications that don't have very specific requirements to start with providing you're able to get good user feedback throughout the development cycle.

To achieve this, there often needs to be some compromises made, which is highlighted in one of the key principles of RAD, the 80-20 rule:

In certain situations, a usable 80% solution can be produced in 20% of the time that would be required to produce a total solution.

In a nutshell, the RAD process includes the following steps:

1. Brainstorm initial specifications.
2. Prototype system and have client review.
3. Update application.
4. Conduct user reviews (repeat step 3 as necessary).
5. Create project analysis (optional).
6. Finalize application.

Now this, of course, sounds very compelling, but is that really possible? Bringing RAD into practice requires quite some discipline on the part of the developer, specifically in regards to scheduling reviewing user comments. To best achieve this, you should work with milestones for your project. After an initial brainstorm session with the client, provisional specifications are outlined and implemented in a *prototype system*.

You can't expect a nontechnical client to give you feedback on source code, so you need to have a basic working prototype version of the application (be it limited in functionality) for them to play around with and give feedback on. This prototype system is the first milestone of your project and is typically just reviewed by the client to finalize the requirements and feature set and start the actual application development.

At this stage scheduling becomes increasingly important, and you need to bring out application updates at a regular interval for users to review. The development cycle is driven by feedback so it is very important that you can get timely and complete feedback from your users. The cycle of update and review is repeated as long as is deemed necessary and feasible given the deadline. Ideally, reviewing the application would not happen by the client or yourself but by the actual user the application is targeting, which always gives you the most useful feedback on the flow of the application.

Once the development cycle is closed, you can move on to an optional analysis stage. Analysis of the project gives your client the opportunity for a final review. While the analysis stage is not a requirement in RAD, it certainly is recommended practice when the project relies on tight integration with another application or a degree of security needs to be implemented.

After the development cycle or project analysis, the code is finalized and prepared for deployment. If no analysis was done before this final stage, it is important that no further changes to the source code are made; if there was an analysis stage, changes to the code should be limited to any problems that came up.

RAD is a very useful programming methodology that you'll no doubt be using quite a lot for typical ActionScript 2.0 projects. The concept of Flash components fits in well with this process, so be sure to read more about v2 component development in Chapter 15. If you think about it, Flash is really a great tool for doing RAD. It allows you to do quick prototyping, design and code are managed using the same IDE, it has a relatively low learning curve, and it is a highly portable, which helps tremendously with the testing and reviewing process.

Extreme Programming

Extreme **P**rogramming (XP) is another interesting programming methodology and is, far more so than RAD, applicable when working with a team of developers.

Breaking down the XP development process into steps is not as straightforward as with RAD, but roughly translates into the following sequence:

1. Define an initial release plan.
2. Put together an iteration plan based on user stories.
3. Use pair programming to develop an iteration.
4. Run acceptance tests on the completed iteration (repeat step 3 as necessary).
5. Project is finished when the code has passed all acceptance tests.

Throughout XP there are a number of practices that all rely on principles of *simplicity* and *communication*. One of the most obvious differences the XP methodology introduces is the way it handles a team. The client is actually part of the team and works with the developers on a daily basis helping to steer everything in the right direction, defining priorities and further outlining the requirements for the project.

There are no strict roles in the team but rather personal expertise; everyone can contribute to the project within their area of expertise. A team can consist of anywhere from 2 to 15 people, though this methodology generally works better with small teams. As you can well imagine, this type of setup can be prone to a mild form of anarchy when not focused properly, and it is therefore often advisable to have a person designated to coordinate the process.

Another major part of XP is planning. There are two types of planning that XP uses, *release planning* and *iteration planning*. The release planning outlines the schedule for the overall project, while iteration planning uses this release plan for scheduling individual iterations of the project during the development process. The way release plans are created is by evaluating *user stories* that the client in the team supplies.

Each user story is basically a short description of a task that the application needs to perform. Those user stories are basic nontechnical and user-centric descriptions of a task that will need to be reviewed by developers in the team to ascertain how much development time it would need. As an alternative to a long requirement document, these user stories are used to make up iterations and plans that fall within the constraints of the release plan.

User stories are used to compile an iteration and to base *acceptance tests* on. Acceptance tests are scenarios outlined by the client and are used to verify whether the application returns the expected result based on the input. If these acceptance tests are passed, the user story is considered complete; if not, the issue will need to be addressed in the following iteration. If an iteration becomes too heavy to handle (usually due to failed acceptance tests in earlier iterations), you can meet with the client and reschedule the user stories in following iterations.

The way development works in a XP environment is using *pair development*. Two developers sit side by side at the same machine and work. The idea behind this is that you get better code because it is continuously monitored by a second developer. Recent studies have also confirmed that $1 + 1 > 2$ when it comes to programming. Pair development takes a while to get used to and requires the developers in question to work well together; if that is not the case, this technique can cause accelerated production of gray hair.

Refactoring, another concept that XP strongly supports, involves breaking down code to the simplest level possible, only keeping the necessary functionality in there. Doing this avoids bloated and difficultly managed code down the line. Repeating the refactoring process might look very harsh, but it will definitely pay off in the end.

So far, so good. You'll notice that with XP the team setup is open and dynamic, while the project itself is scheduled and monitored very strictly. This certainly helps keep the project on track along with automated *unit testing*. Automated tests are very important in XP; they help monitor your code and run objective tests independent of anyone in the team. Based on the results of the automated tests, the development process is tweaked until all user stories are addressed and application is considered final.

XP goes beyond simply being a programming methodology in that it requires you to not only follow a certain project workflow, but also actually organize practical aspects of your business to have them fit in with an XP development environment.

Throughout these various steps, members in the team might take on various roles and contribute in a variety of ways. Communication and planning are very important to have this work properly and should not be ignored at any stage of the development process.

Applying XP techniques to your programming workflow is certainly a good idea. While you might not be able to go for the full package, individual techniques like pair programming or unit testing are certainly worth considering!

I myself recently started using a remote form of pair programming for a number of ActionScript projects. While it may not be as effective as physically sitting at the same computer with a co-developer, I've had great experiences with getting specific code issues worked out.

One instance I can remember was when writing a Flash application that handles shared calendars. There were some problems getting recurring events validated for all users subscribed to the same group calendar. Myself and another developer were initially working separately on finding a solution for this and just compared notes. Unfortunately, that didn't really resolve the issue until we started to do a couple of shared coding sessions.

Using Flash Communication Server we set up a little application through which we could in turn work on the same piece of ActionScript code while the other one checked syntax and comments on the approach. After just a couple of those sessions, and what could not have been more than half a day's work, we found the key to solving the problem on what had earlier took us several days to work on individually. It's quite amazing how effective pair programming can be in some instances, even with your fellow developer located all the way across the ocean.

Usability testing

Usability testing is an often underestimated process that allows you to get real-world information about the way a target user handles your application.

What do you attempt to find out with usability tests? That is a valid question—not all information you can get from users is relevant for evaluating a project. One thing you do know is that you want to make sure users are able to independently perform the tasks that the application was built for. Building on that information, you can find out how easy it was for a user to navigate through the application and complete various required steps.

Often usability tests are thought of as a means of evaluating a project near the end of its development cycle. Nothing is further from the truth. Usability tests can (or dare I say should) be used throughout the entire project workflow. All too often this step is neglected, resulting in bad user experience which in turn influences *return on investment* for the project.

Usability tests during the development cycle don't have to be very elaborate, but they do differ from simple reviews of your application. Remember, the tests serve to get feedback from actual users; it would be bad practice for yourself or the client to take part. When working with multiple user tests, make sure not all people participating in the test have taken part in one or an earlier version. It is important to have users test an application without any prior knowledge, so while it may be interesting to see how previous testers handle the new version, the information you need to act upon is always that of the new people in the test group.

So how do you put together a usability test? First, make sure you have clearly defined the target audience and try to represent that as closely as possible in your test group. Users are each representative for a significant number of people. While you might think that an application that reaches 1,000 users will need more usability testers than one for 100 people, this doesn't appear to be the case. In fact, statistics indicate that groups of just five people give the best overall results. What that means in practical terms is that it's more effective to invest in multiple limited usability tests than a couple of large ones.

When you've got your user test group together, you need to address the questions that you want answered with the usability test. Tests can include questions based on *information* users can get from the application; you can also ask about their *experience* of using the application or have them perform *tasks* with the application to time how efficiently they can get to the desired information.

Let's say we've got a car configurator application that we're running a usability test on. The application lets users choose a model car and customize it to their liking with any accessories, finally to be presented with the total price of their ideal car. Questions and tasks for this type of project might be

- What colors can you get the latest model of a BMW in?
- How much does it cost to include a GPS system with the car?
- What model car would you first look at when searching for a family vehicle?
- Would you be more likely to buy a particular model car after trying the car configurator?
- Locate the car dealer closest to your home.
- Find all car models that come with built-in air conditioning.

Important with asking these questions is that you don't guide users through it. Try not to suggest an answer with the way you ask your question, and before having users take the test simply explain what the application is without discussing how to use it. Monitor users objectively and compare statistics between different releases. Doing that gives you a good indication of how far the changes you made based on prior feedback have been successful.

When handled properly, usability tests are an invaluable tool to make sure your applications do what you want them to do and increase user experience. In the end, that's what it's all about. An application is not just a collection of features, but a way for you to present data in a format that is most efficient and enjoyable for the end user.

What's next?

This chapter discussed aspects of the project workflow that will help you organize and handle your projects most effectively. In the next chapter I'll discuss some more practical considerations when working with ActionScript 2.0, such as commenting, naming conventions, and other best practices.

6 BEST PRACTICES

In the previous chapter we looked at some important aspects of managing a project work-flow. Now we'll specifically explore best practices for working with ActionScript. Best practices aim to make your programming experience as comfortable as possible and outline some standardized methods to structuring and managing code.

The coding practices and naming conventions that will be discussed here are in no way legally binding (I promise I won't sue—unless of course you forget to comment your code!), but I can't stress enough the importance of writing consistent and readable code. What you'll find here can be thought of as the common denominator of best programming practices; be sure to read through these best practices and apply them as much as possible to your project.

External ActionScript

As you know after reading Chapter 3 on ActionScript 2.0 programming, all ActionScript classes you code must be placed in external `.as` files. You might think of this as a bit of an annoyance, but it actually does have a number of advantages such as the ability to work with class packages.

Class packages allow you to organize classes in a folder structure and organize by the specific tasks they perform. One of the main reasons you use class packages is to help avoid naming conflicts; by "packaging" classes in a unique folder structure, you can be sure that you don't accidentally use a class with the same name in the classpath.

Let's say you've written a bunch of classes that deal with user management. Putting those classes in the same folder with classes that handle date functions would not be the most efficient approach. Rather than doing that, you would make two class packages and structure those as follows:

```
com.friendsofed.users
com.friendsofed.date
```

We'll look more into this package naming convention in more detail later on in this chapter, but for now it is good to see that you organized your classes in a folder with a name that best corresponds with the task they perform. In the case of your user management classes, those are put in the folder named users and the classes dealing with dates are put in a date folder. Those two folders are themselves subfolders of the friendsofed package that is a package of com. This again might look a bit convoluted but it makes good sense, as Figure 6-1 illustrates.

Figure 6-1. Package folder structure

ActionScript 2.0 features an `import` keyword that can use a wildcard character (*) to load an entire class package in with a single statement. The `com.friendsofed.users` package might contain 20 different classes but a single line of code will do all that work for you:

```
import com.friendsofed.users.*
```

Now, let's not get too excited—there are a couple of "buts" that you should take into consideration. Let's say you wanted to import both the `com.friendsofed.users` and `com.friendsofed.date` packages. Trying to avoid RSI, my inherent developer instinct would tell me to make that into one import statement:

```
import com.friendsofed.*
```

No such luck, however; that statement will load all classes in the `com.friendsofed` package but no classes that are located in a folder below that. If you need both packages, you will need to use

```
import com.friendsofed.users.*
import com.friendsofed.date.*
```

Another point to make is that import statements only make temporary references to the package in question. If you have an import statement on Frame 1 of your timeline, and you wanted to use it again in the next frame, it would not work. To achieve that, you'd need to use the `import` statement again.

That's all well and good, but keeping in mind the limitations, is it really necessary to use class packages? The answer there is a definite YES! Working with class packages in itself is perfect when doing OOP because it helps you work in a more organized and structured way. Should you use `import` statements is a different question altogether. My personal take on this is that you only need them when using more than one or two instances of the class in your frame and you're working with long package names. In other situations, import statements don't serve that much of a purpose, and it's just as easy to instantiate classes by their fully qualified class package name. We'll compare the two options next:

Using the `import` statement:

```
import com.friendsofed.users.*
var userInfo:UserProfile = new UserProfile();
```

Using the full package name:

```
var userInfo:UserProfile = new com.friendsofed.users.UserProfile();
```

The preceding examples assume we have a class called `UserProfile` in the `com.friendsofed.users` package and clearly show that when you're not extensively instantiating classes, there is no real use to the import statement (in fact, in this case it will give you slightly more code to write). Of course, there will be situations where you're dealing with more complex scripts that will require you to make lots more class instances, and in those cases you could certainly consider using the `import` keyword.

6

I would, however, recommend always using `import` when coding your ActionScript 2.0 classes; adding the `import` statement on top of your `.as` file will allow you to find all class dependencies at a single glance as soon as you open up the file.

Let's move on to another very important subject that is often underestimated and happily ignored: commenting your code.

About commenting

Comments are notes that programmers insert into their code to clarify important aspects of the application. With all the new technology these days, comments seldom get the attention they deserve. Many trainers assume that if you can write a simple program, you must know how to write comments. Not true. I want to bring comments back to the foreground and tell you the correct way to use them.

Some programmers don't write comments. Ever. Others write so many comments, it's nearly impossible to read their code. There's a better way, with neither too few nor too many comments. To maintain the middle course, just remember the word *why*.

Ideally, comments should answer the question *why* (not *what*). The code already demonstrates *what* it is doing, but it may not be clear *why*. When you need to explain *why* in your code, consider including a comment.

> *Some programmers write comments that restate (in their spoken language) what the code already demonstrates. If your code reads n = 10, there's no need to write a comment that reads "Setting the variable named n equal to 10." The real comment should be "n represents the number of seconds until the rocket launches." Ultimately, strive to write naturally self-descriptive code. If you write code such as secondsToLaunch = 10, then you don't need to include a comment in the first place.*

Comments in ActionScript are ignored when your project is compiled down to a `.swf` file, so you definitely don't need to worry about bloating file size of the finished application. There are two ways by which you can add comments to your ActionScript code. The first one is used for small notes that take no more than one single line.

```
// This is a single-line comment
```

When you need multiple lines of comments, it's best to use a comment block by using a combination of the /* and */ characters.

```
/*
    This is a comment block.
    Everything in here is a comment.
*/
```

Now that you know how to add comments to your code, let's consider when you should add them. I personally use the following commenting style when writing classes:

```
/*
UserProfile
Author: Peter Elst
Revision: 1.2
Description: The UserProfile class manages personal user information
To-do: add method for deleting a profile property
*/
```

The preceding example shows what I add on top of all my classes: the class name, author, revision number, and description. The to-do information is optional and helps you remember what functionality you planned on adding. If you're faced with a nasty bug, you might also want to flag that up in this comment block.

There is no need to go overboard with commenting; not every method in a class needs additional info. This is certainly the case if you make use of the naming conventions that I'll discuss later on. In theory, your code should be fairly legible with that in place as well as keeping to the advice that I gave in the introduction to OOP where you strictly have one task for one method.

Classes do usually have a couple of methods that are worth commenting. Those are typically the ones where a lot of the data processing happens or those that rely on very specific information to be passed to them. In those instances, I use another short comment block that describes a method's specific task.

```
/*
buildProfile builds an XML document from the user profile
information stored the userData object
*/
```

I generally don't like adding inline comments (comments within functions) because those clutter the code. The only times I use them is when flagging bug locations or development notes.

```
function buildProfile() {
   // Note: for-in loops through object in reverse order
   for(var i in userProfile) {
      ...
   }
}
```

Development notes are just small single-line comments that I put in as reminders when I know I'll be tweaking a specific method. They usually pertain to a very specific part of code and are better placed inline than above the method. The next time I open up the class, I'll find what functions need my attention in the to-do list comment block at the top of the file, and when I move down to that function there will likely be some notes there that help me get started.

6

The commenting styles I use are not based on any particular guideline but have grown from my own experience with coding ActionScript 2.0 classes. You might well want to use a slightly different approach and of course you're free to do so. There are a few benchmarks you can use to check how effective your commenting style is:

1. Do your comments increase readability of the code?

2. Is your commenting style consistent throughout all classes?

3. Do your comments help you be more productive when revising a class?

Those are three very basic questions that will help your determine the quality of your comments. If one or more answers to these questions is "no," then you should really consider changing the way you document your code. If they're all a big fat "yes," then sit back and relax—you've just earned yourself a cup of coffee.

Comments are finally getting the recognition they deserve. Over the last few years several initiatives have been set up that have given commenting best practices a new lease of life. One such initiative is JavaDoc, a tool developed by Sun Microsystems for automatically generating HTML documentation by extracting comments from class source files. This type of commenting has gained ground with many Flash developers since the release of ActionScript 2.0. To read more about this be sure to visit http://java.sun.com/j2se/javadoc/.

Naming conventions

I remember following a discussion on naming conventions when ActionScript 2.0 first came out. Many people were wondering if strong typing and context-sensitive code hints would now make naming conventions obsolete. Definitely not! If anything, naming conventions have become more important with the introduction of things like private and public scope.

Imagine being faced with a property called "foo" in a class with several hundred lines of code with no idea what type it is (unless you cheat and try to use code hints on it), if it is a public or private property, etc. I've had to deal with classes like that before and let me tell you, it's not a pretty sight. If there's one way to get a fellow developer lose his nerve, this is it.

After a while reading ActionScript code becomes like a second language. Naming conventions play a big part in this; they provide the developer with a lot of background information on properties and method names that allow him or her to work in a much more convenient and productive way.

Enough promotion, let's get to it! The naming conventions discussed here are very common throughout most programming languages and are ideal for working with ActionScript 2.0.

Variables

Variables are namespaces to which you can assign a particular datatype and assign values. Names for variables can contain letters, numbers, the dollar sign ($), or an underscore (_).

Things to consider are that variable names cannot start with a number, and there are a number of reserved words such as class and import that are also not allowed.

In general, variable names consisting of more than one word are written in *camel case*, starting with a lowercase letter and using an uppercase letter for every new word like so: thisIsMyVariable. This is by far the most common practice, and I would certainly recommend using this.

An example of a variable declaration is var countSheep:Number = 500;.

Constants

Constants are variables whose value does not change after they have been initialized. An example of a built-in constant in the Math object is Math.PI.

The naming convention for constants is using all uppercase and separating words with underscores. An example of a constant declaration is var MAX_SHEEP:Number = 500;.

Functions

Functions are reusable containers for code; they can be used throughout an application and usually return a value based on one or more parameters that is passed to them.

Function names follow the same convention as variables do. Names for functions usually consist of two parts; the first is a verb that describes the task it performs, and the second is a noun that defines the object it applies that task to. That sounds much more difficult than it actually is; here are a couple of examples:

```
getProfile();
validateEmail();
parseFeed();
```

Classes

Classes are essential building blocks for doing object-oriented programming. They provide a collection of variables and functions (respectively called *properties* and *methods* in this context) from which multiple independent instances can be created.

The naming convention for classes is camel case, but with an initial uppercase letter. Usually names for classes just consist of a single nonplural noun. It is important to keep your class names as descriptive as possible; try to avoid too generic terms.

Some example of class names are

```
Ball
Sheep
UserProfile
```

6

71

Methods

Methods are essentially functions defined inside a class, and as such they use largely the same naming convention. The difference with methods is that they can have a public or private scope, and some developers like to prefix the name with a dollar or underscore sign to designate it as private. This naming convention is not essential, but it can make your classes more readable, which is always a good thing.

Some examples of method names are

```
buildTable()
$processData()
_parseFeed ();
```

Properties

Properties are variables defined inside a class, and as such use the same naming convention. Just like methods, properties can be assigned a public or private scope. To show what properties are private, you can use the dollar or underscore sign.

Some examples of property names are

```
$profileID
_indexCounter
```

I personally choose to use the dollar sign for private methods and the underscore sign for private properties. Feel free to make your own choice; the two are widely in use with ActionScript developers.

Packages

Packages, as discussed earlier in this chapter, are folder namespaces that you can store classes in to give them a unique identifier, and you can use them to sort classes by function and make importing classes easier.

There is a very common naming convention with packages that originally came from languages such as Java. The first part of a package name is com, which is taken from Internet jargon. You could certainly use org or net for this if either is more suitable. Next in the package name is either your company name or the name of the project the classes are used for. These two namespaces form the basis of your package name, and in most cases this corresponds to the domain name of your organization or project.

```
Example: com.friendsofed
```

It is recommended by the software vendor that you use an mx prefix or com.macromedia, which I personally dislike because it can blur the distinction between your work and classes that come with Flash. Once you've got this basis for your package name, you can go on and add your own folders and extend the package name as far as you find necessary.

Some examples of package names are

```
com.friendsofed.sports
com.friendsofed.animals
com.friendsofed.users
```

As discussed earlier, class names are written in camel case and start with an uppercase letter, which might result in the following class import statements:

```
import com.friendsofed.sports.Ball;
import com.friendsofed.animals.Sheep;
import com.friendsofed.users.UserProfile;
```

Applying naming conventions should, just like commenting your code, become an essential part of your ActionScript 2.0 programming practice. I'm sure you'll have noticed how consistent names for the different elements in your application make a huge difference in understanding what they represent and are used for. We'll explore some further aspects of good coding practices next by discussing good programming styles.

6

Programming styles

There's more to writing code than typing instructions from this (or any other) computer book. There's also programming style, which is really essential as you'll notice from an example of sloppy programming that follows.

> *I've mentioned earlier that it is important to remember that it's likely at some stage other developers will be using your code. Being faced with unreadable and/or badly written code is not very pleasant and will only result in frustration. Just a few tweaks and good coding practice will make life easier for everyone involved.*

Sloppy pseudo-code

```
Start of Application
Variable
  Variable
Variable
Start of Function
    Instruction
Instruction
  Instruction
        End of Function
```

```
Start of Function
 Instruction
Instruction
    Instruction
End of Function
  End of Application
```

Cleaning up the preceding example is not that difficult; the things to keep in mind are *consistency* and *spacing*. Just take a look at the improvement when this very same code is spaced consistently in the following example. I put *at least* one blank line between so-called paragraphs of code (groups of related code). I use consistent indentation to illustrate the code's natural hierarchy (what belongs to what).

Cleaned-up pseudo-code

```
Start of Application

    Variable
    Variable
    Variable

    Start of Function
        Instruction
        Instruction
        Instruction
    End of Function

    Start of Function
        Instruction
        Instruction
        Instruction
    End of Function

End of Application
```

The code just discussed is a very generic overview of how to structure an application. Let's bring this into perspective for use with ActionScript 2.0 classes.

Sloppy ActionScript 2.0 class

```
class myClass {
  function myClass() {
    var TextColor:Color = 0x003366;
trace("Constructor");
  }
var userName:String = "Peter";
  var maxcount = 5;
```

```
      var base_url:String = "http://www.friendsofed.com";
private function reverseString(str):String {
    var tmp = str.split("").reverse();
    return tmp.join("");
  }
function set URL(url:String) {
base_url = url;
}
      function loadSite(){
    getURL(base_url,"_blank");
  }
  private var _foundNumber:Boolean;
function $isEvenNumber(num:Number) {
return (num % 2 == 0);
}
private var _countIndex;
  function countLoop(){
    for(var i=1; i<=maxcount; i++) {
      trace("Loop "+i+" of "+maxcount);
    }
  }
  function get URL():String {
return base_url;
}
}
```

The preceding example is rather extreme, but you can see how inconsistent code and lack of spacing and indentation can cause a lot of issues with readability. Now, how difficult is it really to clean that up? Just take a look for yourself; this very same class is listed next, and just a few tweaks have made a huge difference.

Cleaned-up ActionScript 2.0 class

```
class MyClass {

    // Constants
    var MAX_COUNT:Number = 5;
    var BASE_URL:String = "http://www.friendsofed.com";

    // public properties
    var textColor:Number = 0x003366;
    var userName:String = "Peter";

    // private properties
    private var _countIndex:Number;
    private var _foundNumber:Boolean;
```

```
// constructor
function MyClass() {
  trace("Constructor called");
}

// public methods
function loadSite():Void {
  getURL(BASE_URL,"_blank");
}
function countLoop():Void {
  for(var i=1; i<=MAX_COUNT; i++) {
    trace("Loop "+i+" of "+MAX_COUNT);
  }
}

// private methods
private function $reverseString(str:String):String {
  var tmp = str.split("").reverse();
  return tmp.join("");
}
function $isEvenNumber(num:Number):Boolean {
  return (num % 2 == 0);
}

// getter/setter methods
function get URL():String {
  return BASE_URL;
}
function set URL(url:String):Void {
  BASE_URL = url;
}

}
```

If you look at the preceding code, you'll notice something very important to a clean programming style, which is *grouping*. By grouping properties and methods according to their scope and function within the class, you can quickly find whatever you're looking for, and this increases the overall readability of your code. Just like with our pseudo-code earlier, a couple of blank lines between these various sections of code make it even easier to navigate through. The example shown previously is the way I usually structure my ActionScript 2.0 classes; it is not set in stone, and you can certainly tweak it to your own style and preference.

The key to successful programming is often hidden in the details. You can teach any old monkey OOP (well, at least smart, genetically modified monkeys), but that does not guarantee good and readable code. Never underestimate what things like comments, naming conventions, and good programming styles can do for you.

Alternative programming styles

Peter: As mentioned earlier, developers often have their own distinctive guidelines and best practices for writing their code and defend those with their life. There's nothing wrong with that and thinking about how to best structure code can only lead to a more efficient development process.

When in the process of writing this book, we discovered that myself, Todd, and Sas have slightly different code styles and best practices for coding ActionScript 2.0. Rather than force each other to adhere to a style we don't particularly agree or feel comfortable with, we opted to each outline our best practices and code style and explain why we use those.

You've read about my practices for ActionScript 2.0 development earlier on in this chapter, so I'll leave it up to Todd and Sas to show you theirs here. This should hopefully spark some ideas of your own on how you want to structure application code.

Coding practices: Todd Yard

I would first start off by saying that there is a difference in my mind between good coding techniques and code formatting. I believe it is in the latter issue where many, or even most, developers disagree. For instance, a debate could continue on for years on how code should best be indented or whether a space should appear between a for or if keyword and its following parenthesis, but this does not really affect the quality of the code. One developer may use the following format for a function:

```
function myFunction()
{
}
```

while another developer uses the following:

```
function myFunction() {
}
```

Neither in my opinion is more correct than the other. As long as the intention of the code is clear and it is done in a way that balances both optimal performance and readability, then it is good code. Everything that Peter has laid out for good practices in this chapter does just that. What is left then is differing opinion on naming conventions and formatting.

In the code I present later in this book, I use the following conventions that might at times differ from those of either Peter or Sas:

1. Private properties have a double underscore prefix. No distinction is made for a private property defined in a child class versus a super class (e.g., if I defined a Shape class with the property __fillColor, a Rectangle class that inherited from Shape would access __fillColor and not use some distinction to note that the property was defined in the super class).

2. Local variables use descriptive words written in camel case. The lack of a double underscore distinguishes these from private properties.

3. I do not normally use public properties in a class and instead expose private properties through getter/setter methods. Because of this, no distinction usually needs to be made for the naming of public properties.

4. On a similar note, I use getter/setter methods more often than get__() and set__() methods since the former allows for easier integration into the components inspector.

5. I do not use the keyword this in a class file. This is done mostly for readability's sake, as a color-coded file peppered with this distracts from the unique code around it. For instance, of the following two lines, I feel the second one is much easier to digest when perusing code:

```
this.__area = this.__width * this.__height;
```

```
__area = __width * __height;
```

With the double underscore denoting private properties, I feel the this becomes redundant.

6. Most classes I write are structured with the properties declared at the top, followed by the constructor, the private methods, and then the public methods, separated by comment blocks.

7. Personally, I'm not a big fan of comments and, when not writing for a book, I must admit I don't use them all that often. This probably stems from the fact that too often, comments are overused and distract from the actual code, which, if written with descriptive methods, properties, class, and instance names in a clear and straightforward manner, should be fairly readable without the extra comments. Whenever it is NOT possible to accomplish this with the code, for instance, in lines of complex mathematical calculations, or where there is some backwards logic that needs to be applied for a case not readily apparent, then comments become useful or even necessary. However, I do like to use comments to break of up blocks of code, whether it be for separating private from public methods, or grouping logical aspects of an application. I also take advantage of comments to make notes to myself or other developers for future development or refinement.

8. I do not use super() in my constructor unless it is necessary to pass variables to the super class's constructor, since the line is already implied. If there is a question about whether a class inherits from another, I need only look to the class definition a few lines above, which gives better information as to what the super class is.

9. I usually choose to shorthand the creation of Object and Array instances, using the syntax more often for the first of the following two lines:

```
var myArray:Array = [];

var myArray:Array = new Array();
```

Again, I feel if the code is readable and clear in intent and accomplishes its purpose, then it is hard to argue with. There is nothing confusing about the intent of that first line, even if it uses the shortcut.

All of these points, though, are completely subjective, and alternative viewpoints and arguments may be equally valid (or even more so in the mind of the person with the alternative viewpoint!).

Coding practices: Sas Jacobs

I follow many of the coding best practices that Peter outlines in this chapter. Like Peter, I prefer to use import statements so that I can avoid using fully qualified class package names. I think it makes my code much easier to read. I always locate the statements together at the top of the class file so I can easily find them again later. I am also very particular about writing properly indented code blocks because I think it makes the lines much easier to read.

I have a couple of different coding styles from Peter. These differences are in my commenting and naming conventions.

Commenting code

I also like to comment blocks of code and, unlike Peter, I'm happy to use inline comments. In fact, I'll often write the class structure and pseudo-code using comments. Then, when I write the code, it is already commented by my pseudo-code lines. For example, I might start my class file by writing the following:

```
class ClassName {

  //declare private properties

..//constructor
  function ClassName() {

  }

  //public methods:
  //init
    //create components
    //size components
    //position on stage
```

```
      //loadFile
        //create LoadVars
        //parse and assign to arrays
....//loop through arrays and populate components

      //private methods
        //format date - returns a long date string from a date object
    }
```

I'd then start writing the code under the comments, testing as I go. For me, this provides me with a roadmap when I'm writing code. The comments serve as markers to specific blocks of code and they help to refresh my memory when I come back to a project that I haven't seen for months.

From the preceding code, you can see that I also like to organize my class file into sections. I start by declaring my private variables, then write the constructor function and public methods, and finish with private methods.

Naming conventions

I use the following naming conventions because they make my code easier to understand:

1. Private properties start with a double underscore, e.g., __parentContainer_mc. I don't preface these variables with this because I think it makes the variable names harder to read (e.g., this.__parentContainer_mc).

2. Variable names are descriptive, start with a lowercase letter, and use camel case (e.g., var returnValue:Number).

3. When referring to components, I usually use a name that indicates the component type (e.g., product_txt or __item_lbl).

4. Function names use a verb and noun (e.g., createBinding, loadProduct).

5. Class names are descriptive, start with an uppercase letter, and use camel case (e.g., FeaturedProduct).

6. Package names start with com, include the company name, and use a descriptive name (e.g., com.aip.products).

Looking through my conventions, I realize that I don't have a standard for distinguishing between public and private method names. I guess that shows that even experienced coders are inconsistent at times!

What's next?

This chapter concludes Part Two of the book, which covered object-oriented programming guidelines. You've learned how to plan, model, and manage projects. I covered an introduction to version control, some common programming methodologies, usability testing, and best practices for ActionScript 2.0.

In Part Three of the book, you'll get a more in-depth insight into the various aspects of OOP I outlined in Chapter 1 of the book. First up is encapsulation. I'll discuss what it exactly is, when to use it, and how to apply it in ActionScript 2.0.

6

PART THREE **CORE OOP CONCEPTS**

7 ENCAPSULATION

In this chapter, I create an example to demonstrate encapsulation in Flash. This is the first of four chapters that demonstrate encapsulation, classes, inheritance, and polymorphism using step-by-step instructions.

If you haven't read the introduction to encapsulation in Chapter 1, I would advise you to do so now before we get into the practicalities of applying the concept to an ActionScript 2.0 project. Just to recap, encapsulation helps you to hide the details of your object-oriented code. You just provide the methods that do the job and don't require any other classes to know the internal workings of your code.

I'll show you an example of encapsulation in action next, and start off by setting up the graphics.

Setting up encapsulation

This section describes the manual work—drawing the shapes and parts needed in the encapsulation example. Let's start with a blank FLA:

1. Launch Flash.

2. Choose Flash Document from the Create New menu on the Start Page (see Figure 7-1).

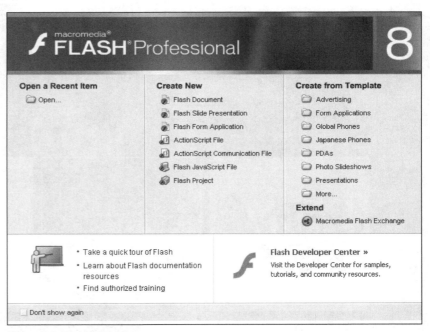

Figure 7-1. Flash 8 Start Page

3. Save the blank document as Encapsulation.fla.

If you have the Start Page in Flash 8 disabled you should—depending on your settings—be presented with either a new blank FLA, last edited FLAs, or nothing at all when you launch the application. If it gives you a blank FLA, simply follow step 3 and save it as Encapsulation.fla; in the other cases you create a new blank FLA by going to File ➤ New and choosing Flash Document from the General tab. The source files for this example are also available from the friends of ED website (www.friendsofed.com) if you don't feel like setting it up yourself.

Creating new layers

In previous chapters I often referred to the idea of a bouncing ball. Let's now put this into practice and start by drawing a ball and a simple background. First, create two new layers in the timeline to hold them:

1. Display the timeline (select Window ➤ Timeline) if it isn't visible.

2. Double-click Layer 1 and rename it Background.

3. Create a new layer in the timeline (select Insert ➤ Timeline ➤ Layer), as shown in Figure 7-2.

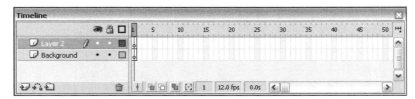

Figure 7-2. Create layer in Timeline panel

4. Double-click Layer 2 and rename it Ball.

5. Create a new layer in the timeline (select Insert ➤ Timeline ➤ Layer).

6. Double-click Layer 3 and rename it ActionScript (see Figure 7-3).

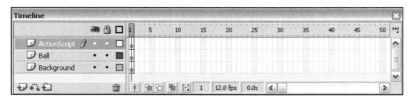

Figure 7-3. Rename layer in Timeline panel

7. Select Frame 1 of the ActionScript layer.

8. Open the Actions panel (select Window ➤ Development Panels ➤ Actions).

7

9. Add the following ActionScript code in the Actions panel (see Figure 7-4):

stop();

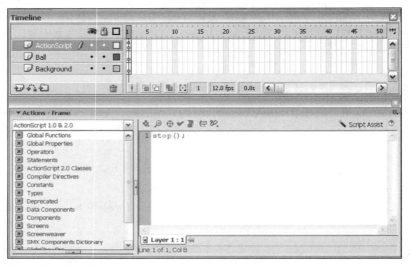

Figure 7-4. ActionScript panel

10. Open the Document Properties panel (select Modify ➤ Document).

11. Set Frame rate to 30 (see Figure 7-5).

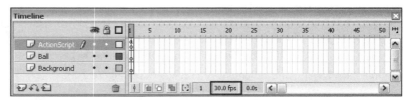

Figure 7-5. Timeline frame rate setting

12. Click OK.

You'll now have three layers in your timeline. From top to bottom, the layers should read ActionScript, Ball, Background (see Figure 7-6).

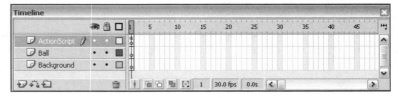

Figure 7-6. After creating and organizing layers in the timeline

Drawing a background

Let's put a filled rectangle into the Background layer:

1. In the Tools panel (select Window ➤ Tools), click the Rectangle tool (see Figure 7-7).

2. In the Properties panel (select Window ➤ Properties), select hairline for the Line Style, select black for the Line Color, and select the black-to-white radial fill for the Fill Color (see Figure 7-7).

Figure 7-7. Anatomy of a filled rectangle

3. In the timeline, click Frame 1 of the Background layer.

4. Draw a rectangle somewhere on the stage. When you release the mouse button, a filled rectangle appears. Your stage should look something like the one in Figure 7-8.

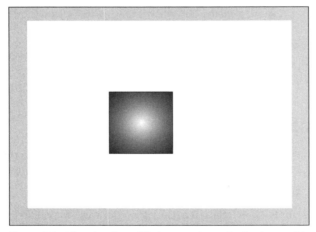

Figure 7-8. After drawing a filled rectangle on the Background layer

Aligning and locking the background

Here's an easy way to make the rectangle fill the stage perfectly:

1. In the timeline, click Frame 1 of the Background layer (this selects the rectangle you just drew).

2. In the Align panel (select Window ➤ Align) click the To Stage button (see Figure 7-9). This is a toggle button. Clicking it once presses it down. Clicking it again releases it. It appears white when it is pressed down and gray when it is released. It must be pressed down for the next step.

Figure 7-9.
The Align panel

3. In the Align panel, click three buttons: the match width and height button (the third button under Match size), and the align left and align top buttons (the first and fourth buttons under Align).

4. Lock the Background layer to protect it while you draw on other layers. Click the Background layer's lock column (see Figure 7-10). When the padlock icon is visible, the layer is locked (clicking the lock column repeatedly locks and unlocks a layer).

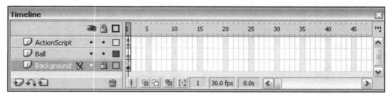

Figure 7-10. Locking the Background layer

Drawing a ball

Let's draw a filled circle to represent the ball. The steps are just like those you performed to draw the background, except you'll use the Oval tool instead of the Rectangle tool:

1. In the timeline, click Frame 1 of the Ball layer.

2. In the Tools panel, click the Oval tool (located immediately to the left of the Rectangle tool).

3. In the Properties panel, select hairline for the Line Style, select black for the Line Color, and select the black-to-green radial fill for the Fill Color.

4. While you hold down the *SHIFT* key on your keyboard, draw an oval in the center of the stage (the *SHIFT* key yields a perfect circle). Try to match the size shown in Figure 7-11.

Figure 7-11. After drawing a filled circle (black to green) on the Ball layer

Converting the ball into a Library symbol

Symbols are reusable content stored in the Library (every Flash document has its own internal Library for storage). Let's convert the ball into a symbol:

1. In the timeline, click Frame 1 of the Ball layer (this selects the circle). Another option is to double-click the ball shape on the stage.

2. Convert the circle into a symbol (select Modify ➤ Convert To Symbol).

3. In the Name field, type the word Ball (see Figure 7-12).

Figure 7-12. The Convert to Symbol dialog box

4. For Behavior, select Movie Clip (see Figure 7-12).

5. Ensure the black registration mark is in the center (see Figure 7-12).

6. Click OK.

> *Symbols are reusable. You can use multiple copies (instances) of any symbol in the Library, without increasing the size of the final published document.*

7. Confirm that the Ball symbol is stored in the Library (select Window ➤ Library), as shown in Figure 7-13.

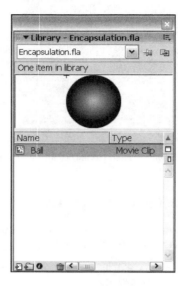

Figure 7-13.
The Ball symbol

8. Save the document (select File ➤ Save).

Content summary

There are three layers in the timeline. The following table summarizes the existing content.

Timeline Layer Name	Content Description
ActionScript	This is the top layer in the timeline. It contains ActionScript code to prevent the timeline from advancing to the next frame.
Ball	This is the middle layer in the timeline. It contains an instance (an on-screen copy) of the Ball movie clip (the Ball movie clip is a symbol stored in the Library).
Background	This is the bottom layer in the timeline. It contains a simple filled rectangle that acts as a decorative background.

That completes the manual work for Encapsulation.fla. Next, you'll write ActionScript code to control the ball.

Writing the code

The Ball is a movie clip symbol stored in the Library (you chose Movie Clip for the Ball's behavior when you converted it to a symbol). For all practical purposes, *movie clips* are independent little Flash movies. Every movie clip has its own timeline and plays independently no matter what happens on the document's timeline.

Movie clips are object oriented; they have their own dedicated properties and functions. Suppose a movie clip named *George* is located at 100, 200 (stage coordinates), and another named *John* is at 300, 400. You could type the following ActionScript code:

```
trace("George is located at "+ George._x +", "+ George._y);
trace("John is located at "+ John._x +", "+ John._y);
```

The output would be as shown in Figure 7-14.

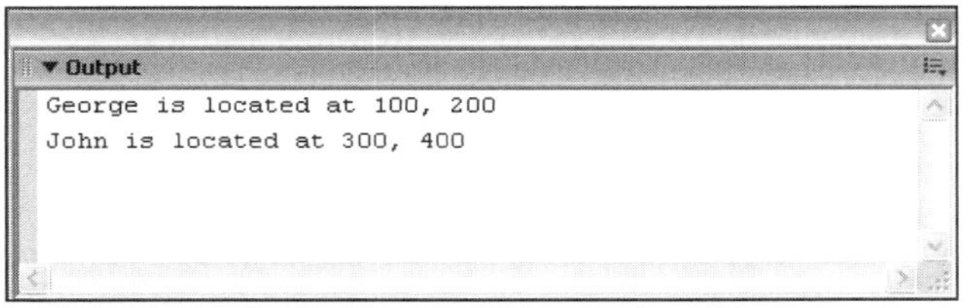

Figure 7-14. Output panel

All movie clips contain the built-in properties _x and _y. The _x property is the horizontal stage location of the movie clip, and _y is the vertical stage location. Movie clips contain other properties too; you'll see more of them later.

Creating an event handler

You were briefly introduced to event handlers in Chapter 4. We'll now be using an event handler to control the Ball. In this document, Flash will attempt to broadcast 30 enterFrame messages per second (because the document's frame rate is 30). If the Ball listens for enterFrame messages, you can create the illusion of movement by changing its position each time it receives a message.

> Setting the document's frame rate to 30 doesn't guarantee 30 frames per second (if that were true, you could just set the frame rate to 8,000 and write a fancy 3D game). It really depends on the computer's performance and how many actions run concurrently.

Let's put an event handler into the Ball. Notice that the layers in the timeline are currently Background, Ball, and ActionScript. When you edit the Ball symbol in just a moment, the timeline will appear to change:

1. In the Library panel, click the Ball to select it.
2. Edit the Ball (select Edit ➤ Edit Symbols).

Now the timeline contains a single layer named Layer 1. That's because you're viewing the Ball's timeline (not the document's timeline). The Ball is a movie clip with its own independent timeline. Let's prepare it for the event handler:

1. In the timeline, click Layer 1 to select it.
2. Rename Layer 1 to Circle.
3. Create a new layer (select Insert ➤ Layer).
4. Rename the new layer ActionScript (select Modify ➤ Layer).
5. The Ball's timeline should match the one shown in Figure 7-15.

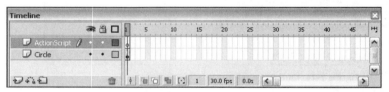

Figure 7-15. The Ball's timeline

Now you're ready to create the event handler:

1. Click Frame 1 of the ActionScript layer.
2. Display the Actions panel (select Window ➤ Development Panels ➤ Actions) if it isn't visible.
3. Type the following code into the Actions panel:

```
stop();

var onEnterFrame:Function = doSomething;

function doSomething():Void {
  trace("Hello from doSomething");
}
```

4. Save the document (select File ➤ Save).

The Actions panel should match the one shown in Figure 7-16.

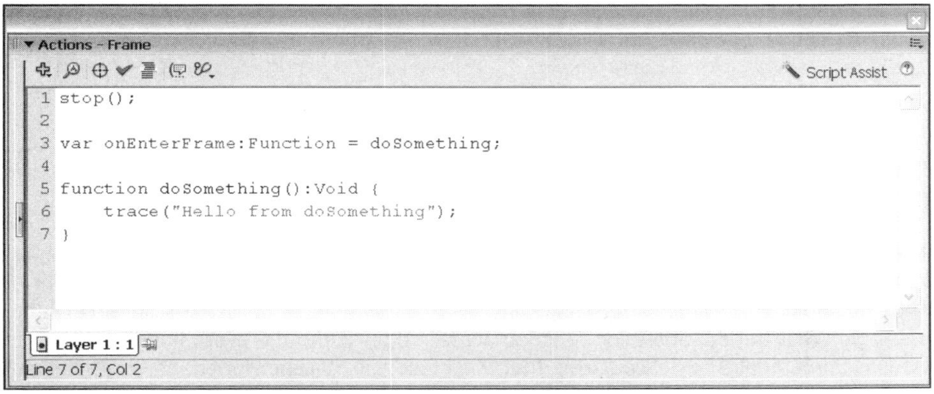

```
  Actions - Frame
1 stop();
2
3 var onEnterFrame:Function = doSomething;
4
5 function doSomething():Void {
6     trace("Hello from doSomething");
7 }

  Layer 1 : 1
Line 7 of 7, Col 2
```

Figure 7-16. The Ball's event handler

The preceding code is used to easily illustrate a simple event handler in action; it is not the way you would typically handle objects in your applications. Once the code gets more complex, you'd start looking at writing ActionScript 2.0 classes and associating that to your movie clip.

7

What about encapsulation?

If you're wondering what happened to the main topic of this chapter (a fair question), it's right in front of you in the code listing of step 3 in the preceding example. Conceptually, encapsulation is shielding (hiding) the internal details of the doSomething function from the Ball's event handler. Here are the details:

```
01  stop();
02
03  var onEnterFrame:Function = doSomething;
04
05  function doSomething():Void {
06      trace("Hello from doSomething");
07  }
```

Line 01 calls the stop function (stop is a built-in function—you don't have to define it, you just use it), line 03 defines the event handler, and lines 05 through 07 define the doSomething function.

The stop function at line 01 prevents the timeline from advancing to the next frame (you don't want it to advance because there's no content after Frame 1). The stop function does not stop the application, nor does it prevent the code in Frame 1 from finishing (all the code in Frame 1 runs, no matter where you put the stop function).

The event handler begins and ends at line 03. To create a movie clip event handler in Flash, you can use the following syntax (as line 03 demonstrates, but this is one of several ways):

```
var FlashMovieClipEvent:Function = myFunctionName;
```

All movie clips support the onEnterFrame event; to use it, you need to provide your own function name. The net result: every time this movie clip receives an *enterFrame* message from Flash, the onEnterFrame event handler calls the doSomething function.

The doSomething function at line 05 is simple enough—it displays Hello from doSomething. It doesn't matter how simple or complex the doSomething function is. That's the point of encapsulation! The event handler calls doSomething whenever it receives an enterFrame message. What the doSomething function actually does (from the event handler's point of view) is immaterial. The doSomething function could call 50 other functions, and the event handler would never know it.

This type of encapsulation is very narrow (existing only at the function level). Encapsulation also exists at wider levels (in a single class or multiple classes, sometimes called *services* or *components*). The concept, however, is identical: The internal behavior of a function, class, or service is hidden (encapsulated) from the caller. The caller is only responsible for knowing which functions, classes, or services are available, not how they operate internally.

Testing the event handler

Test the movie by selecting Control ➤ Test Movie. The output is an endless stream of Hello from doSomething messages (see Figure 7-17). Each Hello from doSomething represents a call to the doSomething function (so the event handler is calling the doSomething function properly).

Figure 7-17. Testing the event handler

When you've seen enough doSomething messages, close the test file (select File ➤ Close) to return to Flash.

Whenever you test a movie, you're actually viewing a published file. You must close it to return to Flash.

Updating the Ball

Movie clips have _x and _y properties to describe their location on the stage. The Ball is a movie clip, so what happens when you change these properties? Update your code to match the following listing:

```
stop();

var onEnterFrame:Function = doSomething;

function doSomething():Void {
  _x++; // Same as _x = _x + 1;
  _y++;
}
```

The Actions panel should match Figure 7-18.

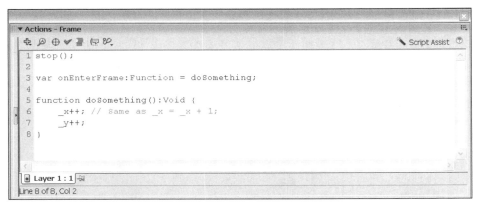

Figure 7-18. Updated code in the Actions panel

Test the movie by selecting Control ➤ Test Movie. The Ball moves 1 pixel down and 1 pixel to the right each time the event handler calls the update function. Close the test file (select File ➤ Close) to return to Flash.

The ++ in _x++ is an increment operator (it increases the value of the variable by 1). This is a shorter way of writing _x = _x + 1 or _x += 1. This is how the Ball moves 1 pixel at a time (there's nothing preventing the Ball from moving off the screen, so it will).

Save your document by selecting File ➤ Save.

Improving the code

The Ball has a working event handler. That's a good start, but you can get the code closer to the plans from the last chapter. First, rename the doSomething function to update (make sure you change the event handler *and* the function) like this:

```
stop();

var onEnterFrame:Function = update;

function update():Void {
  _x++;
  _y++;
}
```

The Actions panel should match Figure 7-19.

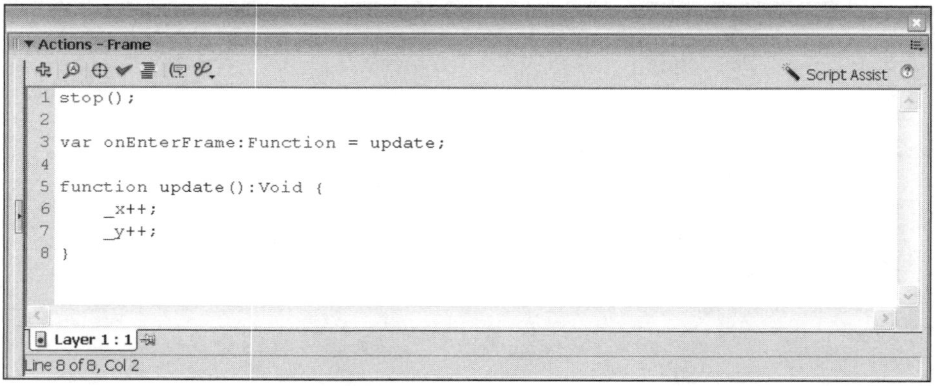

Figure 7-19. After renaming doSomething to update

Enhancing behavior with properties

All movie clips have properties (you've seen _x and _y so far). *Properties* are variables dedicated to a specific instance of a given object. Currently, there's one instance of the Ball, but what if there were 50? Doesn't matter. Every instance has its own independent copy of _x and _y. You aren't limited, however, to the built-in movie clip properties—you can invent your own. Please modify your code to match the following listing:

```
stop();

var onEnterFrame:Function = update;

var xv:Number = 1; // Initial x velocity.
var yv:Number = 1; // Initial y velocity.
```

```
function update():Void {
    _x += xv; // Same as _x = _x + xv;
    _y += yv;
}
```

The Actions panel should match Figure 7-20.

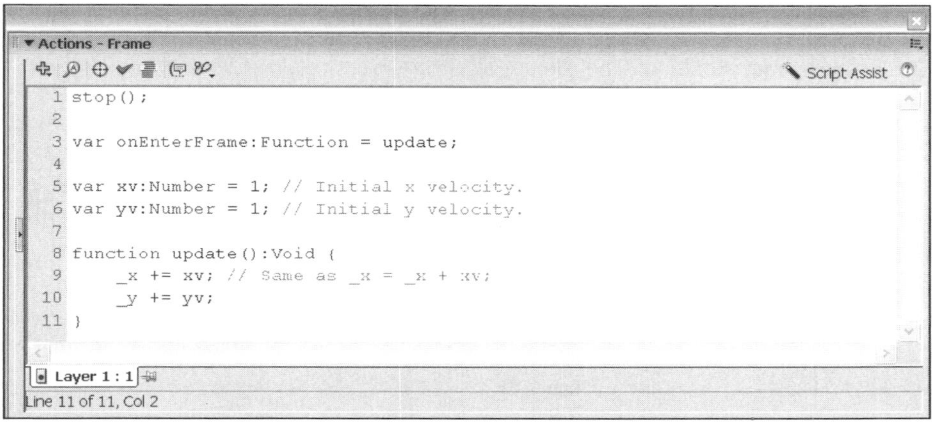

Figure 7-20. Using custom properties

Test the movie by selecting Control ➤ Test Movie. It behaves exactly as it did before. Instead of hard-coding the velocity directly inside the move function, you can store it in a property. This may not seem like an advantage right now, but trust me. Close the test file (select File ➤ Close) to return to Flash.

> *Portability is another advantage of encapsulation. Remember, the event handler doesn't care what the update function does or how it works (as long as there's an update function to call, it's happy). This will become even more apparent when I introduce classes in the next chapter.*

Narrowing the focus with functions

The golden rule of functions is this: one task per function. Right now, the update function is rather vague. What does it update? To clarify, update your code to match the following listing:

```
stop();

var onEnterFrame:Function = update;

var xv:Number = 1; // Initial x velocity.
var yv:Number = 1; // initial y velocity.
```

```
function update():Void {
  updatePosition();
}

function updatePosition():Void {
  _x += xv;
  _y += yv;
}
```

The Actions panel should match Figure 7-21.

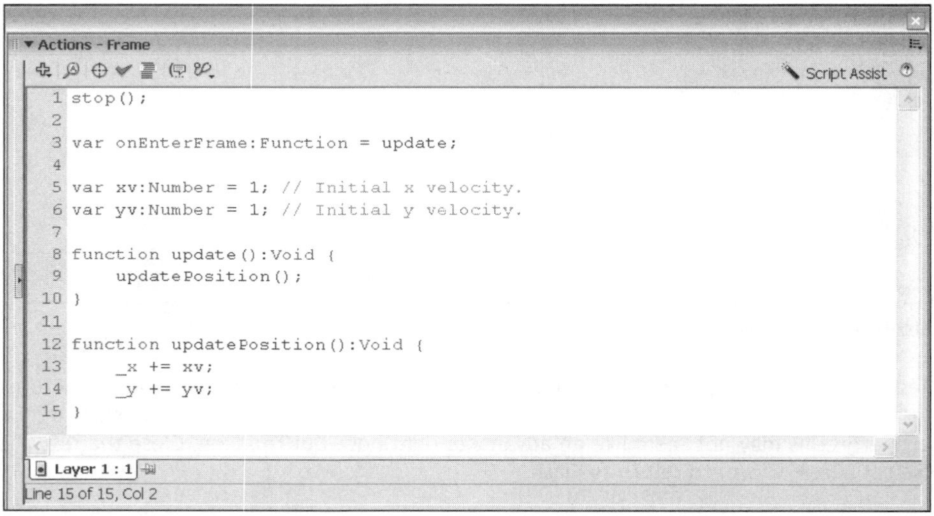

Figure 7-21. Narrowing the focus with functions

Save the document (select File ➤ Save) and test the movie (select Control ➤ Test Movie). The behavior is the same as before, but you've introduced a more descriptive function named updatePosition. Close the test file (select File ➤ Close) to return to Flash.

The name updatePosition is more descriptive than update. The code is now more self-descriptive than before, but was it worth creating another new function? Shouldn't you just rename the update function to updatePosition (and be done with it)?

In OOP, a group of simple functions is better than a single complex function. Think of the update function as an umbrella function. You could write a series of simple functions (updatePosition, updateVelocity, updateFriction). Each function handles one (and only one) task. Eventually, you could have this kind of update function:

```
function update() {
  updatePosition();
  updateVelocity();
  updateFriction();
}
```

Now you know what the update function does, but you don't need to know how the details work. It's a nice overview and you don't even need to see the rest of the code. Encapsulation simplifies development and makes the code naturally self-descriptive. The byproduct is easy-to-read code.

Encapsulation summary

Encapsulation is all about simplification, hiding the details, and distributing the workload. *Abstraction* is another way to describe encapsulation. You can take a complex set of behaviors and *abstract* them into a series of simple functions. For example:

```
var onEnterFrame:Function = update;

function update():Void {
  updatePosition();
  updateVelocity();
  updateFriction();
}

function updatePosition() {
  // internal details of updatePosition
}

function updateVelocity() {
  // internal details of updateVelocity
}

function updateFriction() {
  // internal details of updateFriction
}
```

In this case, the event handler depends only on a function named update. Beyond that, the event handler doesn't know or care what the details are. It has no idea how the update function works or how many other function calls may be involved. That's encapsulation.

> *Consistency is another great benefit of encapsulation. All objects using the* update *function will either succeed or fail in exactly the same way. If there's a bug in the application, I can fix it in exactly one place. With encapsulation, the application behaves consistently—bugs or not.*

In generic terms, encapsulation involves the abstraction of various tasks into one entity. Functions are an example of this as they can contain a series of instructions that you need not know anything about to use it.

Just like in the real world, simple actions can be much more difficult than you'd expect. Let's take opening a door for example.

```
function openDoor() {
  approachDoor();
  grabDoorKnob();
  twistDoorKnob();
  pushDoorOpen();
}
function approachDoor() {
  // internal details of approachDoor
}
function grabDoorKnob() {
  // internal details of grabDoorKnob
}
function twistDoorKnob() {
  // internal details of twistDoorKnob
}
function pushDoorOpen() {
  // internal details of pushDoorOpen
}
```

We've all been conditioned to see the task of opening the door as one simple action, though as you can clearly see from this example it is not. This is a form of abstraction and encapsulation we use in our daily lives; the same applies to object-oriented programming.

When communicating between different blocks of code or classes, as we'll see in the next chapters, you try to keep the message very straightforward. In this case you just want the door to be opened, which is why there is a generic openDoor function. Your code should not be required to know what actions are needed to open the door, or care how this is done. For all you know the door is opened by using a key, swiping an electronic badge, performing some silly little magic dance, or forcing it with a crowbar. All that matters to your code is that the door is "somehow" opened.

Encapsulation may look like a very simple concept, but it is tremendously powerful when doing object-oriented programming to create clean and easily reusable code. The aim with encapsulation is to provide an interface through which other classes can communicate without them needing to know anything else about the internal workings; for example, a Car class could have the method startEngine, a NuclearPlant class could have the method generateElectricity, and so on.

Thank heavens for that. This same encapsulation allows me to use complex Math classes without having to wreck my brain figuring out how to get the required result. I don't know about you, but anything that helps me to focus on the actual tasks rather than the intricate details when writing code gets my stamp of approval!

What's next?

There's nothing wrong with the current version of this document, but before I add more functionality, you should understand classes. Next, I introduce ActionScript 2.0 classes and upgrade the encapsulation example at the same time. Please save your document if you haven't already.

8 CLASSES

I want to update the encapsulation example from the last chapter, so this is the perfect time to introduce ActionScript 2.0 classes. Classes were briefly discussed in Chapter 3 in comparison with the prototype-based approach of ActionScript 1.0. We'll look at that difference again, but focus here on the differences in syntax. Just like languages such as C# or Java, ActionScript 2.0 now supports a class-based approach that makes it much more consistent with other languages that typically use OOP techniques.

Classes vs. prototypes

Prior to the 2.0 release of ActionScript, the language used a prototype-based syntax that was able to simulate classes but didn't have the formal syntax to show this. In many ways this method was a bit of a fraud; you would manipulate the prototype object to do inheritance, there was no support for public and private scope, etc. This is not to say that it wasn't effective. In many ways the prototype-based approach was a good way to quickly and easily extend built-in and custom classes.

Let's see how a Motion class would look in a prototype-based language such as Action-Script 1.0:

```
function Motion() {
}
Motion.prototype.updatePosition = function() {
  this._x++;
  this._y++;
}
```

You can see that by adding the prototype keyword before setting the function name, you actually add it to every instance that is instantiated from the Motion *prototype class* through the new keyword (see the following code).

```
ballMotion = new Motion();
onEnterFrame = ballMotion.updatePosition;
```

Now, how does ActionScript 2.0 handle classes? Take a look at the following syntax:

```
class Motion extends MovieClip {
  function Motion() {
  }
  function updatePosition():Void {
    this._x++;
    this._y++;
  }
  function onEnterFrame():Void {
    this.updatePosition();
  }
}
```

Nice. You can immediately see that this ActionScript 2.0 class looks quite a bit different from the ActionScript 1.0 prototype version. Don't worry, I'll walk you through it. First of all, the code for our Motion class shown previously should be saved as the file `Motion.as`.

The most important difference is that we now have a formal `class` keyword, which is very useful as it shows you what exactly is part of your class. Everything that you'll find between the curly braces of the class statement is part of that class.

Because our Motion class is going to make use of some properties (`_x` and `_y`) and an event handler (onEnterFrame) of the built-in MovieClip class, we need to use the `extends` keyword which allows us—yes, you've guessed it!—to extend the MovieClip class. This behavior is called *inheritance*, and I'll discuss it in greater detail in the next chapter.

You'll notice an empty function in our class called `Motion` (notice it uses the same name as our class). This is the constructor for our class (more about this later on in this chapter).

The next function we defined in the Motion class is updatePosition. Just like in the prototype example, we just increment the built-in `_x` and `_y` properties that position the movie clip on the stage.

Finally, we define the onEnterFrame function and call updatePosition from there. Remember, the onEnterFrame event handler was inherited from the MovieClip class, so it will still be called once every frame.

OK, so far so good—you'll have noticed that the ActionScript 2.0 class does exactly what our prototype class did. Now we only need to instantiate it. For this, you need to associate a movie clip with a class. From reading Chapter 3 you probably know how this is done, but I'll recap and run you through it again.

8

1. Launch Flash.
2. Choose Flash Document from the Create New menu on the Start Page (or select File ➤ New and click Flash Document if the Start Page is disabled).
3. Save the blank document as `Motion.fla` in the folder where you saved `Motion.as`.
4. Rename Layer 1 to Shape.
5. Draw any shape you want on the Shape layer.
6. Convert your shape on the Shape layer to a movie clip (Modify ➤ Convert to Symbol).
7. Set the Behavior to Movieclip and give it the name MotionShape.
8. If the Linkage area isn't visible in the Convert to Symbol panel, click the Advanced button.
9. Select the check box Export for ActionScript.
10. Set the AS 2.0 class for this movie clip to Motion.
11. Click OK.
12. Test the Flash movie (Control ➤ Test Movie).

If all went well, you should now see your shape moving across the screen. Now, that wasn't too difficult, was it? In a nutshell, what you did was simply associate a movie clip with a class. The settings for the symbol we created should look like Figure 8-1.

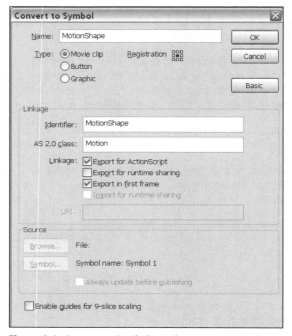

Figure 8-1. Convert to Symbol panel

Now that we've seen that ActionScript 2.0 supports a class-based syntax, there are a couple of concepts you'll need to learn about to write your own custom classes: constructors, methods, and events. That is exactly what I'll be discussing next.

Constructors

A constructor is a function just like any other with the exception that it is called automatically when a class instance is instantiated. Let's look at an example:

```
var myPhoneList:Array = new Array();
```

The class is Array. The instance of the Array class is myPhoneList. The constructor function is Array(). If you could look at the source code for the built-in classes, you would find an Array class constructor function similar to this:

```
class Array {
  function Array() {
    // Internal details of Array class constructor.
  }
}
```

As you can see, there's nothing to discern a constructor function from any other function. There's not a special keyword to mark the start of a constructor function. The only giveaway is that the class name (Array in this case) has the exact same name as the constructor function. So, if you'd look at the constructor for the built-in Date class, you would also see a function called Date. Also worth mentioning is that, although ActionScript 2.0 does not enforce this, the constructor is generally the first function in a class.

Let me put this into context. The following code shows a Motion class.

```
01 class Motion extends MovieClip {
02   function Motion() {
03     trace("Motion class instantiated");
04   }
05   function updatePosition():Void {
06     this._x++;
07     this._y++;
08   }
09   function onEnterFrame():Void {
10     this.updatePosition();
11   }
12 }
```

To show that the constructor function gets called automatically any time that particular class is instantiated, I added a trace statement. Now let's make a couple of instances and see what that does.

```
var spaceship:Motion = new Motion();
var rocket:Motion = new Motion();
```

If we test this movie with the Motion class in place in the same directory, the items shown in Figure 8-2 get displayed in the Output panel.

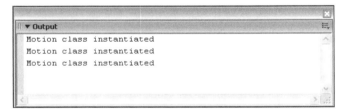

Figure 8-2. Motion class Output panel

We created two instances of the Motion class, and the constructor was called once for each instance. That makes sense, but where does the third line come from? Easy, because we have a movie clip on the stage associated with the Motion class that itself is also an instance of the class that gets instantiated. Now, of course, the class doesn't do anything because we didn't associate it with a movie clip, but it does show you what we were after.

The class is Motion. The objects are spaceship and rocket. The constructor function is Motion(). All Motion objects have an _x property and a _y property and an onEnterFrame event handler that they've inherited from the MovieClip class that it extends.

Constructors are functions, so you'd think there would be nothing stopping you from adding parameters to the constructor. Unfortunately, when using classes that are associated with movie clips, you cannot pass anything to the constructor. The way you would bypass this is by adding an init method that handles this as the following example shows you:

```
class Motion extends MovieClip {
  function Motion() {
  }
  function init(x:Number,y:Number) {
    this._x = x;
    this._y = y;
  }
  function updatePosition():Void {
    this._x++;
    this._y++;
  }
  function onEnterFrame():Void {
    this.updatePosition();
  }
}
```

You'll notice that the only thing I did was add a function, init, that sets the _x and _y properties of the movie clip to the x and y parameters that are passed to it. What you'll have to do next is give the movie clip you associated with the Motion class the instance name motionShape in the Properties panel (select Window ➤ Properties) after which you can add the following code to the main timeline of your document to call the init function:

```
motionShape.init(100,50);
```

What this code does is call the init method for the motionShape instance of the Motion class and pass x and y parameters that determine the initial position our movie clip starts moving from.

Classes that are not associated to movie clips can have parameters passed to the constructor. I'll show a quick example of this here:

```
class MultiplyNumbers {
  function MultiplyNumbers(num1:Number,num2:Number) {
    trace(num1*num2);
  }
}
```

The preceding class should be saved in a file called MultiplyNumbers.as, and in a blank FLA in the same directory you could add the following code:

```
var myMaths:MultiplyNumbers = new MultiplyNumbers(5,4);
```

When you test this movie, the output will show 20.

So far so good—you've just learned about constructors. Before we move on to discussing other class methods, it's good to know something more about the use of the this keyword in ActionScript 2.0.

About this

The this keyword in ActionScript 1.0 was one of the few things that would indicate whether you were dealing with a normal function or a class. In ActionScript 2.0, the use of the this keyword has become optional—more about this later—but it is nonetheless important to know what it represents and why it is used.

When dealing with classes in OOP, you know that there can be multiple instances of that class at one time in your project. Let's take the Motion class; for example, we could have a circle movie clip and a rectangle movie clip both subscribing to our class. If we use the init method discussed earlier and give those movie clips an initial _x and _y position, they can be completely different for both instances.

```
circle.init(10,10);
rectangle.init(50,50);
```

Now, that's interesting—how does our class know the difference between the circle's _x property and the rectangle's _x property? The class doesn't know . . . this does.

When you run the application, this points to different physical locations inside the computer's memory. It's really not much more than a reference to the current instance of a class. Therefore, the circle's version of this points to one location in memory, but the rectangle's version of this points to another. That's why the circle's this._x is 10, but the rectangle's this._x is 50. That's powerful! With this, class properties require zero management (it's completely automatic).

> Important to note is that ActionScript 2.0 supports the use of static class properties. Static properties are shared between all instances of a class. When using this on a static property, this will not refer to the instance but rather to the class. More about this later on in the chapter when I introduce class scope.

As I mentioned earlier, ActionScript 2.0 does not force you to use the this keyword. I would, however, strongly recommend you keep using it for a number of reasons—the most important being it prevents you from confusing local variables (for example in a for-in loop) with class properties.

Confusion.as

```
class Confusion {

  var currentNumber:Number = 50;

  function Confusion() {
    trace("this.currentNumber = "+this.currentNumber);
    trace("currentNumber = "+currentNumber);
    countToTen();
  }

  function countToTen() {
    for(var i=0; i<10; i++) {
      currentNumber = i+1;
      trace(currentNumber);
    }
    trace("currentNumber outside the loop: "+currentNumber);
    delete currentNumber;
    trace("local currentNumber deleted: "+currentNumber);
  }
}
```

The preceding code needs to be saved as the file Confusion.as, and you can instantiate the class by using the following code in an FLA in the same folder:

```
myConfusion = new Confusion();
```

Now what does that code do? First, a currentNumber variable is initialized of type Number and given a value 50. In the constructor method I've added a trace command that will show you that both this.currentNumber and currentNumber will output the same value.

Next in the constructor the method countToTen is called, which loops through the numbers 0 to 9. In that loop, a local variable is initialized with the name currentNumber that increments this by one, thus giving us the numbers 1 through 10 as an output.

After that loop has finished, we trace out the value of currentNumber, delete it, and then trace out the value of currentNumber again. If you run this code, you'll see the results shown in Figure 8-3 in the Output panel.

Now that's what I call confusing! Of course, the first point to make here is that you should never give a local variable a name that is already taken by a class property. It does show you why it can be important to use the this keyword; it explicitly states which of the two you are targeting. The problem with this code is not just limited to the use of the this keyword, but also involves not making a local variable in the function scope for the currentNumber class property. Let's clean up this code and look at what that gives us:

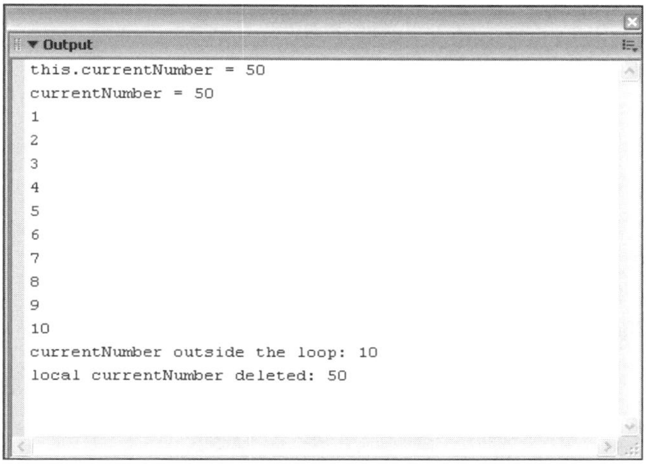

Figure 8-3. Confusion class Output panel

Clarity.as

```
class Clarity {

  var currentNumber:Number = 50;

  function Clarity() {
    trace("this.currentNumber = "+this.currentNumber);
    trace("currentNumber = "+currentNumber);
    countToTen();
  }

  function countToTen() {
    for(var i=0; i<10; i++) {
      var currentNumber = i+1;
      trace("local variable: "+currentNumber);
      trace("class property: "+this.currentNumber);
    }
  }
}
```

The preceding code needs to be saved as the file Clarity.as, and you can instantiate the class by using the following code in an FLA in the same folder:

```
myClarity = new Clarity();
```

If we run this code, we would now have the output shown in Figure 8-4.

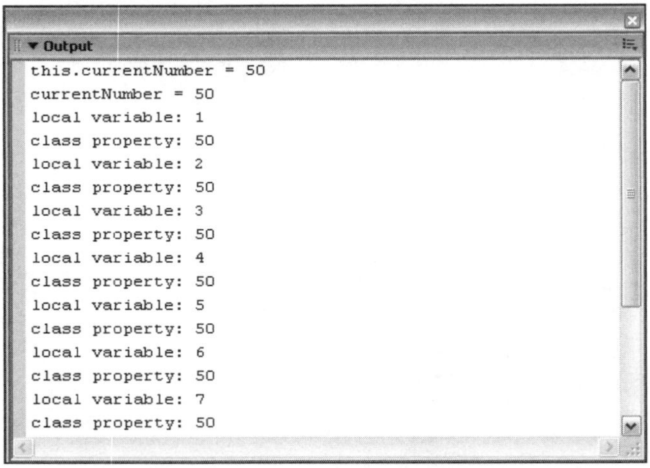

Figure 8-4. Clarity class Output panel

Now isn't that much better? Using this for your class properties and declaring your local variables with the var keyword, you'll never run into variable scope problems. It also increases the overall readability of your code, which is an absolute must when doing any OOP project. Next up we'll be looking at class methods, without which a class wouldn't do much at all.

Methods

A class is more than a template for potential data; it's also a template for potential data *handling*. You've seen class properties (they describe the data). To provide data handling, you need to attach functions to the class. That is where the class methods come in. Here's the syntax:

```
class Car {
  function intendedFunctionName() {
    // Function instructions go here.
  }
}
```

Suppose you want to attach a crash function to a Car class. Here's how:

```
class Car {
  function crash() {
    trace("Boom!");
  }
}
```

The code that follows shows a complete example:

Car.as

```
class Car {
  var speed:Number;
  var direction:String;

  function Car(speed,direction) {
    this.speed = speed;
    this.direction = direction;
  }

  function showVelocity() {
    trace("The car's velocity is "+this.speed+" KPH "+this.direction);
  }
}
```

The preceding code needs to be saved as Car.as and can be instantiated by using the code that follows in an FLA located in the same folder:

```
var yugo = new Car(10, "North");
yugo.showVelocity();
```

If you run the preceding code, the output shown in Figure 8-5 is generated.

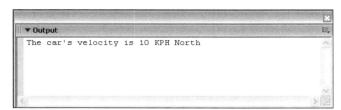

Figure 8-5. Car class Output panel

Aside from these normal class methods, you can actually have something called *anonymous functions*, which are mostly used for event handlers. We'll look at these next.

Anonymous functions

An *anonymous* function is a temporary function without a name. Wait. How can there be a function without a name? How would you call it? You can't . . . at least not directly. Take a look at this simple example:

```
onEnterFrame = function() {
  trace("This is called every frame");
}
```

If you think about it, in the preceding example what we really assign to onEnterFrame is the following code:

```
function() {
  trace("This is called every frame");
}
```

The function we assign to onEnterFrame has no reference by which we can call it; if we were to write the same code with a named function, it would look like this:

```
function callOnEnterFrame() {
  trace("This is called every frame");
}
onEnterFrame = callOnEnterFrame;
```

Now, what is the difference between the two? When you overwrite onEnterFrame when using anonymous functions, that previous function is lost forever; there is no way you can retrieve it because there is no reference by which to call it. Using that last approach, you can still use callOnEnterFrame as a separate function or reassign it to onEnterFrame whenever you want.

Anonymous functions are often used for assigning functions to event handlers. They also provide a quick and easy way to add events to a class.

Car.as

```
class Car {
  var speed:Number;
  var direction:String;
  var onSpeedChange:Function;
  var onDirectionChange:Function;

  function Car(speed,direction) {
    this.speed = speed;
    this.direction = direction;
  }

  function increaseSpeed() {
    this.speed += 10;
    this.onSpeedChange();
  }

  function setDirection(direction) {
    this.direction = direction;
    this.onDirectionChange();
  }
}
```

The preceding code needs to be saved as Car.as, and the following code needs to be used in an FLA in the same folder:

```
var ferrari = new Car(50, "West");
ferrari.onSpeedChange = function() {
    trace("The car now has a speed of "+this.speed+" KMH");
}
ferrari.onDirectionChange = function() {
    trace("Now driving in the following direction: "+this.direction);
}
ferrari.increaseSpeed();
ferrari.setDirection("East");
```

If you run this code, you'll see the output shown in Figure 8-6.

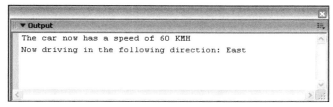

Figure 8-6. Car class Output panel

The code in our Car class is very interesting in that we initialize two variables of a Function type (onSpeedChange, onDirectionChange) but don't specify them as being a method in our class. Instead, we define anonymous functions in the FLA for these function references:

```
function() {
  trace("The car now has a speed of "+this.speed+" KMH");
}
```

and

```
function() {
  trace("Now driving in the following direction: "+this.direction);
}
```

By triggering the onSpeedChange and onDirectionChange references in the class, we're actually running the code that we associate with it from outside the class.

> *The method discussed previously is an easy way to simulate events, though there are certainly more flexible and generally accepted methods of handling events through the latest ActionScript 2.0 class framework as I'll show in Chapter 15.*

That completes the initial tour of classes. Right now, let's use classes to update the encapsulation example from the last chapter.

8

Implementing a class

When you think about the Motion class we discussed at the beginning of this chapter, there are a couple of difficulties with applying it to movie clips. For example, the class needs to be associated with a particular movie clip, and there is no easy way to start or stop the movement.

The way around this is to make a more abstract class that can handle this by passing parameters to its constructor method. I'll show how to handle this next by introducing the Mover class.

The Mover class

Every class needs a constructor. Since you're creating a Mover class, you need to have a constructor function named Mover.

```
class Mover extends MovieClip {

  var targetMC:MovieClip;

  function Mover(targetMC:MovieClip) {
    this.targetMC = targetMC;
  }

  function updatePosition() {
    this._x++;
    this._y++;
  }

  function startMoving() {
    this.targetMC.onEnterFrame = this.updatePosition;
  }

  function stopMoving() {
    this.targetMC.onEnterFrame = null;
  }
}
```

The preceding code needs to be saved as Mover.as and the following steps need to be done to see the class in action:

1. Launch Flash.

2. Choose Flash Document from the Create New menu on the Start Page (or select File ➤ New and click Flash Document if the Start Page is disabled).

3. Save the blank document as Mover.fla in the folder where you saved Mover.as.

4. Set Frame rate to 30.

5. Draw a circle on stage and convert it to a symbol (Modify ➤ Convert to Symbol).

6. Select Movie clip as the behavior and give it a name of circle.

7. Draw a rectangle on stage and convert it to a symbol (Modify ➤ Convert to Symbol).

8. Give the circle instance on stage the instance name "circle".

9. Give the rectangle instance on stage the instance name "rectangle".

10. Rename Layer 1 to Stage.

11. Add a new layer to the timeline and rename it to ActionScript.

12. Add the following code to Frame 1 of the ActionScript layer:

```
var myMover:Mover = new Mover(circle);
myMover.startMoving();
```

If you run Test Movie (Control ➤ Test Movie), you'll see the circle movie clip moving across the screen. The beauty about this version of our class is that we can start and stop the movement at any time by using the startMoving and stopMoving methods.

Now we can easily apply our class to any movie clip without having to associate it in the Flash IDE. It's just as easy to apply it to our rectangle as it was to the circle as you'll see from the following code:

```
var myMover:Mover = new Mover(rectangle);
myMover.startMoving();
```

If you run Test Movie now (Control ➤ Test Movie), you'll see the rectangle movie clip moving across the screen instead. Of course, it's also possible to use multiple instances of this Mover class to apply it to multiple movie clips at the same time. You'll find an example of this here:

```
var circleMover:Mover = new Mover(circle);
var rectangleMover:Mover = new Mover(rectangle);
circleMover.startMoving();
rectangleMover.startMoving();
```

Running the preceding code, we've got both movie clips on stage moving at the same time. Enough examples of the class in action—let's look at how it handles this movement.

The constructor of our Mover class accepts a single parameter that references a movie clip. The movie clip reference is stored in a class parameter called targetMC. Next up we've got our updatePosition method that handles the actual movie clip positioning by using the _x and _y properties.

Notice that this function uses this._x and this._y and yet it targets our targetMC movie clip. You might be wondering why this isn't written as this.targetMC._x and this.targetMC._y. The answer to the question is *scope*, which is a subject that will be discussed in great detail in the following chapters.

Now we have two functions (startMoving and stopMoving) that respectively add and remove our updatePosition method from the targetMC movie clip onEnterFrame handler.

By calling the startMoving method, we assign updatePosition to the target movie clip onEnterFrame, which consequently starts moving; by calling the stopMoving method, we overwrite the target movie clip onEnterFrame, which makes it stop moving.

> *This class is still a work in progress and could do with another couple of updates. That is exactly what I'll be doing throughout the following chapters. For example, it's generally not considered very good practice to overwrite the onEnterFrame event of a target movie clip because that may already be running some code.*

What's next?

Now you know the basics of encapsulation and classes. Next, I cover class inheritance. Using inheritance, you can add new capabilities and extend the current code without even touching the Mover class.

9 INHERITANCE

In this chapter, I'll walk you through an example to demonstrate inheritance in ActionScript 2.0. Whenever you write a new class to extend or enhance an existing class (without actually altering the existing class), you're using inheritance. Inheritance can introduce new capabilities without the fear of breaking existing applications.

About class hierarchy

Inheritance groups two or more classes together into a hierarchy (much like the folder structure on your computer). The first class in the hierarchy is the *base class* (like a top-level folder). The next class is a *subclass* (like a subfolder). Each subsequent class inherits from the previous one, so every subclass has a definite parent.

Look at the following class hierarchy:

Animal Class   **(this is the base class, it has no parent, its child is Mammal)**

  Mammal Class   **(this is a subclass, its parent is Animal, its child is Whale)**

    Whale Class (this is a subclass, its parent is Mammal, it has no children)

Classes range from general to specific. The base class is the most general; subclasses are more specific (for example, a *whale* is a specific *mammal*). Class hierarchies can be simple or complex. Here's another example:

	Life Class		
Plant Class		**Animal Class**	
Tropical Class	**Desert Class**	**Insect Class**	**Mammal Class**
Banana Class	**Cactus Class**	**Ant Class**	**Whale Class**

Life is the base class (the most general); everything else is a subclass (more specific). The Ant class inherits from the Insect class. The Whale class inherits from the Mammal class. The Ant and Whale classes inherit (indirectly) from the Animal class, but they don't even know it! The Ant class only communicates with the Insect class, and the Whale class only communicates with the Mammal class.

> This is natural inherited behavior in OOP—a class may only communicate with its parent (not its grandparent). ActionScript 2.0 provides a special keyword, super, to establish child-to-parent communications.

A quick inheritance test

Let's do a quick inheritance test. Using the Mover class we built in the previous chapter, let's now extend it to include some bounce behavior. Just to remind ourselves, this is the code for the Mover class:

```
class Mover extends MovieClip {

  var targetMC:MovieClip;

  function Mover(targetMC:MovieClip) {
    this.targetMC = targetMC;
  }
  function updatePosition() {
    this._x++;
    this._y++;
  }
  function startMoving() {
    this.targetMC.onEnterFrame = this.updatePosition;
  }
  function stopMoving() {
    this.targetMC.onEnterFrame = null;
  }
}
```

Before we move any further, it is important to add a little functionality that allows our Mover class to do something more than just move at the same speed both horizontally and vertically. To do this, we'll add three properties: xVel and yVel, which store the velocity at which our targetMC moves in any given direction; and objectRef, which acts as a reference to our class.

```
var xVel:Number;
var yVel:Number;
var objectRef:Object;
```

Next, we add two additional parameters to the constructor method:

```
function Mover(targetMC:MovieClip, xVel:Number, yVel:Number) {
  this.targetMC = targetMC;
  this.targetMC.objectRef = this;
  this.xVel = xVel;
  this.yVel = yVel;
}
```

Finally, the updatePosition method needs to be tweaked to read as follows:

```
function updatePosition() {
  this._x += this.objectRef.xVel;
  this._y += this.objectRef.yVel;
}
```

The reason why we're using this objectRef property is because the updatePosition method is called from the scope of our targetMC, when we use this.xVel in that function, it looks for a property called xVel inside the movie clip. Using this.objectRef.xVel, things are different; this.objectRef is a reference to our class, and as a result it looks for the property xVel in the Mover class scope, which is exactly what we need.

9

> *There are more convenient ways to handle scope issues such as this. I'll talk about those in Chapter 15 when discussing handling events using the EventDispatcher class.*

Having made these tweaks, we can now have our Mover class move any movie clip with any given horizontal and vertical velocity. Pretty neat! The full code of the Mover class now looks as follows:

```
class Mover extends MovieClip {

  var objectRef:Object;
  var targetMC:MovieClip;
  var xVel:Number;
  var yVel:Number;

  function Mover(targetMC:MovieClip, xVel:Number, yVel:Number) {
    this.targetMC = targetMC;
    this.targetMC.objectRef = this;
    this.xVel = xVel;
    this.yVel = yVel;
  }
  function updatePosition() {
    this._x += this.objectRef.xVel;
    this._y += this.objectRef.yVel;
  }
  function startMoving() {
    this.targetMC.onEnterFrame = this.updatePosition;
  }
  function stopMoving() {
    this.targetMC.onEnterFrame = null;
  }
}
```

When you want to create an instance of this new Mover class, you would use the following code:

```
var myMover:Mover = new Mover(circle, 2, 3);
```

This code moves our circle movie clip at a velocity of 2 pixels horizontally and 3 pixels vertically once every frame.

Now, the next step is writing our Bouncer class, which extends (or inherits) the new Mover class code. The code for this is listed here:

Bouncer.as

```
class Bouncer extends Mover {
  function Bouncer(targetMC:MovieClip, xVel:Number, yVel:Number) {
    super(targetMC,xVel,yVel);
  }
}
```

The preceding code needs to be saved in a file called Bouncer.as in the same folder as Mover.as.

What you'll need to do next is get a copy of Mover.fla and save it as Inheritance.fla in the folder where Bouncer.as and Mover.as are located. Open up Inheritance.fla and on Frame 1 of the ActionScript layer change the code to

```
var myBouncer:Bouncer = new Bouncer(circle, 2, 3);
myBouncer.startMoving();
```

Feel free to delete the rectangle movie clip from the stage, as we'll not be using this just now. Test the movie (select Control ➤ Test Movie) and you'll see that the circle on stage is now moving, just as was the case with the Mover class. Nothing spectacular, you say? Well, remember, you're now instantiating the Bouncer class, which shows you that it has inherited the functionality of the Mover class by its ability to use the startMoving method and the targetMC property. Inheritance in action, what an awe-inspiring sight!

About inheritance syntax

Let's look at what syntax we used to initiate class inheritance in ActionScript 2.0. First of all, you'll need to have the extends keyword when defining the class.

```
class Bouncer extends Mover {
  ...
}
```

After the extends keyword, you define what class it inherits from, in this case Mover. Important to note is that a class can extend only one class at a time, and this class needs to be specified by its full package name.

As soon as this extends syntax is added to the class statement, all methods and properties of that inherited class are available in the current class. This brings up an important point: what if we define a method or property with the same name in the Bouncer class? It's easy enough to give this a try—add the following code to the Bouncer class:

```
function startMoving() {
  trace("startMoving function called in Bouncer class");
}
```

9

125

If we use Test Movie now, we get the following line in the Output panel, but our circle movie clip does not move at all:

startMoving function called in Bouncer class

That's not good at all. We also want to have access to the startMoving method that was defined in the Mover class. This is where the super keyword comes in; it specifically tells a class to look for a method or property in its *parent* class, our *superclass*. Using this keyword, we can tweak the startMoving method in the Bouncer class to read as follows:

```
function startMoving() {
  trace("startMoving function called in Bouncer class");
  super.startMoving();
}
```

Testing our movie now gives us a much better response: we get both the trace statement in the Output panel and our circle is moving on the stage. It's getting more and more interesting by the minute—we've just extended a method and in the process used an important concept in OOP called **polymorphism** (more about this in the next chapter).

When you look at the code of our Bouncer class, you'll notice that the constructor also uses the super keyword but actually calls it as you would with any other method. It passes the targetMC, xVel, and yVel parameters we got in the Bouncer class down to the constructor of the Mover class.

In other words, a call to super() calls the superclass constructor; in this case, it was needed because Mover required a targetMC property to be passed to its constructor.

The Bouncer class

Using inheritance, you can safely extend existing classes with new or alternative behavior without breaking existing applications. Existing applications continue to work because they do not interact with (or even know about) the newer classes (they use the existing classes as always).

Currently, the Bouncer class behaves just like the Mover class. Next, we'll add new behavior to the Bouncer class. This new behavior will consist of a bounceAtBorder method that bounces our movie clip when it hits the end of the stage.

```
function bounceAtBorder() {
  if (this._x > Stage.width-(this._width/2)) {
    trace("Bounce at right edge");
    this._x = Stage.width-(this._width/2);
    this.objectRef.xVel *= -1;
  }
  if (this._y > Stage.height-(this._height/2)) {
    trace("Bounce at bottom edge");
    this._y = Stage.height-(this._height/2);
    this.objectRef.yVel *= -1;
```

```
      }
      if (this._x < this._width/2) {
        trace("Bounce at left edge");
        this._x = this._width/2;
        this.objectRef.xVel *= -1;
      }
      if (this._y < this._height/2) {
        trace("Bounce at top edge");
        this._y = this._height/2;
        this.objectRef.yVel *= -1;
      }
    }
```

When you look at the bounceAtBorder method, you'll find that it has four if statements, one for each edge of the screen. Each of the if statements checks the _x or _y position of targetMC against the minimum or maximum width and height. To do this, we use the built-in Stage.width and Stage.height methods that return the available width and height of the stage. Because the registration point of our movie clip is in the center, we need to accommodate the maximum and minimum width with the targetMC's _width and _height properties. Take a look at the following table to see how these minimum and maximum positions are calculated:

Right edge	Width of the stage minus half the width of the targetMC movie clip
Bottom edge	Height of the stage minus half the height of the targetMC movie clip
Left edge	Half the width of the targetMC movie clip
Top edge	Half the height of the targetMC movie clip

The only thing that's left for us to do now is tweak the startMoving method; instead of just calling updatePosition in the onEnterFrame event, we want to call both updatePosition and bounceAtBorder. The revised code for startMoving in the Bouncer class is as follows:

```
function startMoving() {
  this.targetMC.updatePosition = this.updatePosition;
  this.targetMC.bounceAtBorder = this.bounceAtBorder;
  this.targetMC.onEnterFrame = function() {
    this.updatePosition();
    this.bounceAtBorder();
  };
}
```

The preceding code makes local references in the targetMC movie clip to the updatePosition method (inherited from the Mover class) and bounceAtBorder method (from the Bouncer class) in our class. After that, we can call the updatePosition and bounceAtBorder methods as local in the targetMC onEnterFrame handler using this. updatePosition and this.bounceAtBorder.

The complete code for our Bouncer class now looks as follows:

```
class Bouncer extends Mover {

  function Bouncer(targetMC:MovieClip, xVel:Number, yVel:Number) {
    super(targetMC, xVel, yVel);
  }
  function startMoving() {
    this.targetMC.updatePosition = this.updatePosition;
    this.targetMC.bounceAtBorder = this.bounceAtBorder;
    this.targetMC.onEnterFrame = function() {
      this.updatePosition();
      this.bounceAtBorder();
    };
  }
  function bounceAtBorder() {
    if (this._x>Stage.width-(this._width/2)) {
      trace("Bounce at right edge");
      this._x = Stage.width-(this._width/2);
      this.objectRef.xVel *= -1;
    }
    if (this._y>Stage.height-(this._height/2)) {
      trace("Bounce at bottom edge");
      this._y = Stage.height-(this._height/2);
      this.objectRef.yVel *= -1;
    }
    if (this._x<this._width/2) {
      trace("Bounce at left edge");
      this._x = this._width/2;
      this.objectRef.xVel *= -1;
    }
    if (this._y<this._height/2) {
      trace("Bounce at top edge");
      this._y = this._height/2;
      this.objectRef.yVel *= -1;
    }
  }
}
```

You can now save Bouncer.as and take a look at Inheritance.fla. Make sure Frame 1 of the ActionScript layer reads as follows:

```
var myBouncer:Bouncer = new Bouncer(circle,2,3);
myBouncer.startMoving();
```

Save Inheritance.fla and run Test Movie, and you should now see the circle movie clip moving across the screen with a horizontal velocity of 2 pixels per frame and 3 pixels per frame vertically. As soon as the movie clip hits an edge, a trace statement is executed showing that in the Output panel, and it bounces off in the opposite direction.

Great work—we've just seen inheritance in action and built our very own Bouncer class by extending the Mover class!

The Gravity class

Let's create a Gravity class to help the Ball move in a natural manner. You'll use inheritance again, but this time you'll extend the Bouncer class.

Create a new file called Gravity.as and save it in the same folder as the Bouncer and Mover classes. We'll start off with the basic code as follows:

Gravity.as

```
class Gravity extends Bouncer {
  var strength: Number;
  function Gravity(targetMC:MovieClip,  xVel:Number, yVel:Number,
strength) {
    super(targetMC, xVel, yVel);
    this.strength = strength || 1;
  }
}
```

The Gravity class constructor takes the three parameters we know are needed for the Bouncer class as well as a strength parameter that defines the strength of the gravitational pull. We pass the first three parameters to the superclass, and the third is assigned to our class scope using the following syntax:

```
this.strength = strength || 1;
```

You might be wondering what's happening there. This is just shorthand syntax for writing the following statement:

```
if(strength == undefined) {
  this.strength = 1;
} else {
  this.strength = strength;
}
```

It essentially sets a default value of 1 in case no strength parameter gets passed to the Gravity class. The next thing we'll do is add the startMoving method to the Gravity class, which will now include two new methods, applyGravity and applyFriction (we'll be writing those in a minute), in the targetMC onEnterFrame handler. You can see how that startMoving method now looks:

```
function startMoving() {
  this.targetMC.updatePosition = this.updatePosition;
  this.targetMC.bounceAtBorder = this.bounceAtBorder;
  this.targetMC.applyGravity = this.applyGravity;
```

9

```
        this.targetMC.applyFriction = this.applyFriction;
        this.targetMC.onEnterFrame = function() {
          this.updatePosition();
          this.bounceAtBorder();
          this.applyGravity();
          this.applyFriction();
        };
      }
```

Just like we did in the Bouncer class, we're making a local reference to the applyGravity and applyFriction methods in targetMC and calling those in onEnterFrame.

Now that we've got that sorted, let's focus on these two new methods. The first one we'll look at is applyGravity:

```
      function applyGravity() {
        this.objectRef.yVel += this.objectRef.strength;
      }
```

Doesn't that look easy? That code adds more pull to the vertical movement of our targetMC movie clip. You'll remember that objectRef property from the Mover class we updated; it's nothing more than a reference to the class scope. As you'll see, the applyFriction method will not be much more difficult:

```
      function applyFriction() {
        this.objectRef.xVel *= 0.98;
        this.objectRef.yVel *= 0.98;
      }
```

In this method, we're adding friction to both the horizontal and vertical velocity by decreasing the velocity slightly every frame. We're using 0.98 here because it gives us the best effect. You could add this friction factor as an additional parameter for your Gravity class. Whatever the number is you'll use for this, it should be below 1; otherwise, it would in fact increase velocity.

> *It's nice to think about the friction coefficient as a percentage of the previous velocity. For example, with a coefficient of 0.98, our Mover moves only 98% the speed it did the frame before. Eventually, friction will slow the movement to nothing, just as in the physical world.*

Save the Gravity class and turn your attention to Inheritance.fla. Make sure the code in Frame 1 of the ActionScript layer looks as follows:

```
      var myGravity:Gravity = new Gravity(circle, 2, 3, 5);
      myGravity.startMoving();
```

If you save the document and run Test Movie, you'll see the circle movie clip, moving with a horizontal velocity of 2 pixels and a vertical velocity of 3 pixels per frame, bounce off the edges of the stage and slow down as if gravity were pulling it to the ground, and eventually the targetMC will rest on the bottom of the stage. In this case, the amount of gravity we applied is 5 pixels per frame.

One thing you will notice is that even when the movie clip has come to a standstill at the bottom of the stage, the onEnterFrame event continuously keeps firing the "Bounce at bottom edge" trace statement to the Output panel. To optimize our code and stop this from happening, we'll add a method that monitors the yVel property, and if that is zero, the onEnterFrame event on our targetMC movie clip gets cleared. This method, which we'll call checkForStop, needs the following code:

```
function checkForStop() {
  if (this._y == Stage.height-(this._height/2)) {
    if (Math.round(this._x) == this.objectRef.lastPosX
&& Math.round(this._y) == this.objectRef.lastPosY) {
      this.onEnterFrame = null;
    }
  }
  this.objectRef.lastPosX = Math.round(this._x);
  this.objectRef.lastPosY = Math.round(this._y);
}
```

That's quite a bit of code just to check whether our targetMC is still moving or not, but you'll see what it does in a minute. The first if statement in the checkForStop method checks whether the movie clip is on the bottom edge of the stage. If that is the case, it moves on to an if statement that checks the current _x and _y position of the targetMC against the last position. To do this, two new class properties are introduced: lastPosX and lastPosY, which hold the latest _x and _y position of targetMC. If the current _x and _y position is the same as the last _x and _y position, and the targetMC is on the bottom edge, we can be sure that our movie clip has stopped moving. In that case, we set the onEnterFrame event for the targetMC to null, essentially clearing it out.

That's it—we've just completed the Gravity class! Be sure to save Gravity.as and run Test Movie on Inheritance.fla. You'll see that the previous problem with the onEnterFrame event not stopping after the movie clip finished moving is now solved. The following is the full code of the Gravity class:

Gravity.as

```
class Gravity extends Bouncer {

  var strength:Number;
  var lastPosX:Number;
  var lastPosY:Number;
```

```
        function Gravity(targetMC:MovieClip, xVel:Number, yVel:Number,
     ➥ strength) {
          super(targetMC, xVel, yVel);
          this.strength = strength;
        }
        function startMoving() {
          this.targetMC.updatePosition = this.updatePosition;
          this.targetMC.bounceAtBorder = this.bounceAtBorder;
          this.targetMC.applyGravity = this.applyGravity;
          this.targetMC.applyFriction = this.applyFriction;
          this.targetMC.checkForStop = this.checkForStop;
          this.targetMC.onEnterFrame = function() {
            this.updatePosition();
            this.bounceAtBorder();
            this.applyGravity();
            this.applyFriction();
            this.checkForStop();
          };
        }
        function applyGravity() {
          this.objectRef.yVel += this.objectRef.strength;
        }
        function applyFriction() {
          this.objectRef.xVel *= 0.98;
          this.objectRef.yVel *= 0.98;
        }
        function checkForStop() {
          if (this._y == Stage.height-(this._height/2)) {
            if (Math.round(this._x) == this.objectRef.lastPosX
     && Math.round(this._y) == this.objectRef.lastPosY) {
              this.onEnterFrame = null;
            }
          }
          this.objectRef.lastPosX = Math.round(this._x);
          this.objectRef.lastPosY = Math.round(this._y);
        }
      }
```

> You might remember that we hard-coded the value of 0.98 in the applyFriction
> method of the Gravity class. As an exercise, try updating the code so people can specify
> the amount of friction when instantiating the class. Be sure to have a default value for
> friction. (Hint: study the strength property in the constructor of the Gravity class.)

Inheritance summary

Inheritance extends existing classes with new and alternative behaviors without breaking existing applications. Existing applications continue to work because they do not interact with (or even know about) the newer classes. Inheritance adds capability without breaking compatibility. Look at this sample code:

```
Animal.as

class Animal {
  function Animal() {
  }
  function speak = function(sound) {
    trace(sound);
  }
}

Cat.as

class Cat extends Animal {
  function Cat() {
  }
  function cryBaby = function() {
    for(i = 0; i < 100; i++) {
        super.speak("Meow! Meow! Meow!");
    }
  }
}


var suki:Cat = new Cat();
suki.cryBaby();
```

With just one statement

```
class Cat extends Animal {
  ...
}
```

the Cat class inherits from the Animal class. The Cat class has all the capabilities and characteristics of the Animal class, plus its own unique capabilities. The super keyword enables child classes (such as Cat) to talk to parent classes (such as Animal). If you try the previous code, you'll find out that you can use ActionScript 2.0 to code a very noisy cat.

What's next?

This chapter introduced the major features and benefits of class inheritance. Next, we'll look at the final building block of OOP: polymorphism.

10 **POLYMORPHISM**

The concept of *polymorphism* implies having certain functionality appear in multiple forms throughout your application, but having a unified way to call it. Doing this allows different classes throughout the project to be easily interchangeable.

In this chapter, we'll create some examples to demonstrate polymorphism in ActionScript 2.0. In a visual environment such as Flash, polymorphism is best observed when multiple objects exhibit similar behavior. Behind the scenes, this usually means multiple classes implementing functions of the same name.

I didn't mention this in detail in the previous chapters, but things like the startMoving method in the Mover, Bouncer, and Gravity classes are excellent examples of *polymorphic design*. You could create many different objects from these classes and know that any of them could fulfill the startMoving request (because they're all based on classes that implement that same method). At random, you could request any of them to start moving. With polymorphism, you don't care how things happen, just that they happen. (That sure reminds me of some project managers I've worked with in the past!)

Building a polymorphism example

This section presents a brief, visual demonstration of polymorphism. We're not going to spend a great deal of time creating this example right now, because you'll update this very same example in a later chapter.

To start off, make a copy of Inheritance.fla and name it Polymorphism.fla. Double-click Polymorphism.fla to launch Flash.

The next thing we'll do is populate the stage so we have some movie clips to work with:

1. Delete all items on the stage.
2. Display the Library panel (select Window ➤ Library).
3. Drag three instances of the circle movie clip to the stage.
4. Give the circle movie clips on the stage the following instance names: circle1, circle2, and circle3.
5. Change the code in Frame 1 of the ActionScript layer to read as follows:

```
var myMover:Mover = new Mover(circle1, 2, 3);
var myBouncer:Bouncer = new Bouncer(circle2, 2, 3);
var myGravity:Gravity = new Gravity(circle3, 2, 3, 5);

function startClassMoving(className) {
  className.startMoving();
}
```

The preceding code does not differ much from the code used for instantiating the Mover, Bouncer, and Gravity classes in the previous chapters. The one thing I added is a function, startClassMoving, that accepts a parameter, className. The function itself tries to call a startMoving function on whatever object is passed to it.

To make the difference between all the circle instances more obvious, let's make each a different color. First select the circle1 instance on the stage by clicking it and opening up the Properties panel (Window ➤ Properties). In the Properties panel, select Tint from the Color drop-down menu and choose red with the color picker tool (see Figure 10-1).

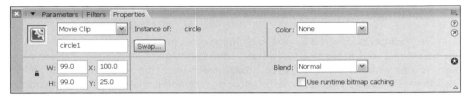

Figure 10-1. Setting the tint color in the Properties panel

Repeat the same for the circle2 and circle3 instances, giving them a blue and green color tint, respectively. When you've finished, Polymorphism.fla's stage should look something like Figure 10-2.

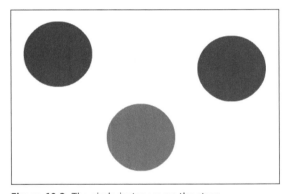

Figure 10-2. The circle instances on the stage

You've probably guessed by now what you'll be doing: passing the names of our class instances to this function should start them moving. Add the following line of code before testing this movie:

```
startClassMoving(myMover);
```

Save the document and use Test Movie (Control ➤ Test Movie) to see this code in action. If all went well, you should now see the circle1 instance moving across the stage. When you change that last line of code to read as follows, you get a different result:

```
startClassMoving(myBouncer);
```

If you run Test Movie now, you'll see circle2 bouncing across the stage. Of course, the same goes for the Gravity class—using the following code, you'll have circle3 bouncing with gravity and friction effect on the stage:

```
startClassMoving(myGravity);
```

10

There is nothing stopping you from using all three at once; as there are three class instances, they can operate completely independently. Try the following code to see all circle instances on stage moving at the same time:

```
startClassMoving(myMover);
startClassMoving(myBouncer);
startClassMoving(myGravity);
```

As you've probably discovered by now, polymorphism is a very easy principle, but applying it in object-oriented projects does wonders for creating reusable code. Polymorphism allows you to write simple code, even though there might be very complex underlying class interaction. You shouldn't have to know or care about that if you use polymorphic design throughout a project—you could even use classes written by another developer without even opening them once.

> *Bear in mind that applying this technique is useful only if you use the same name for functions that perform more or less the same task. There is a danger of going overboard with polymorphism and using very generic function names such as "update", "run", and so forth. Doing so isn't good for code readability, and it might even result in more confusion than clarity. Be sure to refer to Chapter 6, which covers best practices, if you're in doubt about how to handle naming conventions.*

Implementing polymorphism for application reuse

With encapsulation, inheritance, and polymorphism, you have the tools to make software reuse a reality. The sections that follow present examples demonstrating this concept.

Basic concept of polymorphism

Functional polymorphism occurs when multiple classes implement consistent functions. For example, consider the following classes.

Bored.as

```
class Bored {
  function Bored() {
  }
  function doSomething() {
    trace("I'm bored, let's do something!");
  }
}
```

Tired.as

```
class Tired {
  function Tired() {
  }
  function doSomething() {
    this.doNothing();
  }
  function doNothing() {
    trace("I'm tired, I don't want to do anything.");
  }
}
```

Hungry.as

```
class Hungry {
  function Hungry() {
  }
  function doSomething() {
    this.doLunch();
  }
  function doLunch() {
    trace("I'm hungry, let's get lunch!");
  }
}
```

All of these classes implement the doSomething function, so you could write the following in an FLA document located in the same folder:

```
var bob:Tired   = new Tired();
var jill:Bored  = new Bored();
var janet:Hungry = new Hungry();

bob.doSomething();   // Output:  I'm tired, I don't want to do anything.
jill.doSomething();  // Output:  I'm bored, let's do something!
janet.doSomething(); // Output:  I'm hungry, let's get lunch!
```

This is a simple example, and you had to create the objects manually, but what if you could create the objects dynamically? Polymorphism allows you to control dynamic objects without knowing ahead of time which objects you're dealing with.

Functional polymorphism at work

Now let's look at a slightly more useful example of polymorphism. If you were to build a Flash-based tool for a human resources department, a good place to start would be an Employee class, as follows. This base class then holds all properties and methods that are shared by all types of employees the company might have.

Employee.as

```
class Employee {

  var baseSalary:Number = 1000;

  function receivePayment():Number {
    return baseSalary;
  }

}
```

The preceding code shows an Employee class with just one property that contains the base salary of an employee, and a receivePayment method, because that's what we care about most, no?

With this base class in place, you have a starting point to create any number of employee types. Each employee type is a class that inherits from the Employee class and implements its own receivePayment method. For example, the following class defines an Engineer employee type.

Engineer.as

```
class Engineer extends Employee {

  function receivePayment():Number {
    return baseSalary*2;
  }

}
```

The Engineer type has its own receivePayment method, but it is still able to use the baseSalary property it inherited from the Employee class. In a real-world situation, calculating the payment for an individual employee isn't as easy as multiplying the base salary by a given number, but you can see the value of this type of approach for calculating end-of-year bonuses, paid leave, and so forth.

The wonderful thing about polymorphism, as you know by now, is that your code doesn't need to know about all employee types that you create. Because they all implement the same set of properties and methods (either overwritten or inherited from the base class), your project remains flexible and you can easily add new types of employees without needing to restructure your application.

To illustrate this, let's create some more employee type classes, as follows.

UnpaidIntern.as

```
class UnpaidIntern extends Employee {

  function receivePayment():Number {
    return 0;
  }

}
```

Unpaid interns—a vastly underrated asset for any office when it comes to shifting the blame for missed deadlines—are not surprisingly paid nothing.

Manager.as

```
class Manager extends Employee {

  function receivePayment():Number {
    return baseSalary*3;
  }

}
```

Managers in our wonderful company, on the other hand, are paid triple the base salary for their hard work hiring unpaid interns. Again, these classes just represent a specific employee type and implement their own receivePayment method to overwrite the default.

Those classes are all nice to have, but how do you take advantage of this polymorphic design when implementing them in the application? Let's look at a bit of code that you could use to bring together the different employee classes.

Create a new FLA file and save it in the same folder where you have the Employee.as, UnpaidIntern.as, and Manager.as classes stored.

With the FLA open, on the first keyframe of Layer 1 type the following code:

```
function payEmployee(employeeType) {
  return new employeeType().receivePayment();
}

trace(payEmployee(UnpaidIntern)); // outputs 0
trace(payEmployee(Engineer)); // outputs 2000
trace(payEmployee(Manager)); // outputs 3000
```

What is interesting about the preceding code snippet is that the payEmployee function actually takes a reference to an employee class as its argument, after which it instantiates the class, runs the receivePayment method on it, and returns that value.

10

As a side note, because the instantiated employee type class was not assigned to a reference, it will not remain. It is immediately flushed from Flash Player's memory as soon as that statement has ended.

To test this payEmployee function, we create three calls to it, each passing a different employee type class, and have them trace out the values to the Output panel. When you run this code, you'll see the Flash Output panel holds the values 0, 2,000, and 3,000 for the instance of the unpaid intern, engineer, and manager, respectively.

What's next?

The examples in this chapter have given you a glimpse of how polymorphism can be an invaluable tool for your applications. I'm sure you'll be even more convinced of polymorphism's worth when we look at more advanced examples later on in this book.

Encapsulation, inheritance, and polymorphism are the basic building blocks of OOP. Additionally, ActionScript 2.0 supports *interfaces*, which help implement those building blocks. I'll cover that feature in detail in the next chapter.

11 INTERFACES

In the last few chapters we looked at what might be considered the pillars of OOP: encapsulation, inheritance, and polymorphism. With *interfaces*, the topic of this chapter, you're able to bring together those OOP pillars and draw up a template of what your class should look like.

This chapter focuses on what interfaces are, why you should use them, and how to apply them to the code you've written in prior chapters. We'll start by looking at the concept of interfaces and how they're implemented in ActionScript 2.0.

Interfaces overview

Think back to the house-building analogy I used in the first chapter of this book. If you compare a *class* to an architect's blueprint, *class objects* are the houses built from that blueprint, and an *interface* is the contract you sign with the architect.

Despite what you may expect, interfaces do not contain any code at all. Their purpose is to provide a set of methods with corresponding typed parameters and a return datatype that a class must minimally implement to be considered valid. If a class does not conform with the interface(s) it implements, a compile error will be thrown. Interfaces do not, however, support defining properties or private class methods.

Interfaces define the following information for your class:

- The scope of a method (only public is allowed)
- The method name
- The method parameters and their corresponding datatypes
- The method return type

Interfaces do not specify the following:

- Class properties
- Private or static methods
- Any code inside methods

Interfaces help you check if your classes contain all the methods you need them to have available. They are used by the compiler to validate your code and provide you with a means to plan method implementations and APIs at the planning stage of your project.

Typically, interfaces have the most impact when used in projects that use a lot of classes or rely on many different developers to work according to a predefined class structure. Interfaces also help with enforcing polymorphism in all classes that implement it, making your code interchangeable and interoperable.

To quickly familiarize you with interfaces, I'll cover some uses for interfaces and look at a simple example of an interface in the sections that follow.

Interface use-cases

Now, why the heck would you want to use interfaces? At first glance, interfaces seem like a lot of extra work for little in return, but once you start looking at the bigger picture, you'll find situations where you'll want to have interfaces in place.

For example, the previous chapter on polymorphism showed that because the Mover, Bouncer, and Gravity classes all implement the same startMoving method, they are largely interchangeable. You can start movement on any of those classes by calling the same method, and you even used a function on the main timeline to call this for you on the class instance that we passed as a parameter. In that type of situation, you want to be sure the class instance you pass to the function actually has that startMoving method in place, rather than just going forward on good faith. By having these classes implement an interface that defines the startMoving method, you can be sure that all classes have that startMoving method in place, and your code will function.

Other uses for interfaces are when you're designing an API for a class. Oftentimes in large projects, applications are separated into different code modules, and they all need to provide a specific set of methods to communicate with one another. This is where interfaces come in.

In such situations, interfaces can be used as a virtual checklist to ensure all methods are in place and have the correct datatypes and return values applied. Typically in this setup, you would define interfaces during the project planning process and give them to the team as a template to work with.

> *Although you can find many situations in which you can use interfaces—and in which interface usage might even be the recommended practice—most of your of everyday ActionScript OOP will likely not require you to go to the length of creating interfaces. If your code is part of a larger context and will be extended upon in future, or if you're working with a strict method structure for your classes, then interfaces are definitely the way to go.*

11

What an interface looks like

By now you're probably wondering what an interface looks like. You already know it doesn't define any code and that it simply acts as a template of what a class that implements it should look like. Let's examine a sample interface.

First, just as with ActionScript classes, an interface is saved in its own file with an `.as` extension, and it should be called by the name you assign to the interface, for example:

MyInterface.as

```
interface MyInterface {
  public function myFirstMethod(myProperty:String):Void;
  public function mySecondMethod(mySecondProperty:Number):Number;
}
```

The preceding example interface is very simple. You'll notice that it's similar in structure to a class. One of the first noticeable differences is the keyword interface where class would appear. Inside the interface are two public method declarations: myFirstMethod, which accepts a parameter of datatype String named myProperty and has a return type Void, and mySecondMethod, which accepts a Number parameter called mySecondProperty and returns a Number type.

Notice that we aren't using curly braces after the method declaration—it is followed by just a semicolon because, as I stated earlier, interfaces do not need or in fact allow you to specify any code in the method body.

Now that you know what interface are used for and look like, let's build some for the classes discussed in the earlier chapters and cover how they're implemented.

Implementing an interface

In the previous chapters, we built a number of classes to control the movement of a movie clip. We started out by a creating a simple Mover class, which moves the target movie clip with a certain horizontal and vertical velocity.

The key functionality of that class consisted of the startMoving and stopMoving methods, without which our class wouldn't be able to function. With this and the fact that we're planning to extend the class in mind, the Mover class is a good candidate for applying an interface to. Here's what an interface for the Mover class should look like:

IMoveable.as

```
interface IMoveable {
  public function startMoving():Void;
  public function stopMoving():Void;
}
```

Doesn't look very difficult, does it? We create a file called IMoveable.as (more about that naming convention later on), define an interface with that same IMoveable name, and add two lines that show the implementation of startMoving and stopMoving as public methods with a return type of Void.

The only thing left to do is add the implements keyword to the Mover class, as shown in the following code:

Mover.a

```
class Mover extends MovieClip implements IMoveable {

  private var objectRef:Object;
  private var targetMC:MovieClip;
  private var xVel:Number;
  private var yVel:Number;

  function Mover(targetMC:MovieClip, xVel:Number, yVel:Number) {
    this.targetMC = targetMC;
    this.targetMC.objectRef = this;
    this.xVel = xVel;
    this.yVel = yVel;
  }

  public function startMoving():Void {
    this.targetMC.onEnterFrame = this.updatePosition;
  }

  public function stopMoving():Void {
    this.targetMC.onEnterFrame = null;
  }

  private function updatePosition():Void {
    this._x += this.objectRef.xVel;
    this._y += this.objectRef.yVel;
  }

}
```

Just adding implements IMoveable makes sure the class checks that it is compliant with the interface we implemented.

Let's do a quick test to see if our interface does its job. Copy the file Polymorphism.fla from the previous chapter, rename it to Interface.fla, and put it in a folder along with the files Mover.as and IMoveable.as. Double-click Interface.fla to launch Flash.

1. Delete all but one circle movie clip on the stage.

2. Give the remaining circle movie clip the instance name ball.

3. Change the code in Frame 1 of the ActionScript layer as follows:

```
var myMover:Mover = new Mover(ball, 2, 3);
myMover.startMoving();
```

11

OBJECT-ORIENTED ACTIONSCRIPT FOR FLASH 8

If you test the movie, you should see the circle movie clip moving across the stage as normal. That's a good thing—you now know that the class is valid for the interface that it implements. You might be wondering what happens if the class doesn't implement all the interface methods. Well, let's find out!

Open the file IMoveable.as and add another method so it looks like this:

IMoveable.as

```
interface IMoveable {
  public function startMoving():Void;
  public function stopMoving():Void;
  public function getPosition():Object;
}
```

You'll notice that you just added a nonexistent method of getPosition with a return type Object to the interface. You do not have that method in the Mover class, so it would be interesting to see what that gives you. Run Test Movie again and you should see the error message shown in Figure 11-1 pop up.

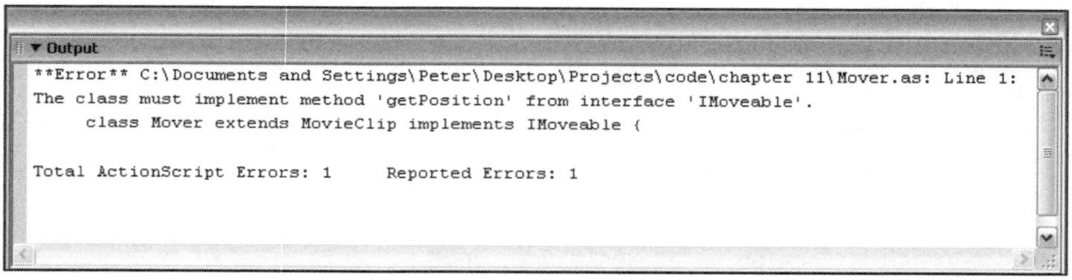

Figure 11-1. Error message for an unimplemented interface method

Don't you just love those descriptive error messages? The class must implement method 'getPosition' from interface 'IMoveable'. This is the type of error you can expect when your classes don't comply with the methods outlined in the interface(s) they implement. With that in mind, you can see that interfaces are used by the compiler only to help you assess if your classes have in place everything that should be there. In fact, interfaces don't get compiled into the SWF whatsoever—they are all checked and converted to bytecode when the project is compiled by using Test Movie or by exporting it.

Let's remove that extra method from the IMoveable interface and look at the next class we worked on. The Bouncer class extends the Mover class and adds a bounceAtBorder method. This method is of a private scope, which means we can't include it in our interface. This is interesting because in a real-world scenario you probably wouldn't go to the trouble of creating an empty interface, but it gives me the chance to outline two practical solutions for implementing interfaces. Here's the first solution:

IBounceable.as

```
interface IBounceable extends IMoveable {
}
```

This isn't much different from the IMoveable interface. We just created an IBounceable interface in the file IBounceable.as. The interface doesn't implement any methods, but the one thing you'll want to notice is the extends keyword. Just like classes, interfaces can extend other interfaces (not classes, mind you), which gives them access to all methods outlined in the superinterface (the interface equivalent of a superclass).

Essentially, we now have a duplicate of the IMoveable interface with the name IBounceable. The next step is to implement it in the Bouncer class.

Bouncer.as

```
class Bouncer extends Mover implements IBounceable {

  function Bouncer(targetMC:MovieClip, xVel:Number, yVel:Number) {
    super(targetMC, xVel, yVel);
  }

  public function startMoving():Void {
    this.targetMC.updatePosition = this.updatePosition;
    this.targetMC.bounceAtBorder = this.bounceAtBorder;
    this.targetMC.onEnterFrame = function() {
      this.updatePosition();
      this.bounceAtBorder();
    };
  }

  private function bounceAtBorder() {
    if (this._x>Stage.width-(this._width/2)) {
      trace("Bounce at right edge");
      this._x = Stage.width-(this._width/2);
      this.objectRef.xVel *= -1;
    }
    if (this._y>Stage.height-(this._height/2)) {
      trace("Bounce at bottom edge");
      this._y = Stage.height-(this._height/2);
      this.objectRef.yVel *= -1;
    }
    if (this._x<this._width/2) {
      trace("Bounce at left edge");
      this._x = this._width/2;
```

11

```
            this.objectRef.xVel *= -1;
        }
        if (this._y<this._height/2) {
          trace("Bounce at top edge");
          this._y = this._height/2;
          this.objectRef.yVel *= -1;
        }
      }


    }
```

Again, just adding implements IBounceable makes sure our class has all the necessary methods implemented when it is compiled. Change the ActionScript on Frame 1 of the ActionScript layer as follows:

```
var myBouncer:Bouncer = new Bouncer(ball, 2, 3);
myBouncer.startMoving();
```

If you run Test Movie, you'll see the Bouncer class functioning as you'd expect it to and bouncing off the edge of the stage. Now, hang on—let's look at that Bouncer class again! We had a stopMoving method defined in the IMoveable interface. Why doesn't our Bouncer.as have this implemented?

It's important to remember that, just like our IBounceable interface, the Bouncer class inherits from the Mover class, which does specify the stopMoving method. This shows you that interfaces don't look at just what methods a specific class has implemented, but also those that it may have inherited from other classes.

Great, we're making progress! I talked about another approach for applying an interface to our Bouncer class. Unlike the extends keyword, classes can implement multiple interfaces, and they just need to be separated by a comma. Let's see how that looks:

Bouncer.as

```
class Bouncer extends Mover implements IMoveable, IBounceable {

  function Bouncer(targetMC:MovieClip, xVel:Number, yVel:Number) {
    super(targetMC, xVel, yVel);
  }

  public function startMoving():Void {
    this.targetMC.updatePosition = this.updatePosition;
    this.targetMC.bounceAtBorder = this.bounceAtBorder;
    this.targetMC.onEnterFrame = function() {
      this.updatePosition();
      this.bounceAtBorder();
    };
  }
```

```
        private function bounceAtBorder() {
          if (this._x>Stage.width-(this._width/2)) {
            trace("Bounce at right edge");
            this._x = Stage.width-(this._width/2);
            this.objectRef.xVel *= -1;
          }
          if (this._y>Stage.height-(this._height/2)) {
            trace("Bounce at bottom edge");
            this._y = Stage.height-(this._height/2);
            this.objectRef.yVel *= -1;
          }
          if (this._x<this._width/2) {
            trace("Bounce at left edge");
            this._x = this._width/2;
            this.objectRef.xVel *= -1;
          }
          if (this._y<this._height/2) {
            trace("Bounce at top edge");
            this._y = this._height/2;
            this.objectRef.yVel *= -1;
          }
        }

      }
```

Instead of just adding implements IBounceable, we used implements IMoveable, IBounceable. We also need to make sure the IBounceable interface does not extend IMoveable, so we'll update that code as follows:

IBounceable.as

```
    interface IBounceable {
    }
```

If you run Test Movie with those changes in place, everything should still function as expected. Now, when should you use what method? Implementing multiple interfaces is generally done when they are not related. For example, say that the Bouncer class, apart from moving, should be able to have some methods to track its position. In such a situation, you might feasibly have an interface called ITrackable that defines certain methods that the class needs to implement.

In the current situation, however, you're extending functionality, so the best practice here would no doubt be to implement one interface that itself extends the other interface. With that in mind, change the code for Bouncer.as and IBounceable.as back to their original forms and let's look at the Gravity class.

The Gravity class is faced with a similar situation as the Bouncer class. Even though it implements several additional methods (applyFriction, applyMethod, and checkForStop), none of those is a public method and therefore can't be added to an interface. We'll nevertheless go ahead and create an empty IGravity interface for the Gravity class to implement.

11

IGravity.as

```
interface IGravity extends IBounceable {
}
```

As you can see, the IGravity interface extends the IBounceable interface, which in turn extends the IMoveable interface. You might be thinking that this looks like some very convoluted code for essentially just having one interface with a startMoving and stopMoving method, and you're not wrong about that. From a simply functional standpoint, the Mover, Bouncer, and Gravity classes could all have implemented the IMoveable interface.

The current approach does have its merits, as we now have a corresponding interface for each of our classes, and should we decide to add some essential methods to the Bouncer class, for example, we can put the method implementation in the corresponding IBounceable interface.

The final step to add interfaces to our classes involves implementing the IGravity interface in the Gravity class as follows:

Gravity.as

```
class Gravity extends Bouncer implements IGravity {

  var strength:Number;

  function Gravity(targetMC:MovieClip, xVel:Number, yVel:Number,
strength) {
    super(targetMC, xVel, yVel);
    this.strength = strength;
  }

  public function startMoving():Void {
    this.targetMC.updatePosition = this.updatePosition;
    this.targetMC.bounceAtBorder = this.bounceAtBorder;
    this.targetMC.applyGravity = this.applyGravity;
    this.targetMC.applyFriction = this.applyFriction;
    this.targetMC.checkForStop = this.checkForStop;
    this.targetMC.onEnterFrame = function() {
      this.updatePosition();
      this.bounceAtBorder();
      this.applyGravity();
      this.applyFriction();
      this.checkForStop();
    };
  }
```

```
    private function applyGravity() {
      this.objectRef.yVel += this.objectRef.strength;
    }

    private function applyFriction() {
      this.objectRef.xVel *= 0.98;
      this.objectRef.yVel *= 0.98;
    }

    private function checkForStop() {
      if (this._y == Stage.height-(this._height/2)) {
        if (Math.round(this._x) == this.objectRef.lastPosX
        ➥ && Math.round(this._y) == this.objectRef.lastPosY) {
          this.onEnterFrame = null;
        }
      }
      this.objectRef.lastPosX = Math.round(this._x);
      this.objectRef.lastPosY = Math.round(this._y);
      }
    }
```

> *A note on the naming convention of interfaces: most developers like to have inter-*
> *face names start with a capital "I" followed by the either the name of the class*
> *+able (IMoveable) if it is a verb or simply the class name if it is a noun (IGravity).*
> *Whatever naming convention you choose for your interfaces, it's a good idea to*
> *make sure those interface names are distinguishable from normal class names*
> *and that the names are descriptive of the types of methods defined.*

What's next?

Don't underestimate the power of interfaces once you start extending existing projects. They can help you code more consistently and will save you time you would otherwise spend on debugging applications because you forgot to add a particular method to one of your classes. Interfaces are quick and easy to build, and will prove to be an essential part of your development workflow once you start developing your own extensive ActionScript 2.0 frameworks.

This chapter concludes a series of chapters in which you learned the core topics of OOP. Before moving on to present more examples of ActionScript 2.0 code, I'm going to introduce you to *design patterns*, which are practical programmatic approaches to solving specific problems and which will help you understand the reasoning behind the way code is structured in upcoming chapters.

11

12 DESIGN PATTERNS

Now that you've read about OOP concepts and best practices, and you've seen OOP applied within some ActionScript 2.0 examples, it's time to get more involved and look at troubleshooting your code and making it more efficient. This is where *design patterns* come in.

> When talking about design patterns, it's almost impossible to ignore one of the most authoritative books on the subject, Design Patterns: Elements of Reusable Object-Oriented Software *by Erich Gamma, Richard Helm, Ralph Johnson, and John Vlissides, who are affectionately called the Gang of Four (GoF). This book first hit the shelves back in 1995 and has contributed tremendously in evangelizing this topic.*

Design patterns provide you with a means to structure your application and streamline communication between classes to effectively deal with common code problems. That being said, there is almost a cult following of developers passionate about the importance and superiority of a very particular implementation of a design pattern. Following the topic of design patterns is actually good entertainment—browse the Web for an afternoon and you'll find endless heated debates on even the most minor and insignificant details. I take a much more pragmatic approach to design patterns, and feel they help developers handle specific code problems in an efficient and OO-friendly way. Whether you call it apples or pears is not what's important; it just needs to do the job. This is also the approach I'll take when I introduce design patterns for OOP with ActionScript 2.0 in this chapter. Rather than focusing on the technicalities and underlying theory, I'll show you some practical implementations of common patterns.

This chapter covers the Observer, Singleton, Decorator, and Model-View-Controller (MVC) patterns that are among the most useful when building ActionScript 2.0 projects. I advise you to read through each example of a design pattern in full in this chapter, and then sit down and try to apply it to one of your projects. By doing so, you'll soon grasp the concepts and better understand the benefits of using certain design patterns in specific situations.

Understanding design patterns

When I first started looking into design patterns for OOP with ActionScript, I must admit that I had some serious difficulties getting my head wrapped around the topic and its implementation in ActionScript. I'm sure the same thing was happening to a lot of other ActionScript developers who don't have a background in low-level OOP languages (as was the case with me).

There's no reason to panic, though; progress has been made since the ActionScript 1.0 days, and the new object-oriented syntax makes it much easier to "borrow" some implementations of design patterns in Java and port them to ActionScript 2.0. That does not mean that you should get carried away with this—ActionScript 2.0 is not Java, and just because something works well in Java does not mean it will automatically be a good thing to do in ActionScript 2.0. While design patterns can help your project, you have to find the balance between what you need and what you can do with them. Failing that, you're stuck with some convoluted and highly restrictive code that hinders your workflow more than it helps with sorting out programming problems. The best way to learn this balance is through understanding design patterns and the role they play in your application.

Design patterns take an abstract description of a situation and talk about the way to handle this in OOP. Now, the interesting thing is that design patterns don't give you ready-made solutions; rather, they simply discuss the different segments of a pattern and how they relate to each other. It's up to you to find an implementation for the pattern and get it embedded in your project. This is really what many people have difficulty with when starting out with design patterns. It is absolutely essential that you have a complete overview of your project and can visualize the relationships of classes and how they communicate with each other. If you're familiar with UML diagrams, they can help tremendously, but in some more complex projects, I recommend using a method that's a bit unorthodox.

In such situations, I suggest taking pieces of paper, each of which represents a class, and spreading them out on a table. On each piece of paper, you then write the class name, a description of its function, and any important methods it implements, and you start walking through the application. You look at a task that the classes need to perform, and keep track of the different steps and roles that your classes play.

When you do that, you'll probably come across some situations where your code isn't as efficient or straightforward as you'd like it to be. You can label those as possible structural failures in your application design and look at how they can be remodeled to behave better.

You'll likely find that many of those instances of potential failures are good candidates for having a design pattern implemented. You can then focus on those specific trouble spots and see what type of situation you're dealing with. Here are some examples of situations in which you might use the design patterns that we'll discuss in this chapter:

- **Observer pattern**: Multiple classes that all depend on the state of a specific class can subscribe to that class and get automatically notified when its state changes. This pattern can be used to keep various elements that use the same data in a project in sync with each other.

- **Singleton pattern**: Classes require only one instance to be available for your entire application. This pattern allows you to have a single centralized point where all information is managed for a project.

- **Decorator pattern**: A class takes in another class instance and adds functionality. This pattern can be used as an alternative to class inheritance.

- **MVC pattern**: Classes are defined as the Model, View, and Controller of your application, which allows you to separate data, programming logic, and presentation. Using this pattern, you can easily make changes to the View, for example, without it affecting the rest of the application.

Once you've found a suitable design pattern that addresses the trouble spot in your application design, you can start to look at a way to implement it. That's exactly what we'll do next. I'll introduce you to each of the design patterns just listed and help you work out a good ActionScript 2.0 implementation for it.

12

Implementing design patterns

There's more than one way to implement design patterns. Finding the best implementation is not just having it adhere to the specifications of the pattern, but also looking at how it best fits in with your project. Even the most useful pattern can become your worst enemy if you're too strict in the way you fit it in. Design patterns shouldn't be looked at as separate from your application, but rather as an integral part of your project model.

In the following sections, we'll look at the design patterns listed earlier and walk through how to apply them to an ActionScript 2.0 project.

Observer pattern

The Observer design pattern is one of the most common patterns you'll find in OOP with ActionScript 2.0 and most other programming languages, for that matter. The theory behind it is simple: class instances can subscribe to a class that uses this Observer pattern and automatically be notified of any changes that occurred. What gives this design pattern its real power is the ability to centralize notifications. Rather than having all classes that rely on a property of a different class continually check for changes, the information is pushed to every subscribing class if and when changes have occurred. This makes the Observer pattern a very efficient way to handle data changes and synchronize events between different classes.

Basic implementation

A basic implementation of the Observer pattern is relatively easy to build. You need an Array class property that keeps track of the class instances that subscribed, methods to add and remove subscribers, and a method that sends out the notifications.

The following Observer class is saved in a file called Observer.as and shows this basic implementation of the Observer pattern.

Observer.as

```
class Observer {

  private var subscribers:Array;

  function Observer() {
    subscribers = new Array();
  }

  public function addSubscriber(classInstance:Object):Void {
    this.subscribers.push(classInstance);
  }
```

```
public function removeSubscriber(classInstance:Object):Void {
  for(var i=0; i<this.subscribers.length; i++) {
    if(this.subscribers[i] == classInstance) {
      this.subscribers.splice(i,1);
        break;
    }
  }
}

public function notifyChanges():Void {
  for(var i in this.subscribers) this.subscribers[i].update();
}

}
```

You'll notice that there is a private variable of an Array type named subscribers, a method called addSubscriber that adds subscribers to the subscribers Array, a removeSubscriber method that removes subscribers from the subscribers Array, and a method called notifyChanges that loops through the subscribers array and calls an update function on all of the instances that subscribed for notifications.

Let's give this class a try and see if it does the trick:

1. Launch Flash.

2. Choose Flash Document from the Create New menu on the start page.

3. Save the blank document in the same folder as Observer.as with the filename Observer.fla.

4. Rename Layer 1 in the Timeline to ActionScript.

5. Open to Actions panel (select Window ➤ Development Panels ➤ Actions).

6. Add the following code to Frame 1 of the ActionScript layer:

```
var myObserver:Observer = new Observer();
var myFirstSubscriber:Object = new Object();
var mySecondSubscriber:Object = new Object();

myFirstSubscriber.update = function() {
  trace("myFirstSubscriber notified by Observer class");
}
mySecondSubscriber.update = function() {
  trace("mySecondSubscriber notified by Observer class");
}

myObserver.addSubscriber(myFirstSubscriber);
myObserver.addSubscriber(mySecondSubscriber);
myObserver.notifyChanges();
```

7. Save the document (select File ➤ Save).

12

By following these steps, you create a new instance of the Observer class named myObserver and two objects named myFirstSubscriber and mySecondSubscriber that each have an update function that traces out a message when called. Then those two object instances are added as subscribers to the Observer class using the addSubscriber method, and finally the myObserver instance calls the notifyChanges method.

If you run Test Movie (Control ➤ Test Movie) now, you should now see both the myFirstSubscriber and mySecondSubscriber instance having their update function called. Congratulations! You've just applied the Observer pattern to some ActionScript 2.0 code (see Figure 12-1).

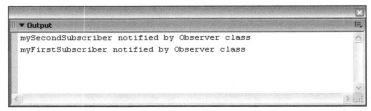

Figure 12-1. Output panel showing the Observer design pattern example

> *When working with the Observer pattern, it's important to note that a class instance is not automatically removed when it gets deleted. If you delete a class instance and don't remove it as a subscriber, Flash will still attempt to call it every time it sends out a notification. For this reason, be sure to unsubscribe a class instance before you delete it to keep your code optimized.*

That's all well and good, but it doesn't look very practical just yet. We'll get to a more practical implementation of the Observer pattern soon, but let's first look at some little tweaks that are required.

The addSubscriber method used in this Observer class doesn't check for duplicate entries. Having the same class instance subscribed multiple times is not very efficient and can easily be avoided. What you'll do is check if the class instance is already added, and if that is the case you'll return a false value; otherwise, you'll add it to the subscribers array and return true. By returning this Boolean true/false value, you also have confirmation of whether or not the class instance was added to the subscribers array.

```
public function addSubscriber(classInstance:Object):Boolean {
    for(var i=0; i<this.subscribers.length; i++) {
        if(this.subscribers[i] == classInstance) {
            return false;
        }
    }
    this.subscribers.push(classInstance);
    return true;
}
```

If you changed the code in Observer.as to have the addSubscriber method look like the preceding code, give it a test in Flash. Make sure you change the code in Frame 1 of the ActionScript layer to read as follows:

```
var myObserver:Observer = new Observer();
var myFirstSubscriber:Object = new Object();
var mySecondSubscriber:Object = new Object();

myFirstSubscriber.update = function() {
  trace("myFirstSubscriber notified by Observer class");
}
mySecondSubscriber.update = function() {
  trace("mySecondSubscriber notified by Observer class");
}

trace(myObserver.addSubscriber(myFirstSubscriber));
trace(myObserver.addSubscriber(mySecondSubscriber));
trace(myObserver.addSubscriber(myFirstSubscriber));

myObserver.notifyChanges();
```

Here, you've added another call to addSubscriber, again passing myFirstSubscriber as a parameter. With the changes you just made to the Observer class, the addSubscriber method now returns a true or false statement indicating whether or not the instance was added to the subscribers array. This was done to avoid duplicate entries. By using the trace statement with these addSubscriber calls, you get the return values traced out to the Output panel when running Test Movie. Let's do just that and check whether that works (see Figure 12-2).

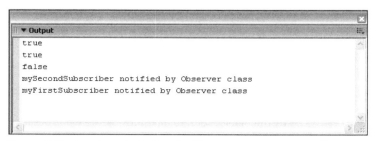

Figure 12-2. Output panel showing the Observer design pattern notification

Great, that seems to work just fine! The first two lines in the Output panel read true, which indicates that myFirstSubscriber and mySecondSubscriber were successfully added to the subscribers array in the Observer class. However, the next line reads false, and if you look at the corresponding line in Frame 1 of the ActionScript layer, that is the result of trying to add myFirstSubscriber to the Observer class again. Finally, you have the last two lines, which you also had last time around, that show that the subscribing instances were notified by the Observer class.

While we're at it, we might as well do the same for the removeSubscriber method. In its current form, this method does not return any value when called. Having it return a Boolean type would be very handy to know if a subscriber was effectively removed from the subscribers array in the Observer class. The code for this looks as follows:

```
public function removeSubscriber(classInstance:Object):Boolean {
  for(var i=0; i<this.subscribers.length; i++) {
    if(this.subscribers[i] == classInstance) {
      this.subscribers.splice(i,1);
      return true;
    }
  }
  return false;
}
```

Make sure you save Observer.as after applying these changes, and you might want to give it a try in your project. Change the code on Frame 1 of the ActionScript layer to read as follows:

```
var myObserver:Observer = new Observer();
var myFirstSubscriber:Object = new Object();
var mySecondSubscriber:Object = new Object();

myFirstSubscriber.update = function() {
  trace("myFirstSubscriber notified by Observer class");
}
mySecondSubscriber.update = function() {
  trace("mySecondSubscriber notified by Observer class");
}

trace(myObserver.addSubscriber(myFirstSubscriber));
trace(myObserver.addSubscriber(mySecondSubscriber));
trace(myObserver.removeSubscriber(myFirstSubscriber));
trace(myObserver.removeSubscriber(myElephant));

myObserver.notifyChanges();
```

The code now has a call to the addSubscriber method for the myFirstSubscriber and mySecondSubscriber instances, and a call to the removeSubscriber method, passing myFirstSubscriber as the instance to be removed from the subscribers array in the Observer class. Finally, you've also added a line that tries to remove a nonexistent myElephant instance as an observer.

If you run Test Movie with this code in place, you'll see the lines shown in Figure 12-3 in the Output panel.

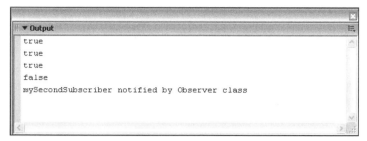

Figure 12-3. Output panel showing addSubscriber and removeSubscriber in action

The first two lines in the Output panel read true, as they correspond with the myFirstSubscriber and mySecondSubscriber instance being added as subscribers to the Observer class. The third line also reads true, which means that the myFirstSubscriber instance was successfully removed from the observers array in the Observer class. The next line reads false because the instance myElephant wasn't found in the subscribers array. Now, this is fun! The final line shows you that mySecondSubscriber was notified by the Observer class. Note that the myFirstSubscriber update method was not called, which also confirms that it was removed from the observers array in the Observer class.

One other minor detail that you might have noticed when first testing the Observer class is that the subscribing instances are called in reverse order. If you look at Figure 12-1, you'll see that mySecondSubscriber was called before myFirstSubscriber, even though it was added after myFirstSubscriber. For most projects, this won't matter too much—at most, the difference between those calls is a couple of milliseconds. If, however, subscriber class instances themselves communicate with each other, the order in which they are notified by the Observer class can be important to ensure they are in sync. Lucky for us, this fix is easily done: the for-in loop iterates in the reverse order as items were added, so adding a simple this.observers.reverse() call before starting this loop should fix things.

```
public function notifyChanges():Void {
  this.subscribers.reverse();
  for(var i in this.subscribers) this.subscribers[i].update();
}
```

If you save the changes to Observer.as, you can go ahead and have the code in Frame 1 of the ActionScript layer read as follows:

12

```
var myObserver:Observer = new Observer();
var myFirstSubscriber:Object = new Object();
var mySecondSubscriber:Object = new Object();

myFirstSubscriber.update = function() {
  trace("myFirstSubscriber notified by Observer class");
}
mySecondSubscriber.update = function() {
  trace("mySecondSubscriber notified by Observer class");
}
```

```
myObserver.addSubscriber(myFirstSubscriber);
myObserver.addSubscriber(mySecondSubscriber);

myObserver.notifyChanges();
```

If you run Test Movie (Control ➤ Test Movie) now, you get the lines shown in Figure 12-4 in the Output panel.

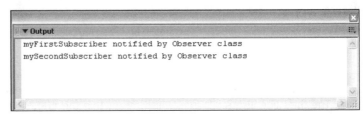

Figure 12-4. Output panel showing notification in the correct order

As you can see, the subscribers are now called in the same order as they were added. The first line shows the myFirstSubscriber and the second line shows the mySecondSubscriber update function being called. If you compare this to Figure 12-1, you will see that this sequencing has now corrected the problem.

So far, so good. With all these tweaks in place, the Observer class now looks as follows:

```
class Observer {

  private var subscribers:Array;

  function Observer() {
    subscribers = new Array();
  }

  public function addSubscriber(classInstance:Object):Boolean {
    for(var i=0; i<this.subscribers.length; i++) {
      if(this.subscribers[i] == classInstance) {
        return false;
      }
    }
    this.subscribers.push(classInstance);
    return true;
  }

  public function removeSubscriber(classInstance:Object):Boolean {
    for(var i=0; i<this.subscribers.length; i++) {
      if(this.subscribers[i] == classInstance) {
        this.subscribers.splice(i,1);
        return true;
      }
    }
  }
```

```
      return false;
    }

    public function notifyChanges():Void {
      this.subscribers.reverse();
      for(var i in this.subscribers) this.subscribers[i].update();
    }

  }
```

Practical implementation

As mentioned earlier, the Observer class isn't very practical as it is used now. For one thing, it needs to have the addSubscriber, removeSubscriber, and notifyChanges functions in place with every class that we want to apply the Observer design pattern to.

By extending the Observer class, we can avoid having to manually add the functions and have a reusable class for our ActionScript 2.0 projects. Next, we'll create an Attendees class that shows how this is done in a typical project.

Attendees.as

```
class Attendees extends Observer {

  private var attendeesList:Array;

  function Attendees() {
    attendeesList = new Array();
  }

  public function addAttendee(name:String):Boolean {
    for(var i=0; i<this.attendeesList.length; i++) {
      if(this.attendeesList[i] == name) {
        return false;
      }
    }
    this.attendeesList.push(name);
    super.notifyChanges();
    return true;
  }

  public function removeAttendee(name:String):Boolean {
    for(var i=0; i<this.attendeesList.length; i++) {
      if(this.attendeesList[i] == name) {
        this.attendeesList.splice(i,1);
        super.notifyChanges();
        return true;
      }
    }
  }
```

12

```
      return false;
   }

   public function getAttendees():Array {
      return attendeesList;
   }

}
```

The Attendees class keeps track of attendees in an Array class property named attendeesList and provides methods to add, remove, and retrieve all attendees. The addAttendee and removeAttendee methods work in much the same way as the Observer class, and because the Attendees class extends this Observer class, it can call the notifyChanges method to send out notifications to subscribing class instances.

Let's see this in action. Save the class in the preceding listing as Attendees.as in the same folder as the Observer class (or get a copy from the downloadable source files on the friends of ED website at www.friendsofed.com) and create a blank FLA called Attendees.fla. With that new blank FLA open, perform the following steps:

1. Rename Layer 1 to ActionScript.

2. Select Frame 1 of the ActionScript layer.

3. Open the Actions panel and add the following code:

```
var myAttendees:Attendees = new Attendees();
var attendeeMonitor:Object = new Object();

attendeeMonitor.update = function() {
   trace("myAttendees sent notification!");
}

myAttendees.addSubscriber(attendeeMonitor);

myAttendees.addAttendee("John Doe");
myAttendees.removeAttendee("John Doe");
```

If you run Test Movie with this code in place, you'll get the lines in the Output panel shown in Figure 12-5.

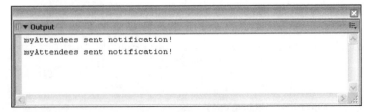

Figure 12-5. Output panel showing the Attendee example using the Observer pattern

Great, we've just managed to get our custom Attendees class to use the Observer class to implement the Observer design pattern! There's just one problem, though: whenever the update function of attendeeMonitor is called, we don't know whether it was caused by the addition or removal of an attendee. More complex implementations of the Observer design pattern have ways of dealing with this, but in this situation we'll use the getAttendees method to get the latest version of the attendeeList array any time it is triggered.

Extending the practical implementation

To do so, we'll make things a bit more interactive and add some controls that allow us to add and remove attendees and show this in a ListBox component. Perform the following steps:

1. Insert a new layer in the Timeline panel (select Insert ➤ Timeline ➤ Layer).
2. Rename Layer 2 to Interface.
3. Open the Components panel (select Window ➤ Development Panels ➤ Components).
4. Drag two instances of the Button component on the stage in the Interface layer.
5. Drag an instance of the List component on the stage in the Interface layer.
6. Drag an instance of the TextInput component on the stage in the Interface layer.
7. Position the components on the stage (see Figure 12-6).

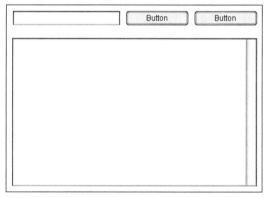

Figure 12-6. Component layout on the stage

12

8. Open the Properties panel (select Window ➤ Properties).
9. Select the List component and give it the instance name attendees_list.
10. Select the TextInput component and give it the instance name attendee_txt.
11. Select the first Button component and give it the instance name add_btn.
12. Select the second Button component and give it the instance name remove_btn.
13. With the first Button selected, set the Label property in the Properties panel to Add.

14. With the second Button selected, set the Label property in the Properties panel to Remove. (See Figure 12-7.)

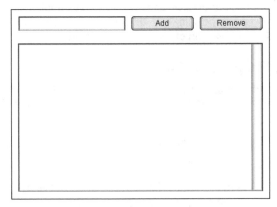

Figure 12-7. Properties panel for the Button component

15. Change the code in Frame 1 of the ActionScript layer to read as follows:

```
var myAttendees:Attendees = new Attendees();
var attendeeMonitor:Object = new Object();

attendeeMonitor.update = function() {
  attendees_list.dataProvider = myAttendees.getAttendees();
}

addPerson = function() {
  myAttendees.addAttendee(attendee_txt.text);
}
removePerson = function() {
  myAttendees.removeAttendee(attendee_txt.text);
}

add_btn.addEventListener("click",addPerson);
remove_btn.addEventListener("click",removePerson);

myAttendees.addSubscriber(attendeeMonitor);
```

The code we now have in place on the first frame of the ActionScript layer does a number of things. First, it creates an instance of the Attendees class (remember, this class extends the Observer class) and creates an Object instance named attendeeMonitor.

This attendeeMonitor object has an update function called by the Attendees class any time an attendee is added or removed from the array. This function sets the dataProvider for attendee_list (the List component on stage) to the array returned by the getAttendees method of the Attendees class. By doing this, we can always be sure that our list on the stage is up to date with the array in the myAttendees instance of the Attendees class.

The next two functions, addPerson and removePerson, call the addAttendee and removeAttendee methods of the myAttendees instance. Those functions are triggered when the Add or Remove button is clicked. To achieve this, we actually use an implementation of the Observer pattern that comes with Flash 8 (more about this in Chapter 15).

When you run Test Movie (Control ➤ Test Movie) with all this in place, you get to interact a little with the Attendees class. To demonstrate, type a name into the TextInput component and click the Add button. You'll see that the List component on the stage gets updated. If you click the Remove button with a name in the TextInput component, that name is removed from the List if it was listed there.

We've sure come a long way! Let's see what actually happens when adding an attendee:

1. When the Add button is clicked, the addPerson function gets called.

2. The addPerson function calls the addAttendee method in the myAttendees instance of the Attendees class and passes it the value of the TextInput component.

3. The addAttendee method in the Attendees class adds the attendee to the attendeesList array, if it is not a duplicate, and calls the notifyChanges method of its superclass, Observer.

4. The attendeeMonitor object has subscribed to notifications of myAttendees and so its update function gets called when notifyChanges is triggered.

5. The update function in the attendeeMonitor object updates the dataProvider of the List component with the latest version of the attendeesList array from the Attendees class by calling the getAttendees method.

Whew—that's quite a few steps for simply updating a List component on the stage! Of course, the same goes for removing an attendee from the Attendees class. Now, you might be wondering if it's worth the trouble to code all that to simply generate a list of attendees. If you are thinking that, you do have a point.

There's no use in applying the Observer pattern when there's just one instance subscribing to the notifications. Imagine the possibilities with the Attendees class, though—without much hassle, you can have a counter that automatically updates the number of attendees every time it receives a notification. You might even have a visual representation of a meeting hall and show the number of seats that are left. That's when things become interesting with the Observer pattern.

As an exercise to try on your own, you might want to add a Label component that automatically shows the number of attendees by subscribing to the Attendees class. You'll find the solution for this exercise in this book's downloadable source files, which you can obtain from the friends of ED website (www.friendsofed.com).

Singleton pattern

The Singleton pattern is used for projects where you want to create classes that can only ever have one instance. "How is that useful?" you may be asking. Well, there are situations in your ActionScript 2.0 projects where you want to have one and only one instance of a class available.

12

Typically, this pattern will be used for manager-type classes that hold data for your entire project. These classes provide you with a centralized, single point of access that you can reach from anywhere in your project. In that sense, classes that implement the Singleton pattern are often simply used as repositories for holding data or references to other class instances.

Basic implementation

So, how exactly do you create a class with the Singleton pattern implemented? First of all, you need to find a way to limit the number of instances a class can create to one. The obvious approach would be to have a property that keeps track of the number of instances a class has. Doing that, you'll soon come across a practical problem: how can you keep count of the number of instances a class has, when class properties are defined on the class instance and not shared throughout the class? Attentive readers will probably have picked up on a possible solution I briefly mentioned in Chapter 8.

Defining a class property as static makes sure it is shared throughout all instances (in this case, just one instance). Knowing that, we can define a static class property of a Number type and in the class constructor (remember, the constructor always gets called immediately when a class is instantiated) increment it. Let's see how that would work.

Singleton.as

```
class Singleton {

  static var instanceCount:Number = 0;

  function Singleton() {
    instanceCount++;
    if(instanceCount == 1) {
      trace("First Singleton class instance");
    } else {
      trace("Singleton class allows only one instance");
    }
  }

}
```

Save the preceding file as Singleton.as and create a blank FLA named Singleton.fla in the same folder. Double-click Singleton.fla to open up Flash and perform the following steps:

1. Rename Layer 1 in the Timeline to ActionScript.

2. Select Frame 1 of the ActionScript layer.

3. Open the Actions panel (select Window ➤ Development Panels ➤ Actions).

4. Add the following ActionScript to the Actions panel:

```
var myFirstSingleton:Singleton = new Singleton();
var mySecondSingleton:Singleton = new Singleton();
```

With this code in place, save the FLA and run Test Movie (Control ➤ Test Movie). You should see the result shown in Figure 12-8 in the Output panel.

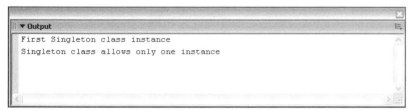

Figure 12-8. Output panel showing the Singleton pattern example

As you can see, the first line of the Output panel reads First Singleton class instance and the second line reads Singleton class allows only one instance. Great, that looks as though you've managed to keep track of the number of classes the Singleton class has. There are a couple of problems with this approach, though.

If you want to add functionality to this Singleton class, you'll need to have a conditional statement that checks the instanceCount property in each and every method. That's not exactly user-friendly, as shown in this example:

Singleton.as

```
class Singleton {

  static var instanceCount:Number = 0;

  function Singleton() {
    instanceCount++;
    if(instanceCount == 1) {
      trace("First Singleton class instance");
    } else {
      trace("Singleton class allows only one instance");
    }
  }

  public function doSomething(){
    if(instanceCount == 1) {
      // do something;
    } else {
      // do nothing
    }
  }

}
```

12

Notice that we have exactly the same conditional as in the class constructor in the doSomething method. That's not exactly a great way to handle the Singleton pattern, and really what the design pattern says is to prevent creating more than one instance. With this implementation, we can create as many instances of the class as we want; it's just the methods that prevent the code from executing by checking that the number of instances hasn't exceeded one.

Let's try something else. If we were to assign a private scope to the constructor method, that would essentially disable us from creating class instances.

Singleton.as

```
class Singleton {

  private function Singleton() {
  }

}
```

Save the preceding class as `Singleton.as`, and in the `Singleton.fla` file open up the Actions panel for Frame 1 of the ActionScript layer and change the code to read as follows:

```
var mySingleton:Singleton = new Singleton();
```

If you run Test Movie (Control ➤ Test Movie) on this code, you'll get what you might expect: an error message in the Output panel (see Figure 12-9).

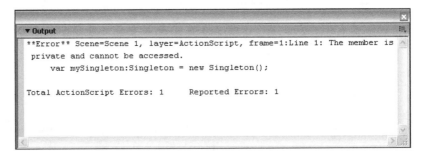

Figure 12-9. Output panel showing the Singleton error message

So how exactly does that code help us with the Singleton pattern? The first attempt allowed multiple instances to be created, and now we can't have any. Not to worry, with a little tweak to that code, we can have a public method in the class control the instantiation of the class.

Singleton.as

```
class Singleton {

  private function Singleton() {
  }

  public static function getInstance():Singleton {
    return new Singleton();
  }

  public function doSomething():Void {
    trace("doing something");
  }

}
```

The preceding code uses a public method named getInstance to return a new instance of the Singleton class. Because it is called from within the class itself, the instantiation isn't blocked by the private scope attribute of the class. Now, you might be wondering how we'll be able to trigger that getInstance method, as we can't create any new instance of the class to call it on. That's where the static keyword comes in again. Any methods that are defined as static can be called by simply using the class name, in this case Singleton. getInstance().

Let's see if this code does what we want it to. Open up Singleton.fla again and change the code in Frame 1 of the ActionScript layer to read as follows:

```
var mySingleton:Singleton = Singleton.getInstance();
mySingleton.doSomething();
```

If you run Test Movie (Control ➤ Test Movie) using the preceding code, you'll see the results Output panel shown in Figure 12-10.

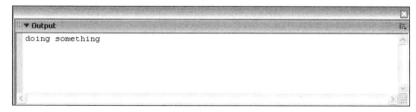

Figure 12-10. Output panel showing the Singleton class in action

We've been able to get an instance of the Singleton class created, and we've called the doSomething method on that instance, which traced out doing something. The only thing that's left to do is add a conditional statement that restricts the number of instances the getInstance method returns to one. This time we'll use a slightly different approach. Rather than keeping track of the number of instances that were created, we'll just store a reference to the Singleton class in the property.

Singleton.as

```
class Singleton {

  private static var instance:Singleton = undefined;

  private function Singleton() {
  }

  public static function getInstance():Singleton {
    if(instance == undefined) {
      trace("Singleton instance created");
      instance = new Singleton();
    } else {
      trace("Singleton instance already exists");
    }
    return instance;
  }

  public function doSomething():Void {
    trace("do something");
  }

}
```

What the preceding code does differently relates to the class property. We've given it a private scope and static property, so it can't be manipulated from outside the class, and given it a value of undefined. In the getInstance method, we then go on to check if this class property is undefined and, if so, we create a new Singleton instance. If the instance class property is not undefined, an instance of Singleton was already created and the existing instance simply gets returned. I added two trace statements to help you see what's going on. Let's try this out in the Singleton.fla Flash file.

Change the ActionScript code on Frame 1 of the ActionScript layer to read as follows:

```
var myFirstSingleton:Singleton = Singleton.getInstance();
var mySecondSingleton:Singleton = Singleton.getInstance();
```

If you run Test Movie (Control ➤ Test Movie) with this code in place, you'll get the result in the Output panel shown in Figure 12-11.

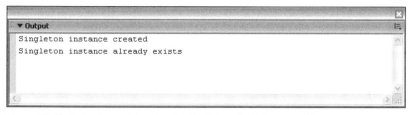

Figure 12-11. Output panel showing the Singleton class's inner workings

The first line of the Output panel reads Singleton instance created, while the second line says Singleton instance already exists. This effectively means that your code to limit the number of instances created using the getInstance method is working properly. If no instance existed, it creates one for you, and if one was already present, it returns a reference to that Singleton instances. Doing that allows you to only ever have one class instance instantiated, and have that instance accessible from anywhere in your application.

Practical implementation

That wasn't too difficult, was it? Now that we've found a good implementation of the Singleton pattern, let's apply it to an ActionScript 2.0 project. Building on the Attendees class we had for the Observer pattern, we'll now work on a MeetingRoomManager class using the Singleton pattern. This class will hold references to MeetingRoom class instances that in turn keep track of the attendees.

The first thing we'll do is use the Singleton class implementation just created as a template for the MeetingRoomManager class.

MeetingRoomManager.as

```
class MeetingRoomManager {

  private static var instance:MeetingRoomManager = undefined;

  private function MeetingRoomManager() {
  }

  public static function getInstance():MeetingRoomManager {
    if(instance == undefined) {
      trace("MeetingRoomManager instance created");
      instance = new MeetingRoomManager();
    } else {
      trace("MeetingRoomMananger instance already exists");
    }
    return instance;
  }

}
```

Next, we'll add some methods for us to be able to add, remove, and retrieve meeting rooms from the MeetingRoomManager class. The methods we'll be using are addMeetingRoom, removeMeetingRoom, and getMeetingRoom. To keep track of the meeting rooms in the MeetingRoomManager class, we have the meetingRooms class property that has a datatype of Array.

MeetingRoomManager.as

```
class MeetingRoomManager {

  public static var meetingRooms:Array = new Array();
  private static var instance:MeetingRoomManager = undefined;

  private function MeetingRoomManager() {
  }

  public static function getInstance():MeetingRoomManager {
    if(instance == undefined) {
      trace("MeetingRoomManager instance created");
      instance = new MeetingRoomManager();
    } else {
      trace("MeetingRoomMananger instance already
exists");
    }
    return instance;
  }

  public function addMeetingRoom(meetingRoomName:String):Void {
    meetingRooms.push({name:meetingRoomName,
    ➥ instance:new MeetingRoom()});
  }

  public function removeMeetingRoom(meetingRoomName:String):Void {
    for(var i=0; i<meetingRooms.length; i++) {
      if(meetingRooms[i].name == meetingRoomName) {
        meetingRooms.splice(i,1);
      }
    }
  }

  public function getMeetingRoom(meetingRoomName:String):MeetingRoom {
    for(var i=0; i<meetingRooms.length; i++) {
      if(meetingRooms[i].name == meetingRoomName) {
        return meetingRooms[i].instance;
      }
    }
  }

}
```

That's an interesting piece of code. As you'll notice in the addMeetingRoom method, we accept a parameter that specifies the name of our meeting room. That name, as well as a new anonymous instance of the MeetingRoom class, form the name and instance properties of an object (note the curly brackets shorthand notation) that gets pushed to the meetingRooms array.

The removeMeetingRoom method also takes this meetingRoomName parameter and uses that to loop through the meetingRooms array, looking for an entry where the name attribute is equal to the parameter. If that is the case, it removes that meeting room from the array. That same approach goes for the getMeetingRoom method, but you'll notice that method has a return type of MeetingRoom. It loops through the meetingRooms array looking for a meeting room where the name is equal to the meetingRoomName parameter and, if found, returns the MeetingRoom instance that was created for that entry in the array.

Before you can do any testing on this, you'll have to create a MeetingRoom class. This class will simply extend the Attendees class (which in turn extends the Observer class), so you have access to the addAttendee and removeAttendee functions and can have instances subscribe when the attendees list is updated for that particular MeetingRoom instance.

MeetingRoom.as

```
class MeetingRoom extends Attendees {

  function MeetingRoom() {
  }

}
```

That's really all that you have to do! Make sure the files MeetingRoomManager.as, MeetingRoom.as, Attendees.as, and Observer.as are in the same folder as Singleton.fla, and let's look at the class in action. When you have the file Singleton.fla open, change the code in Frame 1 of the ActionScript layer to read as follows:

```
// Get an instance of MeetingRoomManager
var myMeetingRoomManager:MeetingRoomManager =
➥ MeetingRoomManager.getInstance();

// Add meeting rooms to MeetingRoomManager
myMeetingRoomManager.addMeetingRoom("boardroom");
myMeetingRoomManager.addMeetingRoom("ballroom");

// Set up listeners for the meeting rooms
boardroomListener = new Object();
boardroomListener.update = function() {
  trace("boardroom attendees: "+
➥ myMeetingRoomManager.getMeetingRoom("boardroom")
➥ .getAttendees());
}
```

12

```
ballroomListener = new Object();
ballroomListener.update = function() {
  trace("ballroom attendees: "+
➥ myMeetingRoomManager.getMeetingRoom("ballroom")
➥ .getAttendees());
}

// Subscribe to updates from MeetingRoom instances
myMeetingRoomManager.getMeetingRoom("boardroom")
.addSubscriber(boardroomListener);
myMeetingRoomManager.getMeetingRoom("ballroom")
.addSubscriber(ballroomListener);

// Add attendees to MeetingRoom instances
myMeetingRoomManager.getMeetingRoom("boardroom")
.addAttendee("John Doe");
myMeetingRoomManager.getMeetingRoom("ballroom")
.addAttendee("Jane Doe");
```

The preceding code looks pretty complex, but you'll soon see that it's not. The first line of code stores the instance of the MeetingRoomManager class in a variable called myMeetingRoomManager. Remember, the MeetingRoomManager class has the Singleton pattern implemented, so it can have only one instance. Next, we add two meeting rooms (boardroom and ballroom) to the MeetingRoomManager class using the addMeetingRoom method.

Following that, we define two object instances that will act as listeners for the meeting rooms we created. For this to work with our implementation of the Observer pattern, the instances need to have an update function defined, which is called when attendees are added or removed. With those two objects in place, we can now subscribe them to the MeetingRoom instances. This is done through the addSubscriber method.

Finally, we add an attendee for both of the MeetingRoom instances. When you save Singleton.fla with these changes in place, or if you grabbed a copy of the source files available from the friends of ED website, you can run Test Movie (Control ➤ Test Movie) and watch the results in the Output panel (see Figure 12-12).

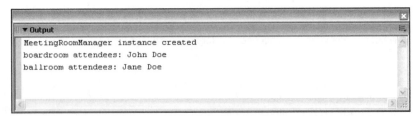

Figure 12-12. Output panel showing the MeetingRoomManager Singleton example

The first line in the Output panel reads MeetingRoomManager instance created, which indicates that there was no earlier instance of the MeetingRoomManager class. The next line, boardroom attendees: John Doe, is the result of notification sent to the boardroomListener update function. The final line in the Output panel, ballroom attendees: Jane Doe, comes from the ballroomListener.

Now, be honest—isn't that some incredibly cool code? One last thing we'll do is build ourselves an interface around this class to add some user interaction.

Building an interface

Get a copy of the file Attendees.fla that was created earlier and rename it to MeetingRoomManager.fla in the folder where all your classes are stored. With MeetingRoomManager.fla open in Flash, perform the following steps:

1. Open the Components panel (select Window ➤ Development Panels ➤ Components).

2. Drag an instance of the ComboBox component to the Interface layer.

3. Give the ComboBox component the instance name meetingrooms_cb (see Figure 12-13).

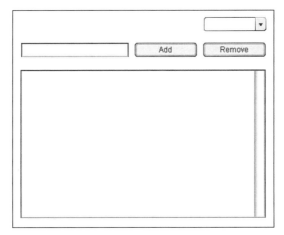

Figure 12-13. Properties panel showing the ComboBox component

4. Change the code in Frame 1 of the ActionScript layer to read as follows:

```
var myMeetingRoomManager:MeetingRoomManager =
 MeetingRoomManager.getInstance();

myMeetingRoomManager.addMeetingRoom("boardroom");
myMeetingRoomManager.addMeetingRoom("ballroom");

meetingrooms_cb.dataProvider =
myMeetingRoomManager.getMeetingRoomList();

attendeeMonitor = new Object();
attendeeMonitor.update = function() {
  attendees_list.dataProvider =
 myMeetingRoomManager.
```

12

181

```
    getMeetingRoom(meetingrooms_cb.text).
    getAttendees();
  }

  addPerson = function() {
    myMeetingRoomManager.
  getMeetingRoom(meetingrooms_cb.text).
  addAttendee(attendee_txt.text);
  }
  removePerson = function() {
    myMeetingRoomManager.
  getMeetingRoom(meetingrooms_cb.text).
  removeAttendee(attendee_txt.text);
  }

  changeRoom = function() {
    attendeeMonitor.update();
  }

  myMeetingRoomManager.getMeetingRoom("boardroom")
  .addSubscriber(attendeeMonitor);
  myMeetingRoomManager.getMeetingRoom("ballroom")
  .addSubscriber(attendeeMonitor);

  add_btn.addEventListener("click",addPerson);
  remove_btn.addEventListener("click",removePerson);
  meetingrooms_cb.addEventListener("change",changeRoom);
```

5. Add the following method to the MeetingRoomManager class in MeetingRoom➡
Manager.as:

```
  public function getMeetingRoomList() {
    var tmp:Array = new Array();
    for(var i=0; i<meetingRooms.length; i++) {
      tmp.push(meetingRooms[i].name);
    }
    return tmp;
  }
```

Once you've completed these steps, save your files and run Test Movie (Control ➤ Test Movie). As with the Observer pattern, you'll now have an interface where you can add and remove attendees. You've just added support for multiple meeting rooms.

The ComboBox component gets filled with the available meeting rooms by assigning the array it gets from the new getMeetingRoomList method you added to its dataProvider. By using the built-in addEventListener method, you can update the List component with attendees as soon as the meeting room in the ComboBox component is changed. The addPerson and removePerson functions that get called when the corresponding Button components are clicked have now been changed to store the attendees in the correct meeting room in the MeetingRoomManager class.

Feel free to play around with this example, just as with the Observer example. You may want to try and add another listener that displays the number of attendees for the selected meeting room. You'll find the solution to this exercise in the downloadable source files that you can obtain from the friends of ED website (www.friendsofed.com).

Decorator pattern

The Decorator pattern is one of my favorite design patterns because it's very flexible and a quick-and-easy alternative to subclassing your code. This pattern adds functionality to an existing class by accepting a class instance as an argument in its constructor.

It's not very difficult to get this pattern to work, so let's start with the basic class structure.

Basic implementation

The following code creates a Decorator that accepts an object instance as an argument and stores that in a private variable named decorateInstance.

Decorator.as

```
class Decorator {

  private var decorateInstance:Object;

  function Decorator(decorateObj:Object) {
    this.decorateInstance = decorateObj;
  }

}
```

If you were to extend the Attendees class, the code on the timeline in Flash would look something like this:

```
var myAttendees:Attendees = new Attendees();
var myDecorator:Decorator = new Decorator(myAttendees);
```

Or if you don't need to have a reference to the Attendees instance and just want to work with the Decorator class, an anonymous instance would also work:

```
var myDecorator:Decorator = new Decorator(new Attendees);
```

The way the Decorator pattern works is it defines all additional methods it wants to add to the existing functionality of the decorateInstance object and overrides any methods it wants changed. All other method calls to the Decorator class should just be relayed to the decorateInstance object. Let's take the Attendees class as an example again and see how that would look.

12

Decorator.as

```
class Decorator {

  private var decorateInstance:Object;

  function Decorator(decorateObj:Object) {
    this.decorateInstance = decorateObj;
  }

  public function addAttendee(name:String) {
    this.decorateInstance.addAttendee(name);
  }

  public function removeAttendee(name:String) {
    this.decorateInstance.removeAttendee(name)
  }

  public function getAttendees() {
    this.decorateInstance.getAttendeeList();
  }

  public function clearAttendees() {
    this.decorateInstance.attendeesList = new Array();
  }

}
```

As you can see from the preceding code, the Decorator class implements all methods that the decorateInstance object has and relays the methods through to that class instance. In this example, we also added a clearAttendees method that resets that attendees array. By doing this, we can now use the Decorator class and have all functionality of the Attendees class, as well as being able to use the clearAttendees method. The code on the Timeline in Flash to work with this class would look something like this:

```
var myDecorator = new Decorator(new Attendees());
myDecorator.addAttendee("John Doe");
myDecorator.clearAttendees();
```

Practical implementation

"Hang on a minute," you may be thinking. "You said this pattern was quick and easy, and how can you possibly call this flexible?" You're absolutely right—even though the preceding code works well, it's not the most convenient way to implement the Decorator pattern. Luckily, ActionScript comes to the rescue and provides us with an invaluable feature: the __resolve method.

If you define a function named __resolve in your class (note the double underscore character), any methods that were not found in the class will be captured by that method. This __resolve method also has a parameter of datatype `String` that gives you the name of the method that wasn't found. Now that is interesting!

Decorator.as

```
class Decorator {

  private var decorateInstance:Object;

  function Decorator(decorateObj:Object) {
    decorateInstance = decorateObj;
  }

  public function __resolve(methodName:String) {
    if(decorateInstance[methodName]) {
      decorateInstance[methodName]();
    } else {
      trace(methodName+" method does not exist!");
    }
  }

}
```

This is more like it! Create a blank FLA and save it in the same folder as `Decorator.as` and `Attendees.as`. With this file open in Flash, rename Layer 1 in the Timeline to ActionScript and add the following code to Frame 1:

```
var myDecorator:Decorator = new Decorator(new Attendees());
myDecorator.paintPinkElephant();
```

Seeing that neither the Decorator or the Attendees class has a `paintPinkElephant` method implemented, the __resolve method should catch this and trace out the message paintPinkElephant method does not exist!. Let's give this a try by running Test Movie (Control ➤ Test Movie).

Oh dear, running that code seems to bring up an error in the Output panel (see Figure 12-14).

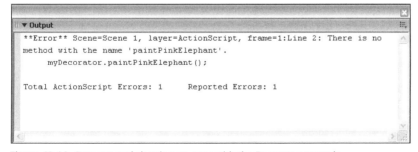

Figure 12-14. Output panel showing an error with the Decorator example

185

As you can see, the error in the Output panel says there is no method with the name 'paintPinkElephant'., but of course we already knew that. What is really causing the problem is the fact we typed the Decorator class instance as a Decorator. The compiler checks that all methods we call on that instance are actually implemented. When we have that __resolve method in place, checking that the methods we call are implemented is the last thing we want to do. So, simply removing the Decorator type from the myDecorator class instance helps us sort out this problem:

```
var myDecorator = new Decorator(new Attendees());
```

Run Test Movie (Control ➤ Test Movie) again (see Figure 12-15).

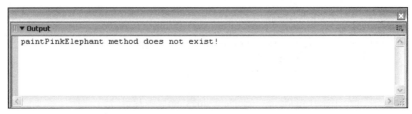

Figure 12-15. Output panel showing the Decorator example in action

That did the trick! We now have a line in the Output panel saying paintPinkElephant method does not exist!. If we were to add a paintPinkElephant method to either the Decorator or Attendees class, that message should disappear and the function in question should be called.

> It's important to note that if both the Decorator class and the decorateInstance object implement the same method, only the method in the Decorator class will get called.

Applying the Decorator pattern

Next, let's check that the Decorator class can act as a replacement for the Attendees class. We should be able to call any and all methods the class has implemented, and even take advantage of the Observer class it extends.

```
var myDecorator = new Decorator(new Attendees());

listenObj = new Object();
listenObj.update = function() {
  trace(myDecorator.getAttendees());
}

myDecorator.addSubscriber(listenObj);
myDecorator.addAttendee("John Doe");
myDecorator.addAttendee("Jane Doe");
```

If you run Test Movie (Control ➤ Test Movie) with this code in place, you'd expect this to work as the Attendees class and have the listenObj trace out the list of Attendees. Unfortunately, nothing happens when you run this code. The reason for that is that the Decorator class does not pass any arguments to the methods it forwards using the __resolve method.

To fix that problem, we'll use another great piece of ActionScript code. The apply method can be used to call another method, and it accepts two arguments. The first argument defines the object to which it is applied; the second argument accepts an array with arguments that you want passed to the method it calls.

Decorator.as

```
class Decorator {

  private var decorateInstance:Object;

  function Decorator(decorateObj:Object) {
    decorateInstance = decorateObj;
  }

  public function __resolve(methodName:String) {
    if(decorateInstance[methodName]) {
      return function() {
        return decorateInstance[methodName].
apply(decorateInstance,arguments);
      }
    } else {
      trace(methodName+" method does not exist!");
    }
  }

}
```

As you can see, the only tweaks done to the preceding code relate to the __resolve method. Remember, if a particular method isn't found in the Decorator class, it calls the __resolve method with that method name as an argument. What we do in the __resolve method is check if this method exists in the decorateInstance object and, if not, we trace an error message.

If the method exists in the decorateInstance object, we return a function that calls the method on the decorateInstance object using the apply method just discussed. The first argument of this apply method is decorateInstance, which essentially means we want to run the method on the decorateInstance object. The second argument refers to the arguments object. Each and every method or function in ActionScript has an arguments object defined in its local scope.

12

187

That arguments object is an array with all the arguments that were passed to the function. For example, arguments[0] would be the first argument passed to a function. The arguments object also has a number of properties: caller (a reference to the function that called the current function), callee (a reference to the current function), and length (the number of arguments passed to the function).

By using this arguments object as the second argument in the apply method, we pass on all arguments that were applied to the method called through __resolve back to the decorateInstance object.

Save the file Decorator.as and with the following code in Frame 1 of the ActionScript layer, try to run Test Movie (Control ➤ Test Movie) again (see Figure 12-16 for the results):

```
var myDecorator = new Decorator(new Attendees());

listenObj = new Object();
listenObj.update = function() {
  trace(myDecorator.getAttendees());
}

myDecorator.addSubscriber(listenObj);
myDecorator.addAttendee("John Doe");
myDecorator.addAttendee("Jane Doe");
```

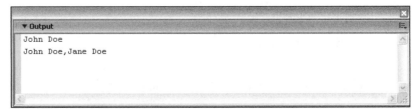

Figure 12-16. Output panel for the Decorator pattern example

That's now running like a train: the listenObj is now subscribed to the myDecorator instance, and its update function gets called any time we run addAttendee. With this Decorator implementation in place, we can now have a working copy of the Attendees class and add additional functionality.

So, why exactly is the Decorator pattern more flexible than subclassing? Well, the most important reason is you can extend functionality of a class at runtime by assigning a class instance as an argument for the Decorator class constructor. But be aware that there is a downside to using this technique: it doesn't work on class properties. To decorate class properties, you'll need to create methods that set and retrieve this property. I personally don't have a problem with this, as I quite like to use methods for getting and setting class properties rather than directly manipulating the properties themselves.

Let's apply the Decorator pattern to something useful in ActionScript 2.0. For example, say we want to add some functionality to the Array class.

Array2.as

```
class Array2 {

  private var decorateInstance:Object;

  function Array2(decorateObj:Object) {
    decorateInstance = decorateObj;
  }

  public function __resolve(methodName:String) {
    if(decorateInstance[methodName]) {
      return function() {
        return decorateInstance[methodName].apply
        ➥ (decorateInstance,arguments);
      }
    } else {
      trace(methodName+" method does not exist!");
    }
  }

  public function checkDuplicate(name:String):Boolean {
    var count:Number = 0;
    for(var i=0; i<decorateInstance.length; i++) {
      if(decorateInstance[i] == name) {
        count++;
      }
    }
    if(count > 1) {
      return true;
    } else {
      return false;
    }
  }

  public function removeDuplicate(name:String):Void {
    var count:Number = 0;
    for(var i=0; i<decorateInstance.length; i++) {
      trace(decorateInstance[i]);
        if(decorateInstance[i] == name) {
          count++;
          if(count > 1) {
          decorateInstance.splice(i,1);
        }
      }
    }
  }
}
```

12

As you can see in the preceding code, the same Decorator template created earlier is used, and the class name and constructor method are simply changed to Array2. Next, we add two new methods, checkDuplicate and removeDuplicate, that loop through the Array instance to which a reference is stored in the decorateInstance class property.

Both methods take an argument that defines what entry they look for in the Array and have a local count variable that keeps track of the number of times it encounters that entry. The checkDuplicate method returns a Boolean value indicating whether or not an entry has duplicates in the Array. The removeDuplicate method removes any duplicate entries that occur in the Array after the first occurrence.

Create a new blank FLA in the same folder where you saved Array2.as and name it Array2.fla. With Array2.fla open in Flash, perform the following steps:

1. Rename Layer 1 in the Timeline to ActionScript.
2. Select Frame 1 of the ActionScript layer.
3. Open the Actions panel (select Window ➤ Development Panels ➤ Actions).
4. Add the following ActionScript to the Actions panel:

```
var myArrayDecorator = new Array2(new Array());

myArrayDecorator.push("Jane Doe");
myArrayDecorator.push("John Doe");
myArrayDecorator.push("Jane Doe");

trace("John Doe: "+myArrayDecorator.checkDuplicate("John Doe"));
trace("Jane Doe: "+myArrayDecorator.checkDuplicate("Jane Doe"));

trace("Remove Jane Doe duplicates");
myArrayDecorator.removeDuplicate("Jane Doe");

trace("John Doe: "+myArrayDecorator.checkDuplicate("John Doe"));
trace("Jane Doe: "+myArrayDecorator.checkDuplicate("Jane Doe"));
```

If you save Array2.fla and run Test Movie (Control ➤ Test Movie), you'll get the result shown in Figure 12-17.

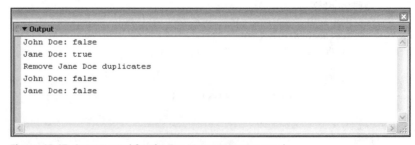

Figure 12-17. Output panel for the Decorator pattern example

The code we use adds three items to the Array: one "John Doe" entry and two "Jane Doe" entries. Using the checkDuplicate method, we check for duplicates of "John Doe" and "Jane Doe" in the Array, and the results of this are traced out in the first two lines of the Output panel. For John Doe, the result of this is false and for Jane Doe it's true.

Next, we use the removeDuplicate method to remove all duplicates of "Jane Doe" in the Array. We add a trace statement saying Remove Jane Doe duplicates.

Finally, we run the checkDuplicate method again for "John Doe" and "Jane Doe," and watch the result in the Output panel. This time, the checkDuplicate method returns false for both entries, which means there are no more duplicate entries.

That's it! You've just created a working implementation of the Decorator pattern and extended an Array object. Now, have some fun and try adding a couple more methods to the Array2 class. For example, you could have a method that uses the checkDuplicate and removeDuplicate methods to automatically remove all duplicates from the array. You can find the solution to this exercise in the downloadable source files for this chapter on the friends of ED site.

Model-View-Controller pattern

The MVC pattern is, technically speaking, not really a design pattern; rather, it's a collection of various patterns that form an architectural framework. That distinction is not all that important for us at the moment, as we're more interested in what the pattern does and how we can apply it to ActionScript 2.0 code.

Using the MVC pattern, we are able to separate the Model (the class that holds the data of the application), the View (the visual presentation of the application), and the Controller (the class that handles user interaction).

Of course, separating a project into these three entities does not help us all that much. What is important is the way the Model, View, and Controller interact.

The MVC pattern specifies the way the different classes can communicate with each other as follows:

- **Model**: Implements the Observer pattern and sends notifications to the View when there are changes to the data it holds.
- **View**: Holds a reference to the Model and the Controller, and is only allowed to connect to the Model to retrieve information when it receives notification from the Model. When user interaction occurs, the View calls the appropriate method on the Controller.
- **Controller**: Holds a reference to the Model and updates that Model through the methods that are called from the View.

12

Basic implementation

Knowing these specifications, we can create a class template for the Model, View, and Controller, as follows:

Model.as

```
class Model extends Observer {

  function Model() {
  }

  public function registerView(view:Object):Void {
    super.addSubscriber(view);
  }

}
```

The Model class extends our Observer class, so it can add, remove, and notify subscribers when changes occur in the data it holds. Our Model class template also holds a method called registerView, which subscribes that View instance to receive notifications.

View.as

```
class View {

  private var model:Object;
  private var controller:Object;

  function View(model:Object,controller:Object) {
    this.model = model;
    this.controller = controller;
    this.model.registerView(this);
  }

  function update() {
  }

}
```

The View class accepts two arguments in its constructor. Those arguments are an instance of the Model class and an instance of the Controller class. A reference to the Model and Controller instances are stored in private class properties called model and controller. Using the model class property, we register this instance of the View class with the Model instance so it subscribes to updates. We defined an empty update function that will be used to respond to notifications sent from the Model.

Controller.as

```
class Controller {

  private var model:Object;

  function Controller(model:Object) {
    this.model = model;
  }

}
```

The Controller class accepts one argument in its constructor: a reference to the Model instance it can modify. A reference to this Model class instance is stored in a private class property called model.

With those classes in place, we can use the following code on the Timeline in Flash:

```
var myModel:Model = new Model();
var myController:Controller = new Controller(myModel);
var myView:View = new View(myModel,myController);
```

The easiest way to see the MVC pattern in action is to apply it to the example we've been working with for the Observer and Singleton patterns.

Practical implementation

We'll be using the Attendees class as our Model, and we'll write new classes to manage the View (the components on the stage) and the Controller (the user interaction that updates the Model). Let's see what the Attendees class looks like and how we'll be applying our Model class template to it:

```
class Attendees extends Observer {

  public var attendeesList:Array;

  function Attendees() {
    attendeesList = new Array();
  }

  public function addAttendee(name:String):Boolean {
    for(var i=0; i<this.attendeesList.length; i++) {
      if(this.attendeesList[i] == name) {
        return false;
      }
    }
    this.attendeesList.push(name);
    super.notifyChanges();
    return true;
  }
```

12

193

```actionscript
public function removeAttendee(name:String):Boolean {
  for(var i=0; i<this.attendeesList.length; i++) {
    if(this.attendeesList[i] == name) {
      this.attendeesList.splice(i,1);
      super.notifyChanges();
      return true;
    }
  }
  return false;
}

public function getAttendees():Array {
  return attendeesList;
}

}
```

To make the code a little more readable, let's rename the class to AttendeeModel and make the necessary changes to make it fit in with our Model class template.

AttendeeModel.as

```actionscript
class AttendeeModel extends Observer {

public var attendeesList:Array;

function AttendeeModel() {
  attendeesList = new Array();
}

public function registerView(view:Object) {
  super.addSubscriber(view);
}

public function addAttendee(name:String):Boolean {
  for(var i=0; i<this.attendeesList.length; i++) {
    if(this.attendeesList[i] == name) {
      return false;
    }
  }
  this.attendeesList.push(name);
  super.notifyChanges();
  return true;
}

public function removeAttendee(name:String):Boolean {
  for(var i=0; i<this.attendeesList.length; i++) {
    if(this.attendeesList[i] == name) {
```

```
        this.attendeesList.splice(i,1);
        super.notifyChanges();
        return true;
      }
    }
    return false;
  }

  public function getAttendees():Array {
    return attendeesList;
  }

}
```

All code that appears in bold shows you changes or additions made to the class. The tweaks we made to this class now make it conform with the MVC Model class specifications.

For the View, we'll need to create a new class, as we didn't previously use a class to work with the components. Sticking to the same naming convention, we'll call this class AttendeeView.

AttendeeView.as

```
import mx.utils.Delegate;

class AttendeeView {

  private var model:Object;
  private var controller:Object;

  function AttendeeView(model:Object,controller:Object) {
    this.model = model;
    this.controller = controller;
    this.model.registerView(this);
    _root.add_btn.addEventListener("click",
    Delegate.create(this,addPerson));
    _root.remove_btn.addEventListener("click",
    Delegate.create(this,removePerson));

  }

  public function update() {
    _root.attendees_list.dataProvider =
    this.model.getAttendees();
  }

  public function addPerson():Void {
    this.controller.addPerson(_root.attendee_txt.text);
```

12

```
      _root.attendee_txt.text = "";
    }

    public function removePerson():Void {
      this.controller.removePerson(_root.attendee_txt.text);
      _root.attendee_txt.text = "";
    }

  }
```

The preceding class makes use of the Delegate class, which we'll discuss in the coming chapters. It allows us to call functions in a different scope than the one it is defined in. In the AttendeeView constructor we use addEventListener to listen for the click event of add_btn and remove_btn. The update function receives notifications from the Model when data has changed, and this then assigns that new data to the attendees_list data provider. The addPerson and removePerson methods forward the method to the Controller instance and clear the attendee_txt TextInput component.

AttendeeController.as

```
  class AttendeeController {

    private var model:Object;

    function AttendeeController(model:Object) {
      this.model = model;
    }

    public function addPerson(name:String):Void {
      this.model.addAttendee(name);
    }

    public function removePerson(name:String):Void {
      this.model.removeAttendee(name);
    }

  }
```

The AttendeeController class basically just holds a reference to the Model instance that was passed as an argument to its constructor and calls the necessary methods on the Model through the methods that get called by AttendeeViewer.

Bringing together the Model, View, and Controller

OK, so now we have the three necessary classes ready: AttendeeModel, AttendeeView, and AttendeeController. All that's left for us to do is prepare the Flash file. Place the files AttendeeModel.as, AttendeeView.as, AttendeeController.as, and Observer.as in the same folder, and get a copy of the file Attendees.fla you created when building the earlier example of the Observer pattern.

Rename `Attendees.fla` to `AttendeesMVC.fla`, open it up in Flash, and make the following changes to Frame 1 of the ActionScript layer:

```
var myAttendeeModel:AttendeeModel = new AttendeeModel();
var myAttendeeController:AttendeeController =
new AttendeeController(myAttendeeModel);
var myAttendeeView:AttendeeView =
new AttendeeView(myAttendeeModel,myAttendeeController);
```

Save `AttendeesMVC.fla` and run Test Movie (Control ➤ Test Movie) to see the MVC example in action (see Figure 12-18).

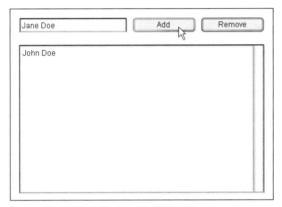

Figure 12-18. Attendee Model-View-Controller pattern example

We've now applied the MVC pattern to our Attendees example. One of the key benefits of this pattern is you can easily assign a different Model to a View, or swap the Controller class to deal with user interaction in a different way.

As an exercise, you might want to try to make the MeetingRoomManager class we created when discussing the Singleton pattern a Model for the AttendeeView can subscribe to. You'll also need to update the Controller class to have this work properly. You can find the solution to this exercise in the downloadable source files for this chapter on the friends of ED site.

12

Design patterns summary

This chapter introduced you to the concept of design patterns and how to apply them to ActionScript 2.0 projects. The Observer, Singleton, Decorator, and MVC patterns we discussed will certainly help you to write better code and make your projects more manageable.

The important thing to remember when applying any of these design patterns is that they need to become an integral part of your application, and stricter implementations of a pattern don't necessarily mean better implementations. Although design patterns are very useful in making your project more efficient, there is no amount of pattern implementation that can save a badly planned application.

Using design patterns in projects once again boils down to best practices and good planning. If you're looking to implement design patterns in your OOP projects with ActionScript 2.0, read up on best practices and project planning, and with that little extra time you invest I'm sure you'll be pleased with the results.

What's next?

This chapter concludes Part 3 of this book. We've now covered OOP concepts in depth. The next chapters will look at the built-in ActionScript 2.0 class framework, which will lead up to Chapter 15 when component development is discussed.

The following chapter will introduce you to the ActionScript 2.0 framework and its functionality. It's essential that you read this chapter to understand how the class structure works and to have the necessary background information to start doing component development.

13 CASE STUDY: AN OOP MEDIA PLAYER

In the previous chapters, we explored many important OOP concepts including encapsulation, classes, inheritance, polymorphism, interfaces, and design patterns. Conceptualization can only go so far, though, so it's important we solidify these ideas by implementing them in the Flash environment. Many of the previous examples of these concepts have been completely virtual, as is often the case when discussing programming ideas. Since Flash is such a visual tool, however, we'll work through this chapter on a more visual implementation of OOP techniques, namely the building of a class to handle displaying media that can be loaded into Flash, including SWFs, FLVs, and MP3s (all right, the last is hardly visual, but it fits in nicely with the others and, as they say, "two out of three..."). As we progress through this chapter, we'll touch on each of the topics discussed in the preceding section, beginning, of course, at the planning stage.

Planning the player

You've learned better than to jump right in and start coding (as tempting as that may seem at the outset!). The best way to begin a project with any scope is to spend a little time planning how to approach it.

Picking a pattern

The media player we'll build in this chapter will utilize a form of the Model-View-Controller framework discussed in Chapter 12, as illustrated in Figure 13-1. In this case, the model will be the media itself that is loaded into Flash. A controller class will be built to manipulate this media, by telling it to play, stop, seek a position, set volume, etc., when it's prompted to do so by the view. The view, for the purposes of this tutorial, will be the Flash timeline, which will display the media as it changes and call methods in the controller class to affect the media. As the media changes, the view is updated.

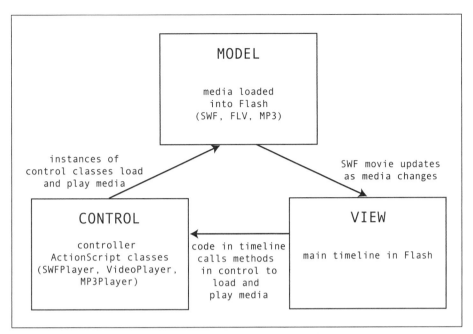

Figure 13-1. The Model-View-Controller interaction for the media player

Guaranteeing methods and datatypes with an interface

Because we wish all three media types to respond to the same methods, it makes sense to create some simple interfaces to define those methods. That way, even though in ActionScript you tell an MP3 to play with start() and an FLV or a SWF to play with play(), we can trust (and guarantee to those using our classes) that calling a single specified method will play each of the media types the same way. To guarantee this, our media controllers will implement two interfaces: IPlayable for controlling playback of media and IAudible for controlling audio properties.

Examining class structure

There will be a number of classes combining to form the finished media player. One important class that falls outside of the scope of the media classes themselves is a base class to control the dispatching of events, which of course is necessary for the Observer pattern utilized by the controller media classes. This class, Broadcaster, which implements IEventDispatcher (an interface to define how to build a class that will broadcast events), will be useful as a separate class, since it's one that may be used often and may act as the base class for any other class that will need to broadcast events. We have built a similar class in previous chapters, and will build a modular variation here.

Broadcaster will act as the base class for MediaController, which will define the common methods and properties for all three of the separate media type controllers. These three controllers, SWFPlayer, VideoPlayer, and MP3Player, will inherit from MediaController these common methods and properties, but implement the media controller methods (specified in IPlayable) in ways appropriate to their media type, acting as a nice example of polymorphism. A developer calling playMedia() on any of these three classes can expect that the appropriate media type will play, despite the different ways Flash plays media. The classes will hide the implementation of these methods through encapsulation.

Finally, there will be a unique static class, IntervalManager, which will help manage all intervals called by our classes. This demonstrates an implementation of the Singleton pattern as presented in Chapter 12, but here, instead of creating an instance as in the previous chapter, we'll simply make the class methods static so that they must be accessed through the class itself. A class handling all interval function calls becomes useful in larger projects where clips are attached and removed with any significant frequency. By keeping references to interval calls stored in a central object as opposed to in the instances themselves, we prevent "orphaned intervals" from occurring. An interval may be orphaned when a reference to the interval call is stored on an object that is then deleted or removed. There is then no way to stop that interval call, which can cause issues if the same setInterval() method is called again.

That's the basic breakdown of the classes we'll be building throughout the rest of the chapter. For a better understanding of how it all fits together, be sure to look at the UML diagram in Figure 13-2 detailing the model for the media player. Once you are confident with the structure, open up Flash and prepare to code!

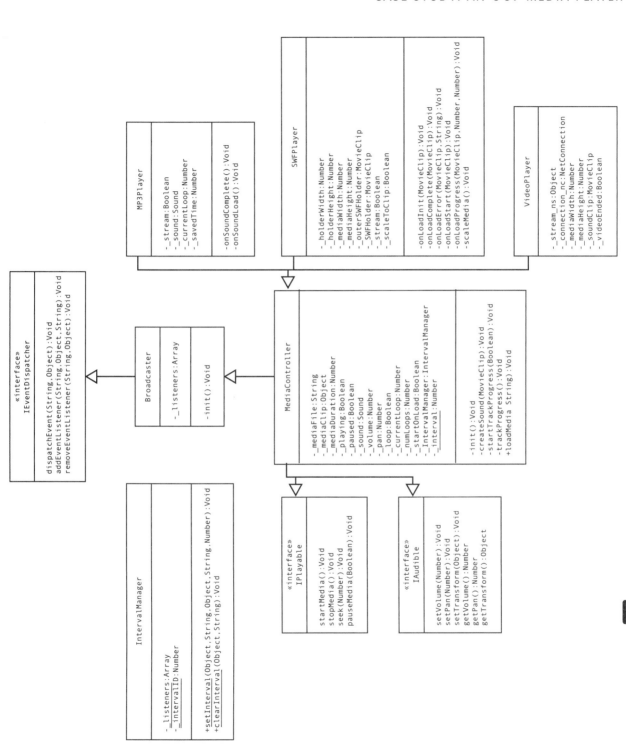

Figure 13-2. The UML diagram for the media player classes

Building the media player

We'll begin this project with the IntervalManager, which will hold reference for every setInterval() call. This is a class that will prove useful for further development throughout the rest of this book. Before we can do this, however, we need to define the package for our classes.

Find the configuration directory for your Flash installation on your machine. On a Windows system, this is located at C:\Documents and Settings*user*\Local Settings\ Application Data\Macromedia\Flash MX 2004*language*\Configuration\. If you are using a Mac, the directory can be found at Hard Disk/Users/user/Library/Application Support/Macromedia/Flash 8/language/Configuration/. Select the Classes folder within this directory and create a new folder named com. Within com, create another folder named oop, and within oop create three folders named core, managers, and media, respectively. See Figure 13-3 for the result. com.oop will be the package for all of the classes we create throughout the rest of the book. We'll create classes within the core, managers, and media packages in this tutorial.

Figure 13-3. A new directory has been added to the Flash Classes directory

IntervalManager

Create a new ActionScript file in Flash. Save it into the managers folder as IntervalManager.as. Add the following lines of code:

```
class com.oop.managers.IntervalManager{

    static private var __listeners:Object = {};
    static private var __intervalID:Number = 0;

    function IntervalManager() {};

}
```

This is the beginning of the IntervalManager class to hold references to all intervals being run. As you can see, it begins with the class keyword and the fully qualified class name.

Within the class definition, we create two static private properties (we'll use the double underscore to denote private properties in our code—notice that it's two underscores, not one). The first, __listeners, will hold references to all objects that have called setInterval. The second, __intervalID, will increment for any non-MovieClip instance calling setInterval (more on that in a moment). The constructor function follows, but doesn't require any code within its block.

Now add the following lines in bold to the IntervalManager class:

```
class com.oop.managers.IntervalManager{

    static private var __listeners:Object = {};
    static private var __intervalID:Number = 0;

    function IntervalManager() {};

    static public function setInterval(
        connection:Object,
        intName:String,
        path:Object,
        func:String,
        time:Number
    ):Void {
      clearInterval(connection, intName);
      if (connection instanceof MovieClip) {
        if (__listeners[connection] == undefined) {
          __listeners[connection] = {};
        }
        __listeners[connection][intName] =
➥ _global.setInterval(path, func, time, arguments[5],
➥ arguments[6], arguments[7], arguments[8],
➥ arguments[9], arguments[10]);
```

```
      } else {
        if (connection.intervalID == undefined) {
          connection.intervalID = "int" + (__intervalID++);
        }
        __listeners[connection.intervalID] = {};
        __listeners[connection.intervalID][intName] =
➥ _global.setInterval(path, func, time, arguments[5],
➥ arguments[6], arguments[7], arguments[8],
➥ arguments[9], arguments[10]);
      }
    }

  }
```

Although setInterval normally requires three arguments, our special manager class will require two more. The first argument, connection, will indicate how the interval call will be stored. This will be a reference to a MovieClip instance or to another class instance (one that doesn't inherit from MovieClip) that is calling the function. intName is a string name for the interval, which again controls how the interval call will be stored. path indicates the path to the function that is to be called, func is the name of the function to be called on that path, and time is the number of milliseconds between each call.

The first thing that occurs within this function is that any interval that might currently be stored at the same location is cleared (using clearInterval(), a function to be written next). This saves the developer from having to clear an interval before setting it (an often necessary task for an interval that is called repeatedly but not consistently). The conditional statement that follows checks to see whether the connection argument is a MovieClip instance or not. If it is, then a reference to that instance is saved into the static __listeners object if it doesn't already exist. This is possible with a MovieClip instance, but not a non-MovieClip class instance. The _global.setInterval function is then called and the reference to the call is stored in the __listeners object under the connection and intName arguments. This prevents the orphaned intervals mentioned earlier. Notice that six additional arguments are also passed to the setInterval() function, allowing the coder to send additional information along in the interval call.

If the connection argument isn't a MovieClip instance, then an ID needs to be generated. This is set using the __intervalID property. Then setInterval() is called just as it was for a MovieClip instance.

The final step for our manager class is to add a clearInterval method. Add the following lines after the setInterval method, which clears any interval saved using the IntervalManager.

```
    static public function clearInterval(
      connection:Object,
      intName:String
    ):Void {
        if (connection instanceof MovieClip) {
        _global.clearInterval(__listeners[connection][intName]);
```

```
  } else {
    _global.clearInterval(
➥ _listeners[connection.intervalID][intName]);
  }
}
```

Now, to implement the IntervalManager, you would use code similar to the following:

```
import com.oop.managers.IntervalManager;

IntervalManager.setInterval(this, "test", this, "testInterval", 1000);

function testInterval():Void
{
  trace("one second passed");
  IntervalManager.clearInterval(this, "test");
}
```

This will prove invaluable as we build more complex applications.

Defining the interfaces

There will be three interfaces used by the classes in this tutorial. The first, IEventDispatcher, will define methods to be used by any class that will need to broadcast events. The other two interfaces, IPlayable and IAudible, will define how media is to be controlled. Let's start with IEventDispatcher.

Dispatching events

We'll start here building our own code library by creating a class to dispatch events. I'll note that, like many of the classes we will code through this and later chapters, you can find fully implemented and working classes with similar functionality either in the component library (EventDispatcher in this case) or through commercially available or freeware components available online. Why code your own? Greater control, greater understanding, and, when something doesn't work the way you wish, greater ease in getting what you want. The best way to learn OOP is to go in from the ground up. With that said, create a new ActionScript document and save it into the com/oop/core directory as IEventDispatcher.as. Enter the following lines of code:

```
interface com.oop.core.IEventDispatcher {

  public function dispatchEvent(
    evnt:String,
    params:Object
  ):Void;
```

13

```
public function addEventListener(
    evnt:String,
    lstnr:Object,
    mappedTo:String
):Boolean;

public function removeEventListener(
    evnt:String,
    lstnr:Object
):Boolean;

}
```

Here you can see that the interface defines three methods for classes implementing the interface. addEventListener() will allow objects to register to hear events from a class, removeEventListener() will remove objects registered to hear events from a class, and dispatchEvent() will be fired to send event notifications to objects registered to hear such events.

Before moving on to the media interface, let's see how such an interface would be implemented by creating a Broadcaster class. Create a new ActionScript file named Broadcaster.as in the com/oop/core directory. Enter the following lines into the file:

```
class com.oop.core.Broadcaster implements
➥ com.oop.core.IEventDispatcher {

  private var __listeners:Array;

  function Broadcaster()
  {
    init();
  }

// PRIVATE
// _____

  private function init():Void
  {
    __listeners = [];
  }

// PUBLIC
// _____

}
```

You can see, the first line of code specifies that this class will implement the IEventDispatcher interface. A private property named __listeners is then defined to hold references to objects registered to hear events from instances of this class. The constructor follows and simply calls the private init() method. In the init(), the __listeners property is assigned an empty array. The IEventDispatcher methods will be public and will be defined next.

Add the following bold lines to the Broadcaster code:

```
// PUBLIC
// _____

  public function addEventListener(
    evnt:String,
    lstnr:Object,
    mappedTo:String
):Boolean {
    var ev:String;
    var li:Object;
    for (var i in __listeners) {
      ev = __listeners[i].event;
      li = __listeners[i].listener;
      if (ev == evnt && li == lstnr) return false;
    }
    __listeners.push(
      {
      event:evnt,
      listener:lstnr,
      mappedTo:mappedTo
      }
    );
    return true;
  }

  public function removeEventListener(
    evnt:String,
    lstnr:Object
):Boolean {
    var ev:String;
    var li:Object;
    for (var i = 0; i < __listeners.length; i++) {
      ev = __listeners[i].event;
      li = __listeners[i].listener;
      if (ev == evnt && li == lstnr) {
        __listeners.splice(i, 1);
        return true;
      }
    }
    return false;
  }

}
```

13

Now we get to it! These are two of the three necessary functions to implement IEventDispatcher. addEventListener() is sent an event to register for, the object to be registered, and the function to call upon notification of that event. The instance of Broadcaster then runs through its current listeners to see whether the object sent is already registered for the specified event (we wouldn't want the same object listed twice to receive notification of a single event), and if so, exits the function. Otherwise, the three arguments are pushed into the __listeners array.

removeEventListener() works in a similar fashion, but in reverse. __listeners is looped through and the specified object is removed if it exists in the array.

Now that objects can be added and removed as listeners, it's time to define the method that will inform these listeners when the appropriate event has fired. Add the following bold lines to the Broadcaster file:

```
public function removeEventListener(
  evnt:String,
  lstnr:Object
):Boolean {
  var ev:String;
  var li:Object;
  for (var i = 0; i < __listeners.length; i++) {
    ev = __listeners[i].event;
    li = __listeners[i].listener;
    if (ev == evnt && li == lstnr) {
      __listeners.splice(i, 1);
      return true;
    }
  }
  return false;
}

public function dispatchEvent(
  evnt:String,
  params:Object
):Void {
  var evtObj = {type:evnt, parameters:params};
  for (var i:String in __listeners) {
    if (__listeners[i].event == evnt) {
      __listeners[i].listener[evnt](evtObj);
      __listeners[i].listener[__listeners[i].mappedTo](evtObj);
    }
  }
  this[evnt + "Handler"](evtObj);
}

}
```

dispatchEvent() will be fired to inform listeners when an event has occurred. The name of the event and any additional parameters are sent to the function. The __listeners are then looped through to find objects registered to hear that event. Instances of Broadcaster will allow listeners two different ways to hear events. One is to have a method with the same name as the event, so that an object listening for a release event from a button can have a release method defined. However, sometimes it may be useful to have the event fire off a specific method in the listener. In these cases, where a separate function is defined to receive notification of the event, the function stored in mappedTo is fired.

Once all of the listeners have been notified, the Broadcaster instance will call its own method for that event, defined as the name of the event with "Handler" appended. This might not always be used, but is useful to have defined when necessary.

To test this new Broadcaster class, create a new Flash document and put the following lines in Frame 1:

```
import com.oop.core.Broadcaster;

var testBroadcaster:Broadcaster = new Broadcaster();

var listener1:Object = {};
listener1.notify = function(infoObj:Object):Void {
  trace("listener1 notified");
}

var listener2:Object = {};
listener2.hearEvent = function(infoObj:Object):Void {
  trace("listener2 notified");
}

testBroadcaster.addEventListener("notify", listener1);
testBroadcaster.addEventListener("notify", listener2, "hearEvent");

testBroadcaster.dispatchEvent("notify");
```

First, the Broadcaster class is imported so that we can reference it by just using its class name, then a new instance of Broadcaster is created. Next, two new objects are created, listener1 and listener2, the former with a notify() function and the latter with a hearEvent() function. Both objects are added as listeners for testBroadcaster's notify event, but with listener2, the notification will be mapped to hearEvent() since that is specified as the third argument. The final line tells testBroadcaster to dispatch its notify event. If you test this, the Output panel should show the results of both listener1 and listener2's trace calls, as shown in Figure 13-4.

13

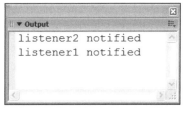

Figure 13-4.
The event listeners tested and working

Media interfaces

The next two interfaces will define how to interact with media. The first, IPlayable, lists four methods for controlling playback of media. Create a new ActionScript file and save it as IPlayable.as in the com/oop/media directory. Enter the following code:

```
interface com.oop.media.IPlayable {

    public function startMedia():Void;

    public function seek(offset:Number):Void;

    public function stopMedia():Void;

    public function pauseMedia(b:Boolean):Void;

}
```

startMedia() will set media playing, stopMedia() will halt its progress and return its position to the beginning, seek() will find a certain point in the media, and pauseMedia() will halt the media's progress but leave its position at the current location.

Moving on to the audio properties of media, create a new ActionScript file named IAudible.as and save it into the same com/oop/media directory. Enter the following code:

```
interface com.oop.media.IAudible {

    public function getVolume():Number;

    public function setVolume(v:Number):Void;

    public function getPan():Number;

    public function setPan(p:Number):Void;

    public function getTransform():Object;

    public function setTransform(obj:Object):Void;

}
```

These are the six functions to control the audio component of any media. As you can see, they are the same as the ActionScript commands for the Sound object. They are defined here in an interface, since each of the three types of media we'll be controlling (SWF, MP3, and FLV) all implement the control of the media's sound in slightly different ways, and we want to guarantee a consistent interface for all three.

Controlling media

With all of the interfaces and event dispatching taken care of, we can finally begin the coding of the media classes to control the playback of media loaded into Flash. MediaController will act as a base class for all the media type controllers and contain the common methods and properties for all.

Defining properties

Create a new ActionScript file and save it as `MediaController.as` into the `com/oop/media` directory. Enter the following code:

```
import com.oop.core.Broadcaster;
import com.oop.media.IAudible;
import com.oop.media.IPlayable;
import com.oop.managers.IntervalManager;;

class com.oop.media.MediaController extends Broadcaster
➥ implements IAudible, IPlayable {

  private var __mediaFile:String;
  private var __mediaClip:Object;
  private var __mediaDuration:Number;
  private var __playing:Boolean;
  private var __paused:Boolean;
  private var __sound:Sound;
  private var __volume:Number;
  private var __pan:Number;
  private var __loop:Boolean;
  private var __currentLoop:Number;
  private var __numLoops:Number;
  private var __startOnLoad:Boolean;

  static private var __interval:Number = 40;

  private function MediaController() {}

// PRIVATE
// _____

// PUBLIC
// _____

}
```

The first three lines of code import the Broadcaster and IntervalManager classes and the IPlayable and IAudible interfaces so that we may reference them in the code by just the name of each. We then define the MediaController class, which inherits from the Broadcaster event dispatching class and implements the two media control interfaces.

What follows is a list of private properties utilized in the class. With decent naming of properties, it should be evident what each is for.

- __mediaFile holds the name of the file to be loaded.
- __mediaClip is the view through which to display the media.
- __mediaDuration is the total time for the media loaded.
- __playing and __paused define the current status of the media.
- __volume and __pan hold values for the sound properties.
- __sound holds a reference to the Sound object controlling the __volume and __pan properties.
- __loop is a flag to determine whether the media should loop.
- __currentLoop is just that, the current number in a series of loops.
- __numLoops is the total number of times to loop the media.
- __startOnLoad is a flag to determine whether the media should play as soon as it's loaded into the Flash player, or if a further startMedia() command needs to be called.
- __interval, the static property that follows the main list, is a property that resides on the MediaController class itself (not an instance) and holds the length of milliseconds for repeated interval calls.

After the properties are defined, the constructor appears, but doesn't require any code within the block. Remember that the MediaController class inherits from Broadcaster, which calls the init() method for that class. Because of this, we don't need any code within the MediaController constructor in order to call an init() method there.

Notice as well that the constructor is given the private modifier. This will ensure that an instance of this class cannot be instantiated by code and must instead be extended to a new public class. We do this because the MediaController class in itself won't function on its own—its code merely contains common methods and properties of the distinct media type controller classes.

Private methods

Add the following code in bold to the MediaController class:

```
function MediaController() {}

// PRIVATE
// _____

private function initController(
  obj:Object
):Void {
  __volume = 100;
  __pan = 0;
  __paused = false;
  __playing = false;
```

```
      __mediaClip = obj;
      __startOnLoad = true;
    }

    private function createSound(
      m:MovieClip
    ):Void {
      __sound = new Sound(m);
    }

    private function startTrackProgress(
      b:Boolean
    ):Void {
      if (b) {
        dispatchEvent("mediaStart");
        IntervalManager.setInterval(
          this,
          "trackInterval",
          this,
          "trackProgress",
          __interval);
      } else {
        dispatchEvent("mediaStop");
        IntervalManager.clearInterval(this, "trackInterval");
      }
    }

    private function trackProgress():Void
    {
      dispatchEvent("progress");
    }

// PUBLIC
// _____
```

Here are the three private methods for MediaController. init() will need to be called from any subclass when an instance is created. In the function, the properties holding the status of the media are assigned the default values. Notice that the initController() method is sent an Object instance as an argument. This will be a reference to the view where the media will be displayed (or, in the case of MP3s, the movie clip instance in which to load the file).

createSound() is a simple method that creates an internal Sound object instance to control the sound of the media loaded.

startTrackProgress() is sent a true or false value depending on whether the media is being started or stopped. If the media is being started, a new interval is created in the static IntervalManager. The method trackProgress will be called every 40 milliseconds (the value for __interval). If the media is being stopped, the interval is cleared.

The final private method, trackProgress(), simply dispatches an event to any listeners that wish to know that the media is playing and act accordingly (imagine that this might be used by a playhead progressing, or perhaps a running collection of subtitles that need to be updated as the media progresses).

Public methods

The private methods defined previously will only be used internally by this class and any class that extends MediaController. This next set of methods can be called from any object and will be used to control the properties of the media. Add the following bold code to the MediaController class:

```
// PUBLIC
// _____

    public function loadMedia(
      file:String
    ):Void {
      __currentLoop = 1;
      __mediaFile = file;
      setVolume(__volume);
      setPan(__pan);
      __paused = false;
    }

    public function startMedia():Void
    {
      __playing = true;
      startTrackProgress(true);
    }

    public function seek(
      offset:Number
    ):Void {
      dispatchEvent("progress", {position:offset});
    }

    public function stopMedia():Void
    {
      __playing = false;
      startTrackProgress(false);
    }

    public function pauseMedia(
      b:Boolean
    ):Void {
      __playing = !b;
      __paused = b;
      startTrackProgress(!b);
    }

}
```

The first method listed, loadMedia(), will be called to load an external media file for the controller to play. Since the three types of media are all loaded in separate ways, the actual loading will have to take place in the classes we write to handle those media types. Here in this base class, the file name is saved, the __currentLoop property is reset, and the sound is set to the current values for __pan and __volume.

The next four methods are necessary when implementing the IPlayable interface. Again, since the control of different media types is implemented differently, the classes extending MediaController will take care of the brunt of the work. Here, the values for __playing and __paused are set when appropriate, and events are broadcast (using Broadcaster's dispatchEvent()) to let registered listeners know the status of the media has changed.

Add these next several methods to the public methods defined earlier (that's between the pauseMedia() method and the class's closing brace):

```
public function get mediaFile():String
{
  return __mediaFile;
}

public function get mediaClip():Object
{
  return __mediaClip;
}

public function get mediaPosition():Number
{
  return 0;
}

public function get mediaDuration():Number
{
  return __mediaDuration;
}

public function get paused():Boolean
{
  return __paused;
}

public function get playing():Boolean
{
  return __playing;
}
```

These methods we've just added are simply getter methods for other objects to retrieve values for the MediaController instance's properties. A getter method allows an object to call the method as if it was a property. This simply means that instead of using

```
var isPlaying:Boolean = mediaController.playing();
```

13

to retrieve the value of the __playing property, the following must be used instead:

```
var isPlaying:Boolean = mediaController.playing;
```

Getter methods don't accept any arguments and must return a value. Notice for each of the preceding getters, the private property value is simply returned. However, for mediaPosition, the value of 0 is returned. This is because the value will be constantly changing, and the classes extending MediaController will simply return the current position of the media as opposed to storing a value in a property.

The next set of public methods will allow objects to set and retrieve values for the sound properties of the media. Enter the following code below the getter methods we just defined, but before the class's closing brace:

```
public function getVolume():Number
{
  return __sound.getVolume();
}

public function setVolume(
  v:Number
):Void {
  __sound.setVolume(v);
  __volume = v;
}

public function getPan():Number
{
  return __sound.getPan();
}

public function setPan(
  p:Number
):Void {
  __sound.setPan(p);
  __pan = p;
}

public function getTransform():Object
{
  return __sound.getTransform();
}

public function setTransform(
  obj:Object
):Void {
  __sound.setTransform(obj);
}
```

These are the necessary methods for classes implementing the IAudible interface. Each sets or retrieves the values for the internal __sound object. To go with these methods, we'll also define some getter and setter methods for easier access to these properties. Since getters and setters cannot be defined in an interface, we are unable to make them a part of IAudible, but we can add them here. Add the following below the methods defined earlier (after setTransform() but before the class's closing brace):

```
public function get volume():Number
{
  return getVolume();
}

public function set volume(
  v:Number
):Void {
  setVolume(v);
}

public function get pan():Number
{
  return getPan();
}

public function set pan(
  p:Number
):Void {
  setPan(p);
}
```

So now the developer can use the methods defined in IAudible or these getter/setter methods to control the audio. Setters work similarly to getters, but must receive a value and cannot return anything. A developer would access a setter with

```
mediaController.volume = 50;
```

The final batch of public functions includes the getter/setter methods for the remaining properties. Add these lines below the code entered previously:

```
public function get loop():Boolean
{
  return __loop;
}

public function set loop(
  b:Boolean
):Void {
  __loop = b;
}
```

13

```
public function get numLoops():Number
{
  return __numLoops;
}

public function set numLoops(
  n:Number
):Void {
  __numLoops = n;
}

public function get startOnLoad():Boolean
{
  return __startOnLoad;
}

public function set startOnLoad(
  b:Boolean
):Void {
  __startOnLoad = b;
}
```

The private properties __loop, __numLoops, and __startOnLoad can be set and retrieved using the preceding methods.

This completes the code for our base MediaController class. Since it was presented in bits, be sure to check your file against the MediaController.as file included with the download files for this chapter.

Controlling FLVs

The first class we'll create to control a specific media type is VideoPlayer. Create a new ActionScript file and save it as VideoPlayer.as into the com/oop/media directory. Add the following code to the file:

```
import com.oop.media.MediaController;
import com.oop.managers.IntervalManager;

class com.oop.media.VideoPlayer extends MediaController {

  private var __stream_ns:Object; // NetStream
  private var __connection_nc:NetConnection;
  private var __mediaWidth:Number;
  private var __mediaHeight:Number;
  private var __sound_mc:MovieClip;
  private var __videoEnded:Boolean;
```

```
    public function VideoPlayer(
      v:Video
    ) {
      initController(v);
    }

  // PRIVATE
  // _____

  // PUBLIC
  // _____

    }
```

The first few lines should be familiar to you after the previous classes we have created. The VideoPlayer will extend the MediaController class and so inherit all of its methods. The list of properties that follows applies specifically to video clips. __stream_ns holds a reference to a NetStream object. (The reason that NetStream isn't used for the datatype is that we'll be utilizing a method that isn't included in the NetStream's definition. Therefore, if we defined the datatype as NetStream, Flash would report an error.) __connection_nc holds a reference to a NetConnection object. Both NetStream and NetConnection instances are necessary to stream in FLV files.

The __mediaWidth and __mediaHeight properties hold values for the dimensions of the media being loaded in, which is stored as metadata in an FLV. __sound_mc holds a movie clip reference for creating the Sound instance to control the FLV's audio properties. __videoEnded is a Boolean flag to determine whether the end of the FLV has been reached.

Finally, the constructor is defined. As you can see, a video instance is passed to the constructor, and this is sent to the initController() method. If you look back at the MediaController class, you'll note that the initController() method accepts an object instance (and Video inherits from Object), and that instance is stored in the __mediaClip property.

There will only be one private method for the VideoPlayer class. Add the following bold lines:

```
  // PRIVATE
  // _____

    private function trackProgress():Void
    {
      if (mediaPosition == mediaDuration || __videoEnded) {
        __videoEnded = false;
        if (__loop && __currentLoop < __numLoops) {
          startMedia();
        } else {
          super.stopMedia();
          __stream_ns.pause(true);
```

13

```
        }
        dispatchEvent("mediaComplete",
➥{type:"swf", loop:__currentLoop});
        __currentLoop++;
      }
      super.trackProgress();
    }

// PUBLIC
// _____
```

As a video file plays, trackProgress() will be called (this was handled in MediaController's startTrackProgress() method). If the position of the media equals the length of the media, then a loop has completed (note that the two getter functions for mediaPosition and mediaDuration are used). If a loop has completed, we check whether the file is supposed to loop (the __loop Boolean flag) and, if so, whether the current loop isn't equal to the total number of loops. If another loop is supposed to occur, startMedia() is called. Otherwise, stopMedia() is called. An event is broadcast to listeners informing them that the media is complete (whether it's looping or not). Finally, super.trackProgress() is called to take care of any code that needs to be run in the super object, which takes care of broadcasting a progress event.

The public methods for this as well as the other media type controllers are where most of the code lies. Add the bold lines of code to the public block of the VideoPlayer.

```
// PUBLIC
// _____

  public function loadMedia(
    file:String
  ):Void {
    super.loadMedia(file);
    __connection_nc = new NetConnection();
    __connection_nc.connect(null);
    __stream_ns = new NetStream(__connection_nc);
    __mediaClip.attachVideo(__stream_ns);
    __sound_mc.attachAudio(__stream_ns);
    var videoPlayer = this;
    __stream_ns.onMetaData = function(data) {
      videoPlayer.__mediaDuration = data.duration;
      videoPlayer.__mediaWidth = data.width;
      videoPlayer.__mediaHeight = data.height;
    };
    __stream_ns.onStatus = function(data) {
      if (data.level == "error") {
        videoPlayer.dispatchEvent("loadError",
➥{message:"file not found"});
      } else if (data.code == "NetStream.Play.Stop") {
        videoPlayer.__videoEnded = true;
      }
```

```
    };
    startMedia();
    if (!__startOnLoad) IntervalManager.setInterval(
➡this, "pauseInterval", this, "pauseMedia", 200);
  }
```

The loadMedia() function will be called to load an FLV and play using a VideoPlayer instance. The file location as a string is sent as an argument. The super.loadMedia() is invoked, then a new NetConnection is created and its connect() method is passed null, which is necessary for streaming in FLV files. A new NetStream instance is created with the __connection_nc passed in the constructor. Whatever Video instance is stored in __mediaClip and whatever MovieClip instance is stored in __sound_mc are passed a reference to the NetStream object. Now whatever is streamed in will be connected to those instances.

The next several lines look to two handlers that are fired by a NetStream instance. onMetaData() is fired when an FLV is loaded and the file's metadata is received. This contains info on the FLV's total time, its width, and its height. These are stored in the appropriate properties of the VideoPlayer instance (which is available in the scope of the two handlers since it was defined above them as a local variable). onStatus() is fired when the status of the NetStream instance changes, such as when it's closed or if there is an error in loading. It's in this latter instance that an event is broadcast informing registered listeners of the error.

After the two handlers are defined, startMedia() is called to load in the video. startMedia(), which will be defined in a moment, will invoke the proper NetStream methods to load the video and start it playing. However, if the __startOnLoad property is set to false, an interval is created to pause the media almost immediately. Unfortunately, this cannot be called immediately, so a 200-millisecond delay is set.

The loadMedia() method is a good example of polymorphism and encapsulation at work. The developer using the VideoPlayer class doesn't need to know how this method is implemented, nor how the implementation differs from loading a SWF or an MP3. All that a developer needs to know is that loadMedia() will load the specified media file.

The next lines of code are another example of polymorphism at work with our media classes. These are the methods defined in IPlayable for controlling playback of the media. Add the lines after the loadMedia() method.

```
    public function startMedia():Void
    {
      __videoEnded = false;
      IntervalManager.clearInterval(this, "pauseInterval");
      if (__paused) {
        __stream_ns.pause();
      } else {
        __stream_ns.play(__mediaFile);
      }
      super.startMedia();
    }
```

13

```
public function seek(
  offset:Number
):Void {
  __videoEnded = false;
  var t:Number = Math.round(offset*1000)/1000;
  __stream_ns.seek(t);
  super.seek(t);
}

public function stopMedia():Void {
  __stream_ns.seek(0);
  __stream_ns.pause(true);
  super.stopMedia();
}

public function pauseMedia(
  b:Boolean
):Void {
  IntervalManager.clearInterval(this, "pauseInterval");
  super.pauseMedia(b);
  __stream_ns.pause(b);
}
```

startMedia() first clears any pause interval that might be running (set in the preceding loadMedia() method). It then checks whether the video is currently paused. If so, it unpauses it by calling the NetStream's pause() method, which acts as a pause/unpause toggle. Otherwise, it simply tells the NetStream instance to play the current media file.

seek() takes a number that indicates the position to find specified in number of seconds. It rounds this to the thousandths, then invokes the seek() method of the NetStream instance. We set the __videoEnded Boolean property to false as a flag so that we know any stopping of the video that occurs here is due to the seek and not because the end of the stream has been reached.

stopMedia() sends the video back to the beginning and pauses it, while pauseMedia() simply invokes the pause() method of the NetStream instance.

The final public methods are the getter/setters for the unique VideoPlayer properties. The following lines should come after the other public methods, but precede the class's closing brace:

```
public function set mediaClip(
  v:Video
):Void {
  __mediaClip.attachVideo(null);
  __mediaClip = v;
  __mediaClip.attachVideo(__stream_ns);
}
```

```
public function set mediaPosition(
  n:Number
):Void {
  seek(n);
}

public function get mediaPosition():Number
{
  return __stream_ns.time;
}

public function get mediaWidth():Number
{
  return __mediaWidth;
}

public function set mediaWidth(w:Number):Void
{
  __mediaClip._width = w;
  __mediaWidth = w;
}

public function get mediaHeight():Number
{
  return __mediaHeight;
}

public function set mediaHeight(
  h:Number
):Void
{
  __mediaClip._height = h;
  __mediaHeight = h;
}

public function get soundClip():MovieClip
{
  return __sound_mc;
}

public function set soundClip(
  m:MovieClip
):Void {
  __sound_mc = m;
  createSound(m);
}
```

Be sure to check your completed VideoPlayer file with the VideoPlayer.as file included with the download files for this chapter.

So now that all the code is complete for VideoPlayer, how does it all work in Flash? Let's try it out and see!

Building a video view

So much coding, and yet we have not until this point been able to see a visual demonstration of the media controllers. All the planning and preparation will pay off now, however, as it becomes clear how easy it now is to load and control playback of an FLV.

Create a new Flash document and save it as videoTest.fla. In the Library, use the menu at the top right to create a new Video symbol, as shown in Figure 13-5. Drag the symbol to the stage and name the instance video in the Properties panel. Make its dimensions 320×240.

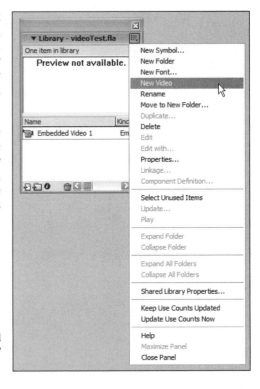

Figure 13-5. Adding a new Video symbol instance to the Library

Name the layer with the video instance video, then create a layer above it named code. Select Frame 1, then open the ActionScript editor and enter the following code:

```
import com.oop.media.VideoPlayer

var videoPlayer:VideoPlayer = new VideoPlayer(video);
videoPlayer.addEventListener("mediaComplete", this);
videoPlayer.loop = true;
videoPlayer.numLoops = 2;
videoPlayer.loadMedia("cyber_minotaur.flv");

function mediaComplete() {
  trace("video complete");
}

function onMouseDown() {
  videoPlayer.pauseMedia(!videoPlayer.paused);
}
```

After importing the VideoPlayer class so that we can use it without typing the full package each time, a new VideoPlayer instance is created, and the video instance on the stage is sent as an argument. The main timeline is added as a listener to the controller for the mediaComplete event, which is fired when a loop is completed. The loop Boolean flag is set to true, enabling the video to be looped, and the number of total loops is set to 2 (twice through). The file cyber_minotaur.flv is passed as the file to load.

When the video completes a loop, the mediaComplete() function will be called and the trace result will appear in the Output panel. Whenever the mouse is clicked in the movie, the video will toggle its pause state.

cyber_minotaur.flv is available in the code download for this book, accessible from www.friendsofed.com. Copy it to the same directory as videoTest.fla. Test the movie to see the video being loaded and controlled by our media classes. The result should appear as in Figure 13-6.

Figure 13-6. The media controller playing back an FLV

Controlling SWFs

Surprisingly, controlling SWF files is actually a little more involved than controlling FLVs. This is because we'll add some functionality for rescaling the loaded SWF files to fit within a movie clip while maintaining the same proportions.

Create a new ActionScript file and save it into the com/oop/media directory as SWFPlayer.as. Add the following code:

```
import com.oop.media.MediaController;
import com.oop.managers.IntervalManager;

class com.oop.media.SWFPlayer extends MediaController {

  private var __holderWidth:Number;
  private var __holderHeight:Number;
  private var __mediaWidth:Number;
  private var __mediaHeight:Number;
  private var __outerSWFHolder_mc:MovieClip;
  private var __SWFHolder_mc:MovieClip;
  private var __stream:Boolean;
  private var __scaleToClip:Boolean;

  public function SWFPlayer(
    m:MovieClip
  ) {
    initController(m);
  }

// PRIVATE
// _____

// PUBLIC
// _____
```

Nothing should come as a surprise at this point. The SWFPlayer will extend the MediaController class as VideoPlayer did. The width and height of the clip in which to load the SWF will be stored, as well as the width and height of the SWF being loaded. Both __outerSWFHolder_mc and __SWFHolder_mc will be used for loading and resizing the SWF. __stream is a Boolean flag to determine whether to play the SWF before it's fully loaded. __scaleToClip is another Boolean flag to determine whether to rescale the loaded SWF to fit the movie clip it's being loaded into.

After that, the constructor is defined. A MovieClip instance is passed, which is in turn passed to the initController() method defined in MediaController.

Add the following private methods in bold to the code:

```
// PRIVATE
// _____

  private function onLoadInit(
    target:MovieClip
  ):Void {
```

```
      __mediaDuration = __SWFHolder_mc._totalframes;
      if (__startOnLoad) {
        startMedia();
      } else {
        __SWFHolder_mc.gotoAndStop(1);
      }
      if (__scaleToClip) {
        __outerSWFHolder_mc._visible = false;
        IntervalManager.setInterval(this, "scaleInterval",
➥this, "scaleMedia", 50);
        scaleMedia();
      } else if (__stream) {
        __outerSWFHolder._visible = true;
      }
      dispatchEvent("loadInit");
    }

    private function onLoadComplete(
      target:MovieClip
    ):Void {
      if (!__stream) __outerSWFHolder_mc._visible = true;
      dispatchEvent("loadComplete");
    }

    private function onLoadError(
      target:MovieClip,
      errorCode:String
    ):Void {
      dispatchEvent("loadError", {errorCode:errorCode});
    }

    private function onLoadStart(
      target:MovieClip
    ):Void {
      dispatchEvent("loadStart");
    }

    private function onLoadProgress(
      target:MovieClip,
      loadedBytes:Number,
      totalBytes:Number
    ):Void {
      dispatchEvent("loadProgress",
➥{loadedBytes:loadedBytes, totalBytes:totalBytes});
    }

// PUBLIC
// _____
```

13

231

These methods will be called by the MovieClipLoader instance used to load the SWF. The last four methods simply pass on the event to any registered listeners. onLoadInit(), which is fired after the first frame of the SWF is fully loaded, stores the number of frames in the SWF, then, depending on the value of __startOnLoad, either stops or starts the SWF playing. If the SWF is to be rescaled, the scaleMedia() method is called and an interval is set up to call the scaleMedia() method in another 50 milliseconds. This is necessary since there are times that a clip is supposedly fully loaded, yet its width and height are still undetermined values, which makes it impossible to rescale. The interval is merely a failsafe.

Let's take a look at the scaleMedia() method. Add the following lines to the block of private methods:

```
private function scaleMedia():Void
{
  if (mediaWidth == undefined || mediaWidth < 1) return;
  __IntervalManager.clearInterval(this, "scaleInterval");
  if (__stream) __outerSWFHolder_mc._visible = true;
  var mw:Number = mediaWidth;
  var mh:Number = mediaHeight;
  var sw:Number = __holderWidth;
  var sh:Number = __holderHeight;
  var ch:Number;
  if (sw > sh) {
    ch = sh/mh;
    if (mh < mw) {
      ch = ((mw*ch < sw) ? ch : sw/mw);
    }
  } else {
    ch = sw/mw;
    if (mw < mh) {
      ch = ((mh*ch < sh) ? ch : sh/mh);
    }
  }
  __SWFHolder_mc._width *= ch;
  __SWFHolder_mc._height *= ch;
  __SWFHolder_mc._x = (sw - __SWFHolder_mc._width)/2;
  __SWFHolder_mc._y = (sh - __SWFHolder_mc._height)/2;
}
```

In the first line of the function, we check to see whether mediaWidth is still an undefined value. If so, this method cannot yet run and is exited. However, if this value exists, we use some math to compare the width and height of the loaded media and the width and height of the clip it's loaded into. Using some comparisons, we rescale the __SWFHolder_mc movieclip (the instance holding the loaded SWF) to match the holder movie clip. In addition, the _x and _y are set to center the loaded SWF in the holder.

The final private functions take care of tracking progress of a playing SWF. Add the following lines below scaleMedia():

```
    private function startTrackProgress(
      b:Boolean
    ):Void {
      if (b) {
        dispatchEvent("mediaStart");
        var controller = this;
        __SWFHolder_mc.onEnterFrame = function() {
          controller.trackProgress();
        };
      } else {
        dispatchEvent("mediaStop");
        __SWFHolder_mc.onEnterFrame = null;
      }
    }

    private function trackProgress():Void
    {
      if (mediaPosition == mediaDuration) {
        if (__loop && __currentLoop < __numLoops) {
          startMedia();
        } else {
          stopMedia();
          __SWFHolder_mc.gotoAndStop(mediaDuration);
        }
        dispatchEvent("mediaComplete",
➥{type:"swf", loop:__currentLoop});
        __currentLoop++;
      }
      super.trackProgress();
    }
```

startTrackProgress() needs to be different here than its implementation in the super class, since SWFs use frames instead of time. We need to use an onEnterFrame function to determine progress instead of an interval, so we override the method here in SWFPlayer. As you can see, when a SWF begins to play, an onEnterFrame handler is used to call trackProgress() in the SWFPlayer instance. When the SWF stops, the handler is deleted.

trackProgress() is similar to VideoPlayer's implementation. If the current position matches the total duration, it's determined whether a loop needs to occur and the media is stopped or started accordingly.

The public functions are similar to VideoPlayer as well, though of course their implementation differs slightly due to the different media type. Add the following lines in bold:

```
    // PUBLIC
    // _____

    public function loadMedia(
      file:String
    ):Void {
```

13

```
        super.loadMedia(file);
        __holderWidth = __mediaClip._width;
        __holderHeight = __mediaClip._height;
        if (__mediaClip.__SWFHolder_mc == undefined) {
            __outerSWFHolder_mc =
➡️__mediaClip.createEmptyMovieClip("__SWFHolder_mc ",
➡️__mediaClip.getNextHighestDepth());
            __SWFHolder_mc =
➡️__outerSWFHolder_mc.createEmptyMovieClip("__SWFHolder_mc ", 0);
        }
        createSound(MovieClip(__mediaClip));
        __outerSWFHolder_mc._visible = false;
        var loader_mcl:MovieClipLoader = new MovieClipLoader();
        loader_mcl.addListener(this);
        loader_mcl.loadClip(file, __SWFHolder_mc);
    }
```

loadMedia() is sent the path of the SWF file to load. The width and height of the holder clip are saved to be used for resizing of the loaded file. A new MovieClip instance is created, then another is created nested inside. This is done so that the outer clip can be made invisible as the inner clip loads the file. createSound() is then called to create a new Sound instance on the __mediaClip's timeline. Remember that createSound() is a method defined in the super class, MediaController, so we can access it from here since SWFPlayer inherits from MediaController. Finally, a new MovieClipLoader is created to handle the loading of the file.

Next we have the IPlayable methods to control the playback of the SWF. Add these lines below loadMedia():

```
    public function startMedia():Void
    {
        super.startMedia();
        __SWFHolder_mc.play();
    }

    public function seek(
        offset:Number
    ):Void {
        offset = Math.round(offset);
        if (__playing) {
            __SWFHolder_mc.gotoAndPlay(offset-1);
        } else {
            __SWFHolder_mc.gotoAndStop(offset);
        }
        super.seek(offset);
    }
```

```
public function stopMedia():Void
{
  __SWFHolder_mc.gotoAndStop(1);
  super.stopMedia();
}


public function pauseMedia(
  b:Boolean
):Void {
  super.pauseMedia(b);
  if (__paused) {
    super.stopMedia();
    __SWFHolder_mc.stop();
  } else {
    startMedia();
  }
  startTrackProgress(!__paused);
}
```

As you can see, these control the playhead of the SWF using the standard ActionScript commands for movie clip timelines. The final methods for SWFPlayer are the getter/setters for its unique properties. Add these to the end of the public methods, but before the class's closing brace:

```
public function set mediaClip(
  m:MovieClip
):Void {
  __SWFHolder.removeMovieClip();
  __mediaClip = m;
}

public function get mediaPosition():Number
{
  return __SWFHolder._currentframe;
}

public function set mediaPosition(
  n:Number
):Void {
  seek(n);
}

public function get mediaWidth():Number
{
  return __SWFHolder._width;
}
```

13

```
public function set mediaWidth(
  w:Number
):Void {
  __SWFHolder._width = w;
}

public function get mediaHeight():Number
{
  return __SWFHolder._height;
}

public function set mediaHeight(
  h:Number
):Void {
  __SWFHolder._height = h;
}

public function get scaleToClip():Boolean
{
  return __scaleToClip;
}

public function set scaleToClip(
  b:Boolean
):Void {
  __scaleToClip = b;
  if (b) scaleMedia();
}

public function get stream():Boolean
{
  return __stream;
}

public function set stream(
  b:Boolean
):Void {
  __stream = b;
}
```

That finishes up all the code for the SWFPlayer class. Once again, you can check your files against the SWFPlayer.as file included with this chapter's download files. With inheritance doing a lot of the heavy lifting for us, that wasn't so bad, now was it?

Building a SWF view

Once again, we get to the fun part of seeing the fruits of all this labor. Let's build the visual component so we can see what we've accomplished!

Create a new Flash document and save it as swfTest.fla. Give the movie a 30 fps frame rate. Rename the default layer mc, then draw a black rectangle on the stage and size it 320×280. Convert this rectangle into a movie clip symbol named SWF screen with its registration point in the upper-left corner, as demonstrated in Figure 13-7. Name the SWF screen instance on stage swf in the Properties panel.

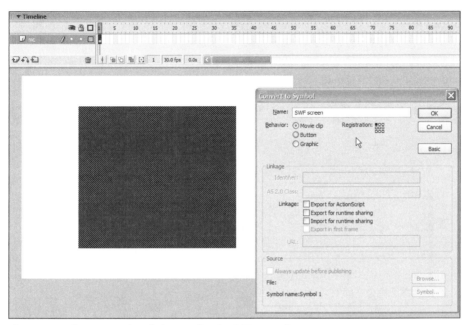

Figure 13-7. The stage and symbol set up for the SWF controller

Now create a new layer above mc and name it code. Select its first frame and type the following code:

```
import com.oop.media.SWFPlayer;

var swfPlayer:SWFPlayer = new SWFPlayer(swf);
swfPlayer.scaleToClip = true;
swfPlayer.stream = true;
swfPlayer.loop = true;
swfPlayer.numLoops = 3;
swfPlayer.addEventListener("mediaComplete", this);
swfPlayer.loadMedia("bookworm.swf");

function mediaComplete() {
  trace("swf complete");
}

function onMouseDown() {
  swfPlayer.pauseMedia(!swfPlayer.paused);
}
```

13

As with the code in `videoTest.fla`, we create a new media controller instance and pass the clip through which to view the media to the constructor. `scaleToClip` is set, which will resize the media to fit the movie clip holder. `stream` will start the playing of the SWF immediately. `loop` is set to true, and the number of loops is set to 3. The main timeline is added as a listener for the `mediaComplete` event, then the SWF file is loaded.

When the SWF has completed each loop, the `mediaComplete` function will be called and trace a message to the Output window. If you click the screen as the SWF is playing, the pause state for the SWF will be toggled.

Make sure that `bookworm.swf` is saved into the same directory as this file. Test your movie and see the result! It should resemble what you see in Figure 13-8.

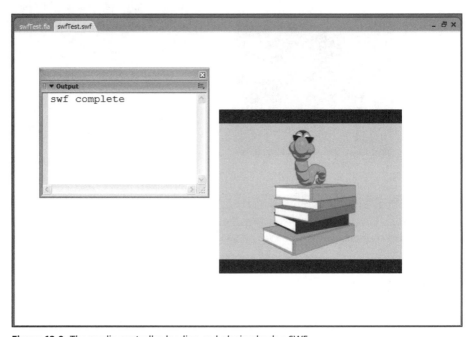

Figure 13-8. The media controller loading and playing back a SWF

Controlling MP3s

There is of course one last media type, but as you have already been through two, I think you've probably typed enough! The `MP3Player.as` can be found in the code download (in the `com/oop/media` folder). I would encourage you to open it up and peruse its code. There is actually less code than either SWFPlayer and VideoPlayer, and its implementation of the same methods is so similar that it should be nothing you can't handle.

The methods used in Flash to load and play MP3 files are slightly different from what we have used so far with SWFs and FLVs (both of which were different from the other). With MP3s, the Sound object's loadSound() is used to bring the file into the player. start(), stop(), and seek() are used to control playback, and position and duration are used to note time. When a sound has completed playing, an onSoundComplete() handler is called.

What this means is that when dealing with sounds, these would be the methods used behind the scenes. However, to anyone using MP3Player, the same methods used for VideoPlayer and SWFPlayer (startMedia(), stopMedia, loadMedia(), etc.) would be implemented. This is the beauty of polymorphism. With it, we can hide the implementation of different methods while exposing the same API.

Summary

After all of the concepts of the previous section, it's helpful to see a practical and visual demonstration of what you've learned. This case study has walked through the planning and building of classes to control a very important aspect in Flash development—externally loaded media. Interfaces were defined to guarantee that methods to control media would not change from type to type. A base class was built to hold common functionality for all three media type controllers. These controllers then used inheritance to extend the functionality of the base class. All of the methods to load and control the media were encapsulated in these controller classes, classes that demonstrated polymorphism by implementing the methods defined by the IPlayable interface in different ways. And that is some Flash OOP at work!

What's next?

Now that the general OOP concepts have been discussed, the next part of this book will delve into more Flash-centric ideas on implementing OOP in development, from building components to interacting with live data and Web servers. The next chapter looks at component architecture by exploring the version 2 component framework. Be prepared for some exciting possibilities!

13

PART FOUR **BUILDING AND EXTENDING A DYNAMIC FRAMEWORK**

14 FRAMEWORK OVERVIEW

The next logical step after learning the OOP and design patterns basics is to look at *frameworks* and how they fit into effective ActionScript programming practices. Before we investigate this more closely, I think it's important to know that lately the term "framework" has become something of an overly used—perhaps even abused—buzzword. What exactly defines a framework and how does it differ from just any old collection of classes?

In the context of this chapter, I describe a framework as a set of logically related classes that provide a solid structure through an API that promotes encapsulation, and consists of one or more base classes that you extend to build your application code on. As such, frameworks often, if not always, use practical design patterns to link together the various classes to create an optimized structure for specific code problems.

When you think about ActionScript 2.0 frameworks in Flash 8, the first candidate that comes to mind is the v2 component architecture that the built-in components use and you can extend to create your own components (more about this in Chapter 16). The v2 framework makes use of a number of base classes that implement core functionality, as we will discuss later on in this chapter.

Let's take this v2 component architecture as an example and walk through its functionality to get started with the concept of frameworks, before we move on to develop our own framework in later chapters.

Introducing the framework

Looking at the hierarchy chart in Figure 14-1, you can see that all UI components that come with Flash 8 essentially derive from four base classes: MovieClip, UIObject, UIComponent, and View.

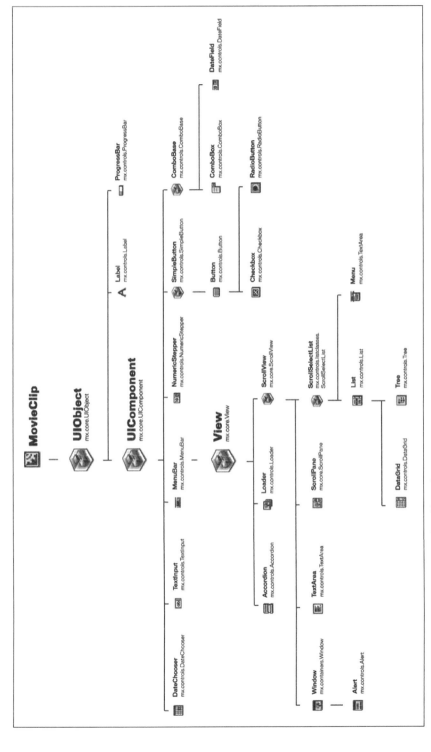

Figure 14-1. v2 component architecture class hierarchy
Image courtesy of Macromedia. Used with permission.

14

Those four classes extend each other, with MovieClip as the topmost class and View as the most specialized, as you can see from the tree structure shown in Figure 14-2.

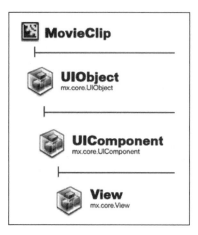

Figure 14-2.
V2 framework base classes hierarchy

When you study Figure 14-1 more closely, you'll notice that the component classes extend only the base classes from UIObject onward; there isn't a single component that directly extends MovieClip. Although that would certainly be possible, the MovieClip class is the most basic building block available in Flash 8 and as such doesn't provide any additional information for the component to make use of.

Anyone that has had the Flash IDE open for more than 15 minutes will have come across the concept of *movie clips*. The MovieClip class is nothing more than its representation in code form. Having said that, you're probably already eagerly browsing your hard disk to find this MovieClip class. Look no further. You'll find it in the First Run/Classes folder in your installation directory.

If you open up MovieClip.as, you'll notice something strange in the class definition: intrinsic. You may be thinking, "Now what the heck is that and why didn't you tell me about this earlier?" The answer is simple: it isn't really a class in the way we know it; rather, it's a file that defines datatype information for enforcing strict typing for built-in classes (or, in fact, ActionScript 1.0 classes that, as you know, don't support datatyping). By creating such an intrinsic class, the compiler knows what datatype it should expect for each property and method, and can give us more meaningful error messages should something go wrong when we try to compile a Flash project.

What this tells us about the MovieClip class is that it is built into Flash Player and not compiled into the SWF at authoring time. This, of course, makes perfect sense, as movie clips are so common in all Flash projects.

Intrinsic classes aren't something you'll use all that often unless you'd like to add strict typing functionality for ActionScript 1.0 classes. Doing that is very easy indeed, so I'll just give you a quick example:

WordUtils.as

```
intrinsic class WordUtils {
  function getLetters(word:String):Array;
  function reverseWord(word:String):String;
}
```

Flash timeline

```
var WordUtils = function() {
}
WordUtils.prototype.getLetters = function(word) {
  return word.split("");
}
WordUtils.prototype.reverseWord = function(word) {
  return this.getLetters(word).reverse().join("");
}

var myWord:String = "Intrinsic class";
var myWordUtils:WordUtils = new WordUtils();
trace(myWordUtils.reverseWord(myWord));
trace(myWordUtils.getLetters(50)); // type error
```

With the WordUtils class in the same folder as an FLA with the ActionScript 1.0 WordUtils class on the main timeline, try running Test Movie and see what happens. As expected, the call to getLetters gives a type mismatch error when trying to compile (see Figure 14-3).

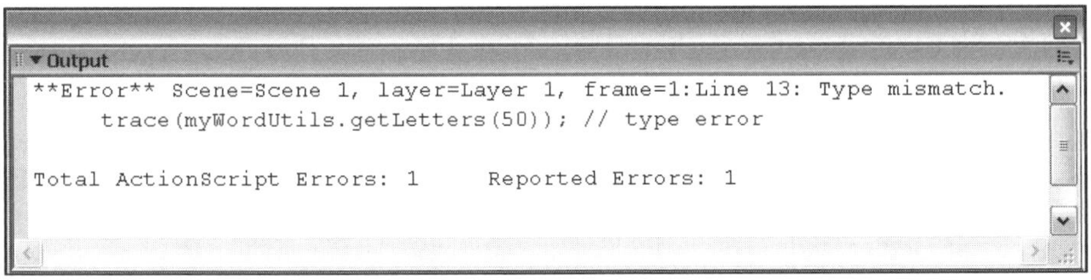

Figure 14-3. Type mismatch error in the Output panel

14

245

If you comment out the line of code that calls getLetters and try to compile again, everything runs just fine, the reverseWord result is returned for the myWord string ssalc cisnirtnI (see Figure 14-4).

Figure 14-4. The Output panel showing the result of running reverseWord

That's pretty cool. Without having to rework all your ActionScript 1.0 classes to ActionScript 2.0, you can now take advantage of intrinsic classes to add strict typing support.

Next up, we'll walk through the various base classes of the v2 component architecture, look at specific uses for the classes, and obtain a reference to its API.

Understanding the MovieClip class

As discussed earlier, the MovieClip class is really at the core of all Flash application development. If you've ever done Flash development, try to imagine what it would be like to not have access to movie clips. Every time you create a new movie clip symbol, you're essentially instantiating a new instance of the MovieClip class. In fact, it is common to use the terms "movie clip" and "movie clip instance" interchangeably, as I do throughout this book.

Earlier on in this book, you learned that classes can be linked to movie clips—without this feature, many of the examples featured here would simply not work. The same goes for building visual components, which we'll discuss in Chapter 16. They require you to use a movie clip to assign your class to and serve as a container for your graphical elements.

By now I hope I've managed to convince you (if you weren't already) that movie clips are a very important aspect of Flash development. Knowing that the MovieClip class is built into Flash Player, we can't get access to the actual code, but we are able to look up its methods, properties, and events by looking at its intrinsic class (if you like to show off your geeky skills) or look at the ActionScript Reference panel if you're a mere mortal.

Tables 14-1, 14-2, and 14-3 provide a reference of the methods, properties, and events that the MovieClip class has available for us to use.

Table 14-1. Overview of the methods of the MovieClip class

Method	Description
attachMovie(id:String,name:String, depth:Number,initObject:Object)	Attach a movie clip with the specified linkage ID.
beginFill(rgb:Number,alpha:Number)	Begin filling a shape drawn using the drawing API.
beginGradientFill(fillType:String, colors:Array,alphas:Array, ratios:Array,matrix:Object)	Begin gradient fill for a shape drawn with the drawing API.
clear()	Remove everything drawn using the drawing API within the movie clip.
createEmptyMovieClip(name:String, depth:Number)	Create a new, empty movie clip at runtime.
createTextField(instanceName:String, depth:Number,x:Number,y:Number, width:Number,height:Number)	Create a new text field at runtime.
curveTo(controlX:Number, controlY:Number,anchorX:Number, anchorY:Number)	Draw a curve using the drawing API.
duplicateMovieClip(name:String, depth:Number,initObject:Object)	Duplicate a movie clip that is located on the stage.
endFill()	End a fill for a shape drawn using the drawing API.
getBounds(bounds:Object)	Get the minimum and maximum x and y positions of the movie clip.
getBytesLoaded()	Get the number of bytes loaded into a movie clip when executing a load request.
getBytesTotal()	Get the total number of bytes that need to be loaded into a movie clip to complete the load request.
getDepth()	Get the depth of the movie clip.
getInstanceAtDepth(depth:Number)	Get the reference to an instance located at a specified depth.

14

(Continued)

Table 14-1. Overview of the methods of the MovieClip class *(Continued)*

Method	Description
getNextHighestDepth()	Get a depth higher than the highest used depth for an instance on the stage.
getSWFVersion()	Get the version of the SWF that is loaded into a movie clip instance.
getTextSnapshot()	Get a TextSnapshot object of all static text in the movie clip instance.
getURL(url:String,window:String, method:String)	Direct the browser to a specified URL.
globalToLocal(pt:Object)	Convert coordinates from the stage to be relative to the movie clip instance.
gotoAndPlay(frame:Object)	Move the playhead to a frame number or label and start playing.
gotoAndStop(frame:Object)	Move the playhead to a frame number or label and stop playback.
hitTest()	Check if another movie clip or coordinate overlaps with the movie clip instance.
lineStyle(thickness:Number, rgb:Number,alpha:Number)	Set the style of lines that are drawn with the drawing API.
lineTo(x:Number,y:Number)	Draw a line using the drawing API.
loadMovie(url:String,method:String)	Load an external SWF or JPEG into a movie clip.
loadVariables(url:String,method:String)	Load an external text file in name/value pair format into a movie clip.
localToGlobal(pt:Object)	Convert coordinates from the movie clip to be relative to the stage.
moveTo(x:Number,y:Number)	Set the x and y coordinates from where to start drawing using the drawing API.

Method	Description
nextFrame()	Move the playhead to the next frame on the timeline of the movie clip.
play()	Start playback for the timeline of the movie clip instance.
prevFrame()	Move the playhead to the previous frame on the timeline of the movie clip.
removeMovieClip()	Remove the movie clip instance from the stage and from memory.
setMask(mc:Object)	Set the specified movie clip instance as a mask for the movie clip instance calling the method.
startDrag(lockCenter:Boolean, left:Number,top:Number,right:Number, bottom:Number)	Start dragging the movie clip instance.
stop()	Stop playback for the timeline of the movie clip instance.
stopDrag()	Stop dragging a movie clip instance.
swapDepths(mc:Object)	Swap the depth of the current movie clip instance with the depth of the specified movie clip instance (or a depth level if a number is instead provided in the argument).
unloadMovie()	Unload content loaded into the movie clip instance.

Table 14-2. Overview of the properties of the MovieClip class

Property	Description
_alpha:Number	Get or set the opacity of the movie clip instance.
_currentframe:Number	Get the current frame the playhead is located on in the timeline of the movie clip instance (read-only).

(Continued)

14

Table 14-2. Overview of the properties of the MovieClip class *(Continued)*

Property	Description
_droptarget:String	Get a reference to the path of the movie clip instance the current movie was dropped on (read-only; uses slash syntax).
_focusrect:Boolean	Specify whether yellow focus rectangles are shown when tabbing between buttons or movie clips (this setting is global and applies to the entire Flash movie).
_framesloaded:Number	Get the number of frames loaded in the timeline of the movie clip instance (read-only).
_height:Number	Get the height of the movie clip instance.
_lockroot:Boolean	Set the movie clip scope to be the _root for all code included in the movie clip or any nested movie clips.
_name:String	Get or set the instance name of the movie clip.
_parent:MovieClip	Get a reference to the parent timeline (movie clip) of the movie clip.
_quality:String	Get or set the quality setting for the movie clip.
_rotation:Number	Get or set the rotation for the movie clip.
_soundbuftime:Number	Get or set the number of seconds the audio buffers for SWFs or MP3s loaded in globally.
_target:String	Return the path of the movie clip instance (read-only; uses slash syntax).
_totalframes:Number	Get the total number of frames in the timeline of the movie clip (read-only).
_url:String	Get the URL for the content that was loaded into the movie clip (read-only).
_visible:Boolean	Get or set the visibility of the movie clip instance.
_width:Number	Get or set the width of the movie clip instance.
_x:Number	Get or set the horizontal position of the movie clip instance.
_xmouse:Number	Get the horizontal mouse position relative to the movie clip (read-only).
_xscale:Number	Get or set the horizontal scale for the movie clip.

Property	Description
_y:Number	Get or set the vertical position of the movie clip.
_ymouse:Number	Get the vertical mouse position relative to the movie clip (read-only) .
_yscale:Number	Get or set the vertical scale for the movie clip.
enabled:Boolean	Set the movie clip to click events to be enabled or disabled, or retrieve its current value.
focusEnabled:Boolean	Allow or disallow a movie clip to get focus.
hitArea:Object	Set another movie clip instance to be the hit area for the current movie clip for any button events.
tabChildren:Boolean	Enable or disable nested movie clips to be part of the automatic tab ordering.
tabEnabled:Boolean	Enable or disable the movie clip to be part of the automatic tab ordering.
tabIndex:Number	Get or set the index for the sequence in which the tab ordering should occur.
trackAsMenu:Boolean	Enable or disable mouse release events for the movie clip.
useHandCursor:Boolean	Enable or disable the hand cursor when rolling over the movie clip.

Table 14-3. Overview of the events of the MovieClip class

Event	Description
onData	Triggered when data is loading into a movie clip
onDragOut	Triggered when the mouse is dragged outside the bounds of the movie clip while pressed
onDragOver	Triggered when the mouse is dragged over the movie clip instance while pressed
onEnterFrame	Triggered once every frame

(Continued)

14

Table 14-3. Overview of the events of the MovieClip class *(Continued)*

Event	Description
onKeyDown	Triggered when a key is pressed (requires instance being added as listener to static Key object, so it is not really a MovieClip event, though it is listed as one)
onKeyUp	Triggered when a key is released (requires instance being added as listener to static Key object, so it is not really a MovieClip event, though it is listed as one)
onKillFocus	Triggered when the movie clip loses focus
onLoad	Triggered when data has finished loading into a movie clip
onMouseDown	Triggered when the mouse button is clicked
onMouseMove	Triggered when the mouse is moved
onMouseUp	Triggered when the mouse button is released
onPress	Triggered when the mouse button is clicked over the movie clip
onRelease	Triggered when the mouse button is pressed and then released over the movie clip
onReleaseOutside	Triggered when the mouse button is clicked over the movie clip but released outside it
onRollOut	Triggered when the mouse position rolls out of the bounds of the movie clip
onRollOver	Triggered when the mouse rolls over the movie clip instance
onSetFocus	Triggered when the movie clip is given focus
onUnload	Triggered when the movie clip contents are unloaded

You can find a more detailed overview of the MovieClip class in the Flash 8 help files (ActionScript 2.0 Language Reference ➤ ActionScript classes ➤ MovieClip class).

Having looked at the role the MovieClip class plays in ActionScript 2.0 and Flash development in general, its uses, and the available API, let's now examine the next class in the v2 framework hierarchy: UIObject.

Understanding the UIObject class (mx.core.UIObject)

From the UIObject class onward, things start getting interesting in terms of component development with the v2 framework. The UIObject class extends MovieClip and provides additional functionality for things like resizing and applying styles. The class also broadcasts a number of common events that make your life easier by not requiring you to write code to check if your component was moved or resized, or its visibility was changed.

As you'll see when looking at Figure 14-1, the built-in UI components in Flash 8 that extend the UIObject class are Label and ProgressBar.

Tables 14-4, 14-5, and 14-6 provide a reference of all the methods, properties, and events that the UIObject makes available to all classes that extend it, in addition to those inherited from the MovieClip class.

Table 14-4. Overview of the methods of the UIObject class

Method	Description
createClassObject()	Attach an object with a specified class to the stage.
createObject(linkageName:String, instanceName:String, depth:Number, initObj:Object)	Attach an object to the stage.
destroyObject	Delete the object instance.
doLater(obj:Object,function:String)	Postpone a function call to a next frame iteration.
getStyle(property:String)	Get the value of the specified style.
invalidate()	Postpone a redraw of the object to the next frame to increase performance.
move(x:Number,y:Number)	Move the object to a new x and y position.
redraw()	Force the object to be redrawn in the current frame.
setSize(width:Number,height:Number)	Resize the object to a new width and height.
setSkin(tag:Number,linkageName:String, initObj:Object)	Assign a movie clip linkage ID to a specified skin.
setStyle(prop:String,value:Variant)	Assign a value to a specified style.

14

Table 14-5. Overview of the properties of the UIObject class

Property	Description
bottom:Number	Available space from the object to the bottom of the stage (read-only)
height:Number	Height of the object (read-only)
left:Number	Available space from the object to the left of the stage (read-only)
right:Number	Available space from the object to the right of the stage (read-only)
scaleX:Number	Horizontal scale percentage of the object
scaleY:Number	Vertical scale percentage of the object
top:Number	Available space from the object to the top of the stage (read-only)
visible:Number	Visibility of the object
width:Number	Width of the object (read-only)
x:Number	X position of the object on the stage (read-only)
y:Number	Y position of the object on the stage (read-only)

Table 14-6. Overview of the events of the UIObject class

Event	Description
draw	Broadcast when the object is about to draw its graphics.
hide	Broadcast when the object is set as invisible.
load	Broadcast when the object is loaded.
move	Broadcast when the object is moved.
resize	Broadcast when the object is resized.
reveal	Broadcast when the object is set as visible.
unload	Broadcast when the object is unloaded.

You can find a more detailed overview of the UIObject class in the Flash 8 help files (Components Language Reference ➤ UIObject class).

The UIObject class brings us into the realm of v2 component development. The next class in the hierarchy is UIComponent and, as the name implies, it is just the thing for working on full-fledged component classes.

Understanding the UIComponent class (mx.core.UIComponent)

When extending the UIComponent class, you start getting down to business. Apart from all the functionality UIComponent inherits from UIObject and indirectly from MovieClip, it adds methods, properties, and events for keyboard input, focus management, enabled and disabled states for the component, and more advanced resizing.

Built-in UI components that directly extend UIComponent are DateChooser, TextInput, MenuBar, and NumericStepper. There are also two base classes that extend UIComponent, SimpleButton and ComboBase, which in turn serve as base classes for the Button, ComboBox, and DateField UI components.

Tables 14-7, 14-8, and 14-9 provide a reference of all the methods, properties, and events that the UIComponent class offers to classes that extend it.

Table 14-7. Overview of the methods of the UIComponent class

Method	Description
getFocus()	Get the object currently in focus.
setFocus()	Set focus to the object.

Table 14-8. Overview of the properties of the UIComponent class

Property	Description
enabled:Boolean	Set the object state to enabled or disabled.
tabIndex:Number	Get or set the tabbing order index for the object.

14

255

Table 14-9. Overview of the events of the UIComponent class

Event	Description
focusIn	Broadcast when the object receives focus.
focusOut	Broadcast when the object loses focus.
keyDown	Broadcast when a key is pressed.
keyUp	Broadcast when a key is released.

You can find a more detailed overview of the UIComponent class in the Flash 8 help files (Components Language Reference ➤ UIComponent class).

You can see from the preceding tables that the UIComponent class will serve you well as a foundation for building full-fledged components. There is yet another class that extends on this functionality and is particularly useful for components that act as containers for other assets: the View class.

Understanding the View class (mx.core.View)

The View class is the final class in our v2 component base class hierarchy, and is specifically used for creating, destroying, and managing child objects. *Child objects* can be either other movie clips in the SWF that are attached or external content that is loaded in at runtime.

Built-in UI components that directly extend the View class are Accordion and Loader. Another class that extends View is ScrollView, which acts as a base class for the Window, TextArea, and ScrollPane components.

Tables 14-10 and 14-11 present the methods and properties that the View class exposes to all classes that extend it (the class does not provide any additional events). Remember, as the last class in this base class hierarchy, the View class inherits from UIComponent, which in turn inherits from UIObject and MovieClip.

Table 14-10. Overview of the methods of the View class

Method	Description
createChild(className, instanceName:String, initProps:Object)	Add a new child object.
destroyChildAt(childIndex:Number)	Destroy a child object at the specified index.
getChildAt(index:Number)	Get a child object with the specified index.

Table 14-11. Overview of the properties of the MovieClip class

Property	Description
numChildren	Return the number of child objects.
tabIndex	Get or set the tabbing order index for the object.

Framework summary

With the preceding reference section, we'll conclude our look at the available APIs for each of the v2 component framework base classes.

I'm pretty excited about what this framework has to offer and the way it is structured. It provides us with basic and more specialized base classes, and adds appropriate methods and properties for each. Of course, there is nothing stopping you from building your own base classes and extending the v2 framework yourself, as classes like SimpleButton, ComboBase, and ScrollView do.

This chapter has given you a good insight into the concept of frameworks, using the v2 component architecture as an example. You covered the intrinsic classes and how they are used to provide strict typing support for built-in or ActionScript 1.0 classes. You also looked at a reference to the methods, properties, and events of each of the major v2 component architecture base classes.

After seeing all those methods, you might be feeling a little overwhelmed at this point. Not to worry, though, as we'll delve into those in more detail in the next chapters, where we look at hands-on examples of extending the various base classes.

What's next?

In this chapter, we explored the v2 component architecture as an introduction to frameworks. To truly understand frameworks and how to develop them using the best OOP practices for Flash, we'll find our own solution and develop our own component framework in the coming chapters, building upon some of the work from Chapter 13's case study. By approaching the problem from the ground up and coding all of our own classes, we will explore further and expand upon the OOP concepts introduced in the previous chapters.

14

15 MANAGER CLASSES

The last chapter explored the foundation of the v2 component framework. Developers can choose to use the components and classes that utilize this framework and build new classes to fit within the framework, or developers can create a unique framework from the ground up on which to build their components. The benefits of using the component framework is obvious: the code is already written and the components are ready to drag and drop into your interface. If you need a quick solution, this is a great way to go, as interface prototypes can be rapidly developed and demonstrated. However, the greatest benefit of developing your own components from scratch is that you have a deep understanding of what each component can do and how to extend it with new functionality. This is obviously possible with these components, but not without a lot of work scrutinizing others' code. If work is to be invested, why not work to build something you have complete control over and can more easily extend and modify? This and the next two chapters will show you how to begin.

Planning the framework

What exactly is needed to build a working framework? Although we could jump right in and start building buttons, which is arguably the simplest Flash widget to create, if we instead plan a solid course of action for an entire component set, we'll save time in further development of more complex components (and save ourselves from inevitably having to rework that same simple button).

The framework we'll build in this book will consist broadly of widgets (the UI controls visible on the stage), manager classes (classes to control specific overall functionality of widgets or the interface), and utilities (helper classes to be used by both manager classes and widgets for common functions). The next chapter concentrates on interface widgets and the one that follows that on utility classes. This chapter will focus on the classes to manage an entire collection of widgets in an interface or application.

What to manage

When considering manager classes, imagine the tasks that you'll need performed throughout the interface or for the entirety of the interface where having a single class instance or even a static class will ease development and/or allow for centralized modifications. In Chapter 13's case study, we already created an IntervalManager class to handle storing interval identifiers in order to prevent orphaned interval calls. It wouldn't make sense to have multiple instances of an IntervalManager. What additional classes could we create to centralize other tasks?

One great candidate for a manager class is a StyleManager. Multiple interfaces utilizing components will require different styles (colors for widget elements for different states), and having a centralized class to handle styles for all components will only speed later development as components are appropriated in new interfaces. In addition, if ever styles should be defined by values from a database, having the styles stored within a single class or instance will allow for smoother integration with the back-end.

For similar reasons, a SoundManager is a good candidate for a manager class as well. Many widgets can be enhanced by sounds (a button click would be the most obvious example), and instead of coding event listeners to play sounds for every instance, we can build into our components an interface with a global SoundManager. Within this SoundManager would be the definitions for all component event sounds and the Sound objects to create those sounds.

Additional managers that would fit nicely within a component framework for building interfaces in Flash are a FocusManager to handle tab navigation within views, perhaps a ContextMenuManager to handle creating right-click context-sensitive menus, and a ToolTipManager for creating pop-up tooltips for components. As applications grow and become more complex, a DragManager to handle drag-and-drop functionality and a DialogManager to handle the creation of pop-up dialog boxes would be great development aids. In each of these manager class examples, it's cleaner to have a centralized class with visual definitions, behavior, and functionality reside where individual components or timelines could call. This will keep the individual component code slimmer and more manageable.

Diagramming the classes

As always, it's helpful to map out classes before beginning to code. We've discussed UML diagrams and used them to describe classes in earlier chapters, so you should be starting to feel more comfortable taking in such a diagram and referring to it as a blueprint. Peruse Figure 15-1 for the classes we'll explore in this chapter and look back to it for reference as we begin to code.

15

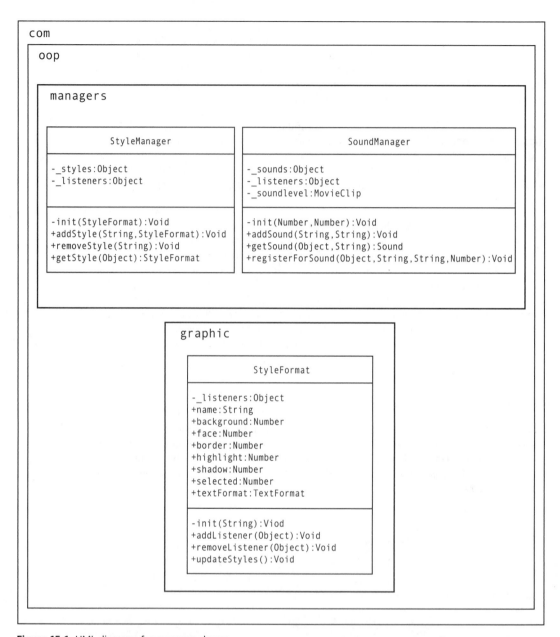

Figure 15-1. UML diagrams for manager classes

We'll continue to build within the package structure we created in Chapter 13's case study. As you can see in the diagram, we'll be adding two classes to the com.oop.managers package, StyleManager and SoundManager. The StyleManager itself will be managing multiple instances of style formats, so we create a StyleFormat class for this purpose within a new com.oop.graphic package.

Once you're comfortable with the structure proposed in the class diagram, fire up Flash and get ready for some framework coding!

Building managers

Individual component widgets are all well and good, but it's the centralized means of controlling the look and feel of those widgets that can make working with components a breeze (as well as speed up the creation of new and unique interfaces!). These next two manager classes and the StyleFormat class will go a long way in making our components reusable from interface to interface without making everything appear the same.

StyleFormat

The first class we'll create to manage the look of our components is StyleFormat. Instances of this class will hold values for a number of visual properties for components and will be used to assign a style to a component instance, a whole class, or the entire set of components.

To begin, create a new ActionScript file and save it into the com/oop/graphic class directory (you'll need to create the new graphic folder) as StyleFormat.as. Enter the following code into the Script pane:

```
dynamic class com.oop.graphic.StyleFormat {

  public var name:String;
  public var background:Number;
  public var face:Number;
  public var border:Number;
  public var highlight:Number;
  public var shadow:Number;
  public var selected:Number;
  public var textFormat:TextFormat;
  private var __listeners:Array = [];

  public function StyleFormat(name:String) {
    init(name);
  }

}
```

Notice the use of the dynamic modifier for the class. This will allow developers using the StyleFormat class to add new properties to the instances when needed without Flash throwing a compile error. The properties that we do define are the most common and will have default values assigned to them in the next step. As you may see, the constructor gets passed a string for the format name, which is in turn passed to the init() method. Let's add that next.

15

```
dynamic class com.oop.graphic.StyleFormat {

  public var name:String;
  public var background:Number;
  public var face:Number;
  public var border:Number;
  public var highlight:Number;
  public var shadow:Number;
  public var selected:Number;
  public var textFormat:TextFormat;
  private var __listeners:Array = [];

  function StyleFormat(name:String) {
    init(name);
  }

// PRIVATE
// _____

  private function init(nm:String):Void {
    name = nm;
    background = 0x454545;
    face = 0x999999;
    border = 0x000000;
    highlight = 0xFFFFFF;
    shadow = 0x666666;
    selected = 0xCCCCCC;
    textFormat = new TextFormat("Arial", 10);
  }

}
```

The bold code in the preceding code is the only private method for this class, an initialization method that assigns default gray color values to the properties. An instance of this class will default to these unless new values (and thus a new look) are assigned. The power of this class will come when component instances register themselves with a StyleFormat instance and update their graphical look to match its style values. This functionality is added with the public methods for the class, added next.

```
// PRIVATE
// _____

  private function init(nm:String):Void {
    name = nm;
    background = 0x454545;
    face = 0x999999;
    border = 0x000000;
    highlight = 0xFFFFFF;
    shadow = 0x666666;
```

```
        selected = 0xCCCCCC;
        textFormat = new TextFormat("Arial", 10);
    }

// PUBLIC
//  _____

    public function addListener(obj:Object):Void {
        obj.styleFormat.removeListener(obj);
        obj.styleFormat = this;
        for (var i in __listeners) {
          if (__listeners[i] == obj) return;
        }
        __listeners.push(obj);
    }

    public function removeListener(obj:Object):Void {
      var len:Number = __listeners.length;
      for (var i:Number = 0; i < len; i++) {
        if (__listeners[i] == obj) {
          __listeners.splice(i, 1);
          break;
        }
      }
      delete obj.styleFormat;
    }

    public function updateStyles():Void {
      for (var i:String in __listeners) {
        __listeners[i].updateStyles();
      }
    }

}
```

The public methods include an addListener() and removeListener() method, which simply add or remove a component instance to a list of listeners stored in a StyleFormat class instance. The methods also add or remove a new property, styleFormat, to the listener object. This property holds a reference to the StyleFormat instance.

updateStyles() is where the true power lies as all of the listeners can be easily updated with changes to the StyleFormat instance. Using this class alone, you could assign styles to any object that implements an updateStyles() method (Hmmm, does that sound like a good use for an interface, perhaps?) and control the look of multiple clips. However, it will require using addListener() for every single instance you want to assign a format to. That means if there are 20 buttons in your interface and you want them all to look the same, you'll need to add 20 addListener() calls. What would help immensely is a class that manages this process for all the components. Which brings us nicely to the next topic . . .

15

StyleManager

The StyleManager will handle the registering and format assignment for all components in our framework. The concept is that a single StyleManager instance will hold references to all the StyleFormat instances in a movie. Component instances that we create will automatically "check in" with the StyleManager to see which format they should apply. Let's step through the code to see how to create this.

Create a new ActionScript file in the com/oop/managers directory and name it StyleManager.as. Add the following code:

```
import com.oop.graphic.StyleFormat;

class com.oop.managers.StyleManager {

  private var __styles:Object = {};
  private var __listeners:Object = {};

  public function StyleManager(defaultFormat:StyleFormat) {
    if (_global.StyleManager) return;
    _global.StyleManager = this;
    init(defaultFormat);
  }

}
```

These lines set up the StyleManager class. There are two private properties, __styles and __listeners, to hold references to StyleFormat instances and components, respectively. Next, in the constructor method, we first check to ensure a StyleManager doesn't already exist. If it doesn't, we set a global property to hold a reference to this instance and send the default StyleFormat sent in the constructor to the init() method, which we'll add next.

This is an example of one way to use the Singleton pattern for a global manager class. With this class, there can only ever be one instance present and used. If the constructor is attempted a second time, it's exited out of. Placing the newly created instance in the _global object allows access to it from any timeline.

Additional ways a Singleton manager could be accomplished are having the class consist of static methods where no instance is created at all, or perhaps having a static method that returned an instance of the class, something like getManager(), which would only create an instance the first time the method was called and would return that same instance for any additional calls. All three of these methods have their pros and cons, but what we've done here is perhaps the easiest to implement for our examples.

```
import com.oop.graphic.StyleFormat;

class com.oop.managers.StyleManager {

  private var __styles:Object = {};
  private var __listeners:Object = {};

  public function StyleManager(defaultFormat:StyleFormat) {
    if (_global.StyleManager) return;
    _global.StyleManager = this;
    init(defaultFormat);
  }

// PRIVATE
// _____

  private function init(defaultFormat:StyleFormat):Void {
    if (defaultFormat == undefined)
      var defaultFormat:StyleFormat = new StyleFormat();
    addStyle("default", defaultFormat);
  }

// PUBLIC
// _____

  public function addStyle(name:String, format:StyleFormat):Void {
    __styles[name] = format;
    format.styleReference = name;
  }

  public function removeStyle(name:String):Void {
    delete __styles[name];
  }

}
```

init() calls the addStyle() method and passes the default StyleFormat, which is the format that will apply to all components unless others are assigned. If no default was passed in, a new StyleFormat instance is created for this purpose.

In the addStyle() method, the format passed in is placed in the __styles object property under the name of the format for easy reference. It also stores the reference as styleReference in the format itself so that the instance may know how it is stored in the StyleManager. removeStyle() simply deletes this value for the object.

15

The final two methods take care of assigning StyleFormat instances to individual components.

```
// PUBLIC
// _____

public function addStyle(name:String, format:StyleFormat):Void {
  __styles[name] = format;
}

public function removeStyle(name:String):Void {
  delete __styles[name];
}

public function style(obj:Object):Void {
  getStyle(obj).addListener(obj);
  obj.updateStyles();
}

public function getStyle(obj:Object):StyleFormat {
  if (obj.styleFormatName != undefined) {
    if (__styles[obj.styleFormatName] != undefined)
      return __styles[obj.styleFormatName];
  }
  var classes:Array = obj.classes;
  for (var i:Number = classes.length-1; i > -1; i--) {
    if (__styles[classes[i]] != undefined) {
      return __styles[classes[i]];
    }
  }
  return __styles["default"];
}
```

style() will be called by every component internally. style() in turn calls getStyle(), which determines which of the StyleFormat instances should be applied to the object passed in. The way this is determined is broken down into the following steps:

1. If the object has a specific styleFormatName value and that refers to a StyleFormat instance stored in the StyleManager, use that style.

2. Otherwise, if the object belongs to a class and that class has an associated StyleFormat instance stored in the StyleManager, use that style.

3. If neither of the previous cases is true, use the default StyleFormat instance.

When we build component classes in the next chapter, we'll plug them into the StyleManager and StyleFormat to better illustrate how the style hierarchy works. However, we can test out the concept without having to create full component classes. The next section demonstrates how.

Adding style

To try out the two classes explored in the last section, create a new movie and save it as `styleTest.fla`. Rename the default layer graphics and add a second layer above it named code, as shown in Figure 15-2.

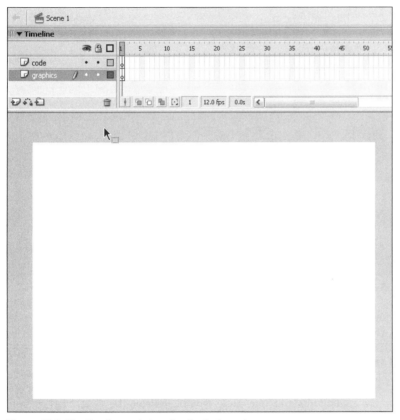

Figure 15-2. The timeline and stage for the test movie

15

On the graphics layer, draw a gray circle with a 4-point black stroke. Convert the fill to a movie clip symbol named fill and the stroke to a movie clip symbol named stroke (if you do it in that order, the stroke will remain above the fill, which is what we want for our example). Name the two instances on stage stroke and fill, respectively, as well. Now select both the stroke and fill instances together and convert them into a single movie clip symbol named circle ("square" just didn't make sense). Duplicate this instance on stage three more times and name the four instances c0, c1, c2, and c3, respectively, as shown in Figure 15-3.

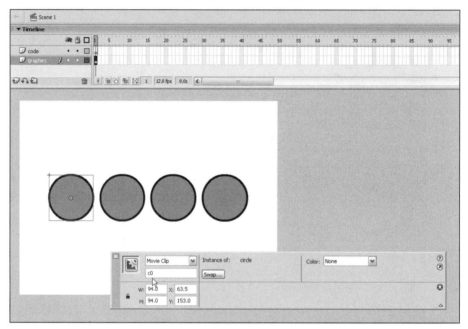

Figure 15-3. Four circle instances all in a row

We're now going to add code inside our symbol, a practice not normally encouraged due to the troubles that can arise from having code spread out into multiple timelines throughout a movie. However, there is nothing wrong with doing it when testing functionality as we're doing here. Next chapter, we'll implement what we're testing here inside external class files. But before we do that, we should ensure this small piece works!

Enter symbol editing mode for the circle symbol. Rename the default layer graphics and create a layer above this and name it code. On the code layer, add the following lines to your ActionScript editor:

```
StyleManager.style(this);

function updateStyles() {
  (new Color(fill)).setRGB(styleFormat.face);
  (new Color(stroke)).setRGB(styleFormat.border);
}
```

Remember how I mentioned that objects looking to use StyleFormat instances needed to implement an updateStyles() method? Well, here it is. In the method, we define how the internal movie clips will use the style properties to color the clips. The first line in the code block calls the style() method in the global StyleManager (if one exists) to assign the proper StyleFormat instance to this object.

Now return to the main timeline and select Keyframe 1 in the code layer. Add the following code to your ActionScript editor:

```
import com.oop.graphic.StyleFormat;

defaultFormat = new StyleFormat("defaultFormat");
defaultFormat.face = 0xFF0000;
defaultFormat.border = 0x0000FF;

new com.oop.managers.StyleManager(defaultFormat);
```

Here we create a new StyleFormat instance with a face and border value. We then instantiate a new StyleManager and pass this default format. Test your movie to see all four circles take this color format, as shown in Figure 15-4.

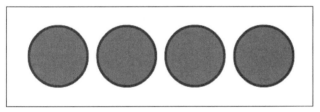

Figure 15-4. The circle instances with StyleFormats applied (though grayscale doesn't do it justice)

Imagine if these circles represented button instances. In a few simple lines of code, we could recolor every single instance. But what if we wished one instance to be colored differently? With the manager we've set up, we only need to add a few extra lines, and it's all taken care of for us behind the scenes.

```
import com.oop.graphic.StyleFormat;

defaultFormat = new StyleFormat("defaultFormat");
defaultFormat.face = 0xFF0000;
defaultFormat.border = 0x0000FF;

reverseFormat = new StyleFormat("reverseFormat");
reverseFormat.face = 0x000FF;
reverseFormat.border = 0xFF0000;

new com.oop.managers.StyleManager(defaultFormat);
StyleManager.addStyle("reversed", reverseFormat);
c2.styleFormatName = "reversed";
```

15

If you test the movie again you'll see that the c2 circle has now taken a format different from its companions, as shown in Figure 15-5, though all four are instances of the same symbol with the same code. What we've created is a centralized means of managing the styles for all aspects of an interface, which is a powerful demonstration of the usefulness of a global managing class.

Figure 15-5. Individual StyleFormats can easily be set.

SoundManager

With the appearance of widgets being controlled by a centralized manager class, our next step will be to create a similar manager for sounds in the interface. In much the same way that the StyleManager holds references to style formats, the SoundManager will hold references to Sound object instances. Individual objects can then request a sound to play for a certain event. Using this concept, we'll be able to limit the number of Sound object instances—if all buttons should produce the same click when pressed, why create multiple Sound object instances when one will suffice? All that's necessary is a way to manage this for an entire interface, which is where the SoundManager comes in.

Create a new ActionScript file and save it into the com/oop/managers directory as SoundManager.as. Enter the following code into the Script pane:

```
class com.oop.managers.SoundManager {

  private var __sounds:Object = {};
  private var __listeners:Object = {};
  private var __soundLevel:MovieClip;

  public function SoundManager(level:MovieClip, depth:Number) {
    if (_global.SoundManager) return;
    _global.SoundManager = this;
    init(level, depth);
  }

// PRIVATE
// _____

  private function init(level:MovieClip, depth:Number):Void {
    __soundLevel = level.createEmptyMovieClip("__soundLevel", depth);
  }

}
```

In the initial lines for the class, we create three private properties to hold references to the Sound object instances (_sounds) and the objects listening for sounds (_listeners) as well as a movie clip in which we'll create individual movie clips to hold the paths for the Sound object instances (more on the reasoning for that when we create these instances). In the constructor, we first check to see whether a SoundManager already exists, and if so exit. Otherwise, we send the level and depth values passed in the constructor to the init() method.

The init() method itself merely creates a new movie clip in the level and at the depth specified. Why do we need this? All will be explained with the next block of code!

```
// PRIVATE
// _____

  private function init(level:MovieClip, depth:Number):Void {
    _soundLevel = level.createEmptyMovieClip("_soundLevel", depth);
  }


// PUBLIC
// _____

  public function addSound(soundName:String, soundPath:String):Void {
    _sounds[soundName] = soundPath;
  }

  public function registerForSound(
    listener:Object,
    soundName:String,
    event:String,
    volume:Number
  ):Void {
    var depth:Number = _soundLevel.getNextHighestDepth();
    var clip:MovieClip =
    _soundLevel.createEmptyMovieClip("s" + depth, depth);
    var sound:Sound = new Sound(clip);
    if (volume == undefined) var volume:Number = 100;
    var path:String = _sounds[soundName];
    if (path.substr(0, 5) == "file:") {
      sound.loadSound(path.substr(5));
    } else {
      sound.attachSound(path);
    }
    sound.setVolume(volume);
    if (_listeners[listener] == undefined) _listeners[listener] = {};
    _listeners[listener][event] = sound;
  }

}
```

15

The addSound() method is what will be used to add sounds to the list to be managed. This simply stores the name of the path to the sound (we'll make it so you can use a sound in the library or in an external MP3 file) by the name used to reference the sound.

registerSound() is the workhorse of this class. For arguments it takes the name of the object listening for the sound, the name of the sound to receive, the event for which to receive the sound, and the volume at which the sound should be played. A new movie clip is then created in the __soundLevel movie clip at the next highest depth. The clip is used as the target for the sound. This allows us to have volume control for every single sound that is registered.

Next in the method, if no volume has been passed in, the volume for this sound is saved at 100. The following conditional block checks to see whether the path passed in begins with "file:", which will indicate the sound is located in an external file. If so, loadSound() is called. Otherwise, attachSound() attaches the sound from the movie's library.

The last lines in the method check to see whether the listener has already been added to the __listeners object to hear a sound for another event. If this is the first sound for the listener, a new object is created for the listener in the __listeners array, then the Sound object instance is saved into that new object to be referenced by the event name. This will allow a single object to register for sounds for different events, such as both rollOver and press events.

One final bit of code left before we can test our new manager. Add the following lines to the class between the registerForSOund method and closing class brace:

```
public function getSound(listener:Object, event:String):Sound {
  if (__listeners[listener] != undefined) {
    if (__listeners[listener][event] != undefined)
      return __listeners[listener][event];
  }
  var classes:Array = listener.classes;
  var clss:String;
  for (var i:Number = classes.length-1; i > -1; i--) {
    clss = classes[i];
    if (__listeners[clss] != undefined) {
      if (__listeners[clss][event] != undefined)
        return __listeners[clss][event];
    }
  }
  return;
}
```

This last method is what will be called by all of the object instances (such as components) when they wish to play a sound. The method will be sent a reference to the listener as well as the event for the sound. Using these parameters, and in a similar way to how the StyleManager returned style formats to objects, the SoundManager first checks to see whether there is a sound for that event specifically stored for the instance calling, and if so returns the Sound object instance. If, however, no sound exists for that listener and that event, the listener's classes are checked to see whether there are sounds registered for those particular classes. In this way, we can assign a single sound to all button clicks, all window pop-ups, all check box toggles, etc. Let's see how that works by returning to our earlier test file.

Sounding off

Open `styleTest.fla` and resave it as `soundTest.fla`. Drop the sound file CLICK2.mp3 into the same directory. Next, within the Flash file, import the sound file CLICK8.mp3 into the library. Right-click it in the library and choose to export it for ActionScript as CLICK8.mp3 as well, as shown in Figure 15-6.

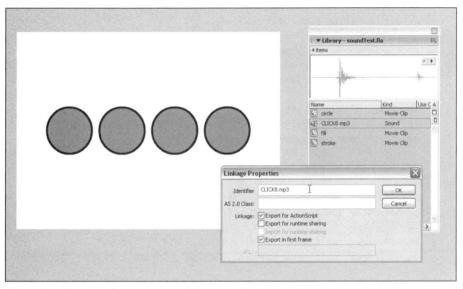

Figure 15-6. Exporting the sound symbol from the Library

Now enter symbol editing mode for the circle symbol and add the following bold lines to the code layer:

```
classes = ["Button"];
StyleManager.style(this);

function updateStyles() {
  (new Color(fill)).setRGB(styleFormat.face);
  (new Color(stroke)).setRGB(styleFormat.border);
}

function onPress() {
  SoundManager.getSound(this, "press").start();
}
```

15

Nothing too extreme here. We've simply created a new array to hold the names of the classes for this symbol (this will be built into the components we make and is used here to simulate it). Next, we add an onPress() handler to give the symbol button events. All we do in the handler is ask the global SoundManager for the relevant sound for this object's press event.

Now let's jump back to the main timeline to instantiate our new SoundManager. Add the bold lines to the code layer on the main timeline:

```
import com.oop.graphic.StyleFormat;

defaultFormat = new StyleFormat("defaultFormat");
defaultFormat.face = 0xFF0000;
defaultFormat.border = 0x0000FF;

reverseFormat = new StyleFormat("reverseFormat");
reverseFormat.face = 0x0000FF;
reverseFormat.border = 0xFF0000;

new com.oop.managers.StyleManager(defaultFormat);
StyleManager.addStyle("reversed", reverseFormat);
c2.styleFormatName = "reversed";

new com.oop.managers.SoundManager(_level0, 16001);

SoundManager.addSound("kiss", "file:CLICK2.mp3");
SoundManager.addSound("click", "CLICK8.mp3");

SoundManager.registerForSound("Button", "kiss", "press", 50);
SoundManager.registerForSound(c2, "click", "press", 80);
```

After creating the SoundManager instance (and telling it to create its sound holder movie clip at depth 16001 on _level0) we add two sounds, "kiss" found in an external file and "click" found in the library. We then register the "kiss" sound to be played for all "Button" instances when they call with a "press" event. However, for the c2 movie clip, we register the "click" sound to be played on the "press" event. Test your movie out to see, or rather hear, the result. Let's hear it for the SoundManager!

> *It's important to note that by explicitly setting the SoundManager's depth to 16001, any subsequent calls to getNextHighestDepth() for _level0 will result in depths above this, despite the fact that no clips are currently at depths 0 to 16000. If you use getNextHighestDepth() frequently, you would perhaps want to put the SoundManager at a lower depth or consider not having movie clips placed directly on the _root timeline. For instance, you could create a single movie clip on the _root to act as a graphic container and add all subsequent clips to that, allowing use of getNextHighestDepth() without consideration of where the SoundManager was placed.*

Summary

I hope that this chapter has demonstrated how useful a centralized manager class can be when handling multiple movie clips. This will become even more apparent as we build actual drag-and-drop components and use them in an interface. By having the functionality common to all widgets stored within and referenced in a single class, we have much more control of the overall look and feel of an interface. Altering that functionality or changing an interface's appearance then becomes a cinch, as updating the manager instance propagates changes throughout the entire component set.

What's next?

This chapter explored manager classes for a Flash component framework. The next chapter examines how to build visual components to handle standard UI functionality, leveraging the work done here on the manager classes. Unlike the classes created in this chapter, these new components will exist in the Library and plug into the Components and Properties panels in the IDE, yet still take advantage of the framework we have begun in this chapter. To paraphrase Al Jolson, you ain't seen nothin' yet!

15

16 UI WIDGETS

When it comes to a user interface, the most obvious components are the visual *widgets* that allow the user to interact with the application. These include, to name but a few in their simplest form, buttons, sliders, and input fields. Individually, each can be created rather easily and quickly using the built-in tools in Flash, but how do you create a set of these widgets that can seamlessly work within and integrate into the architecture of an entire application? To do this requires some OOP forethought and the creation of classes that standardize how widgets may be interacted with, through inheritance and polymorphism.

In this chapter, I'll show you what it takes to lay down the foundation for a framework containing UI widgets and how OOP can help create a structure that allows for common code interfaces with these widgets. Together, we'll build upon the work begun in the previous chapters with our event broadcasters and Singleton manager classes to start a component library that could be used for a multitude of applications. In doing this, you'll learn the process of creating custom components in Flash and hooking into the Component Inspector.

> It should be noted once more that there already exists a number of components and component frameworks, including the component framework that comes bundled with Flash. We are building from the ground up instead of using a prebuilt set for a number of reasons. First, it'll allow you to more easily go in and add or modify the code to do exactly what you need without having to wade through others' code to see what is possible. Second, you can ensure the functionality is exactly what you need in your own projects and optimize the code for that purpose. For instance, some find the components bundled with Flash difficult to reskin, and if this is something you feel you'll need to do often, it makes good sense to develop a framework that allows you to do so more easily. Third, if bugs arise, it's far easier to go in and fix your own code than that of others, where changing functionality might have more of a ripple effect than you may suspect. Finally, this is a book about learning and using OOP in your own Flash projects. There is no better way to learn than to get in and code the object-oriented interaction from scratch.

Diagramming the classes

As always, we'll begin by mapping out the classes we'll be building before we start in on the code. This gives us an idea of what is necessary, brings to light initial problems we must address, and gives us a clear goal for what we are trying to accomplish. A few extra moments at the start will save a world of frustration later down the line!

UIObject

Let's consider some of the properties and methods that will be important for all visual UI elements. We can place this common functionality into a super class from which all of our widgets will inherit, UIObject.

The purpose is, at this phase, not to envision every possible method and property that would ever be needed and lock it down, but to come up with a plan on how to approach coding a base class for all UI widgets. Our goal here is to break down the problem into its smallest blocks and solve those blocks. We want to code a class that can be used for visual UI widgets, so what issues will be common to all visual user interaction elements?

Obviously, position and scale come near the top of the list. For position, the _x and _y properties of MovieClip (from which all visual elements, and thus our super class, will inherit) will work, but we can add the useful properties top, left, right, and bottom, which will make easier the placement of other elements in relation to a widget. In addition, we can take advantage of the new Point object for setting a widget's position in a single property, perhaps named position. This would allow for one element to be placed at the coordinates of another by using elementA.position = elementB.position. As for scale, unfortunately the built-in _xscale, _yscale, _width, and _height properties can be problematic for resizing since they can cause distortion and don't allow for reflow of internal graphics in a widget. We'll overcome this by giving each widget a setSize() method to be used for resizing and then providing width and height properties for retrieving size information. It would also be a good idea to include initialWidth and initialHeight properties to allow a component to be sized correctly upon initialization when being attached without requiring an additional setSize() call (more on this when we actually implement it).

That takes care of positioning and scale. What other useful methods and properties might apply to all UI widgets? Since what we are laying the foundation for here are more complex components and applications, it follows that a widget will often have to attach subcomponents to its timeline (e.g., a text input field may attach a scrollbar, which in itself is made up of multiple buttons). It will quickly become important to have a good way to attach, remove, and manage these internal components. For this purpose, a children array property would come in handy, which would hold references to all movie clips that were created or attached. This array could be populated by using two special methods: createObject(), which takes care of attaching a movie clip and pushing it into the children array, and createClassObject(), which would create an instance of a specific class and push it into the children array. We could also add a createEmptyObject(), which would act as createEmptyMovieClip() does, but would instead create an empty UIObject instance and push it into the children array. The counter to these would be removeChild(), and a remove() method could go through and remove all internal children, as well as remove the component itself, which would make for good housekeeping. Finally, getChild() would be handy in order to retrieve any child of a component without having to access the component's timeline.

We'll eventually need a way for our widgets to broadcast events, since the whole point is responding to user interaction. The Broadcaster created in the Chapter 13 case study and used in the last chapter as well will do nicely. UIObject can create a Broadcaster instance and use that to dispatch all events, implementing the IEventDispatcher interface with addEventListener(), removeEventListener(), and dispatchEvent() all going through the internal Broadcaster instance. An alternative would be to have Broadcaster serve as the super class of UIObject, but that would require Broadcaster to inherit from MovieClip, which isn't ideal since there will be many event broadcasting classes that don't need the MovieClip properties and methods (as you saw with the StyleManager and SoundManager last chapter).

The final methods that will be useful at the base level of our component architecture are getEnabled() and setEnabled(). The built-in enabled property in itself will enable and disable a component, but using these new methods will allow us to program visual feedback when a widget is disabled.

Of course, additional properties and methods will come to light as we program (incorporating styles immediately comes to mind as something that will need addressing), and this class may continue to grow as it's used and built upon. The functionality we've addressed here is a good starting place, though, so let's start with our diagram, shown in Figure 16-1.

Figure 16-1. The class diagram for UIObject

Block

Once our base class, UIObject, is created, we can easily extend it to other classes. The first and most useful class will be the simplest graphic form used by all other widgets. We can call this Block, and it'll serve as the graphic aspect of all other components. For instance, a button would attach a single Block instance to serve as its graphic. A slider might attach a Block instance for its slider well and another for its slider button. As long as we program a way for a Block instance to take different skins, it could be used anywhere a graphic is required. Putting all the graphic-attaching code into a single class will make managing styles and skins so much easier when we come to it, since it'll all be handled within a single class.

So what methods might Block have in addition to those of UIObject? attachGraphics() is a fine candidate, since that is Block's main purpose. This method will attach another movie clip to serve as the Block's skin, making reskinning possible and easy to implement. Hand-in-hand with this will be the property __blockGraphic, which will be the linkage identifier for the movie clip to be attached as a skin. Finally, it would help if Block could handle multiple states, like _Up, _Down, and _Over. Otherwise, widgets like buttons would require multiple Block instances for different states. It would be better to have one Block instance that could change its appearance based on its state. Figure 16-2 shows what our diagram of this would look like.

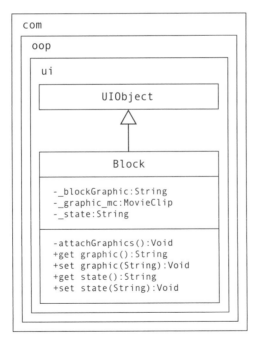

Figure 16-2. The class diagram for Block

Not too bad, is it? With UIObject taking on so much useful functionality, child classes become much more easy to write.

SimpleButton

The final class we'll be looking at for our component foundation is for the simplest user interaction widget, the button. That said, a button can actually be fairly complex, with toggling capability and label and icon placement, so we'll create a simpler button named SimpleButton that will handle changing visual states based on user interaction and broadcasting events when this interactivity occurs. A Button class can handle the bells and whistles such as toggling, labels, and icons.

For SimpleButton, the actual button events offButton(), overButton(), pressButton(), and releaseButton() will be the most important methods. Add to that attachGraphics(), which will attach a Block instance for the button's graphic, and the property __blockGraphic, which will hold the name of the identifier used for the button's skin. We also have two Boolean properties to keep track of certain button states, __overButton and __pressedButton. Since SimpleButton will have states and a single graphic, we could have it inherit from Block, but it was a personal choice to have Block act as the single class that attaches skins, and having SimpleButton inherit from that would cause some muddiness in this clear intention.

The diagram is shown in Figure 16-3.

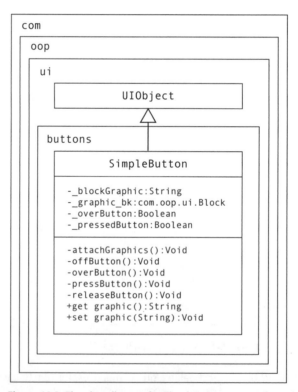

Figure 16-3. The class diagram for SimpleButton

Making the foundation

With all the initial classes diagrammed, we can now get into the ActionScript needed to code our component foundation. The first thing we need to do to our class library created in the previous chapters is add the appropriate directories to our file system. Navigate to your classes directory, first created in Chapter 13, and add a new folder named com/oop/ui. Inside ui, add the folder buttons. The UIObject and Block classes will be in the com.oop.ui package and SimpleButton will be in com.oop.ui.buttons. The classes directory structure should look like Figure 16-4.

Figure 16-4.
The classes directory for the component framework

Open Flash, create a new ActionScript file named UIObject.as, and save it into the com/oop/ui directory. Add the following code, which creates the blueprint of our base class:

```
import com.oop.core.IEventDispatcher;

class com.oop.ui.UIObject extends MovieClip
➥ implements IEventDispatcher {

  function UIObject() {
    init();
  }

// PRIVATE
// _____

  private function init():Void {}

// PUBLIC
// _____

  public function dispatchEvent(evnt:String, params:Object):Void {}

  public function addEventListener(
    evnt:String,
    lstnr:Object,
    mappedTo:String
  ):Boolean {}

  public function removeEventListener(
    evnt:String,
    lstnr:Object
  ):Boolean {}
```

285

As you can see from the class definition, the UIObject will inherit from the MovieClip class, which means it'll have all of the properties and methods belonging to MovieClip. It also means that it'll need to be connected with a symbol in the Library in order to be instantiated. We'll look at this more closely when we get to Block.

Also note that UIObject implements the IEventDispatcher interface, and you'll see at the bottom of the preceding code block that the three methods required by the interface are included (though they don't yet do anything). The only other piece is the constructor, which calls a private init() method.

Now, before we get into the initialization, let's declare the member properties for the UIObject. Once again, we'll use the double underscore for private properties.

```
import com.oop.core.IEventDispatcher;
import com.oop.core.Broadcaster;

class com.oop.ui.UIObject extends MovieClip
➡ implements IEventDispatcher {

  private var __enabled:Boolean;
  private var __width:Number;
  private var __height:Number;
  private var __initialWidth:Number;
  private var __initialHeight:Number;
  private var __children:Array;
  private var __dispatcher:Broadcaster;

  function UIObject() {
    init();
  }
```

At the top before the constructor we declare and type all of the properties we diagrammed earlier. With the properties declared, we can now begin the initialization methods for the class. Add the following lines to the init() method:

```
private function init():Void {
  __children = [];
  __dispatcher = new Broadcaster();
  __enabled = true;
  tabEnabled = false;
  focusEnabled = false;
  tabChildren = true;
  _focusrect = false;
  useHandCursor = false;
  __width = __initialWidth || _width;
  __height = __initialHeight || _height;
  _xscale = _yscale = 100;
}
```

Here we initialize the __children array, create a new Broadcaster instance to handle the event dispatching, and set the __enabled property to true. The remaining lines set default values for a number of built-in properties for movie clips. The settings for tab and focus properties prevent automatic focusing and tabbing to UIObject instances. Ideally, we would want control over how our applications are navigated, and so we are preventing the default yellow bounding box being drawn about a widget. As this framework is developed further, a FocusManager would be a necessary addition to handle this now-disabled functionality.

The last three lines of the function set the __width and __height properties based on either the __initialWidth and __initialHeight passed in, or, if these values are undefined, the _width and _height of the movie clip itself. In these two lines, the || (OR) operator is used as a shortcut to set the property on the left with the first variable on the right that has a defined value. The way that this works, in the instance of the first line, is that __initialWidth || _width will evaluate to __initialWidth if that is defined, OR _width if it isn't. This value will then be assigned to __width. After these values are set, we set the _xscale and _yscale of our component to 100% to prevent any distortion. This is necessary for clips that are placed and resized on the stage in the IDE. After recording the __width and __height that the clip has been sized to, we can set its scaling back to 100%.

The next step is to fill in the event dispatching methods. Mostly these will simply pass on the arguments to the __dispatcher we created in the init() method.

```
public function dispatchEvent(evnt:String, params:Object):Void {
  var info:Object = params || {};
  info.target = this;
  __dispatcher.dispatchEvent(evnt, info);
}

public function addEventListener(
  evnt:String,
  lstnr:Object,
  mappedTo:String
):Boolean {
  return __dispatcher.addEventListener(evnt, lstnr, mappedTo);
}

public function removeEventListener(
  evnt:String,
  lstnr:Object
):Boolean {
  return __dispatcher.removeEventListener(evnt, lstnr);
}
```

As you can see, the addEventListener() and removeEventListener() methods merely need to pass on their arguments to the dispatcher. The dispatchEvent() does the same, but after first adding a target property to the params object. Objects subscribing to hear events should be informed which object is firing the event, and in this case we'll put

UIObject instances into a target property of the params object. The first line in dispatchEvent is a shortcut that assigns the params argument to info if it doesn't equal null/undefined, in which case it assigns a new Object instance.

Moving on through our class, the next methods that were listed in our diagram are fairly straightforward in implementation.

```
public function setEnabled(bool:Boolean):Void {
  __enabled = enabled = bool;
}

public function getEnabled():Boolean {
  return __enabled;
}

public function setSize(w:Number, h:Number):Void {
  __width = w;
  __height = h;
  _xscale = _yscale = 100;
  dispatchEvent("resize");
}

public function get width():Number {
  return __width;
}

public function get height():Number {
  return __height;
}
```

getEnabled() and setEnabled() merely need to get and set the __enabled (and built-in enabled) property. Classes that inherit from UIObject will perhaps redraw when disabled or enabled, but the UIObject itself doesn't need to do anything since it doesn't contain any visual elements.

The setSize() method sets the private __width and __height properties, as well as ensures the scaling of the component remains 100% (preventing distortion if you resize the component in the IDE). Again, it'll be up to the classes that inherit from UIObject to redraw themselves when setSize() is called. You'll see this implemented in both Block and SimpleButton. Notice that we also dispatch an event here since it's an event that other objects might need to be aware of for repositioning, for example.

The final two methods are getter methods that return the current __width and __height values. There are no corresponding setter methods, as the setSize() takes care of both properties in a single call. Otherwise, if you required each property be set individually, there is the possibility that a component would have to redraw itself twice and waste processes.

Speaking of wasted processes, we include a few additional properties to prevent just that, __initialWidth and __initialHeight. Without these properties, when a component is attached to the stage through code, it first sizes itself based on its default size in the Library, then must be resized through the setSize() method. This is fine with smaller components, but when a lot of calculations exist in setSize(), which perhaps calls other methods, this can mean a lot of unnecessary work for Flash. These properties will allow components to be attached with the desired size passed in the initObj parameter of attachMovie(). No second resizing will then be required, and we'll have saved Flash some cycles. Here are those methods, which are straight setters:

```
public function set initialWidth(n:Number):Void {
   __initialWidth = n;
}

public function set initialHeight(n:Number):Void {
   __initialHeight = n;
}
```

The next methods all correspond to the positioning of the component.

```
public function get position():Point {
  return new Point(_x, _y);
}

public function set position(pos:Point):Void {
  _x = pos.x;
  _y = pos.y;
}

public function get top():Number {
  return _y;
}

public function get bottom():Number {
  return _y + __height;
}

public function get right():Number {
  return _x + __width;
}

public function get left():Number {
  return _x;
}
```

Have a look through these positioning methods. Nothing too surprising here. The first two use the new Point object, which holds an x and y property, conveniently. For this to work, you'll either need to list the full package or import the class at the top of the code:

```
import flash.geom.Point;
```

I haven't included corresponding setter methods for left, top, right, and bottom, as I feel having a single coordinate position to set is simpler in the long run. Feel free to add these if you feel they would be useful.

The final methods that we mapped out in the diagram are those to handle the adding, removing, and managing of child clips for a component. The first set we'll look at are those for adding child objects.

```
public function createObject(
  linkageID:String,
  name:String,
  depth:Number,
  initObj:Object
):MovieClip {
  if (depth == null) var depth:Number = getNextHighestDepth();
  var p:MovieClip = attachMovie(linkageID, name, depth, initObj);
  __children.push(p);
  return p;
}

public function createClassObject(
  theClass:Function,
  name:String,
  depth:Number,
  initObj:Object
):UIObject {
  var linkageID:String = "empty class";
  Object.registerClass(linkageID, theClass);
  var p:UIObject = UIObject(
    createObject(linkageID, name, depth, initObj)
  );
  return p;
}

public function createEmptyObject(
  name:String,
  depth:Number
):UIObject {
  return createClassObject(UIObject, name, depth);
}
```

createObject() is the heart of these three methods. This simply uses MovieClip's built-in attachMovie() method, first grabbing the next depth if no depth is defined. It then pushes the new movie clip instance into the __children array.

createClassObject() offers a little more complexity, as it allows you to instantiate a specific class that inherits from UIObject. This is a powerful method because it provides the means to create many UI widgets without requiring the individual symbols in the Library. Instead, all it requires is a single symbol in the Library exported with the unique identifier empty class. How is this done? By using Object.registerClass(), we can associate any class with a certain symbol in the Library. empty class has been hard coded as that symbol. When this method is called, it associates the specified class with the "empty class" symbol in the Library, then calls createObject(), which attaches the symbol. We cast the returned movie clip instance as a UIObject and return it out of the function.

The last method listed is createEmptyObject(), which acts as a replacement for createEmptyMovieClip(). This attaches an empty clip as well, but one that is a UIObject and not just a MovieClip, giving us the additional UIObject properties and methods.

With all the attaching methods added, we can look to the counterparts that remove clips.

```
public function remove():Void {
  var children:Number = __children.length;
  var child:MovieClip;
  for (var i:Number = children-1; i > -1; i--) {
    child = __children[i];
    if (!UIObject(child)) {
      child.removeMovieClip();
      child.unloadMovie();
    } else {
      child.remove();
    }
  }
  _parent.removeChild(this);
  this.removeMovieClip();
  this.unloadMovie();
}

public function removeChild(child:MovieClip):Boolean {
  var children:Number = __children.length;
  for (var i:Number = 0; i < children; i++) {
    if (child == __children[i]) {
      __children.splice(i, 1);
      return true;
    }
  }
  return false;
}
```

remove() can be called in the place of removeMovieClip() and relied upon to do better cleanup after a movie clip has left the building, so to speak. As you can see, it runs through the __children array and, in the case of MovieClip instances, simply removes them and unloads them from memory, and in the case of UIObjects calls the child's own remove() method (which will in turn call its children's remove() methods, etc., working its way down through nested clips). The method then calls the removeChild() method on the parent timeline and removes and unloads the clip. removeChild() goes through the __children array and removes the reference from the array. For actually removing the clip, the remove() method should instead be called.

The only method we listed in the diagram earlier that we haven't yet added is getChild(), which would return a reference to the child object. This is easily accomplished with the following code:

```
public function getChild(name:String):MovieClip {
  return this[name];
}
```

Why provide this method at all instead of simply requiring direct access of a movie clip through the component's timeline? Well, right now there is nothing stopping the direct access (e.g., componentInstance.childObject), but encapsulating this functionality within this method would allow us at a later point, if it became necessary, to use different names internally for the attached movie clips without having to change any code that was accessing those clips externally. Perhaps an ID will have to be appended to all clips, or we might want to allow for case insensitivity. Thinking ahead to these situations will save us many a headache later on, and so in general we would want to avoid in our classes having any properties (including attached movie clips) directly accessed by external objects.

Since the UIObject code was pieced together as we went along, be sure to take a look at the finished class available in this chapter's download files and check it against your own code.

Basic building block

The previous section had plenty of code, but we as of yet haven't been able to see any result. This is because we don't have any visual component for the UIObject, which only serves as a super class for all the visual widgets, but doesn't have any visual elements itself (which makes sense, seeing as how all visual elements will require different graphic aspects). In this section we'll look at Block, which will serve as the graphic building block for all widgets. With one class handling skins, making components skinnable will be easier later on (in this chapter!). The best part about this point onwards is that the majority of our code is common and so housed in the UIObject class. Block, by comparison, will be around a quarter of the number of lines. That's the beauty of inheritance!

We'll start out with the class declaration and the constructor. We'll include declaring the properties we know about and setting up the init() method, which we know is called in the super class's constructor.

```
import com.oop.ui.UIObject;

class com.oop.ui.Block extends UIObject {

  private var __graphic_mc:MovieClip;
  private var __blockGraphic:String;
  private var __state:String;

  function Block() {}
```

```
// PRIVATE
// _____

  private function init():Void {
    super.init();
    attachGraphics();
  }

  private function attachGraphics():Void {}

// PUBLIC
// _____

}
```

There's nothing too surprising yet. We start with the class declaration which, as you can see, has Block inheriting from UIObject. Several properties are then declared. __graphic_mc will be the movie clip symbol attached as a skin. We'll need some way to give Block the linkage identifier for that symbol, and for this we have __blockGraphic. Finally, to allow a Block instance to have multiple states, __state will keep track of the current state.

We've already called attachGraphics(), which will attach the symbol to the timeline of the component, so we'll fill that in next.

```
private function attachGraphics():Void {
  var initObj:Object =
    {
    width:__width,
    height:__height,
    state:__state,
    component:this
    };
  createObject(__blockGraphic, "__graphic_mc", 0, initObj);
}
```

Here we use the createObject() method we defined in UIObject to attach a movie clip symbol from the Library to the component's timeline. The linkage identifier is found in the __blockGraphic property. Note that we pass to the attached clip the width, height, state, and a reference to the component itself. This can be used by the attached symbol to size and draw itself, which we'll look at when we go about skinning the component.

Would you believe that's already half of the necessary code for our Block class? In fact, let's just look at the rest of it all in one batch.

```
public function setSize(w:Number, h:Number):Void {
  super.setSize(w, h);
  __graphic_mc.setSize(__width, __height);
}
```

```
public function get graphic():String {
  return __blockGraphic;
}

public function set graphic(str:String):Void {
  __blockGraphic = str;
  attachGraphics();
}

public function get state():String {
  return __state;
}

public function set state(s:String):Void {
  __state = s;
  __graphic_mc.changeState(__state);
}
```

The setSize() method first calls the super class's setSize(), which sets the __width and __height properties, then calls the setSize() method on the attached graphic (so it's important to note that an attached skin needs a setSize() method).

The remaining methods are all getter/setters for the __graphic and __state properties. Setting _graphic calls attachGraphics() once again to replace the current __graphic_mc with a new one. Setting __state calls changeState() on the attached clip (so we see we need this method to be included in an attached skin as well).

That's the class, folks! It's nice seeing that once you have laid the foundation properly and then take advantage of inheritance, creating new classes really can be quick and painless. Here we've created a new graphic class that can be used within any visual component, and we kept it around 50 lines of code (with some comments and lots of spaces!). So let's test it out.

Building a component

Create a new Flash document named Block_test.fla. Create a new movie clip symbol named Block and export it for ActionScript as Block as well. The important bit is associating a class with this symbol, and you do that in the AS 2.0 class text field. Enter the value com.oop.ui.Block, since we want any instance of this symbol to be an instance of Block. Your dialog box should look like Figure 16-5.

Once you click OK to create the symbol, you'll be placed in symbol editing mode for the Block symbol. In Frame 1 of its default layer, draw a 25×25 pixel gray rectangle with no stroke, placing its top-left corner on the symbol's registration point. This will be the bounding box for our symbol, which we can use to size the component when we place it on the stage (if it had no internal graphics, we could not give it a width and height in the IDE). In fact, make the rectangle into a movie clip symbol named bounding box and name the instance on stage boundingBox_mc. The resulting timeline should look like Figure 16-6.

Figure 16-5. Associating a class with a symbol

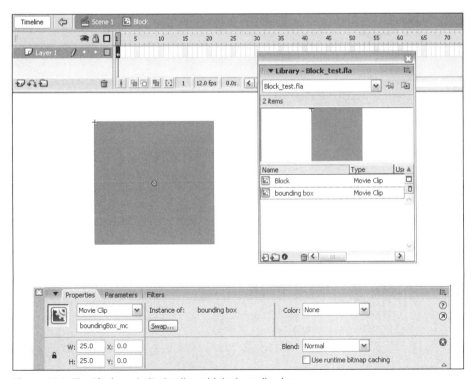

Figure 16-6. The Block symbol's timeline with its bounding box

Return to the main timeline and drag three instances of Block from the Library onto the stage. Size each of them to a different dimension. If you test your movie now, you should see three gray rectangles, each sized at 100%, as shown in Figure 16-7. We have to do a few things more to our Block and UIObject first before they display their usefulness.

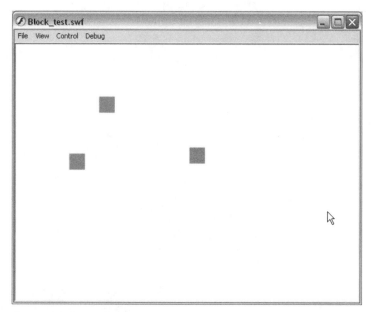

Figure 16-7. Three Block instances at runtime

First, we need to allow for a way to specify a skin to be loaded for a Block instance. We can do this by placing special metatags in our class file that plug into the Component Inspector in Flash. Head back to the Block.as file and enter the following bold lines:

```
[Inspectable(type="String", defaultValue="")]
public function set graphic(str:String):Void {
  __blockGraphic = str;
  attachGraphics();
}

public function get state():String {
  return __state;
}

[Inspectable(type="String", defaultValue="")]
public function set state(s:String):Void {
  __state = s;
  __graphic_mc.changeState(__state);
}
```

By placing these tags before our setter functions, we tell Flash to display these properties in the IDE (placing them before the getters works just as well, but logically it makes more sense to me to group these with setter functions, since that is their purpose as well). Within the brackets and Inspectable keyword, we define the parameters type as a String and set its default value to be an empty string. In addition to String, you could specify the type as Number, Boolean, Object, or Array.

Now go back to Block_test.fla and right-click the Block symbol in the Library. Select Component Definition and in the AS 2.0 Class field enter com.oop.ui.Block. Also be sure to select the Display in Components panel option at the bottom of the dialog box (enter a tooltip if you desire, but it's not necessary). The dialog box should look like Figure 16-8.

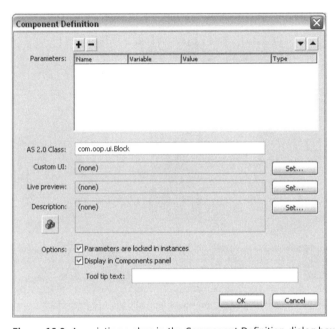

Figure 16-8. Associating a class in the Component Definition dialog box

Click OK to exit the dialog box, and you'll notice that the symbol in the Library now has a new icon to denote that it is a component. What does that mean? Select one of the Block instances you already placed on stage and open the Component Inspector (*ALT+F7*) and you'll see that graphic and state are now configurable options, as shown in Figure 16-9.

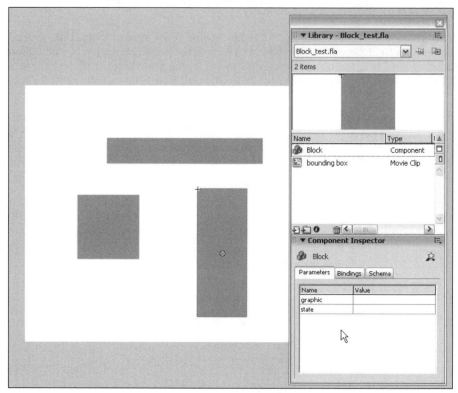

Figure 16-9. The Block symbol with a component icon and an instance selected with its configurable properties shown in the Component Inspector

For all of the Block instances, set the graphic property to circleSkin. Now create a new movie clip symbol named and exported for ActionScript as circleSkin. Draw a 50×50 red circle with the top left of its bounding box at the symbol's registration point. Convert this circle into a movie clip symbol named circle with its registration at the top-left corner. Name the instance inside circleSkin circle_mc, as shown in Figure 16-10.

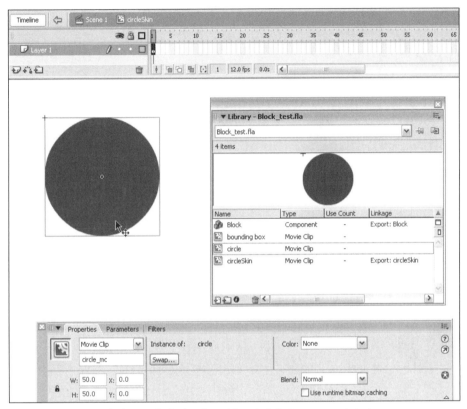

Figure 16-10. The circleSkin symbol's timeline with a circle instance named circle_mc

Test your movie and you'll see that the circle has been attached for all clips, but there are two issues, as is obvious from Figure 16-11. First, the bounding box for Block is still visible despite the new skin, and second, the circles don't resize to match the dimensions of the Block instances. Let's look at these problems in order of complexity.

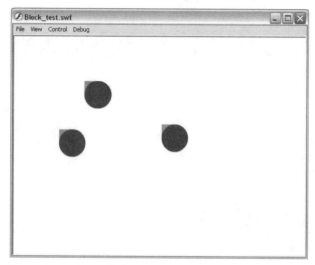

Figure 16-11. The circleSkin is attached to the Block instances, with undesirable results

We need the bounding box in Block in order to size the component correctly in the IDE, but once the component is initialized and the _width and _height are stored, we no longer need the box. Return to UIObject.as and add a new property with the other property declarations.

```
class com.oop.ui.UIObject extends MovieClip implements IEventDispatcher
{

    private var boundingBox_mc:MovieClip;
    private var __enabled:Boolean;
    private var __width:Number;
```

At the end of the init() function, once the dimensions of the clip have been stored, we can remove the bounding box.

```
    private function init():Void {
        __children = [];
        __dispatcher = new Broadcaster();
        __enabled = true;
        tabEnabled = false;
        focusEnabled = false;
        tabChildren = true;
        _focusrect = false;
```

```
        useHandCursor = false;
        __width = __initialWidth || _width;
        __height = __initialHeight || _height;
        _xscale = _yscale = 100;
        boundingBox_mc.unloadMovie();
    }
```

Test your movie again and you'll see the bounding boxes have been removed.

As for the sizing of the skin, we saw that in Block.as, we call a setSize() and a changeState() method in the attached skin. We can use the former to resize any internal graphics. This can be as complex or as simple as a skin requires. For our purposes here, we can simply set the height and width of the skin to match the Block instance's own __width and __height.

Enter symbol editing mode for circleSkin and create a new layer named code. On this layer, still in the first and only frame, enter the following script:

```
setSize(width, height);

function setSize(w:Number, h:Number):Void {
    circle_mc._width = w;
    circle_mc._height = h;
}
```

The setSize() function receives a width and height, and we use those to size the circle_mc movie clip. When the skin is attached, though, the setSize() isn't called (this only occurs when the Block's setSize() method is called at runtime), so we call it here so it'll run upon initialization. If you test your movie now, you might be surprised by the result, shown in Figure 16-12.

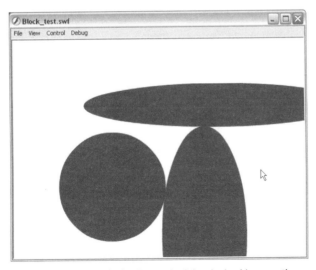

Figure 16-12. The circleSkin is attached, but is sized incorrectly.

Although resizing is definitely occurring, the sizes of the circles are way off. The reason for this lies in the following code:

```
[Inspectable(type="String", defaultValue="")]
public function set graphic(str:String):Void {
  __blockGraphic = str;
  attachGraphics();
}
```

attachGraphics() is called whenever the graphic property is set. Because we've set the graphic property to be Inspectable, this method is invoked *before* the initialization of the object (that's just the way it works—it sets the property so that it's available with its new value upon the initialization of the object). We need a way for attachGraphics() to be called only if the component has completed its initialization (and thus called through code, not from the Component Inspector). We can accomplish this by making a new variable flag, __initialized, that is set to true at the end of the UIObject's init() method.

Return to UIObject.as and add the __initialized property to the declarations.

```
private var __children:Array;
private var __dispatcher:Broadcaster;
private var __initialized:Boolean;

function UIObject () {
  init();
}
```

Now at the end of the init() method, set the flag to true.

```
  _xscale = _yscale = 100;
  boundingBox_mc.unloadMovie();
  __initialized = true;
}
```

Finally, back in Block.as, add the following check to the graphic setter:

```
[Inspectable(type="String", defaultValue="")]
public function set graphic(str:String):Void {
  __blockGraphic = str;
  if (__initialized) attachGraphics();
}
```

Test your movie again to see the skins sized correctly, as in Figure 16-13.

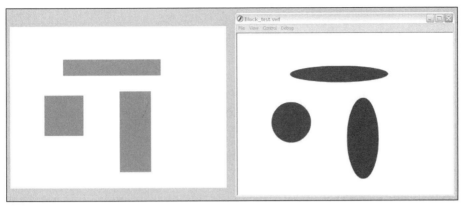

Figure 16-13. The circleSkins attached and sized to match the Block instances

Skinning a widget

Right now, we have all three Block instances set to use the circleSkin graphic, and to do that we had to set the graphic property on all three instances. If we had 50 blocks on the stage, having to set each one would become a frustration we could easily do without. Since all Block instances come from the same class, there should be a way to let them all know to use a certain graphic. Then, only when needed, we could set an individual instance separately, which would override the default graphic for that instance.

The simplest solution for this is to have a static property on the Block class that will hold the name of the default graphic. We'll set this after the other property declarations in Block.as.

```
static private var sClass:String = "Block";
private var __graphic_mc:MovieClip;
private var __blockGraphic:String;
private var __state:String;

static public var globalGraphic:String = "Block graphic";

function Block() {}
```

We've assigned this static property the value Block graphic, which means we'll want to have this clip available in the Library for when it's needed. First, though, we'll look at how a Block instance will determine whether to use this default graphic or not. Return to Block.as and change the attachGraphics() method to the following:

```
private function attachGraphics():Void {
  var initObj:Object =
    {
    width:__width,
    height:__height,
    state:__state,
```

```
        component:this
    };
    var g:String = getGraphic("__blockGraphic");
    createObject(g, "__graphic_mc", 0, initObj);
}
```

Instead of automatically using the value in __blockGraphic, we now call another method that will determine the name of the symbol to attach. This new method, getGraphic(), to which we pass the name of the graphic property to check, will reside in UIObject. We'll put this method there since it's one that all visual components will utilize to determine their graphics. This is the reason we pass the name of the graphic property as well. Although Block only has one graphic, other components might have many.

Go to UIObject.as and add this new getGraphic() method below the init() method. We also create a stub method, resolveGraphic(), which will need to be defined in each child class.

```
private function resolveGraphic(graphic:String):Void {}
```

```
private function getGraphic(graphic:String):String {
    var g:String = this[graphic];
    return (g != undefined && g != "") ? g : resolveGraphic(graphic);
}
```

getGraphic() first checks the property on the instance itself (so it'll look at this __blockGraphic for each Block instance). If this value exists, then it'll return this value as the identifier to use to attach a skin. This value can be unique to the component instance. If this value doesn't exist, however, then resolveGraphic() is called and passed the name of the property to check for. Since different components will have many different graphic properties, we'll leave this method to be overridden by each child class, as we'll do now with Block.

Returning to Block.as, add the following method below attachGraphics():

```
private function resolveGraphic(s:String):String {
    return Block.globalGraphic;
}
```

Since Block only has one static graphic property, we know that this function will only be called for that, so we can return it directly.

Now, how do these functions translate? Basically, when a Block instance is initialized, it'll call its attachGraphics() method. In this method, it calls getGraphic() to determine the name of the symbol this particular instance should attach as its skin. If the instance has a value stored in __blockGraphic, it'll use this. If not, then getGraphic() calls resolveGraphic(), which for Block simply returns the value of the static globalGraphic property, Block graphic.

Obviously, this means we need to create a movie clip symbol exported as Block graphic. Return to Block_test.fla and create a new movie clip symbol named and exported for ActionScript as Block graphic. On the default layer, first frame, place the following code:

```
setSize(width, height);

function setSize(w:Number, h:Number):Void {
  width = w;
  height = h;
  drawRect();
}

function drawRect():Void {
  var color:Number = 0xFF0000;
  clear();
  beginFill(color, 100);
  lineTo(width, 0);
  lineTo(width, height);
  lineTo(0, height);
  lineTo(0, 0);
  endFill();
}
```

This code begins like our circleSkin did, but instead of resizing a predrawn graphic, this skin draws it dynamically using the Drawing API. When setSize() is called, the width and height are set and drawRect is called to draw a rectangle of the desired dimensions. If you test your movie now, you'll see no difference, since each instance has its graphic property set to use circleSkin. However, if you delete the value in the graphic property for each Block instance using the Component Inspector and test the movie again, you'll see that all instances use the Block graphic skin and draw a red rectangle, as demonstrated in Figure 16-14.

Figure 16-14. The default Block graphic drawn for all Block instances

So we know the default works, but how would you override this on a global level? (You already have seen that you can override this on individual instances by setting the graphic property.) We only need to set the value of Block's globalGraphic property to a new value. Create a new layer on the main timeline named code and add the following line:

```
com.oop.ui.Block.globalGraphic = "circleSkin";
```

However, if you test your movie now, you'll see no difference. The Block graphic rectangle is still attached. The reason for this is that the components' code is run before the code on the main timeline, so the globalGraphic property isn't set until after the Block instances have finished their initialization. To fix this, we could call some sort of update function after setting the new skin, but this would mean that the instances would initialize and run through all their code, attaching their default skin, then have to run through all of the graphic code a second time to attach a new skin. It's best to keep the processes limited, so a better solution is simply to move the component instances to the second frame and place a stop(); action there, as shown in Figure 16-15. That way, the skin value is set in the first frame, then the playhead reaches the second frame, where it stops as the component instances initialize with the new globalGraphic property. Try this to see the Block instances using the circleSkin graphic.

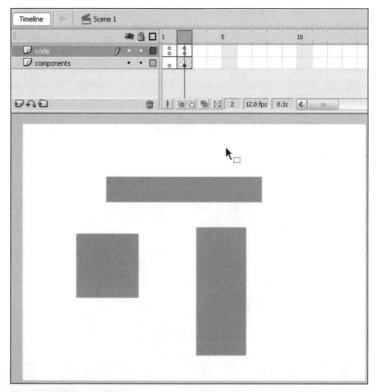

Figure 16-15. A two-frame movie set up with initialization code in the first frame and components in the second

Another possible solution is to have all the components internally wait until the next frame to draw themselves. Using this method would allow you to keep the main timeline one frame long and simply shift the two-frame concept to the ActionScript, where components would initialize but would not render themselves until the following frame, at which point all of the styles and skins would be set. One issue with this, however, is that there would be a delay between instantiation and rendering that could have unwanted effects when components are instantiated through ActionScript as opposed to using the IDE. It also creates a number of intervals within the components themselves, either enterFrame handlers or setInterval calls, which is easier and less buggy not to have to manage.

Changing state

You might have noticed that we've had a state property for a while but have yet to use it. This property can be used by skins to alter their appearance based on the value. We'll use the Block graphic default skin to demonstrate this.

First, it's important that you delete or comment out the line in the first frame of the movie that sets the globalGraphic static property for Block. We want all instances to take the default so you may see how the state property works.

The next step is to go inside the Block graphic movie clip symbol and add to the code.

```
function changeState(s:String):Void {
  state = s;
  drawRect();
}

function drawRect():Void {
  var color:Number;
  switch (state) {
    case "_Over":
      color = 0xFF9999;
      break;
    case "_Down":
      color = 0x660000;
      break;
    default:
      color = 0xFF0000;
  }
  clear();
  beginFill(color, 100);
  lineTo(width, 0);
  lineTo(width, height);
  lineTo(0, height);
  lineTo(0, 0);
  endFill();
}
```

We know that Block calls changeState() in the skin whenever it changes state, so we use this to set a state property, then call drawRect(). Inside drawRect(), instead of using a single color, we determine a color based on the state.

Go back to the main timeline and for one of your Block instances, use the Component Inspector to set its state to _Over. For another instance, set its state to _Down. Test your movie now to see how the graphic renders its different states. The result should look similar to Figure 16-16.

Figure 16-16. The Block graphic uses the state property to draw different tones.

Adding some style

In the last chapter, we created a StyleManager class to handle the styling of multiple components. It's now time to take advantage of our previous work and use the StyleManager to style our Block instances.

On the first frame of the main timeline (while the components still reside in the second frame, since the same issues we saw with the skins will apply to styles as well), place the following code:

```
import com.oop.graphic.StyleFormat;

blueFormat = new StyleFormat("blueFormat");
blueFormat.face = 0x7F9BE8;
blueFormat.highlight = 0xB4CBFE;
blueFormat.selected = 0x596BA3;
```

```
redFormat = new StyleFormat("redFormat");
redFormat.face = 0xE05A5A;
redFormat.highlight = 0xFFA1A1;
redFormat.selected = 0xA14040;

greenFormat = new StyleFormat("greenFormat");
greenFormat.face = 0x54BF4C;
greenFormat.highlight = 0x8DDB87;
greenFormat.selected = 0x337832;

styleManager = new com.oop.managers.StyleManager(blueFormat);
styleManager.addStyle("red", redFormat);
styleManager.addStyle("green", greenFormat);
```

There should be no need to go over this in depth since it was covered thoroughly last chapter. This merely creates three StyleFormat instances and adds them to the global StyleManager. But how do we tie these to our components? Since styles will apply to all visual components, it makes sense to add the code to UIObject.

In UIObject.as, add the following classes to the top of the file:

```
import com.oop.core.IEventDispatcher;
import com.oop.core.Broadcaster;
import com.oop.managers.StyleManager;
import com.oop.graphic.StyleFormat;
import flash.geom.Point;
```

Now that we can use them throughout the file without having to specify the package, add the following new properties as well as a new line in the constructor:

```
private var __dispatcher:Broadcaster;
private var __initialized:Boolean;
[Inspectable]
public var styleFormatName:String;
public var styleFormat:StyleFormat;

function UIObject() {
  if (!_global.StyleManager) new StyleManager();
  init();
}
```

styleFormatName and styleFormat are made to be public properties that can be accessed directly. With the former, we make it inspectable so that it'll appear in the Component Inspector. Note that we don't have to include its type, since that is present in the property's declaration and its value will default to an empty string.

In the first line of the constructor, we check to see whether a StyleManager exists and create one if it doesn't. This is just a safety check, since the majority of the time, if not all, the StyleManager will be created before any components appear on the stage.

If you recall from last chapter, or flip back to take a look, the StyleManager determines the appropriate StyleFormat for a component based on whether it has a styleFormatName on the instance, or else on its classes. For instance, for a Block instance, the StyleManager will first check to see whether the instance has a styleFormatName defined and use the StyleFormat saved by that name if it does. If the instance doesn't have a styleFormatName, then StyleManager runs through the component's classes, working up the hierarchy chain until it finds a StyleFormat for that class. For a Block instance, the StyleManager will first check to see whether a StyleFormat has specifically been assigned for Block. If it hasn't, it'll then look to see whether a StyleFormat instance has been assigned to UIObject. If it hasn't, then the default StyleFormat is returned. Here's the relevant code from last chapter:

```
public function getStyle(obj:Object):StyleFormat {
  if (obj.styleFormatName != undefined) {
    if (__styles[obj.styleFormatName] != undefined)
      return __styles[obj.styleFormatName];
  }
  var classes:Array = obj.classes;
  for (var i:Number = classes.length-1; i > -1; i--) {
    if (__styles[classes[i]] != undefined) return
➥__styles[classes[i]];
  }
  return __styles["default"];
}
```

To use this with our components, we need to have all the component's classes stored in a classes property that the StyleManager can access. Let's look to see how we can accomplish this.

Still in UIObject, add the following new static properties to the declarations:

```
class com.oop.ui.UIObject extends MovieClip
➥ implements IEventDispatcher {

  private static var sClass:String = "UIObject";
  private var boundingBox_mc:MovieClip;
  private var __Class:Array;
  private var __enabled:Boolean;
```

__Class will hold all of the classes for a component. This will be populated using the static sClass property stored on each class. This will be populated in the init() method of each class, as we see here with the additional line in UIObject's init() method:

```
private function init():Void {
  __Class = [UIObject.sClass];
  __children = [];
```

So the first index in the __Class array for UIObjects will always be the string UIObject. The next step is to add similar code to Block. Jump back to Block.as and add the following new line in the properties declarations:

```
class com.oop.ui.Block extends UIObject {

    static private var sClass:String = "Block";
    private var __graphic_mc:MovieClip;
    private var __blockGraphic:String;
    private var __state:String;
```

We then need to push this value into the __Class array. This needs to occur *after* the super's init() method is called, since that is what initializes the array, and this class name should follow the super's class name.

```
    private function init():Void {
      super.init();
      __Class.push(Block.sClass);
      _global.StyleManager.style(this);
      attachGraphics();
    }
```

After pushing the class name into the __Class array, we call StyleManager's style() method, which will determine the appropriate StyleFormat for this instance. Remember though that the StyleManager was looking for an array named classes. We need to create a getter function in UIObject for this array. Jump back to UIObject.as and add the following new methods to work with the StyleManager:

```
    public function get classes():Array {
      var a = [];
      for (var i:Number = 0; i < __Class.length; i++) {
        a.push(__Class[i]);
      }
      return a;
    }

    public function updateStyles(sf:StyleFormat):Void {
      if (sf != undefined) {
        if (sf != styleFormat) sf.addListener(this);
      }
      dispatchEvent("restyle");
    }
```

When StyleManager accesses classes, it'll get returned a copy of the __Class array (it's always a good idea to return copies of arrays unless you want to allow manipulation of the arrays to external objects). updateStyles() is a method that can be called by a StyleFormat in order to update its listeners when its values have changed (also from last chapter). This method can also be used for UIObjects to change their StyleFormat. This way, you can swap StyleFormats for a component at runtime. For example, an input field might have a default StyleFormat upon initialization, but a StyleFormat with red color values might be swapped in if the field had an error for the user to correct.

The next step, as we near completion of styles, is to program our skin to look at styles when rendering itself. Return to Block_test.fla and enter symbol editing mode. In the drawRect() function, change the following bold lines:

```
function drawRect():Void {
  var color:Number;
  switch (state) {
    case "_Over":
      color = component.styleFormat.highlight;
      break;
    case "_Down":
      color = component.styleFormat.selected;
      break;
    default:
      color = component.styleFormat.face;
  }
  clear();
  beginFill(color, 100);
  lineTo(width, 0);
  lineTo(width, height);
  lineTo(0, height);
  lineTo(0, 0);
  endFill();
}
```

Now instead of hard coding color values into the skin, it looks to the component instance's styleFormat property. If you test your movie out now, you'll see that the Block instances are colored blue hues since that is the default StyleFormat instance for the StyleManager. If we don't want the default format for Block instances, we can tell the StyleManager to style them differently. On the main timeline of the Block_test.fla, add the following bold line to the code in the first frame:

```
styleManager = new com.oop.managers.StyleManager(blueFormat);
styleManager.addStyle("red", redFormat);
styleManager.addStyle("green", greenFormat);
styleManager.addStyle("Block", greenFormat);
```

This tells the StyleManager to style all Block instances with greenFormat unless an instance has a specific styleFormatName. If you test the movie now, you'll see all Block instances take a green hue.

The final test is to give a Block instance an individual styleFormatName. On Frame 2, select a Block instance and look at the Component Inspector. The new styleFormatName property has appeared below graphic and state. Set this value to red and test the movie. Although all other Block instances are taking greenFormat for their style, this one instance should be taking redFormat, as shown in Figure 16-17. That's some fine control!

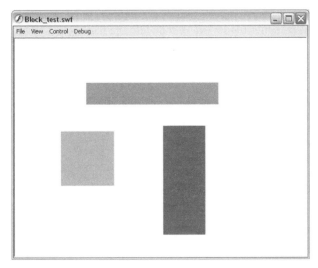

Figure 16-17. The Block graphic skins using StyleFormat instances to color themselves, with all Blocks using a single format unless overridden on the instance level

More ways to skin a cat

What more could we do for our base component structure? One area we might improve upon is the way we are currently skinning the components. Any time we can get away from having code nested within clips, the easier it'll be to maintain and manage. For skins, we can when possible have the drawing code and/or resizing code in an external class file. This makes even more sense when we consider that the Block class requires a couple of methods of skins in order to work with them. When one class expects a certain API with another class, this is a good candidate for an interface to enforce implementation of those methods.

Create a new ActionScript file and save it as `ISkinnable.as` into a new directory `com/oop/graphic/skins/` in your file system. This interface will be short and sweet.

```
interface com.oop.graphic.skins.ISkinnable {

    public function setSize(w:Number, h:Number):Void
    public function changeState(s:String):Void

}
```

We already know that these are the methods required by Block, so this interface is easily defined. The next step is to build a Skin class that implements this interface and can serve as the super class for any skin that is drawn through code.

Create another new ActionScript file and save it into the same com/oop/graphic/skins/ directory as Skin.as. Enter the following code into the file:

```
import com.oop.ui.UIObject;
import com.oop.graphic.skins.ISkinnable;

class com.oop.graphic.skins.Skin extends MovieClip
➥ implements ISkinnable {

  private var __width:Number;
  private var __height:Number;
  private var __state:String;
  private var __component:UIObject;

  function Skin() {
    init();
  }

  private function init():Void {
    __component.addEventListener("restyle", this, "drawRect");
    setSize(__width, __height);
  }

  function draw():Void {}

  public function setSize(w:Number, h:Number):Void {
    __width = w;
    __height = h;
    draw();
  }

  public function changeState(s:String):Void {
    __state = s;
    draw();
  }

  public function set width(n:Number):Void { __width = n; }
  public function set height(n:Number):Void { __height = n; }
  public function set state(s:String):Void { __state = s; }
  public function set component(c:UIObject):Void { __component = c; }

}
```

Notice that the class extends MovieClip and implements the new ISkinnable interface. In the init() method we call addEventListener() on the component attaching this skin. If you look at UIObject's updateStyles() method, it dispatches a restyle event. When this is fired, a Skin instance's draw method will be called automatically.

At this point, setSize() and changeState() call a draw() method that here is merely a stub intended to be overridden. Ideally, any class that inherits from Skin need simply define a single draw() method and nothing else. We can try that by creating a SimpleRect skin.

Create another new ActionScript file and save it into the same com/oop/graphic/skins/ directory as SimpleRect.as. Add the following code:

```
import com.oop.graphic.skins.Skin;

class com.oop.graphic.skins.SimpleRect extends Skin {

  function SimpleRect() {}

  public function draw():Void {
    var color:Number;
    switch (__state) {
      case "_Over":
        color = __component.styleFormat.highlight;
        break;
      case "_Down":
        color = __component.styleFormat.selected;
        break;
      default:
        color = __component.styleFormat.face;
    }
    clear();
    beginFill(color, 100);
    lineTo(__width, 0);
    lineTo(__width, __height);
    lineTo(0, __height);
    lineTo(0, 0);
    endFill();
  }

}
```

Look familiar? It should, as it's almost exactly the same code we had inside the Block graphic's drawRect() method. Now it's simply in an external class, but doing the same thing.

To get this to work in the `Block_test.fla`, go into the Block graphic and either delete or comment out all of the code. Next, right-click the symbol in the Library and select Linkage. In the AS 2.0 class field, type com.oop.graphic.skins.SimpleRect, as shown in Figure 16-18. Now whenever this symbol is attached to the stage, it'll be an instance of the SimpleRect class. If you test your movie now, you'll see the same result as before, but now the skin is being defined by an external class as opposed to a symbol with nested code.

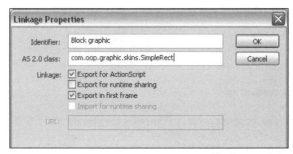

Figure 16-18. The Block graphic associated with the SimpleRect class instead of having code on its timeline

The last tweak we should make for our new skins is to change the type for `__graphic_mc` in the Block class. Right now, it's typed as a movie clip, and although this works, we've now created an interface that all attached skins should adhere to. It would be better to type this now as ISkinnable so that it may be enforced within Block. To do this, go back to `Block.as` and add or change the following bold lines:

```
import com.oop.ui.UIObject;
import com.oop.graphic.skins.ISkinnable;

class com.oop.ui.Block extends UIObject {

    static private var sClass:String = "Block";
    private var __graphic_mc:ISkinnable;
    private var __blockGraphic:String;
    private var __state:String;
```

With Block now completed, be sure to check your code against the class included in the downloadable files for this chapter.

Attaching from scratch

Up until this point, we've been attaching our components to the stage in the IDE. This has the disadvantage of having to place components in the second frame after skin and style initialization, but offers two great advantages to note. First, we can see exactly how the instances are placed and sized in relation to each other. Second, we can plug into the Component Inspector in order to set parameters. There are a number of additional features that we haven't even touched on, such as Live Preview and Custom UIs, as well as two other tabs in the Component Inspector, Bindings and Schema. We'll look at bindings and schema in a later chapter.

As for Live Preview, this allows you to see what your component may look like at runtime. I say "may," since a Live Preview generally can't take into account custom skins or fonts. It also has the disadvantage of requiring you to either precompile your component (which you don't want to do unless you are certain of never needing to update the component's code) or build an external SWF. It can also, with more complex components, slow down your IDE, at which point you can disable the Live Previews altogether. For development, I've generally found that it's better to keep components as we have the Block now—a symbol that isn't compiled and merely has a bounding box for visually resizing when needed. If you are distributing your components to others, compiling them into SWCs, which automatically generates a Live Preview, is a great way to go.

Custom UIs are a fantastically neat feature to explore, but one out of the scope of this book. If you have components that have too many parameters to comfortably be set in the Component Inspector, or if you need to provide a more complex interface to configure your component, a Custom UI can come in extremely handy. Back a few versions ago, I developed a 3D modeling component that allowed the developer to add points, lines, and planes in 3D space, texture the planes, and animate the simple models. That's not really something that can be done in the Component Inspector!

The point of this is that components offer and can do a multitude of things, but for our purposes we are creating components that can work within a framework for developing interfaces and applications. As such, it'll often be the case that we don't use the timeline to place and arrange graphic components, but instead attach and place through code. When we work in this manner, we can keep code in external text files, which can be more easily managed, and we can use the FLAs merely to hold our embedded fonts and graphic skins.

To see how easy it is to use the Block component we've created in such an environment, create a new ActionScript file and save it into a new directory, com/oop/ui/interfaces/, as InterfaceTest.as. The full listing of the class is shown here:

```
import com.oop.ui.UIObject;
import com.oop.ui.Block;
import com.oop.graphic.StyleFormat;

class com.oop.ui.interfaces.InterfaceTest extends UIObject {

  function InterfaceTest() {}

  private function init():Void {
    super.init();
    createStyles();
    attachGraphics();
  }
```

```
private function createStyles():Void {
  var blueFormat:StyleFormat = new StyleFormat("blueFormat");
  blueFormat.face = 0x7F9BE8;
  blueFormat.highlight = 0xB4CBFE;
  blueFormat.selected = 0x596BA3;
  var redFormat:StyleFormat = new StyleFormat("redFormat");
  redFormat.face = 0xE05A5A;
  redFormat.highlight = 0xFFA1A1;
  redFormat.selected = 0xA14040;
  var greenFormat:StyleFormat = new StyleFormat("greenFormat");
  greenFormat.face = 0x54BF4C;
  greenFormat.highlight = 0x8DDB87;
  greenFormat.selected = 0x337832;
  _global.StyleManager.addStyle("Block", blueFormat);
  _global.StyleManager.addStyle("red", redFormat);
  _global.StyleManager.addStyle("green", greenFormat);
}

private function attachGraphics():Void {
  createClassObject(Block, "block0", 0,
    {
    initialWidth:100,
    initialHeight:100
    }
  );
  createClassObject(Block, "block1", 1,
    {
    initialWidth:100,
    initialHeight:100,
    _x:150,
    styleFormatName:"red"
    }
  );
  createClassObject(Block, "block2", 2,
    {
    initialWidth:100,
    initialHeight:100,
    _x:300,
    styleFormatName:"green"
    }
  );
}

}
```

In this class, which inherits from UIObject, we are simply creating a layout for components. The init() method calls createStyles() and attachGraphics(). createStyles() is the same style code that we used in Block_test.fla. attachGraphics() uses createClassObject(), defined in UIObject, to attach three Block instances to the stage. To each it passes an initObj with initialWidth and initialHeight parameters and positions. For the latter two Block instances, it assigns a specific styleFormatName.

To see how this code runs, create a new Flash document and save it as InterfaceTest.fla. Create a new movie clip symbol named and exported as empty class. After that, create a second movie clip symbol, this one named and exported as Block graphic, with its AS 2.0 class text field set as com.oop.graphic.skins.SimpleRect. This makes two symbols in the Library, neither with any graphics, shown in Figure 16-19.

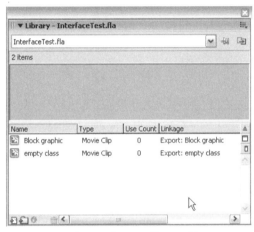

Figure 16-19. The InterfaceTest library with two empty and exported movie clip symbols

Return to the main timeline and in the first frame on the default layer, place the following code:

```
Object.registerClass("empty class",
➥ com.oop.ui.interfaces.InterfaceTest);
attachMovie("empty class", "blocks", 0, {_x:75, _y:150});
```

That's it. We register the empty class symbol in the Library with our InterfaceTest class and then attach the symbol. Once attached, the InterfaceTest class initializes, sets styles, and attaches Block instances, using the same empty class clip in the Library. Implementation is clean and sweet, with everything contained in our external class files. Test the movie to see the result, shown in Figure 16-20.

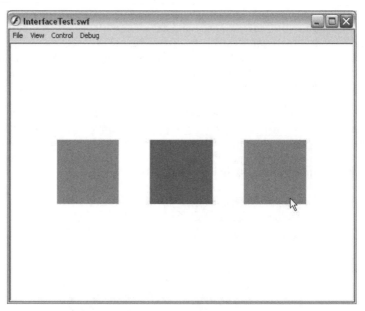

Figure 16-20. The InterfaceTest movie generated by the InterfaceTest class

Tying in events

As we wind down this chapter on UI widgets, it would serve us well to have a component that the user could actually interact with. To this end, we'll extend our UIObject class to create a SimpleButton, using a Block instance inside for the graphic. We mapped out the diagram earlier, so we can begin filling in the class. Create a new ActionScript file and save it as SimpleButton.as into the com/oop/ui/buttons/ directory. Enter the following code:

```
import com.oop.ui.Block;
import com.oop.ui.UIObject;

class com.oop.ui.buttons.SimpleButton extends UIObject {

    static public var sClass:String = "SimpleButton";
    private var __blockGraphic:String;
    private var __overButton:Boolean;
    private var __pressedButton:Boolean;
    private var __graphic_bk:Block;

    static public var globalGraphic:String;

    function SimpleButton() {}

// PRIVATE
//  _____
```

```
    private function init():Void {
      super.init();
      __Class.push(SimpleButton.sClass);
      _global.StyleManager.style(this);
      attachGraphics();
      setEvents();
    }

  }
```

This class starts off similarly to Block. After importing the necessary classes and the class declaration, we define properties, including the static sClass property to hold the name of the class and the globalGraphic property to hold the identifier for the skin, if any, used for all SimpleButton instances. Following the constructor, the init() method calls the super's init() method, then pushes its class name into the __Class array. Next, it has the StyleManager assign the appropriate StyleFormat (up to this point, virtually all UIObject components will use similar code), then calls two new methods, attachGraphics() and setEvents().

Add the attachMethods() and resolveGraphic() methods below the init().

```
    private function attachGraphics():Void {
      createClassObject(
        Block, "__graphic_bk", 0,
        {
        initialWidth:   __width,
        initialHeight:  __height,
        graphic:  getGraphic("__blockGraphic"),
        styleFormatName:  styleFormat.styleReference
        }
      );
    }

    private function resolveGraphic(s:String):String {
      return SimpleButton.globalGraphic;
    }
```

attachGraphics() uses createClassObject() to attach a Block instance. It uses getGraphic(), defined in UIObject, which in turn calls resolveGraphic(), to determine whether a skin should be passed into the Block's graphic property (this was covered with Block's code). Also notice how the styleFormatName is set by whatever the styleReference is for this SimpleButton reference. This is important since we want the Block instance inside SimpleButton to use the SimpleButton instance's StyleFormat, not Block's. Otherwise, we could never style SimpleButton specifically.

The next set of methods all have to do with the user interaction with the SimpleButton, using the built-in mouse events to create button functionality.

```
private function setEvents():Void {
  onRollOver = overButton;
  onRollOut = onReleaseOutside = offButton;
  onPress = pressButton;
  onRelease = releaseButton;
}

private function offButton():Void {
  __graphic_bk.state = "_Up";
  __overButton = false;
  dispatchEvent("rollOut");
}

private function overButton():Void {
  __graphic_bk.state = "_Over";
  __overButton = true;
  dispatchEvent("rollOver");
}

private function pressButton(noCallback:Boolean) {
  __graphic_bk.state = "_Down";
  __pressedButton = true;
  dispatchEvent("press");
}

private function releaseButton(noCallback:Boolean) {
  __pressedButton = false;
  offButton();
  dispatchEvent("release");
  if (__enabled) overButton();
}
```

setEvents(), which was called in the init() method, simply assigns different handlers for the button events. The next four methods are those handlers. In each handler, we dispatch an event that external objects can subscribe to in order to be notified when the events occur. We also set the Block instance's state based on the event. This will allow our skins to respond to the different mouse events.

The final methods are ones we've already seen in Block and UIObject.

```
// PUBLIC
// _____

public function setEnabled(b:Boolean):Void {
  super.setEnabled(b);
  __overButton = false;
  __graphic_bk.state = "_Disabled";
}
```

```
public function get graphic():String {
  return __blockGraphic;
}

[Inspectable(type="String", defaultValue="")]
public function set graphic(str:String):Void {
  __blockGraphic = str;
  if (__initialized) __graphic_bk.graphic = str;
}

public function updateStyles(sf):Void {
  super.updateStyles(sf);
  __graphic_bk.updateStyles(styleFormat);
}
```

setEnabled() changes the state of the Block instance to _Disabled (it would be up to the skin to have a disabled state defined). graphic has a getter/setter set much like Block. Finally, updateStyles() passes the styleFormat on to the Block instance so it can update as well. And that is the SimpleButton complete!

To test this, open the InterfaceTest.as file and add the new class to the top.

```
import com.oop.ui.UIObject;
import com.oop.ui.Block;
import com.oop.ui.buttons.SimpleButton;
import com.oop.graphic.StyleFormat;
```

Then, at the end of the attachGraphics() method, after attaching the three Block instances, add the following code:

```
createClassObject(SimpleButton, "button0", 3,
  {
  initialWidth:50,
  initialHeight:20,
  _x:25,
  _y:40
  }
);
createClassObject(SimpleButton, "button1", 4,
  {
  initialWidth:50,
  initialHeight:20,
  _x:175,
  _y:40
  }
);
createClassObject(SimpleButton, "button2", 5,
  {
  initialWidth:50,
  initialHeight:20,
```

```
        _x:325,
        _y:40
      }
    );
    getChild("button0").addEventListener("release", this,
➥ "onButtonRelease");
    getChild("button1").addEventListener("release", this,
➥ "onButtonRelease");
    getChild("button2").addEventListener("release", this,
➥ "onButtonRelease");
```

Here, three SimpleButton instances are attached, each being given dimensions and coordinates. The final three lines add the InterfaceTest instance as a listener to all three buttons' release event. Now we just need to define the onButtonRelease() handler we specified.

Add the following new method after attachGraphics():

```
private function onButtonRelease(infoObj:Object):Void {
  trace(infoObj.parameters.target._name + " released");
}
```

This would obviously contain more useful code in an actual interface, but here we simply trace the name of the button that has been released so we may ensure that it's working properly. Test the movie now to see it in action; the result should look like Figure 16-21. We now have components that are responding to and firing off events.

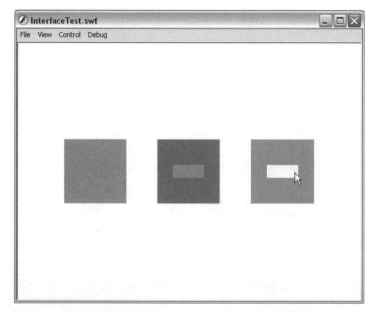

Figure 16-21. InterfaceTest using instances of SimpleButton

Pulling it all together

Throughout this and the previous chapter, I've covered quite a few aspects of a component framework, laying the groundwork for a more complex system. At this point we have a class defining a layout and styling of components and an FLA that instantiates that class and has a Library containing attachable, but empty, clips. We've looked at how we may style and skin different classes and instances of components. Let's bring it all together by creating a new skin and style for the newly attached buttons, and add in the feature of sounds that we explored last chapter with the SoundManager.

The first thing we'll do is create a new skin for the buttons. This will allow for gradient colors and a border to be drawn within a rectangle, as opposed to just the solid fill that SimpleRect offers. To make this skin, create a new ActionScript file and save it as GradientBorderRect.as into the com/opp/graphic/skins/ directory. The following code is the entire listing:

```
import com.oop.graphic.skins.Skin;
import flash.geom.Matrix;

class com.oop.graphic.skins.GradientBorderRect extends Skin {

  function GradientBorderRect() {}

  public function draw():Void {
    var property:String;
    switch (__state) {
      case "_Over":
        property = "highlight";
        break;
      case "_Down":
        property = "selected";
        break;
      default:
        property = "face";
    }
    var colors:Array = [];
    for (var i:Number = 0; i < 4; i++) {
      colors.push(__component.styleFormat[property + i]);
    }
    clear();
    var alphas:Array = [100, 100, 100, 100];
    var ratios:Array = [0, 120, 135, 255];
    var matrix:Matrix = new Matrix();
    matrix.createGradientBox(__width, __height, Math.PI/2, 0, 0);
    lineStyle(0, __component.styleFormat.border, 100);
    beginGradientFill("linear", colors, alphas, ratios, matrix);
    lineTo(__width, 0);
    lineTo(__width, __height);
    lineTo(0, __height);
```

```
        lineTo(0, 0);
        endFill();
    }

}
```

Just like SimpleRect, this class inherits from Skin and only requires a draw() method. In this method, we place four color values into a colors array depending upon the __state property. The for loop is a shortcut for us to put, for example, face0, face1, face2, and face3 into the colors array. Remember that since the StyleFormat class is dynamic, we can add whatever properties we require for the skins.

The rest of the code draws a gradient box with a border. It does utilize the new Matrix class and its built-in createGradientBox() method to create the matrix to pass to the beginGradientFill() method, but the rest is all standard Drawing API.

The next step is to export a clip from the InterfaceTest.fla's Library for this new skin. Return to InterfaceTest.fla and create a new movie clip symbol named and exported as GradientBorderRect. Make sure its AS 2.0 class is set as com.oop.graphic.skins. GradientBorderRect, as shown in Figure 16-22.

Figure 16-22. The GradientBorderRect symbol associated with an external class

With the skin defined in the Library, we need to assign it to all SimpleButton instances. We can do this upon the initialization of InterfaceTest. In the `InterfaceTest.as` file, add the following bold lines:

```
private function init():Void {
  super.init();
  createStyles();
  assignSkins();
  attachGraphics();
}

private function assignSkins():Void {
  SimpleButton.globalGraphic = "GradientBorderRect";
}
```

Pretty straightforward, no? We simply assign the linkage identifier for our new symbol to the globalGraphic property of SimpleButton, which will apply it to all instances.

The last step is to create the new StyleFormat required by the new skin. Add the new lines to the createStyles() method of InterfaceTest.

```
var greenFormat:StyleFormat = new StyleFormat("greenFormat");
greenFormat.face = 0x54BF4C;
greenFormat.highlight = 0x8DDB87;
greenFormat.selected = 0x337832;
var chromeFormat:StyleFormat = new StyleFormat("chromeFormat");
chromeFormat.border = 0x333333;
chromeFormat.face0 = 0xB0DFDE;
chromeFormat.face1 = 0xDAF0F0;
chromeFormat.face2 = 0xEDE9E0;
chromeFormat.face3 = 0xCCBEAA;
chromeFormat.highlight0 = 0xCEAEDE;
chromeFormat.highlight1 = 0xE9DAF0;
chromeFormat.highlight2 = 0xE0E3ED;
chromeFormat.highlight3 = 0xABB2CC;
chromeFormat.selected0 = 0x897394;
chromeFormat.selected1 = 0xB2A7B8;
chromeFormat.selected2 = 0x9FA1A8;
chromeFormat.selected3 = 0x787B8F;
_global.StyleManager.addStyle("SimpleButton", chromeFormat);
_global.StyleManager.addStyle("Block", blueFormat);
_global.StyleManager.addStyle("red", redFormat);
_global.StyleManager.addStyle("green", greenFormat);
```

There are certainly more properties, but there is nothing new in this code. The last new line adds the StyleFormat to the StyleManager using the reference SimpleButton. All SimpleButton instances will get assigned that style (unless they have a `styleFormatName` assigned on the instance level).

Test your movie to see the new skin and style applied. The result should look like Figure 16-23.

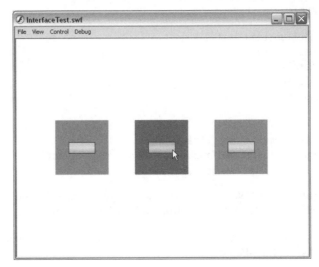

Figure 16-23. The GradientBorderRect skin applied to the SimpleButton instances

As for sounds, there are only two things we need to add to get them to work with our components. First, though, we need the sounds themselves. Included with this chapter's files are CLICK2.mp3 and CLICK8.mp3. Make sure the files are in the same directory as InterfaceTest.fla.

Once the sounds are in place, we need to load and assign them to our components in InterfaceTest.as. We can do this, just like the styles and skins, at initialization. Add the following bold lines to InterfaceTest.as:

```
private function init():Void {
  super.init();
  createStyles();
  assignSkins();
  assignSounds();
  attachGraphics();
}

private function assignSounds():Void {
  var soundManager = new com.oop.managers.SoundManager(this, 16001);
  soundManager.addSound("kiss", "file:CLICK2.mp3");
  soundManager.addSound("click", "file:CLICK8.mp3");
  soundManager.registerForSound("SimpleButton", "kiss",
➥ "press", 80);
  soundManager.registerForSound("SimpleButton", "click",
➥ "release", 80);
}
```

In the `assignSounds()` method, we use almost identical code to that used last chapter. After instantiating the SoundManager, we add two sounds, pointing to the relative files and assigning the files names for reference. The last two lines register SimpleButton to receive sounds on press and release events.

But how exactly does SimpleButton get these sounds? Since we are tying sounds to events, it makes sense to place the relevant code in the one place where we know all UIObject events go through, namely UIObject's `dispatchEvent()` method.

Return to `UIObject.as` and add the following bold line to `dispatchEvent()`:

```
public function dispatchEvent(evnt:String, params:Object):Void {
  _global.SoundManager.getSound(this, evnt).start();
  var info:Object = params || {};
  info.target = this;
  __dispatcher.dispatchEvent(evnt, info);
}
```

That's all it takes, after the work from last chapter, to enable sounds in our components. Since the SoundManager handles all the loading and managing of sounds, instances ask it whenever an event is fired whether a sound needs to play. The SoundManager then checks to see whether that object has registered for a sound at that event, and if it does, it sends the Sound object instance back, at the right volume, to be played.

Summary

Well, that was a pretty full chapter! I've covered developing UI components from a humble diagram through to a skinnable, stylable, configurable, broadcasting (both events and sound!), fully fledged widget. We've explored how to plug a component into the Component Inspector to be manipulated in the IDE as well as being attachable through ActionScript with nothing in the Library but empty clips. Building on the knowledge from throughout this book, we've applied practical OOP to create a basic framework for developing an entire component library, separating function from the visuals as much as possible. Although in the end a simple button might seem a small prize at the completion of so much work, realize that the simple button merely demonstrates the process now by which all other visual widgets may be developed. With all of the hard work creating skinning and styling methods, creating an event broadcasting framework and sound management, building visual widgets of any complexity is made that much easier. Abstract where you can (does a button need to know how it's colored or what sounds it makes?) and the work can be broken up into smaller pieces, much more easier to deal with than the whole.

What's next?

We spent this chapter developing components using movie clip symbols from the Library since we needed visual representation on the stage. In the next chapter, we explore classes that don't have a visual component, but instead alter the visuals of our movie clips using many of the new effects and image manipulation ActionScript available in Flash 8. There are so many new graphic capabilities, and we'll use OOP to help organize and manage these capabilities so we may more easily apply them to great effect (and great fun!).

17 OOP ANIMATION AND EFFECTS

The original purpose of Flash was animation. Using the timelines, animators either drew frame-by-frame graphics to simulate motion or used Flash's tweening capabilities to create animation between keyframes. With the addition of ActionScript, animation did not go out the window. In fact, ActionScript proved to be just another tool, like the timeline, that developers could use to create animation. By altering visual properties of movie clips through code, fluid and complex animation could be created without timelines. But how exactly can we apply OOP to this process of animation in order to make it easier and more manageable?

The first thing to consider is that in the case of animation classes, most likely these classes won't themselves be visible, but will instead handle the animation of other visual objects. For instance, a movie clip class that can tween its position would be extremely useful, but more useful would be a class outside of that movie clip class that handles the tweening animation. This tweening class could then be applied to other objects as well, not just the single movie clip class. If we think of these animation classes as handling animation as opposed to visually animating themselves, we can focus in on the useful pieces that would comprise such classes.

Events being fired when an animation begins, is occurring, or ends would be the most important feature, and this can be handled using the Broadcaster class created in Chapter 13, with perhaps a little enhancement. This could serve as the base class for all of our animation classes. Generally, if we have a class that can broadcast when it's animating and we can pass that class a reference to a clip that we wish to animate, we have the basis for any animation class. How the class handles the animation of the clip through some looping mechanism (perhaps an interval using our centralized IntervalManager) would be up to each animation class individually.

In this chapter, we'll explore a number of different classes to control the animation of movie clips in an object-oriented manner, playing a bit with the functionality of filters and bitmap manipulation new to Flash 8. Making a break from the process of previous chapters, we'll dive right into the code without spending too much time in the planning stages. Sometimes, especially when creating code for animation and effects, a lot of experimentation happens to get what is wanted, and creating too rigid of a box to work in makes it difficult to break out of. After the structure and discipline applied in the previous chapters (and now that you are comfortable with when and how to create UML diagrams to help with the planning), let's give ourselves a little freedom to have some fun in this chapter.

Preparing for animation

The base class of the animators we create will use Broadcaster (from the classes we created in Chapters 13, 15, and 16) in order to dispatch events to listeners detailing when an animation begins, is occurring, and ends. As we won't know any additional information about the type of animation in this superclass, there won't be too much code we need to add.

Animator

The first thing we need to do is create a new package for our animation classes; do this in the class directory that you first created in Chapter 13 (this could be in the Flash configuration directory, in the same directory of whatever FLA you are currently working on, or in some directory you have specified in the Flash IDE). Add a new folder/directory named animation in the com/oop directory, as shown in Figure 17-1. We'll save our animation classes here.

Figure 17-1.
The path to the new animation package

Create a new ActionScript file in Flash and add these lines:

```
class com.oop.animation.Animator extends com.oop.core.Broadcaster {

  function Animator() {}

// PUBLIC
// _____

  public function dispatchEvent(evnt:String, params:Object):Void {
    if (params == undefined) var params:Object = {};
    params.animator = this;
    super.dispatchEvent(evnt, params);
  }

}
```

Save this completed file as Animator.as into the com/oop/animation directory. As I said, there's not much to add to this class on top of the Broadcaster functionality. You can see from the code that it simply inherits from Broadcaster and then overrides the dispatchEvent(). In Animator's dispatchEvent(), it adds a new property to the params object, animator, which stores a reference to the Animator instance itself (note that the

335

first line first checks to see whether a params object was sent to the method and, if not, creates one). The superclass, Broadcaster, then gets its dispatchEvent() method invoked with the altered params object passed in.

It actually makes a lot of sense to add similar functionality to Broadcaster itself, an oversight from its initial coding. In fact, if Broadcaster itself added its reference to all events it dispatched, it would remove the necessity for Animator. However, we'll leave the Animator class for two reasons. First, any animation classes we create can now inherit from Animator instead of Broadcaster, which not only makes more sense in the code, but also gives us the freedom down the line to add additional functionality to all animation classes (and not all broadcasting classes). Second, the property we have added to the params object, animator, will be descriptive and helpful, as we are coding listeners to animator objects. The generic term that we would have to add to Broadcaster ("target" or "broadcaster", perhaps) would not read as clearly in the code.

Tweening properties and values

With the base class coded, it's time to get into some actual animation. The first thing we'll look at is how to tween simple movie clip properties in order to create movement. We can contain this functionality in a single class, named Tweener, which will handle taking an object and changing a specific value for that object over the course of time.

Tweener

Create a new ActionScript file and save it as Tweener.as into the com/oop/animation directory. Let's begin with its basic blueprint.

```
import com.oop.animation.Animator;
import com.oop.managers.IntervalManager;

class com.oop.animation.Tweener extends Animator {

  function Tweener() {}

// PRIVATE
// _____

  private function runTween():Void {
  }

// PUBLIC
// _____

  public function haltTween() {
  }
```

```
    public function tween():Void {
    }

    public function tweenTo():Void {
    }

}
```

At the top of the class, we import the two classes we know will be used, Animator (the superclass) and IntervalManager (to handle the interval calls). The four methods defined are the four that are immediately apparent. tween() and tweenTo() would initiate animation, haltTween() would end an animation, and runTween() would handle altering values to create that animation. The next step would be to decide what you would need to pass in order to start an animation.

```
    public function tween(
      clip:Object,
      prop:String,
      startValue:Number,
      destValue:Number,
      time:Number
    ):Void {
    }
```

To create a tween for an object's property, we would need to know the object, the property to tween, the values to tween, and the time in which that animation should occur. With these values passed in, we can start the process of animation by creating an interval that will be called to change the property over the course of time.

```
    public function tween(
      clip:Object,
      prop:String,
      startValue:Number,
      destValue:Number,
      time:Number
    ):Void {
      clip[prop] = startValue;
      var intName:String = clip._name + "_" + prop;
      if (__intervals[intName] == undefined) __intervals[intName] = {};
      var intObj:Object = __intervals[intName];
      intObj.count = 1;
      intObj.totalInts = Math.floor(time/Tweener.intervalTime);
      intObj.startProp = startValue;
      intObj.endProp = destValue;
      intObj.changeProp = intObj.endProp - intObj.startProp;
      intObj.clip = clip;
      intObj.prop = prop;
      intObj.tweener = this;
```

```
        IntervalManager.setInterval(intObj, "interval",
➥ this, "runTween", Tweener.intervalTime, intObj);
        runTween(intObj);
        dispatchEvent("startTween", {clip:clip, prop:prop});
    }
```

The first thing that is done in this method is the clip passed in immediately gets its property set to the start value passed in. Next, we need a way for Tweener to store the interval that will be passed to the IntervalManager. This is necessary since it's possible that Tweener might handle animating multiple properties or multiple objects, so an individual and unique object will need to be passed to the IntervalManager for each interval that needs to be called. This interval object will be stored in a new property, __intervals, which we'll declare in a moment.

The name of the interval object will be determined by the name of the clip passed in, plus an underscore, plus the name of the property to be tweened. Thus, if a movie clip named "ball" was passed in and the property to tween was its _rotation, then the interval object would be stored in Tweener's __intervals as "ball__rotation".

Once the interval object has been declared as a new object (if it hasn't already been defined), then all of the arguments passed in are stored in that object to be used to calculate and perform the animation. These include the clip, start, and end values of the tween and the property to animate. In addition, we calculate the amount the property must change over the course of the animation and determine exactly how many intervals must be called in order to perform the animation over the course of the specified time, stored in the property totalInts.

How is this totalInts calculated exactly? First, you'll see that it uses a static property of Tweener, intervalTime. Let's go ahead and declare this, along with __intervals, at the top so we can see how the calculation works.

```
    class com.oop.animation.Tweener extends Animator {

        private var __intervals:Object;
        static var intervalTime:Number = 40;

        function Tweener() {
            __intervals = {};
        }
```

intervalTime will dictate the frequency with which the IntervalManager calls the interval, in this case every 40 milliseconds. With that in mind, we can see that if a time of 2 seconds, or 2000 milliseconds, is passed to the tween() method, then the total number of intervals will be 50 (i.e., 2000/40). That means that the runTween() function should be called a total of 50 times in order to complete the animation. We'll keep track of the current interval through the interval object property count.

Finally, after storing a reference to the Tweener instance in the interval object, we call the IntervalManager's IntervalManager () method and pass in the interval object, instructing the IntervalManager to call runTween() on the Tweener instance (this) every 40 milliseconds (Tweener.intervalTime).

With all that work laid down, the tweenTo() method is considerably easier to pull off:

```
public function tweenTo(
  clip:Object,
  prop:String,
  destValue:Number,
  time:Number
):Void {
  tween(clip, prop, clip[prop], destValue, time);
}
```

tweenTo() will handle animating a clip from its current state to a new state. As such, a start value doesn't have to be passed in. However, after that point, the functionality behind the scenes is exactly that of tween(), so all we do is pass the values on to tween() with the clip's current property value being passed as the start value.

Before we get to actually performing the tween, let's add the ability to stop the tween, if needed. This is simply done by calling clearInterval() on the IntervalManager. Since the interval object being used is stored in our Tweener instance using the clip's name and property, that is all we need passed in to halt the interval.

```
public function haltTween(clip:Object, prop:String) {
  IntervalManager.clearInterval(
➥   _intervals[clip._name + "_" + prop], "interval");
}
```

All that's left now is to determine how the tween will be performed in runTween(). To start off easily, we'll perform a linear tween, meaning that the value of the clip's property will change an equal amount each interval. Let's add this to the runTween() method and see how it works.

```
private function runTween(intObj:Object):Void {
  var startProp:Number = intObj.startProp;
  var changeProp:Number = intObj.changeProp;
  var count:Number = intObj.count;
  var total:Number = intObj.totalInts;
  intObj.clip[intObj.prop] = startProp + ((changeProp/total)*count);
  var eventName:String = "tween";
  if (intObj.count++ >= intObj.totalInts) {
    intObj.clip[intObj.prop] = intObj.endProp;
    IntervalManager.clearInterval(intObj, "interval");
    eventName = "endTween";
  }
  dispatchEvent(eventName, {clip:intObj.clip, prop:intObj.prop});
}
```

For better readability, the first four lines simply store the properties of the interval object used to calculate the new property value. This calculation is performed on the fifth line of the function where the clip's property (accessed using bracket notation) is given a new value determined by the current count. This formula works by taking the amount the property needs to change each interval call (changeProp/total) and multiplying it by the current count, adding this to the initial value of the property. It's perhaps a bit easier to see how this formula works by plugging in numbers. For instance, if we were tweening a clip's _x position from 50 to 450 over the course of 2 seconds, then the changeProp value would be 400 and the totalInts would be 50 (2000 milliseconds / Tweener.intervalTime). This means after 1 second has passed, the count would be 25 (half of the total 2 seconds worth of 50 intervals). The formula would then become, after substitution

```
clip._x = 50 + ((400/50)*25);
```

So the clip would be placed at 250, halfway between 50 and 450.

The conditional that follows just checks to see whether the current interval, represented by count, equals or exceeds the allotted number of intervals for the animation. If so, the clip's property is given the destination value and the interval is cleared. The last line of code dispatches an event informing listeners either that a tween or an endTween has occurred.

That's the bare bones of our Tweener class, so let's try it out to see how it performs. Create a new Flash document and save it as tweenerTest.fla. Rename the default layer clip. Draw a circle on the stage, converting it to a movie clip symbol. Name the instance circle_mc, as shown in Figure 17-2.

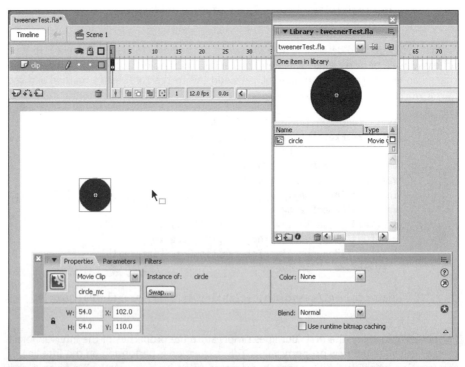

Figure 17-2. The stage set for testing Tweener

Create a new layer named code, and for its first (and only) frame, enter the following code into the ActionScript panel:

```
import com.oop.animation.Tweener;

init();
function init():Void {
  tweener = new Tweener();
  onMouseDown = tweenCircle;
}
function tweenCircle():Void {
  tweener.tweenTo(circle_mc, "_x", _xmouse, 1000);
  tweener.tweenTo(circle_mc, "_y", _ymouse, 1000);
}
```

If you test the movie now, you'll see that the circle performs a linear tween to wherever the mouse is clicked. We use the tweenTo() method to animate the clip from its current _x and _y position to the mouse position over the course of 1 second. Because the Tweener class utilizes the IntervalManager, we don't have to worry about conflicting tweens or interval calls causing any animation irregularities.

What is missing, however, is any type of organic feel to the movement. We can add that in by using a bit of easing, or acceleration/deceleration, to the animated movement.

Easer

It just so happens that someone has already spent the time to write the ActionScript equations that can be used to create easing movement, similar to what we did earlier with the linear animation equation. Robert Penner (www.robertpenner.com) has provided open source easing equations for several versions of Flash now, equations you can download from www.robertpenner.com/easing/ or from this chapter's download files. We'll leverage this useful and excellent code to provide more interesting animation possibilities without a large amount of excess work.

The first thing to do is to install his classes into the same directory as your current class files. The package for the easing equations is com.robertpenner.easing, so you can copy the robertpenner directory right into the com directory of your own classes, as you see in Figure 17-3.

Figure 17-3.
The path to the new robertpenner.easing package

Let's take a look at one of his easing classes, Cubic, reproduced here with kind permission from Mr. Penner.

```
class com.robertpenner.easing.Cubic {
  static function easeIn (t:Number, b:Number,
➡ c:Number, d:Number):Number {
    return c*(t/=d)*t*t + b;
  }
  static function easeOut (t:Number, b:Number,
➡ c:Number, d:Number):Number {
    return c*((t=t/d-1)*t*t + 1) + b;
  }
  static function easeInOut (t:Number, b:Number,
➡ c:Number, d:Number):Number {
    if ((t/=d/2) < 1) return c/2*t*t*t + b;
    return c/2*((t-=2)*t*t + 2) + b;
  }
}
```

Here you can see that a single easing equation type (Cubic) has three different static methods, easeIn(), easeOut(), and easeInOut(). Let's make some modification to our Tweener class so that we may use these equations in our animations.

Go back to the Tweener.as file and add the following bold lines:

```
public function tween(
  clip:Object,
  prop:String,
  startValue:Number,
  destValue:Number,
  time:Number,
  easeFunction:Function
):Void {
  clip[prop] = startValue;
  var intName:String = clip._name + "_" + prop;
  if (_intervals[intName] == undefined) _intervals[intName] = {};
  var intObj:Object = _intervals[intName];
  intObj.count = 1;
  intObj.totalInts = Math.floor(time/TweenerTest.intervalTime);
  intObj.startProp = startValue;
  intObj.endProp = destValue;
  intObj.changeProp = intObj.endProp - intObj.startProp;
  intObj.clip = clip;
  intObj.prop = prop;
  intObj.easeFunction = (easeFunction == undefined) ?
➡ com.robertpenner.easing.Linear.easeNone : easeFunction;
  intObj.tweener = this;
  IntervalManager.setInterval(intObj, "interval",
➡ this, "runTween", TweenerTest.intervalTime, intObj);
  runTween(intObj);
}
```

```
public function tweenTo(
  clip:Object,
  prop:String,
  destValue:Number,
  time:Number,
  easeFunction:Function
):Void {
  tween(clip, prop, clip[prop], destValue, time, easeFunction);
}
```

Here you can see that we now accept another parameter into both the tween() and tweenTo() methods, a function for the ease. We might wish in the future to modify the easing equations to inherit from a single Ease class so that we could type this argument accordingly, but for now we'll type it as Function. In the tween() method, we check to see whether a function has been passed in and, if not, we use the Linear.easeNone method, which you'll notice if you look at that particular method is the linear equation we originally coded ourselves.

Finally, we need to change the way we calculate the clip's property each interval in the runTween() method. Instead of using our single equation, it should use the function passed in.

```
    private function runTween(intObj:Object):Void {
      var startProp:Number = intObj.startProp;
      var changeProp:Number = intObj.changeProp;
      var count:Number = intObj.count;
      var total:Number = intObj.totalInts;
      intObj.clip[intObj.prop] =
➡ intObj.easeFunction(count, startProp, changeProp, total);
      if (intObj.count++ >= intObj.totalInts) {
        intObj.clip[intObj.prop] = intObj.endProp;
        IntervalManager.clearInterval(intObj, "interval");
        dispatchEvent("endTween", {clip:intObj.clip, prop:intObj.prop});
      }
    }
```

Go back to your tweenerTest.fla file and pass in an easing function to see how it works. This particular combination produces a nice effect.

```
    import com.oop.animation.Tweener;
    import com.robertpenner.easing.*;

    init();
    function init():Void {
      tweener = new Tweener();
      onMouseDown = tweenCircle;
    }
    function tweenCircle():Void {
      tweener.tweenTo(circle_mc, "_x", _xmouse, 1000, Cubic.easeOut);
      tweener.tweenTo(circle_mc, "_y", _ymouse, 1000, Cubic.easeIn);
    }
```

Testing the Tweener

Let's set up a little bit more of a structured environment through which to test. This will prove useful as we create more animation classes. Create a new ActionScript file and save it into the same directory as tweenerTest.fla. This class won't be within our class structure, as we'll simply be using it to test some of our code. Add the following lines, which is the entirety of the class:

```actionscript
import com.oop.ui.UIObject;
import com.oop.ui.Block;

class AnimationTest extends UIObject {

  private var __blockHolder:UIObject;

  function AnimationTest() {}

  private function init():Void {
    super.init();
    attachGraphics();
  }

  private function attachGraphics():Void {
    __blockHolder = createEmptyObject("__block", 0);
    __blockHolder.position =
➡ new flash.geom.Point(Stage.width/2, Stage.height/2);
    __blockHolder.createClassObject(Block, "__block", 0,
      {
      initialWidth:50,
      initialHeight:50,
      _x:-25,
      _y:-25
      }
    );
  }

}
```

Here we have a class that will draw an initial graphic, a Block instance, onto the stage so that we may animate it. In the attachGraphics() method, we create an empty UIObject named __blockHolder, and within this we create a Block instance named __block. The reason this is done is so that we may center the Block instance within __blockHolder (its default registration point is at the top left). This will be important if we were to test scaling and rotation animation, since the graphic would then transform from its center as opposed to the top-left corner.

Now create a new Flash document and save it into the same directory as tweenerTest_2.fla. In this file, create an empty movie clip symbol named empty class and export it as empty

class as well, and another movie clip symbol named and exported as Block graphic with its
AS 2.0 class set as com.oop.graphic.skins.SimpleRect, as shown in Figure 17-4.

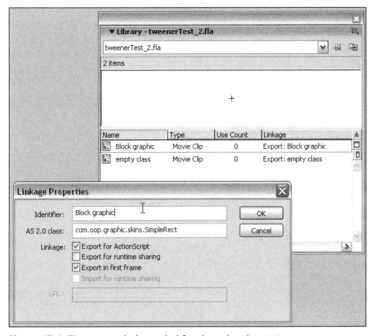

Figure 17-4. The two symbols needed for the animation test

In the only frame on the main timeline, add the following code:

```
Object.registerClass("empty class", AnimationTest);
attachMovie("empty class", "animationTest", 0);
```

If you test your movie now, you'll see a 50×50 gray box drawn onto the middle of the
stage. Now let's try animating it!

Create a new ActionScript file and save it as TweenerTest.as into the same directory as
AnimationTest.as. Add the following lines of code, which show the class in its entirety:

```
import com.oop.animation.Tweener;
import com.robertpenner.easing.*;

class TweenerTest extends AnimationTest {

  private var __tweener:Tweener;
  private var __positions:Array;
  private var __tweenCount:Number;
```

```
function TweenerTest() {}

private function init():Void {
  super.init();
  __tweener = new Tweener();
  __tweener.addEventListener("endTween", this, "startNextTween");
  __positions =
    [
    {x:100, y:100},
    {x:Stage.width-100, y:100},
    {x:Stage.width-100, y:Stage.height-100},
    {x:100, y:Stage.height-100}
    ];
  __tweenCount = 0;
  startNextTween();
}

private function startNextTween():Void {
  var pos:Object = __positions[__tweenCount];
  __tweener.tween(__blockHolder, "_rotation",
➥ 0, 90, 500, Quad.easeInOut);
  __tweener.tweenTo(__blockHolder, "_x", pos.x, 500, Quad.easeIn);
  __tweener.tweenTo(__blockHolder, "_y", pos.y, 500, Quad.easeOut);
  if (++__tweenCount >= __positions.length) __tweenCount = 0;
}

}
```

We are extending AnimationTest here so that we start off with the Block on the stage. In this class's init() method, we create a new Tweener instance and add this TweenerTest instance as a listener to the endTween event, which will call startNextTween() whenever it's fired. We then set four positions in the __positions object that we'll use in our tweens. At the end of the init(), we set the current tween to 0 (__tweenCount) and call startNextTween(), which should start everything rolling.

In startNextTween(), we determine the next position to tween to and store that in the local variable pos. We then set up three tweens, one for rotation and two for position. The rotation tween will go from 0 degrees to 90 degrees each tween, which will look fine considering we are simply rotating a plain gray rectangle. For the two coordinate positions, we use the current values stored in pos. To each of these three tweens, we pass a different easing equation.

The last line of startNextTween() increments __tweenCount. Once the value exceeds the number of positions, the count is set back to 0. In this way, the Block instance will continuously loop through the four positions.

Return to tweenerTest_2.fla and change the lines of code to read as follows:

```
Object.registerClass("empty class", TweenerTest);
attachMovie("empty class", "tweenerTest", 0);
```

Test the movie once more to see the Block performing a number of complex tweens about the stage, all managed by our animation classes. We'll continue to use this setup in our later animation experiments.

Enhancing Tweener

A common need for animation in Flash is tweening the position of clips on the stage, which obviously involves changing not one, but two variables over the course of the animation. To accomplish this, the Tweener class could be used (as we did in the previous exercise), but it would be helpful to have a class that handled specifically the tweening of position. We'll do this in a moment with a new Mover class.

In order to create the Mover class, we'll first add a little enhancement to the Tweener class in order to make it more powerful and useful under more circumstances. Right now, the Tweener is limited to altering one property per call, and that is all done within the scope of the Tweener instance itself. When more complex properties need to be changed, like a Color object or even a multidimensional structure, the Tweener would fail. What we need then is a way to have the Tweener handle multiple and diverse values over the course of an animation. We'll accomplish this with a few new methods whose collective purpose is merely to calculate easing values for any type of object passed in, and then pass these values over the course of an animation to a user-defined method outside of the scope of the Tweener instance. In this way, we'll open up endless possible uses for the Tweener class, from tweening a movie clip's position to altering advanced Color transforms to even performing 3D transformations.

Open up the Tweener class, and add a new callTween() method to the public functions. This will be the method we would call to initiate this new type of interval call.

```
public function callTween(
  clip:Object,
  method:String,
  startParams:Object,
  destParams:Object,
  time:Number,
  easeFunction:Function
):Void {
  var intName:String = clip._name + "_" + prop;
  if (__intervals[intName] == undefined) __intervals[intName] = {};
  var intObj:Object = __intervals[intName];    intObj.count = 0;
  intObj.totalInts = Math.floor(time/Tweener.intervalTime);
  intObj.startParams = startParams;
  intObj.endParams = destParams;
  intObj.changeParams = {};
  for (var i:String in startParams) {
    intObj.changeParams[i] = destParams[i] - startParams[i];
  }
  intObj.easeFunction = (easeFunction == undefined) ?
➥ com.robertpenner.easing.Linear.easeNone : easeFunction;
  intObj.clip = clip;
```

```
        intObj.method = method;
        IntervalManager.setInterval(intObj, "interval",
➥   this, "runTweenCall", Tweener.intervalTime, intObj);
        dispatchEvent("startTween", {clip:clip, method:method});
        runTweenCall(intObj);
    }
```

The arguments passed to this function will be very similar to those passed to tween(). The changes to note are that instead of a property passed in to alter, a method is passed in that the Tweener instance will call every interval. Also, startParams and destParams are objects as opposed to scalar values.

The body of the function is also very similar to that of tween(). A new interval object is created and given all the arguments to store. The changeParams are calculated by running through them all in a loop and finding the differences. You may note that in this case the count is initialized at 0 instead of 1. We do this because in this method we have no way of knowing what to do with the start values of the tween, as they could apply to object properties or something more abstract. However, the Tweener instance doesn't need to know this since the external method that will be called should be set to handle all the numbers and know what to do with them. Instead, the Tweener instance simply sets the count to 0 and immediately calls the runTweenCall() method (the last line of the function) so that the external method might be invoked to handle the animation at the 0 count, which would be the tween's starting values.

Since this function and the tween() function both create the interval object in the exact same way, let's move that functionality into a separate method to clean things up. Add the following to the private methods:

```
        private function getInterval(clip:Object, prop:String):Object {
          var intName:String = clip._name + "_" + prop;
          if (__intervals[intName] == undefined) __intervals[intName] = {};
          return __intervals[intName];
        }
```

With this functionality now removed from the tween() and callTween() methods, we can replace the lines in those two places with a call to this method.

```
        public function tween(
          clip:Object,
          prop:String,
          startValue:Number,
          destValue:Number,
          time:Number,
          easeFunction:Function
        ):Void {
          clip[prop] = startValue;
          var intObj:Object = getInterval(clip, prop);
          intObj.count = 1;
          intObj.totalInts = Math.floor(time/Tweener.intervalTime);
          ...
          etc.
```

```
public function callTween(
  clip:Object,
  method:String,
  startParams:Object,
  destParams:Object,
  time:Number,
  easeFunction:Function
):Void {
  var intObj:Object = getInterval(clip, method);
  intObj.count = 0;
  intObj.totalInts = Math.floor(time/Tweener.intervalTime);
  ...
  etc.
```

Now that the getInterval() is separate, its flaws may become apparent. For instance, the method assumes that the object passed in for the creation of the interval object will have a _name property. However, unless the Tweener always deals with movie clips, this won't be the case. A good example is the new Mover class we'll create, which, like the Tweener, will be an abstract object that doesn't exist on the stage and won't have a _name property like a movie clip. In such a circumstance, we need the Tweener class to be able to have a way to store intervals for these abstract objects. We'll do this by assigning a unique ID to any object that doesn't have a _name and using this value when creating an interval object.

The first thing we need is to create a way to assign these unique IDs for a Tweener instance. This will be accomplished with a new __tweenID property and a getTweenID() method.

```
class com.oop.animation.Tweener extends Animator {

  private var __intervals:Object;
  private var __tweenID:Number = 0
  static var intervalTime:Number = 40;

  function Tweener() {
    __intervals = {};
  }

// PRIVATE
// _____

  private function getTweenID():String {
    return String(++__tweenID);
  }
}
```

Each ID requested will increment the __tweenID count by one. We also return the ID as a string since the interval object names are stored as strings and not numbers.

The next step would be to alter the getInterval() method to handle objects with no _name and instead assign a tweenID.

```
private function getInterval(clip:Object, prop:String):Object {
  var clipName:String = clip._name || clip._$tweenID;
  if (clipName == undefined) {
    clipName = clip._$tweenID = getTweenID();
  }
  var intName:String = clipName + "_" + prop;
  if (__intervals[intName] == undefined) __intervals[intName] = {};
  return __intervals[intName];
}
```

So now instead of immediately assuming a _name exists, the first line assigns the clip._name to a local variable clipName or a special property named _$tweenID if the clip._name doesn't exist. On the second line, if clipName is undefined, we know that the clip doesn't have a _name property and hasn't yet been assigned a special _$tweenID. In this case, we call getTweenID() and assign its return value to both the clipName variable and the clip._$tweenID property, which can then be accessed the next time this object creates a tween. In the third line, the clipName variable is then used to create the name of the interval object.

Of course, with this change in how the interval is stored, we need to alter the haltTween() call as well. Make the following bold changes:

```
public function haltTween(clip:Object, prop:String) {
  IntervalManager.clearInterval(getInterval(clip, prop), "interval");
}
```

The final step to add our more robust functionality to Tweener is to write the runTweenCall() method present in the callTween() code. This is the method that will be called every interval when the callTween() method begins a tween. In this method, the multiple values passed in to callTween() will have their new values calculated, and the external method will be called with these new values passed.

```
private function runTweenCall(intObj:Object):Void {
  var startParams:Number = intObj.startParams;
  var changeParams:Number = intObj.changeParams;
  var count:Number = intObj.count;
  var total:Number = intObj.totalInts;
  var p:Object = {};
  for (var i:String in changeParams) {
    p[i] = intObj.easeFunction(count,
➥ startParams[i], changeParams[i], total);
  }
  if (intObj.count++ > intObj.totalInts) {
    intObj.clip[intObj.method](intObj.endParams);
    IntervalManager.clearInterval(intObj, "interval");
    dispatchEvent("endTween",
➥ {clip:intObj.clip, method:intObj.method});
  } else {
```

```
      intObj.clip[intObj.method](p);
      dispatchEvent("tween", {clip:intObj.clip, method:intObj.method});
    }
  }
```

Much like callTween() was very similar to tween(), runTweenCall() has much in common with runTween(). Within the method, the values within changeParams are run through, and the easing equation is used to calculate their new values. Once that is complete, we determine whether the number of intervals allotted for the tween is up, and if so, the endParams are passed to the external method. If not, then the changed params for this time in the interval are passed to the external method.

With Tweener as complete as we need it for these exercises (you could certainly add more functionality such as the ability to loop or create random fluctuations in motion), here is the entire listing to check your code against:

```
import com.oop.animation.Animator;
import com.oop.managers.IntervalManager;

class com.oop.animation.Tweener extends Animator {

  private var __intervals:Object;
  private var __tweenID:Number = 0
  static var intervalTime:Number = 40;

  function Tweener() {
    __intervals = {};
  }

// PRIVATE
// _____

  private function getTweenID():String {
    return String(++__tweenID);
  }

  private function runTween(intObj:Object):Void {
    var startProp:Number = intObj.startProp;
    var changeProp:Number = intObj.changeProp;
    var count:Number = intObj.count;
    var total:Number = intObj.totalInts;
    intObj.clip[intObj.prop] =
➦ intObj.easeFunction(count, startProp, changeProp, total);
    var eventName:String = "tween";
    if (intObj.count++ >= intObj.totalInts) {
      intObj.clip[intObj.prop] = intObj.endProp;
      IntervalManager.clearInterval(intObj, "interval");
      eventName = "endTween";
```

```
      }
      dispatchEvent(eventName, {clip:intObj.clip, prop:intObj.prop});
    }

    private function runTweenCall(intObj:Object):Void {
      var startParams:Number = intObj.startParams;
      var changeParams:Number = intObj.changeParams;
      var count:Number = intObj.count;
      var total:Number = intObj.totalInts;
      var p:Object = {};
      for (var i:String in changeParams) {
        p[i] = intObj.easeFunction(count,
➡ startParams[i], changeParams[i], total);
      }
      if (intObj.count++ >= intObj.totalInts) {
        intObj.clip[intObj.method](intObj.endParams);
        IntervalManager.clearInterval(intObj, "interval");
        dispatchEvent("endTween",
➡ {clip:intObj.clip, method:intObj.method});
      } else {
        intObj.clip[intObj.method](p);
        dispatchEvent("tween", {clip:intObj.clip, method:intObj.method});
      }
    }

    private function getInterval(clip:Object, prop:String):Object {
      var clipName:String = clip._name || clip._$tweenID;
      if (clipName == undefined) {
        clipName = clip._$tweenID = getTweenID();
      }
      var intName:String = clipName + "_" + prop;
      if (__intervals[intName] == undefined) __intervals[intName] = {};
      return __intervals[intName];
    }

// PUBLIC
// _____

    public function haltTween(clip:Object, prop:String) {
      IntervalManager.clearInterval(getInterval(clip, prop), "interval");
    }

    public function tween(
      clip:Object,
      prop:String,
      startValue:Number,
      destValue:Number,
      time:Number,
      easeFunction:Function
```

```
):Void {
  clip[prop] = startValue;
  var intObj:Object = getInterval(clip, prop);
  intObj.count = 1;
  intObj.totalInts = Math.floor(time/Tweener.intervalTime);
  intObj.startProp = startValue;
  intObj.endProp = destValue;
  intObj.changeProp = intObj.endProp - intObj.startProp;
  intObj.clip = clip;
  intObj.prop = prop;
  intObj.easeFunction = (easeFunction == undefined) ?
➡ com.robertpenner.easing.Linear.easeNone : easeFunction;
  IntervalManager.setInterval(intObj, "interval",
➡ this, "runTween", Tweener.intervalTime, intObj);
  runTween(intObj);
  dispatchEvent("startTween", {clip:clip, prop:prop});
}

public function tweenTo(
  clip:Object,
  prop:String,
  destValue:Number,
  time:Number,
  easeFunction:Function
):Void {
  tween(clip, prop, clip[prop], destValue, time, easeFunction);
}

public function callTween(
  clip:Object,
  method:String,
  startParams:Object,
  destParams:Object,
  time:Number,
  easeFunction:Function
):Void {
  var intObj:Object = getInterval(clip, method);
  intObj.count = 0;
  intObj.totalInts = Math.floor(time/Tweener.intervalTime);
  intObj.startParams = startParams;
  intObj.endParams = destParams;
  intObj.changeParams = {};
  for (var i:String in startParams) {
    intObj.changeParams[i] = destParams[i] - startParams[i];
  }
  intObj.easeFunction = (easeFunction == undefined) ?
➡ com.robertpenner.easing.Linear.easeNone : easeFunction;
  intObj.clip = clip;
  intObj.method = method;
```

```
        IntervalManager.setInterval(intObj, "interval",
➥    this, "runTweenCall", Tweener.intervalTime, intObj);
        dispatchEvent("startTween", {clip:clip, method:method});
        runTweenCall(intObj);
      }

   }
```

Mover

Now that we have added the extra functionality to Tweener, creating unique animators that can handle complex objects is pretty simple. Take for instance the Mover class discussed at the beginning of the last section. Let's look at the code necessary to create such a class using our Tweener.

Create a new ActionScript file and save it as Mover.as into the com/oop/animation directory where Tweener resides. Add the following lines of code, which is the framework of a simple Mover class:

```
import com.oop.animation.Animator;
import com.oop.animation.Tweener;

class com.oop.animation.Mover extends Animator {

   private var __tweener:Tweener;
   private var __clip:MovieClip;

   function Mover() {
      __tweener = new Tweener();
   }

// PRIVATE
// _____

   private function runMoveTween(intObj:Object):Void {
   }

// PUBLIC
// _____

   public function haltTween(clip:Object) {
   }

   public function tween(
      clip:MovieClip,
      startParams:Object,
      endParams:Object,
      time:Number,
      easeFunction:Function
```

```
):Void {
}

public function tweenTo(
   clip:MovieClip,
   endParams:Object,
   time:Number,
   easeFunction:Function
):Void {
}

}
```

As you can see, Mover isn't a Tweener itself, but instead has a Tweener instance that it will use to calculate all of the changed values. tween() and tweenTo() will initiate a tween, runMoveTween() will be the external method called by the Tweener instance, and haltTween() will end the tween when requested. Of course, the methods won't yet do anything, so let's fill them in.

```
public function tween(
   clip:MovieClip,
   startParams:Object,
   endParams:Object,
   time:Number,
   easeFunction:Function
):Void {
   __tweener.addEventListener("endTween", this);
   __clip = clip;
   dispatchEvent("startTween", {clip:clip});
   __tweener.callTween(this, "runMoveTween",
➥ startParams, endParams, time, easeFunction);
}

public function tweenTo(
   clip:MovieClip,
   endParams:Object,
   time:Number,
   easeFunction:Function
):Void {
   tween(clip, {x:clip._x, y:clip._y}, endParams, time, easeFunction);
}
```

With the Tweener instance providing most of the functionality, setting up a tween of multiple properties is relatively easy. Note that in the tween() method, we add the Mover instance as a listener to the Tweener instance. This means that we'll need to define an endTween() method that will be called when the endTween event is dispatched. The remaining lines in the method save a reference to the clip being tweened, dispatch the startTween event, and set up __tweener to call runMoveTween() at every tween interval. The Tweener instance will handle calculating what values should be sent to this method by using the startParams, the endParams, and the easing function passed in.

As before, tweenTo() merely needs to call tween() with the startParams passed in.

Next, let's flesh out the final two methods we defined earlier while adding the new endTween() method that will be called when __tweener completes a tween.

```
// PRIVATE
// _____

  private function endTween(infoObj:Object):Void {
    __tweener.removeEventListener("endTween", this);
    dispatchEvent("endTween", {clip:__clip});
  }

  private function runMoveTween(intObj:Object):Void {
    __clip._x = intObj.x;
    __clip._y = intObj.y;
    dispatchEvent("tween");
  }

// PUBLIC
// _____

  public function haltTween(clip:Object) {
    __tweener.haltTween(this, "runMoveTween");
  }
```

endTween() merely needs to remove the Mover instance as a listener for the endTween event from __tweener. runMoveTween(), which receives values calculated by __tweener, sets the clip's _x and _y properties to the current tween values. Finally, haltTween() calls the haltTween() method on __tweener.

The simple Mover class is complete, so let's try it out. Create a new ActionScript file and save it into the same directory as AnimationTest and TweenerTest from the first section's exercise. Add the following code:

```
import com.oop.animation.Mover;
import com.robertpenner.easing.*;

class MoverTest extends AnimationTest {

  private var __mover:Mover;

  function MoverTest() {}

  private function init():Void {
    super.init();
    __mover = new Mover();
    onMouseDown = moveToMouse;
  }
```

```
    private function moveToMouse():Void {
      __mover.tweenTo(__blockHolder,
➥ {x:_xmouse, y:_ymouse}, 600, Circ.easeInOut);
    }

  }
```

Since AnimationTest, if you recall, draws a Block instance on the stage, MoverTest simply has to decide how to move it about. In the init() method, a new Mover instance is created and moveToMouse() is assigned to the onMouseDown handler. moveToMouse() calls a tweenTo() on the Mover instance, animating __blockHolder to the current mouse position using the Circ.easeInOut easing equation.

To test this out, duplicate the tweenerTest.fla file from the first section's exercise and save it as moverTest.fla. This file has an empty clip in the library and the Block graphic skin. Change the Frame 1 code on the main timeline to the following:

```
Object.registerClass("empty class", MoverTest);
attachMovie("empty class", "moverTest", 0);
```

Test the movie and click the stage to see the Block tween to the clicked position. Not bad! What would be great now is if we could add a little dynamic blur to the fast-moving object in order to create a little more realistic movement. Turns out that in Flash 8, we can!

Motion blur

With the new BlurFilter available in Flash 8, we can add a bit of motion blur to our objects as they move across the stage, a cool little effect with minimal additional work. This won't be a true directional motion blur, but a close approximation. When things are moving fast across the screen in a blur, it will be hard to tell the difference anyway!

What we'll do is calculate the distance an object has traveled since the last interval call and use the distance on each axis to set the blur on each axis, properties of the BlurFilter. Therefore, if an object moves more vertically than horizontally, the blur on the y axis will be greater than the blur on the x axis.

The first thing we'll add to our Mover.as file is the code to import the BlurFilter class and set its default values for Mover.

```
import com.oop.animation.Animator;
import com.oop.animation.Tweener;
import flash.filters.BlurFilter;

class com.oop.animation.Mover extends Animator {

  private var __tweener:Tweener;
  private var __clip:MovieClip;
  public var blur:Boolean = false;
  public var blurFactor:Number = 1;
  public var blurQuality:Number = 1;
```

```
function Mover() {
    __tweener = new Tweener();
}
```

blur will determine whether the Mover uses the BlurFilter on its tweened clip, turned off by default. blurFactor will be used to help determine the blurX and blurY values for the BlurFilter (higher values will produce more blur), and blurQuality will be passed to the BlurFilter as its quality property, controlling how many blur calculations are performed on the object. Higher quality obviously produces better results, but at the cost of more processing cycles.

I have decided to leave these properties public for ease of demonstration here. Feel free to create getter/setter methods for private variables if you so wish. Also, there is the possibility of adding blur values for each individual tween as opposed to for every tween performed by a single Mover instance. That, again, is up to you.

The next step is to add a BlurFilter to the tweened clip when a tween starts (and when blur is set to true). Add these lines to the tween() method:

```
public function tween(
    clip:MovieClip,
    startParams:Object,
    endParams:Object,
    time:Number,
    easeFunction:Function
):Void {
    __tweener.addEventListener("endTween", this);
    __clip = clip;
    if (blur) {
        var f:Array = __clip.filters || [];
        if (f[f.length-1] instanceof BlurFilter) f = f.slice(0, -1);
        f.push(new BlurFilter(0, 0, blurQuality))
        __clip.filters = f;
    }
    dispatchEvent("startTween", {clip:clip});
    __tweener.callTween(this, "runMoveTween",
➥ startParams, endParams, time, easeFunction);
}
```

If blur is set to true, we grab either the filters array currently assigned to the object or, if it doesn't yet exist, create a new array. Then, if the last filter in this array is already a BlurFilter instance, we remove it. This assumes that clips passed to the Mover that should be blurred should not already have a BlurFilter instance applied. Finally, we push a new BlurFilter instance into the filters array with no blur yet applied (0 values for both the blurX and blurY) and reassign this modified array back as the clip's filters. We are now ready to tween!

Now that the BlurFilter is prepared on the tweened clip, we can alter its values each frame to create the motion blur. This will all occur in the runMoveTween() method.

```
private function runMoveTween(intObj:Object):Void {
  __clip._x = intObj.x;
  __clip._y = intObj.y;
  if (blur) {
    if (__clip._$moverLastX != undefined) {
      var f:Array = __clip.filters;
      var bf:BlurFilter = f[f.length-1];
      var factor:Number = blurFactor/10;
      bf.blurX = Math.abs((intObj.x - __clip._$moverLastX)*factor);
      bf.blurY = Math.abs((intObj.y - __clip._$moverLastY)*factor);
      __clip.filters = f;
    }
    __clip._$moverLastX = intObj.x;
    __clip._$moverLastY = intObj.y;
  }
  dispatchEvent("tween");
}
```

Here is the logic applied to create our blur. Each frame, the Mover modifies two special values on the tweened clip, _$moverLastX and _$moverLastY, so named to hopefully prevent any conflict with values already on the clip. These variables will hold the last screen position of the clip on each axis. The first time this method is called, these values don't exist, but every subsequent time we can check the difference of these values and the current position of the clip and use this to calculate the blur. How exactly is that calculated? A factor variable is determined based on the blurFactor property of Mover. The movement on each axis is multiplied by this factor to determine the blur amount, so the larger the factor and the greater the movement, the larger the blur. By default, blurFactor is set to 1, which makes factor resolve to 0.1. Therefore, with these settings, a movement of 50 pixels on the x axis will set the BlurFilter's blurX value to 5. This calculation occurs every time this method is called during a tween to create a dynamic blur.

The last step would be to remove the blur upon completion of the tween. This is taken care of in the haltTween() method.

```
public function haltTween(clip:Object) {
  if (blur) {
    delete __clip._$moverLastX;
    delete __clip._$moverLastY;
    __clip.filters = __clip.filters.slice(0, -1);
  }
  __tweener.haltTween(this, "runMoveTween");
}
```

Once the tween is complete, the special variables used for the tween are deleted, and the BlurFilter, last in the list of filters for the clip, is removed.

To test this in action, return to the MoverTest.as file and set the Mover instance's blur property to true.

```
private function init():Void {
  super.init();
  __mover = new Mover();
  __mover.blur = true;
  onMouseDown = moveToMouse;
}
```

Test your movie, and you should see a subtle blur as you click the stage and tween the clip. To get a more distinct blur (less distinct?), try raising the blur factor.

```
private function init():Void {
  super.init();
  __mover = new Mover();
  __mover.blur = true;
  __mover.blurFactor = 3;
  onMouseDown = moveToMouse;
}
```

With just a little bit of code encapsulated in an animation class, we've now enabled the ability to tween the position of any movie clip object in our movies and have a motion blur applied!

Transitioning views

This next group of classes, we'll explore the transitioning of visual objects from one state to another. By abstracting these transition classes out from the objects themselves, they may be reused over and over from one project to another with little to no additional work. For instance, if you were developing an image slideshow and you wanted a simple fade in/out of all the images, you might consider making a function that uses an onEnterFrame or an interval to change the alpha of one image till it disappeared, then tweens up the opacity of another image to bring it into view. This sort of transition is fairly easy to accomplish and might even be something that you have already copied and pasted from one project to another. How much easier would it be, even for this simple function, to create a transition instance, pass it the clip to be transitioned, and just tell it to start. Once completed, an event would be broadcast so you could have another transition tween in the new image. It becomes more obviously useful when dealing with more complex transitions, as we'll create through the rest of this chapter, using some of the bitmap manipulation available in Flash 8. By separating the transition code from the graphic objects themselves, these classes can be reused in any project with little fuss.

Transition

All transitions will have similar needs, so it makes sense to have a class from which all transitions will inherit. This class will establish the common properties and the start and end events for transitions.

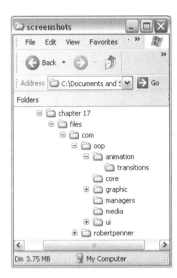

Figure 17-5.
The path to the new transitions package

Create a new directory in the com/oop/animation directory and name it transitions, as shown in Figure 17-5. Now create a new ActionScript file in Flash and save it as Transition.as into the transitions directory. Enter the following code to get started:

```
import com.oop.animation.Animator;
import com.oop.animation.Tweener;
import com.oop.managers.IntervalManager;

class com.oop.animation.transitions.Transition extends Animator {

  private var __tweener:Tweener;
  public var clip:MovieClip;
  public var time:Number = 1000;
  public var direction:String = "up";
  public var easeFunction:Function =
➥ com.robertpenner.easing.Linear.easeNone;
  public var type:String = "in";
  public var startTransform:Object;
  public var endTransform:Object;

  function Transition() {}

  private function init() {
    super.init();
    __tweener = new Tweener();
  }
```

Once again, at the top of the class we import the other necessary classes for the code. Transition will inherit from Animator, so it will have all the event dispatching functionality. In the properties declarations, we leave the __tweener that will be performing the interval calculations private, as it will never have to be accessed externally. The other properties are all configurable, and could be made to be private with getter/setter methods, but have been made public here again for simplicity's sake.

What will these properties determine? clip will be the movie clip instance to transition. time will be the length of time in milliseconds in which to perform the transition. direction will be useful for those transitions that have an obvious direction, like the standard wipe, which could occur left, right, up, down, etc. The easeFunction, discussed much earlier this chapter, can be passed to the Tweener instance to provide different forms of numeric calculations for the transformations. type will determine whether a clip is transitioning in to view, or out of it. Finally, startTransform and endTransform are open-ended and can hold values necessary for each end of a transition (for instance, a color transition might store color values here, whereas a transition using a filter might store filter-specific variables).

After the constructor, the init() method invokes the super method and then instantiates a Tweener instance that will perform the transition calculations when we come to it.

To finish off the Transition class, we need to define the standard methods that a developer would call on any transition. The full listing of the Transition class, with the new lines added in bold, is as follows:

```
import com.oop.animation.Animator;
import com.oop.animation.Tweener;
import com.oop.managers.IntervalManager;

class com.oop.animation.transitions.Transition extends Animator {

  private var __tweener:Tweener;
  public var clip:MovieClip;
  public var time:Number = 1000;
  public var direction:String = "up";
  public var easeFunction:Function =
➥ com.robertpenner.easing.Linear.easeNone;
  public var type:String = "in";
  public var startTransform:Object;
  public var endTransform:Object;

  function Transition() {}

  private function init() {
    super.init();
    __tweener = new Tweener();
  }

  public function start():Void {
    __tweener.addEventListener("endTween", this, "halt");
  }
```

```
    public function halt():Void {
      __tweener.removeEventListener("endTween", this);
      dispatchEvent("endTransition", {clip:clip});
    }

  }
```

When the transition's start() method is called, the transition is added as a listener to the __tweener's endTween event. When the tween completes, the halt() method will be called, removing the listener and dispatching an endTransition event. The classes inheriting from Transition will have to determine the best way for each to halt the transition animation itself—polymorphism at work again.

This class in and of itself won't do anything. Next, we'll build a class that extends Transition in order to perform a visual effect.

FadeTransition

Now that we have the base class functionality, each transition that builds off it merely needs to concern itself with code specific to performing its unique transition. We'll start with one of the easiest examples, an alpha fading transition.

Create a new ActionScript document and save it into the com/oop/animation/ transitions directory as FadeTransition.as. The following is the entire class listing, with explanation to follow.

```
import com.oop.animation.transitions.Transition;

class com.oop.animation.transitions.FadeTransition extends Transition {

  public var startAlpha:Number;

  function FadeTransition() {}

  public function start():Void {
    super.start();
    if (type == "in") {
      var a:Number = startAlpha;
      if (a == undefined) a = 0;
      __tweener.tween(clip, "_alpha", a, 100, time, easeFunction);
    } else {
      var a:Number = startAlpha;
      if (a == undefined) a = clip._alpha;
      __tweener.tween(clip, "_alpha", a, 0, time, easeFunction);
    }
  }
}
```

```
public function halt():Void {
  __tweener.haltTween(clip, "_alpha");
  clip._alpha = ((type == "in") ? 100 : 0);
  super.halt();
}

public function removeTransitionEffects():Void {
  clip._alpha = 100;
}

}
```

When a new FadeTransition is created and its start() method is called, it calls the tween() method on its Tweener instance, tweening the _alpha property of the clip passed in. Whether the tween goes from full opacity to 0, or 0 to full, depends on the type of transition, in or out. You can also see that a startAlpha property was added so that the alpha tween could start at an arbitrary value. This would be useful if you had a clip that was already at 80% opacity and this transition was used to tween it out.

In the halt() method, the __tweener's haltTween() method is called to stop the animation and the clip's _alpha is set to 0 or 100 based on the type of transition. Finally, the super's halt() method is called, where the Tweener listener is removed and the endTransition event is dispatched.

While coding this class, it became apparent that a useful function would be one where any effects placed on a clip by a transition could be removed, hence the original-named method removeTransitionEffects(). Whatever actions a transition has performed on a clip, be they alpha fades or the application of filters, need to be easily removable by the developer, without the developer needing to know what those actions were. In the FadeTransition's case, the clip's _alpha should be restored to its full value.

Since this a method that all transitions should support, let's put it into the base class to be overridden by each subclass. Go back to Transition.as and add the new line in bold:

```
public function halt():Void {
  __tweener.removeEventListener("endTween", this);
  dispatchEvent("endTransition", {clip:clip});
}

public function removeTransitionEffects():Void {};
```

The removeTransitionEffects() is empty here, but at least any code accessing a Transition instance can expect this method to exist without any compile errors being thrown.

Testing transitions

We now have a super Transition class and a FadeTransition inheriting from it, so it's time to see the fruits of our labors and watch a transition! Of course, what that means is we need to prepare a file with a movie clip in it on which to perform the transitions. This file will run through all transitions that we store in an array.

Create a new Flash document and save it as `transitionTest.fla` into the same directory where you placed the earlier `tweenerTest.fla` and `moverTest.fla` files. In the document, create a new movie clip symbol named and exported as empty clip. Finally, import into the library an image that will fit on the stage (the smaller the image, the faster the transitions can perform). You may use the file included in this chapter's download files, `Audrey.jpg`, or any of your own choosing. Once it's in the library, right-click the symbol and in its Linkage dialog box set the symbol's Identifier to something descriptive (I used Audrey, as you see in Figure 17-6).

Figure 17-6. The library set up to test transitions

Now create a new ActionScript file and save it into the same directory as this `transitionTest.fla`. Save this new file as `TransitionTest.as`. Enter the following code:

```
import com.oop.ui.UIObject;
import com.oop.animation.transitions.*;
import flash.display.BitmapData;
import flash.geom.*;
```

```
class TransitionTest extends UIObject {

    private var __imageHolder:UIObject;
    private var __transition:Transition;
    private var __transitionList:Array;
    private var __transitionCount:Number;
    private var __transitioning:Boolean;

    function TransitionTest() {}

    private function init():Void {
        super.init();
        __transitionList =
            [
            FadeTransition
            ];
        __transitionCount = 0;
        var image:BitmapData = BitmapData.loadBitmap("Audrey");
        __imageHolder = createEmptyObject("__imageHolder", 0);
        __imageHolder.createEmptyObject("innerClip", 0);
        __imageHolder.getChild("innerClip").attachBitmap(image, 0);
        __imageHolder.position = new Point((Stage.width-image.width)/2,
➡ (Stage.height-image.height)/2);
        __imageHolder.filters = [
➡ new flash.filters.DropShadowFilter(10, 45, 0x000000,
➡ 40, 5, 5, .7, 1)];
        onMouseDown = transitionImageOut;
        transitionImageIn();
    }
}
```

This is the first half of the class to test the transitions. After the class imports and property declarations, which will be explained in the actual methods, we begin with the init() method. In this, we create a new array named __transitionList, which will hold all transitions to test. Right now, there is only one, FadeTransition. The current transition (the one that will occur next) has its index stored in the __transitionCount variable. The next several lines use the new BitmapData object to attach the JPEG from the library (isn't it fantastic we can do that now?). Be sure to change the name of the bitmap to attach to whatever you named your bitmap symbol in transitionTest.fla. This image is placed inside a UIObject instance named innerClip that is created within the UIObject __imageHolder. The reason for this nesting is so we can center innerClip within __imageHolder, effectively creating a center registration point.

Once the image is attached to innerClip and centered within __imageHolder, we add a nice DropShadow filter to it for a little effect. We then set transitionImageOut() to be called onMouseDown and immediately call transitionImageIn(), which will start the first transition.

These next functions, completing TransitionTest, define the transition functions. Add these below the init() within the class definition.

```
       private function transitionImageIn():Void {
          __transitioning = true;
          __transition.removeEventListener("endTransition", this);
          __transition = Transition(
     ➡ new __transitionList[__transitionCount]());
          __transition.addEventListener("endTransition", this);
          __transition.clip = __imageHolder;
          __transition.start();
       }

       private function transitionImageOut():Void {
          if (__transitioning) return;
          __transitioning = true;
          __transition.addEventListener("endTransition", this);
          __transition.type = "out";
          __transition.start();
          if (++__transitionCount >= __transitionList.length) {
             __transitionCount = 0;
          }
       }

       private function endTransition():Void {
          if (__transition.type == "out") {
             __transition.removeTransitionEffects();
             transitionImageIn();
          } else {
             __transitioning = false;
          }
       }
```

When transitionImageIn() is called, we set a Boolean flag to true so that another transition may not be called until the transition is complete. Then, after removing this instance as a listener to the previous transition, whatever that may have been, we create a new transition instance, using the current __transitionCount to access a function from the __transitionList array. This instance is cast to Transition, as that class holds all the common methods and properties for all transitions. Next, we add this class as a listener to the new transition, pass in a reference to the _imageHolder movie clip, and tell the transition to start().

When the transition is complete, it will call the endTransition() method. At that time, if the current transition was going out, we remove any transition artifacts from the clip and call transitionImageIn() to transition the image in using the next transition. However, if the transition was coming in, then we simply set the transitioning flag to false, meaning that clicking the mouse will start the next transition.

That logic is defined in the transitionImageOut() method, which you'll recall was the onMouseDown handler. This changes the current transition's type to out and starts it up. __transitionCount is then incremented to move on to the next transitions. If the max transitions has been reached, then the count is set back to 0.

Time to test the code! Return to `transitionTest.fla` and add the following lines of code to the single frame:

```
Object.registerClass("empty class", TransitionTest);
attachMovie("empty class", "transitionTest", 0);
```

Figure 17-7. The transition test base image between each transition

Figure 17-8. The FadeTransition applied to the image

Test your movie and the image should begin transitioning in immediately, as you see in Figures 17-7 and 17-8. Once the transition is complete, click with your mouse to see the image fade out, then fade back in. This will continue to loop as long as you keep clicking your mouse. Although this end result might seem paltry after all that code, the beauty of it is that the transition itself now can be accomplished with three little lines of code:

```
var ft:FadeTransition = new FadeTransition();
ft.clip = myMovieClip;
ft.start();
```

This small snippet can be used in any project, and you can expect it to work the same. Plus, since you can configure the time, type, and easing function, you have a number of possible transitions at your disposal.

ColorTransition

The next transition we code will also offer many different ways it can be configured. With the ColorTransition, any advanced Color transform can be used to transform in and out of the view of a clip. This means that an image might transition in from white or black or hot pink. It also means that different color effects might be transitioned through, like a transform from a negative of the image to a positive. The transition can change completely based on whatever is passed in as the startTransform and endTransform. Let's take a look at the code, represented next in its entirety.

```
import com.oop.animation.transitions.Transition;
import flash.geom.*;

class com.oop.animation.transitions.ColorTransition
➥ extends Transition {

  private var __transform:Transform;

  function ColorTransition() {
    startTransform = {ra:0, rb:0, ga:0, gb:0, ba:0, bb:0, aa:1, ab:0};
    endTransform = {ra:1, rb:0, ga:1, gb:0, ba:1, bb:0, aa:1, ab:0};
  }

  private function setTransform(ct:Object):Void {
    __transform.colorTransform = new ColorTransform(
      ct.ra,
      ct.ga,
      ct.ba,
      ct.aa,
      ct.rb,
      ct.gb,
      ct.bb,
      ct.ab
    );
  }
```

17

```
        public function start():Void {
          super.start();
          __transform = new Transform(clip);
          if (type == "in") {
            setTransform(startTransform);
            __tweener.callTween(this, "setTransform",
➥ startTransform, endTransform, time, easeFunction);
          } else {
            setTransform(endTransform);
            __tweener.callTween(this, "setTransform",
➥ endTransform, startTransform, time, easeFunction);
          }
        }

        public function halt():Void {
          setTransform(type == "in" ? endTransform : startTransform);
          __tweener.haltTween(this, "setTransform");
          super.halt();
        }

        public function removeTransitionEffects():Void {
          setTransform({ra:1, rb:0, ga:1, gb:0, ba:1, bb:0, aa:1, ab:0});
        }

      }
```

The ColorTransition tweens the color properties stored in the two transforms, either end determined by the type of transition, in or out. When start() is called, a Transform instance (new to Flash 8) is created to handle the color transforms of the clip. Then the __tweener's callTween() is used to call the ColorTransition instance's setTransform() each interval call, swapping the Transform's colorTransform, effectively coloring the clip.

The halt() function colors the clip with the proper transform depending on the transition type, and then halts the tween of the ColorTransition.

Finally, the removeTransitionEffects() method sets the clip's color transform back to the default with no tinting.

That's a pretty simple implementation for tweening colors (considering we can even use easing functions to make it more interesting)! This is because we have spent the time laying the groundwork elsewhere in the Transition and Tweener classes. We are now getting to the fun part of implementing new effects with very little elbow grease.

To see how this works, add the ColorTransition to your TransitionTest class.

```
private function init():Void {
  super.init();
  __transitionList =
    [
    FadeTransition,
    ColorTransition
    ];
```

Test the `transitionTest.fla` and, after the opacity fade transition, you'll see the image perform a color transition from black to its normal colors. Figure 17-9 gives you an idea of how this will look.

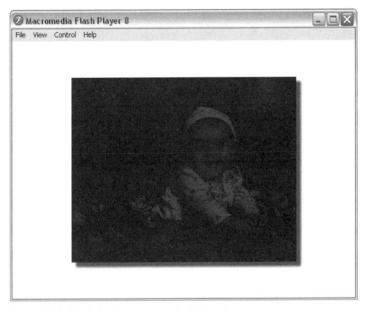

Figure 17-9. The ColorTransition applied to the image

BlurTransition

This next transition utilizes the BlurFilter we already worked with in the Mover class. The transition will be from a blurred image to crisp, or vice versa. Once more, the class is fairly small, since a lot of the work is taken care of elsewhere, so the following represents the complete listing, with explanation to follow.

```
import com.oop.animation.transitions.Transition;
import flash.filters.BlurFilter;

class com.oop.animation.transitions.BlurTransition extends Transition {

  public var quality:Number = 1;
```

```
function BlurTransition() {
  startTransform = {blurX:25, blurY:25};
  endTransform = {blurX:0, blurY:0};
}

private function applyBlur(blur:BlurFilter):Void {
  var f:Array = clip.filters.slice(0, -1);
  clip.filters = f.concat(blur);
}

private function runTransition(transform:Object):Void {
  applyBlur(new BlurFilter(
➡ transform.blurX, transform.blurY, quality));
}

public function start():Void {
  super.start();
  var f:Array = clip.filters || [];
  if (f[f.length-1] instanceof BlurFilter) f = f.slice(0, -1);
  f.push(new BlurFilter(0, 0, quality));
  clip.filters = f;
  if (type == "in") {
    __tweener.callTween(this, "runTransition",
➡ startTransform, endTransform, time, easeFunction);
  } else {
    __tweener.callTween(this, "runTransition",
➡ endTransform, startTransform, time, easeFunction);
  }
}

public function halt():Void {
  if (type == "in") {
    applyBlur(new BlurFilter(
➡ endTransform.blurX, endTransform.blurY, quality));
  } else {
    applyBlur(new BlurFilter(
➡ startTransform.blurX, startTransform.blurY, quality));
  }
  __tweener.haltTween(this, "runTransition");
  super.halt();
}

public function removeTransitionEffects():Void {
  clip.filters = clip.filters.slice(0, -1);
}

}
```

Much of this bears a striking resemblance to what we already coded in the Mover class. When the start() method is called, a new BlurFilter instance is pushed into the clip's filters array (after ensuring that the last filter applied is NOT a BlurFilter instance). Then, depending on the type of transition, the __tweener.callTween() is used to tween from the startParams to the endParams, or vice versa.

The runTransition(), which is called by __tweener every interval with new values, simply calls applyBlur(), a method that removes the last filter in the clip's filters array and adds the BlurFilter instance passed to the method, reapplying this modified array to the clip.

halt() in this transition applies either the start or end blur to the clip and halts the tween. removeTransitionEffects() removes the BlurFilter that was added.

To test, once again return to TransitionTest.as and add the BlurTransition to the __transitionList.

```
private function init():Void {
  super.init();
  __transitionList =
    [
    FadeTransition,
    ColorTransition,
    BlurTransition
    ];
```

Figure 17-10. The BlurTransition applied to the image

Test the `transitionTest.fla` with these changes and see all three transition types playing together (Figure 17-10 shows what the BlurTransition looks like). That's three complete transition effects, each between 30 to 50 lines of code, demonstrating the powers of abstraction, inheritance, and polymorphism. But we can still do more!

NoiseTransition

The NoiseTransition takes advantage of the new BitmapData object and its noise() method, which fills an image with pixel noise. We'll use this to create a sort of TV snow effect, as if a television channel is coming into focus (you know, from the days we still had knobs on our TVs). The code is once again less than 50 lines, so here is the full listing, with its explanation to follow.

```
import com.oop.managers.IntervalManager;
import com.oop.animation.transitions.Transition;
import com.oop.animation.transitions.FadeTransition;
import flash.display.BitmapData;
import flash.geom.*;

class com.oop.animation.transitions.NoiseTransition
➥ extends Transition {

  private var __noiseImage:BitmapData;

  function NoiseTransition() {}

  private function runTransition():Void {
    __noiseImage.noise(getTimer(), 0, 255, 7, true);
  }

  public function start():Void {
    super.start();
    __noiseImage = new BitmapData(
➥ clip._width, clip._height, true, 0x00FFFFFF);
    if (clip.noise_mc) clip.noise_mc.removeMovieClip();
    clip.createEmptyMovieClip("noise_mc", clip.getNextHighestDepth());
    clip.noise_mc.attachBitmap(__noiseImage, 0);
    var t:FadeTransition = new FadeTransition();
    t.clip = clip.noise_mc;
    t.type = ((type == "in") ? "out" : "in");
    t.easeFunction = easeFunction;
    t.time = time;
    t.addEventListener("endTransition", this, "halt");
    t.start();
    IntervalManager.setInterval(
➥ this, "interval", this, "runTransition", 40);
  }
```

```
public function halt():Void {
  IntervalManager.clearInterval(this, "interval");
  if (type == "in") removeTransitionEffects();
  super.halt();
}

public function removeTransitionEffects():Void {
  clip.noise_mc.removeMovieClip();
  __noiseImage.dispose();
}

}
```

When the transition's start() is called, a new transparent BitmapData object is created to match the clip's dimensions. Then, a new movie clip is created on the clip at its next highest depth, and the bitmap is attached to this clip. To have the noise fade in or out, we'll reuse the FadeTransition we created earlier (see how it all fits together nicely now?), passing the noise_mc as its clip to transition. The type will be the opposite of NoiseTransition's type—for instance, if the NoiseTransition is to transition in, then we want the noise itself to fade out. When the FadeTransition instance completes its transition, we specify that it should call the halt() method on this NoiseTransition instance. The last line in the start() method sets up an interval call so that we can animate the noise in the runTransition() method while the noise_mc is fading in or out.

If you look to runTransition(), it's a single line, but with a method new to Flash 8. The noise() method of BitmapFilter simply applies noise to the image. By passing in a different seed value each time (the first parameter—getTimer() ensures that this will never be the same value), the noise is changed each frame, creating the snow animation.

When the FadeTransition instance completes its transition, halt() is called, which clears the animation interval. If the transition type is in, then removeTransitionEffects() is called, which disposes of the __noiseImage BitmapData instance and removes the clip we created to display it.

Return to TransitionTest and add the NoiseTransition into the list of transitions to test.

```
private function init():Void {
  super.init();
  __transitionList =
    [
    FadeTransition,
    ColorTransition,
    BlurTransition,
    NoiseTransition
    ];
```

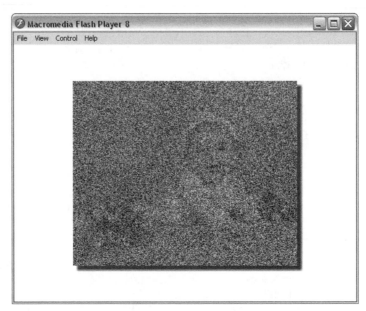

Figure 17-11. The NoiseTransition applied to the image

Test the movie to see all the transitions in action! Figure 17-11 shows how the NoiseTransition appears.

DissolveTransition and WaterTransition

Included to further inspire you are two more transitions that are a bit more complex, using Flash 8 bitmap manipulation features. You can copy these files, available with this chapter's download files, into your class directory and test them in the same TransitionTest class.

The DissolveTransition uses the pixelDissolve() method of the BitmapData class to dissolve an image from a solid image, breaking it down into smaller clumps of pixels, and vice versa. The WaterTransition uses the powerful DisplacementMapFilter and the perlinNoise() method of the BitmapData class to create a water-like effect, rippling the image into a static position. The complete listing of both of these classes follows for your perusal and further discovery. Although they are certainly more complex than the earlier transitions, they are still less than 90 lines of code apiece.

```
// +++++++++++++++++++++++++++++++++++++++++++++++++++++
// DISSOLVE TRANSITION

import com.oop.managers.IntervalManager;
import com.oop.animation.transitions.Transition;
import com.oop.animation.Tweener;
import flash.display.BitmapData;
import flash.geom.*
```

```
class com.oop.animation.transitions.DissolveTransition
➥ extends Transition {

  private var __dissolveImage:BitmapData;
  private var __originalImage:BitmapData;
  public var rate:Number = 5;

  function DissolveTransition() {}

  private function runTransition(intObj:Object):Void {
    __dissolveImage.draw(clip.dissolve_mc, new Matrix());
    intObj.seed = Number(__dissolveImage.pixelDissolve(
➥ __originalImage, intObj.rect, intObj.point,
➥ intObj.seed, intObj.pixels));
    if ((intObj.currentPixels += intObj.pixels)
➥ >= intObj.totalPixels) halt();
  }

  public function start():Void {
    super.start();
    var w:Number = clip._width;
    var h:Number = clip._height;
    __dissolveImage = new BitmapData(w, h, true, 0x00FFFFFF);
    __originalImage = new BitmapData(w, h, true, 0x00FFFFFF);
    if (type == "in") {
      __originalImage.draw(clip.innerClip, new Matrix());
    } else {
      __dissolveImage.draw(clip.innerClip, new Matrix());
    }
    clip.innerClip._visible = false;
    clip.createEmptyMovieClip("dissolve_mc",
➥ clip.getNextHighestDepth())
    var holder_mc:MovieClip =
➥ clip.createEmptyMovieClip("holder_mc", clip.getNextHighestDepth());
    holder_mc.attachBitmap(__dissolveImage, 0);
    var intObj:Object = {};
    intObj.totalPixels = w*h;;
    intObj.pixels = ((w*h)/100)*rate;
    intObj.currentPixels = 0;
    intObj.rect = new Rectangle(0, 0, w, h);
    intObj.point = new Point(0, 0);
    intObj.seed = Number(new Date());
    IntervalManager.setInterval(this, "interval",
➥ this, "runTransition", Tweener.intervalTime, intObj);
  }

  public function halt():Void {
    IntervalManager.clearInterval(this, "interval");
    clip.innerClip._visible = (type == "in");
```

```
      clip.dissolve_mc.removeMovieClip();
      clip.holder_mc.removeMovieClip();
      __dissolveImage.dispose();
      __originalImage.dispose();
      super.halt();
    }

    public function removeTransitionEffects():Void {
      clip.innerClip._visible = true;
    }

  }
```

Figure 7-12 shows how the DissolveTransition should look when you test it.

Figure 17-12. The DissolveTransition applied to the image

```
// ++++++++++++++++++++++++++++++++++++++++++++++++++++
// WATER TRANSITION

import com.oop.managers.IntervalManager;
import com.oop.animation.transitions.Transition;
import com.oop.animation.Tweener;
import flash.filters.DisplacementMapFilter;
import flash.display.BitmapData;
import flash.geom.*;
```

```
class com.oop.animation.transitions.WaterTransition
➡ extends Transition {

  private var __waterImage:BitmapData;
  private var __noiseImage:BitmapData;
  private var __seed:Number;
  private var __offsets:Array;
  private var __displaceFactor:Number;
  public var rate:Number = 15;
  public var maxDisplace:Number = 200;

  function WaterTransition() {
    __offsets = [new Point(), new Point()];
    __seed = Number(new Date());
  }

  private function runTransition(intObj:Object):Void {
    for(var i:Number=0;i<2;++i){
      __offsets[i].x+=rate;
      __offsets[i].y-=rate;
    }
    __noiseImage.perlinNoise(100,100,1,
➡ __seed,false,true,1,false,__offsets);
    var dMap:DisplacementMapFilter=
➡ new DisplacementMapFilter(__noiseImage,
➡ new Point(),1,1,__displaceFactor,__displaceFactor,"clamp");
    var mc:MovieClip=clip.water_mc;
    mc.filters=[dMap];
    if (type=="in") {
      if (intObj.alpha<100)mc._alpha=(intObj.alpha+=10);
      if(__displaceFactor<=0){
        halt();
      } else {
        __displaceFactor-=intObj.displaceRate;
      }
    } else {
      if (intObj.alpha>0)mc._alpha=(intObj.alpha-=intObj.alphaRate);
      if(__displaceFactor>=maxDisplace){
        halt();
      } else {
        __displaceFactor+=intObj.displaceRate;
      }
    }
  }
}
```

```
    public function start():Void {
      super.start();
      __displaceFactor = (type == "in") ? maxDisplace : 0;
      var w:Number = clip._width;
      var h:Number = clip._height;
      __noiseImage = new BitmapData(w*1.2, h*1.2, false, 0xFFFFFFFF);
      __waterImage = new BitmapData(w*1.2, h*1.2, true, 0x00FFFFFF);
      var tempImage:BitmapData = new BitmapData(w, h, true, 0x00FFFFFF);
      clip.innerClip._visible = true;
      tempImage.draw(clip, new Matrix());
      __waterImage.copyPixels(tempImage,
➥ new Rectangle(0, 0, w, h), new Point(w/10, h/10));
      var mc:MovieClip =
➥ clip.createEmptyMovieClip("water_mc", clip.getNextHighestDepth());
      mc.attachBitmap(__waterImage, 0);
      mc._x = -w/10;
      mc._y = -h/10;
      tempImage.dispose();
      var intObj:Object = {};
      mc._alpha = intObj.alpha = ((type == "in") ? 0 : 100);
      clip.innerClip._visible = false;
      var numInts:Number = time/Tweener.intervalTime;
      intObj.displaceRate = maxDisplace/numInts;
      intObj.alphaRate = 100/numInts;
      IntervalManager.setInterval(this, "interval",
➥ this, "runTransition", Tweener.intervalTime, intObj);
      runTransition(intObj);
    }

    public function halt():Void {
      IntervalManager.clearInterval(this, "interval");
      clip.water_mc.removeMovieClip();
      clip.innerClip._visible = (type == "in");
      __waterImage.dispose();
      super.halt();
    }

    public function removeTransitionEffects():Void {
      clip.innerClip._visible = true;
    }

}
```

The WaterTransition should appear as shown in Figure 17-13 when you test it.

Figure 17-13. The WaterTransition applied to the image

Summary

That's another hefty chapter behind you with a lot of good practice creating classes in an OOP manner, utilizing encapsulation to house functionality within the tweening and transition classes that can now be reused in many projects, inheritance to extend base classes to allow for more specific functionality (Broadcaster to Animator to Transition to FadeTransition), and polymorphism to enable multiple transitions to respond to the same method calls in their own unique ways, with the implementation hidden from the user. You developed several animation classes that abstracted the animation from the objects to be animated, making for a powerful and robust animation code library with a multitude of applications.

What's next?

The next chapter starts our exploration of data integration by delving into data binding as a means of sharing content between components. We'll work through several examples that demonstrate how to create both scripted and visual bindings, exploring related topics such as formatters and validators along the way.

PART FIVE **DATA INTEGRATION**

18 INTERRELATIONSHIPS AND INTERACTIONS BETWEEN COMPONENTS

In this chapter, you'll learn how components interact with each other. Specifically, you'll see how you can share data between components using data binding. Within data binding, a property from one component is bound to the property of another. The source component shares the property with the target.

You can bind data between UI components and also between UI and data components or between data components. For example, you can bind two TextInput components so that their text properties are always synchronized. You could also share the results property from an XMLConnector component with a DataSet component or with a TextInput or TextArea component. Throughout this chapter, I'll focus on binding XML data from an XMLConnector component to UI components.

The main advantage of data binding is that you don't have to write ActionScript to create the data associations. In the case of complicated data structures, without data binding you would have to write much more code to achieve the same result. Data binding is a more efficient process, both from a coding and workflow perspective. It also allows you to apply formatters and validators as part of the process.

During the binding process, you can apply a formatter to transform your content. For example, you can use this technique to alter the display of data to add a specific number of decimal places. Several built-in formatters are available, and you can specify your own custom formatter. You can also work with a validator to check that the data meets validation criteria. For example, you could specify a minimum or maximum text length or a range for numeric data.

You can create component bindings visually, using the Bindings tab in the Component Inspector panel. You can also use ActionScript to generate the bindings. Within this chapter, we'll focus on using ActionScript to create component bindings. However, we'll also have a brief look at visual binding. We'll start with an overview of the data binding process.

Data binding

Data binding allows you to associate a bindable property from one component with a bindable property in another component. When the source component property changes, the bound component property changes in response.

The process of data binding involves two components—the source and destination points for the binding. By default, bindings are one-way—one component affects another, but changes in the second don't affect the first component. It is also possible to specify two-way bindings—both components can change each other so that their bound properties remain synchronized.

In order to set up a binding, you need to specify a bindable property from each component. For example, you could specify the results property of an XMLConnector or the text property of a TextArea. You can also specify a path within a property and the event that triggers the binding between the components.

You can implement data binding either though the Bindings tab of the Component Inspector or entirely through ActionScript using the classes in the mx.data.binding package. If you're writing ActionScript to configure your bindings, you'll need to make sure that the data binding classes are available at runtime by including them within your library. Note that the classes are included automatically if you add a binding through the Bindings tab of the Component Inspector.

To include the data binding classes, choose Window ➤ Common Libraries ➤ Classes and drag the DataBindingClasses clip to your Library. You can also drag the clip to the stage, but be aware that it has a visual appearance within Flash movies.

You will also want to import the relevant classes from the mx.data.binding package so that you don't have to refer to them with their fully qualified names in your code:

```
import mx.data.binding.*;
```

The mx.data.binding package

The mx.data.binding package in Flash Professional includes the following classes:

- EndPoint
- Binding
- ComponentMixins
- CustomFormatter
- CustomValidator
- DataType
- TypedValue

The EndPoint class creates the source and destination points for a binding. These objects specify which components to use and how to bind the data, and they can refer to a component property or a constant value. You need to specify two EndPoints—one for the source of the binding and one for the destination. You can also create a two-way binding between the EndPoints. Once you've specified these points, the Binding class creates the binding.

The ComponentMixins class defines the properties and methods that are automatically added to any of the points in the binding.

The CustomFormatter class is the base class that you can use to create custom formatter classes. Custom formatters change the presentation of data during the binding process. We'll look at how to apply them during binding a little later in this chapter in the section "Understanding custom formatters."

The CustomValidator class is the base class for creating custom validator classes. You use custom validators to create your own validation routines for the bindable properties within a component. We'll explore how you can use validation later in the chapter in the section "Including validators."

The DataType class provides read and write access to the data fields of a component property while the TypedValue class provides information used for type conversion within DataType objects. This chapter won't examine these classes, as they're used in more complicated bindings.

We'll start by looking at the ActionScript needed to create a simple binding.

Creating a simple binding

A simple binding uses a source and a destination EndPoint. Simple bindings are one-way—from the source to the destination. The bindable property of the source component sets the bindable property in the destination component. More complicated bindings occur in both directions—from the source to the destination and back again.

You need to create the two EndPoints before creating the binding. In the code that follows, I've assumed that the mx.data.binding package has already been imported.

Creating EndPoints

You can create EndPoint objects using the following EndPoint constructors:

```
var sourcePoint:EndPoint = new EndPoint();
var destinationPoint:EndPoint = new EndPoint();
```

Each EndPoint object has two properties: a component and a bound property. The source EndPoint also has an event property and an optional location property. Instead of using a bound property, you can also specify a constant value.

The component property is the instance name of the component to be used in the binding:

```
EndPoint.component = componentName;
```

The property is a string that specifies which property is involved in the binding:

```
EndPoint.property = "componentProperty";
```

For example, in a TextArea component, you would set the property to text, as there are no other bindable properties. If you were binding an XMLConnector component, you would use the results property, which contains the XML tree.

You can use the location property of the EndPoint to access specific data within the bindable property. This might be useful to pinpoint a specific element within an XML tree, and I'll cover this property in the next section.

The event property for the source component specifies which event will trigger the binding. If you set a single event, the property requires a string value:

```
EndPoint.event = "eventName";
```

The binding can also listen for multiple events by passing an array of strings to this property:

```
EndPoint.event = ["eventName1", "eventName2"];
```

If you want to use a constant value in a source EndPoint, you can use

```
EndPoint.constant = constantValue;
```

Setting this property overrides the other properties set by ActionScript.

You can use objects to pass the data binding settings, rather than setting the EndPoint properties individually:

```
var source:Object = {component: componentName, property:
➥"componentProperty", event: "eventName"};
var destination:Object = {component: componentName, property:
➥"componentProperty"};
```

You can also assign a formatter that transforms the source data before it reaches the destination component property. You'll see that a little later in this chapter in the "Using formatters" section.

Specifying a location

You may need to specify a location within the source data for the binding where you're working with a complex bound property such as the results from an XMLConnector component. You can use the location property to specify the location of the data field in one of four ways:

1. Use an XPath expression.

2. Write an ActionScript path.

3. Use an array of strings.

4. Create an object.

You can only use the first option—an XPath expression—where you're working with data that is provided as an XML object, for example, from the results property of an XMLConnector. XPath is a means of navigating an XML tree. Covering XPath is beyond the scope of this book, but you'll see some examples of XPath expressions a little later in the chapter when we work through the examples.

Where the data is provided within an XML or ActionScript object, you can use a string that contains an ActionScript path to specify the data for binding. The path contains the field names separated by dots:

```
"object.field1.field2";
```

A similar approach is to specify the path using an array of strings:

```
["object","field1","field2"];
```

Again, this approach is appropriate for either an ActionScript object or XML data.

You can't use the final option, specifying an object as the location, with XML data. To use this approach, the object must specify two properties—path and indices.

```
{path: ["[n]","field1","[n]","field2"], indices: [{constant:0},
➥{constant:0}]}];
```

The path is an array of strings as listed in the previous option. You can use "[n]" to refer to multiple occurrences of data. Each time you use "[n]", you must specify a corresponding index in the indices property.

Once you've created the source and destination EndPoints for the binding, it's time to create the Binding itself.

Creating the binding

To create the binding, you'll need to call the constructor for a Binding object:

```
new Binding(source, destination, format, isTwoWay);
```

The last two parameters, format and isTwoWay, are optional. The format parameter specifies formatting information, while the isTwoWay argument is a Boolean value that determines whether the binding is two-way. If you omit this argument, the default value is false.

As an alternative, you can pass all parameters at the same time that you create the binding:

```
new Binding({component: componentName, property: "componentProperty",
➥event: "eventName"}, {component:comonentName, property:
➥"componentProperty"});
```

To my mind, it is much harder to read this code block compared with creating the EndPoint objects separately in code.

Sometimes, you'll need to trigger the binding in response to an event within an unrelated component. For example, the binding might need to respond to a data component receiving results by recognizing the result event. In this case, you can use the execute method instead of assigning an event property to the source EndPoint.

Using the execute method

Instead of configuring the event property for the EndPoint of the binding, an alternative approach is to create the binding and call the execute method at a later stage. The execute method takes a Boolean parameter, reverse, that indicates whether to apply the binding in both directions. If the binding executes successfully, it returns null. Otherwise, the method returns an array of error message strings containing errors.

```
var bindingResults:Array = newBinding.execute(reverse);
```

The code that we've discussed so far will probably make more sense when you see it within an example. During the remainder of the chapter, we'll focus on creating bindings between an XMLConnector component and other UI components. The XMLConnector will load external data and display it in components such as a TextArea, TextInput, or Label.

Working through a simple binding example

Here we'll create a simple binding example that binds XML content to a TextArea compo-
nent. We'll do this using an XMLConnector component to load an external XML document.
When the XMLConnector component triggers, the XML document will appear within a
TextArea component. Because we're working with the data components, you'll need to use
Flash Professional to complete the example.

The example uses a direct binding between the two components. If we were dealing with a
more complicated XML data structure, we could bind the XMLConnector to a DataHolder
or DataSet component first and then bind from that component to one or more UI components. This would require us to specify a schema for the DataSet component, and we'd
need to include other bindings if we wanted the user to be able to update the XML data.

We'll use the following XML document, which contains information about a featured product. The XML document includes details about the product name, description, price, and
contact details of the salesperson. You can create this XML document yourself and save it
with the name `featuredProduct.xml` or use the file from within the resource folder `18-1`,
available for download from www.friendsofed.com.

```
<?xml version="1.0" encoding="UTF-8"?>
<FeaturedProduct>
  <product>
    <productName>Shirt</productName>
    <description>Light weight cotton shirt</description>
    <price>25.7</price>
    <salesFirst>Sas</salesFirst>
    <salesLast>Jacobs</salesLast>
    <salesContact>sas@aip.net.au</salesContact>
  </product>
</FeaturedProduct>
```

Start by creating a new ActionScript file and save it as `FeaturedProduct.as`. Create a Flash
document and save it as `featuredProduct.fla` in the same directory. Include the
`featuredProduct.xml` file within the same folder.

The FeaturedProduct class will allow a user to pass in a container movie clip and display a
TextArea component within that clip that displays the contents of an external XML document. The class will load the XML document using an XMLConnector component, and the
user will be able to pass in the filename of the XML document as well as the position and
size for the TextArea component.

Enter the following code in the `FeaturedProduct.as` file:

```
import mx.controls.TextArea;
import mx.data.binding.*;
import mx.data.components.XMLConnector;
```

18

```
class FeaturedProduct {
  private var __parentContainer_mc:MovieClip;
  private var __productContainer_mc:MovieClip;
  private var __product_txt:TextArea;
  private var __XMLContent:XMLConnector;
}
```

The code imports the classes that we'll need and declares the FeaturedProduct class. Because the class resides in the same folder as the Flash movie, we don't need to use a fully qualified class name.

Within the class declaration, we have declared the private properties that the class will use with two underscore characters at the start of each name. The first property, __parentContainer_mc, keeps track of the parent movie clip that is passed to the class. This allows the Flash file to create the featured product details within any movie clip. The second property, __productContainer_mc, keeps track of the movie clip within __parentContainer_mc that contains the TextArea component. We'll create this movie clip when we initialize the class.

The __product_txt property provides a reference to the TextArea component itself, while the __XMLContent variable refers to the XMLConnector that we'll use to load the external XML data.

Add the class constructor with the following code, shown in bold:

```
import mx.controls.TextArea;
import mx.data.binding.*;
import mx.data.components.XMLConnector;

class FeaturedProduct {
  private var __parentContainer_mc:MovieClip;
  private var __productContainer_mc:MovieClip;
  private var __product_txt:TextArea;
  private var __XMLContent:XMLConnector;

  function FeaturedProduct (parent_mc:MovieClip) {
    __parentContainer_mc = parent_mc;
    __productContainer_mc = __parentContainer_mc.createEmptyMovieClip
      ("product_mc", parent_mc.getNextHighestDepth());
  }
}
```

The constructor function takes the parent movie clip as an argument and sets the private variable __parentContainer_mc as a reference to this clip. It creates an empty movie clip inside the parent to hold the TextArea component and uses the variable __productContainer_mc as a reference.

After the user creates a FeaturedProduct object, they'll initialize it, passing through the width, height, x, and y positions. I could have included these options within the class constructor, but I chose to add them within a separate function, in case we wanted to determine the parameters dynamically at a later stage.

Add the following public function to the class file, before the closing brace:

```
public function init(width:Number, height: Number, xPos:Number,
➡yPos:Number):Void {
  __product_txt = __productContainer_mc.createClassObject(TextArea,
➡  "product_txt", __productContainer_mc.getNextHighestDepth(),
➡  {wordWrap: true});
  __product_txt.setSize(width, height);
  __product_txt.move(xPos, yPos);
}
```

The init function creates a TextArea component using the createClassObject method. This method takes four arguments:

```
createClassObject(className, instanceName, depth, initObject)
```

In the example, we've created the TextArea component within __productContainer_mc. I haven't used the fully qualified name for the class, as I included an import statement earlier. The component has the instance name product_txt and is placed at the next highest depth available. An initialization object sets the wordWrap property of the component to true. To use the createClassObject method, the TextArea component will need to be included within the library of the Flash document using this class.

We'll use the variable __product_txt to refer to the TextArea component. We also set the size and position of the component, using the arguments passed into the function and the setSize and move methods of the component.

The last code block that we'll include creates the public function that connects to the XML document and binds the contents to the TextArea component. The Flash file will call this function and pass the URL of the XML document as an argument.

Add the following public method, loadProduct, within the class declaration.

```
public function loadProduct(XMLFileName:String):Void {
  if (XMLFileName.length > 0) {
    __XMLContent = new XMLConnector();
    __XMLContent.URL = XMLFileName;
    __XMLContent.direction = "receive";
    __XMLContent.ignoreWhite = true;
    __XMLContent.multipleSimultaneousAllowed = true;
    __XMLContent.suppressInvalidCalls = true;

    var sourcePoint:EndPoint = new EndPoint();
    var destinationPoint:EndPoint = new EndPoint();
    sourcePoint.component = __XMLContent;
    sourcePoint.property = "results";
    sourcePoint.location = "/FeaturedProduct";
    sourcePoint.event = "result";
    destinationPoint.component = __product_txt;
    destinationPoint.property = "text";
    new Binding(sourcePoint, destinationPoint);
```

18

```
      __XMLContent.trigger();
    }
  }
```

In this code block, we receive the XML file name as an argument to the function. If the length is greater than 0, we proceed. We're not limiting the input to files that end in .xml, as the user could pass in either an XML file name or the path to a server-side file that creates the XML content.

First, we create the XMLConnector called __XMLContent and set the relevant properties. Note that we can only create this component if it is already present inside the Flash file that will call this method.

The XMLFileName parameter is assigned to the URL property. We set the direction to receive and the ignoreWhite property to true so that Flash ignores any white space in the XML document. We also set the multipleSimultaneousCalls property to true to allow more than one call to the connector at a time and the supressInvalidCalls property to true so that the call is suppressed if the parameters are invalid.

Next, we define the two EndPoints for the binding—sourcePoint and destinationPoint. This will be a one-way binding so that the results property from the XMLConnector is bound to the text property of the TextArea component. In other words, we'll display the contents from the XML document within the TextArea component.

The sourcePoint EndPoint uses the __XMLContent component, the results from the component as the bindable property, and the result event to trigger the binding. Be careful not to confuse the result event with the results property, as they appear very similar.

I've also specified a location property to the root node of the XML document by using sourcePoint.location = "/FeaturedProduct". This value uses XPath notation to refer to the root node of the XML document—<FeaturedProduct>. The path starts with a forward slash to indicate that we start at the top of the XML tree. The destinationPoint EndPoint specifies the __product_txt component reference and the text property.

Finally, the code creates the binding and triggers the XMLConnector.

The following code lists the complete class file:

```
import mx.controls.TextArea;
import mx.data.binding.*;
import mx.data.components.XMLConnector;

class FeaturedProduct {
  private var __parentContainer_mc:MovieClip;
  private var __productContainer_mc:MovieClip;
  private var __product_txt:TextArea;
  private var __XMLContent:XMLConnector;
```

```
  function FeaturedProduct (parent_mc:MovieClip) {
    __parentContainer_mc = parent_mc;
    __productContainer_mc = __parentContainer_mc.createEmptyMovieClip
➡      ("product_mc", parent_mc.getNextHighestDepth());
  }

  public function init(width:Number, height: Number, xPos:Number,
➡yPos:Number):Void {
    __product_txt = __productContainer_mc.createClassObject(TextArea,
➡    "product_txt", __productContainer_mc.getNextHighestDepth(),
➡    {wordWrap: true});
    __product_txt.setSize(width, height);
    __product_txt.move(xPos, yPos);
  }

  public function loadProduct(XMLFileName:String):Void {
    if (XMLFileName.length > 0) {
      __XMLContent = new XMLConnector();
      __XMLContent.URL = XMLFileName;
      __XMLContent.direction = "receive";
      __XMLContent.ignoreWhite = true;
      __XMLContent.multipleSimultaneousAllowed = true;
      __XMLContent.suppressInvalidCalls = true;

      var sourcePoint:EndPoint = new EndPoint();
      var destinationPoint:EndPoint = new EndPoint();
      sourcePoint.component = __XMLContent;
      sourcePoint.property = "results";
      sourcePoint.location = "/FeaturedProduct";
      sourcePoint.event = "result";
      destinationPoint.component = __news_txt;
      destinationPoint.property = "text";
      new Binding(sourcePoint, destinationPoint);
      __XMLContent.trigger();
    }
  }
}
```

To create an object from this class, we'll need to switch to our Flash file, FeaturedProduct.fla. We'll have to start by adding the relevant component and data binding classes to the Library of the Flash file.

Choose Window ➤ Common Libraries ➤ Classes and drag the DataBindingClasses clip to your Library. Drag an XMLConnector and a TextArea to the Library. If you're using Flash MX 2004, you'll have to drag these components to the stage and delete them to add them to the Library.

You can create a FeaturedProduct object by adding the following code to Frame 1 of the only layer in the Flash movie:

```
var myProduct:FeaturedProduct= new FeaturedProduct(this);
```

The code creates a FeaturedProduct object called myProduct on the main timeline. We can then initialize the object and load the featuredProduct.xml file with the following lines:

```
myProduct.init(300, 100, 10, 10);
myProduct.loadProduct("featuredProduct.xml");
```

We've called the methods init and loadProduct, passing in the relevant arguments. The TextArea is 300×100 in size and is placed at 10, 10 on the stage. In this example, we've loaded an XML document, but we could also load a server-side file resulting in an XML document. If so, we'd need to include the full http:// path to the server-side file in the loadProduct method.

Test the Flash file and you should see the TextArea component populated with the XML content from the external document. You can see a screenshot of the finished example in Figure 18-1. The completed files are also available in the resource folder 18-1.

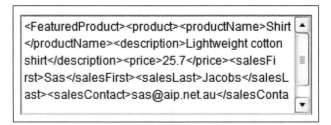

Figure 18-1. The output resulting from the simple binding exercise

If the example doesn't work as expected, it can be a little difficult to find out what's gone wrong. To assist, we can find out a little more about what's happening behind the scenes by turning on the logger. Add the following line at the top of your Flash file:

```
_global.__dataLogger=new mx.data.binding.Log();
```

This line sets up logging and if you test your Flash movie again, you'll see something similar to the screen shot shown in Figure 18-2.

The first line creates the binding from results:/FeaturedProduct to product_mc. product_txt:text. The XMLConnector is then triggered and the results property changes. The binding executes and the new value is assigned to the text property of the TextArea component. Note that the entire XML string from the root node displays in the TextArea component.

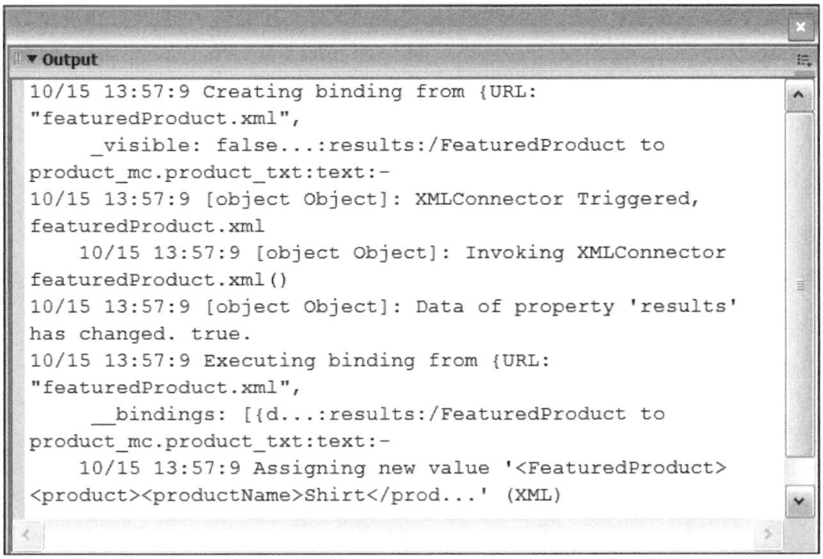

```
10/15 13:57:9 Creating binding from {URL:
"featuredProduct.xml",
     _visible: false...:results:/FeaturedProduct to
product_mc.product_txt:text:-
10/15 13:57:9 [object Object]: XMLConnector Triggered,
featuredProduct.xml
     10/15 13:57:9 [object Object]: Invoking XMLConnector
featuredProduct.xml()
10/15 13:57:9 [object Object]: Data of property 'results'
has changed. true.
10/15 13:57:9 Executing binding from {URL:
"featuredProduct.xml",
     __bindings: [{d...:results:/FeaturedProduct to
product_mc.product_txt:text:-
     10/15 13:57:9 Assigning new value '<FeaturedProduct>
<product><productName>Shirt</prod...' (XML)
```

Figure 18-2. Output from the logger

The display within the TextArea is not very useful as it contains both the data and tags from the XML document. We can improve the readability by using formatters to alter the appearance of the source data. We can also display different elements from the XML document within different components by specifying a location within the source EndPoint of the binding.

Using formatters

Formatters change the appearance of bound data by adding formatting. Formatters apply their changes after data is sent from the source component but before it is received by the target component. This means that formatted data appears in the target component. As with data binding, you can apply a formatter either through the Component Inspector panel or by writing ActionScript. We'll look at applying formatters through ActionScript.

Flash Professional ships with several preset formatters that you can use with your bindings. You can also create a custom formatter to handle more complex data. When we examined the Binding class earlier in the chapter, you saw that you could pass an optional parameter specifying a formatter class and settings.

```
new Binding(source, destination, format, isTwoWay);
```

The format parameter requires an object containing the formatter class and a settings object. The settings object contains settings that are specific to the chosen formatter class.

```
{cls: mx.data.formatters.formatterName, settings: {specific settings}};
```

You can see examples of the settings for each of the formatters in the next section. We'll start by looking at the built-in AS2.0 formatters.

Using built-in formatters

Flash includes the following AS2.0 formatters:

- **Boolean**: Formats a Boolean value as a string
- **Compose String**: Converts one or more data objects to a string using a template
- **Custom Formatter**: Specifies a custom formatter using a class name
- **Date**: Applies a date template to create a string from a date
- **Rearrange Fields**: Creates a new array of objects based on the original array
- **Number Formatter**: Specifies the number of decimal places that appear in a number

Each of the formatters has different settings, and we'll look at them in a little more detail. I'll cover creating a custom formatter a little later in the chapter.

Using the Boolean formatter

The Boolean formatter converts between Boolean and string data. It takes Boolean data from the source component and creates a string representation using a different string for true and false values. For example, you could display the Boolean value true as *affirmative* or *ready to go*.

You must use the following settings for the Boolean formatter:

```
{cls: mx.data.formatters.Bool, settings: {falseString:"Value is
➡false", trueString:"Value is true"}};
```

This formatter works well using the Component Inspector panel. However, its implementation in ActionScript is problematic because working in code accesses the raw value of data items within bindings. In the case of an XML object, Flash accesses the values of true and false as strings, so you can't bind directly from the XMLConnector to another component using the Boolean formatter.

A solution to this problem would be to bind the XMLConnector to a DataSet component first, and create a schema for the datatypes. This would allow you to specify a Boolean datatype before binding the content from the DataSet to a UI component. You could then include a Boolean formatter in the second binding.

Using the Compose String formatter

The Compose String formatter specifies a template for creating string output for the target component. You can specify multiple input fields as well as including fixed text in the template. For example, you might use a Compose Strings formatter to create a full name from a first and last name.

The following code shows how you could use the Compose String formatter in ActionScript:

```
{cls: mx.data.formatters.ComposeString, settings: {template: "My name
➡is <firstName> <lastName>."}};
```

When using this formatter, you need to specify a template containing both fixed text and field references. You can refer to a data field using `<fieldName>` or you can use dot notation to drill down into the fields `<fieldName.childFieldName>`. You can also use `<.>` to indicate the entire data object. You'll see an example of the Compose String formatter a little later in this section.

Using the Date formatter

The Date formatter allows you to specify a date format using a string such as MM/DD/YYYY. This might be useful if you were passing a value that included a time and you only wanted to include the date portion.

The code that follows shows the use of this formatter:

```
{cls: mx.data.formatters.Dte, settings: {format: "MM/DD/YYYY"}};
```

Be careful when using this formatter in ActionScript, as Flash accesses raw data during binding. In this case, Flash interprets the date as a string. If you bind directly from the raw data to a UI component, you won't be able to use this formatter. As with the Boolean formatter, you'd need to bind to a DataSet component first and include a schema that specifies the correct datatype. Then you'd be able to use the Date formatter in a second binding.

Using the Rearrange Fields formatter

The Rearrange Fields formatter only applies to array fields and transforms one array into another using a string template in the following format:

```
outputfield1=inputfield1;outputfield2=inputfield2;
```

You can also specify a template for the input field in the same way as with a Compose String formatter.

A common use for this formatter is to transform an array to assign `label` and `data` properties for use in a ComboBox or List component. The following code shows how this can be achieved:

```
{cls: mx.data.formatters.RearrangeFields, settings: {fields: "label=
➡productName, data=productID"}};
```

Using the Number formatter

The Number formatter allows you to choose the precision for decimal places within a number. This might be useful where you are displaying currency values with less than two decimal points and want to display the cents correctly.

```
{cls: mx.data.formatters.NumberFormatter, settings: {precision:"2"}};
```

18

We'll examine the Compose String and Number formatters by changing the display of data from the previous example.

Working through a simple formatting example

Start by opening the FeaturedProduct.as and featuredProduct.fla files from the previous example. You can also open the resource files from the 18-1 folder. We'll modify the class file to display the content from the XML file in separate components. We'll use formatters to alter the display of the data but leave the TextArea component in place so you can compare the data.

In the FeaturedProduct.as file, we'll add some more bindings to display specific elements in Label components. We'll show the product name and description in Label components and display all of the contact details in a single Label using a Compose String formatter. Finally, the price will display in a Label to two decimal places.

Because we'll create Label components dynamically, we'll import the relevant class at the top of the FeaturedProduct.as file. We'll also import the formatters package so we can refer to the formatters without their fully qualified names.

The complete list of import statements that should appear in the class file follows:

```
import mx.controls.TextArea;
import mx.controls.Label;
import mx.data.binding.*;
import mx.data.formatters.*;
import mx.data.components.XMLConnector;
```

The next step is to add the private variables that will refer to the components that we're going to include in the interface. The following code shows the complete list of private variables with the new items highlighted in bold:

```
private var __parentContainer_mc:MovieClip;
private var __productContainer_mc:MovieClip;
private var __product_txt:TextArea;
private var __item_lbl:Label;
private var __description_lbl:Label;
private var __contact_lbl:Label;
private var __price_lbl:Label;
private var __XMLContent:XMLConnector;
```

The __item_lbl Label component will display the product name, while __description_lbl will display the description. The contact details will appear in the __contact_lbl Label component and the price in __price_lbl.

The initialization function for the interface will need to change. We'll have to create several Label components to display the data from the XML document. To simplify things, we'll add a private function to handle the component creation process. Add the following code:

```
    private function createComponent(compType:Object, instanceName:String,
➥ initObj:Object) {
      return __productContainer_mc.createClassObject(compType,
➥  instanceName, __productContainer_mc.getNextHighestDepth(), initObj);
    }
```

This function returns a component created within __productContainer_mc.

We'll need to change the code within the init function to the following:

```
    public function init(width:Number, height: Number, xPos:Number,
➥yPos:Number):Void {
      var compPlacer:Number = yPos + height;

      __product_txt = createComponent(TextArea, "product_txt",
➥  {wordWrap: true});
      __item_lbl =  createComponent(Label, "item_lbl");
      __description_lbl = createComponent(Label, "description_lbl");
      __contact_lbl = createComponent(Label, "contact_lbl");
      __price_lbl = createComponent(Label, "price_lbl");

      __product_txt.setSize(width, height);
      __item_lbl.setSize(width, 20);
      __description_lbl.setSize(width, 20);
      __contact_lbl.setSize(width, 20);
      __price_lbl.setSize(50, 20);

      __product_txt.move(xPos, yPos);
      __item_lbl.move(xPos, compPlacer);
      __description_lbl.move(xPos, compPlacer+20);
      __contact_lbl.move(xPos, compPlacer+40);
      __price_lbl.move(xPos, compPlacer+60);
    }
```

The code starts by creating a numeric variable that we'll use to set the y position of the components. Then we call the createComponent function five times, passing the component type, instance name, and optional initialization object. This re-creates the original TextArea component and four additional Label components.

The second code block sets the size for each of the components with the setSize method. The final block positions the components within the parent movie clip.

Because I'm going to create multiple bindings, I'll change the loadProduct method to call a private function that creates the bindings. All bindings will come from the same component—the XMLConnector—and be triggered by the same event—result. The only thing that will change for each binding will be the location property within the results and the target component. Because I'll want to add a formatter to some of the bindings, I'll need to pass in an object containing those details.

Add the following private function to the class file:

```
private function createBinding(loc:String, desComp:Object,
➡format:Object):Void{
  var src:Object = {component: __XMLContent, property: "results",
➡  location:loc, event: "result"};
  var des:Object = {component: desComp, property: "text"};
  new Binding(src, des, format);
}
```

This function takes arguments for the location within the XML results (loc), the destination component (desComp), and an object containing the formatting details (format). We declare two EndPoint objects—src and des. Each object contains the relevant properties for the binding. Finally, the function creates the binding from the src and des objects and applies the format object.

We'll call this method from within the loadProduct function so you'll need to modify it as shown. The changed lines appear in bold.

```
public function loadProduct(XMLFileName:String):Void {
  if (XMLFileName.length > 0) {
    __XMLContent = new XMLConnector();
    __XMLContent.URL = XMLFileName;
    __XMLContent.direction = "receive";
    __XMLContent.ignoreWhite = true;
    __XMLContent.multipleSimultaneousAllowed = true;
    __XMLContent.suppressInvalidCalls = true;

    var contactFormat:Object = {cls: ComposeString, settings:
➡    {template:"Contact: <salesFirst> <salesLast>, <salesContact>"}};
    var priceFormat:Object = {cls: NumberFormatter, settings:
➡    {precision:"2"}};

    createBinding("/FeaturedProduct", __product_txt);
    createBinding("/FeaturedProduct/product/productName", __item_lbl);
    createBinding("/FeaturedProduct/product/description",
➡    __description_lbl);
    createBinding("/FeaturedProduct/product", __contact_lbl,
➡    contactFormat);
    createBinding("/FeaturedProduct/product/price", __price_lbl,
➡    priceFormat);

    __XMLContent.trigger();
  }
}
```

The first block of changed lines creates the formatter objects—contactFormat and priceFormat. contactFormat is a Compose String formatter that creates a template for the contact details. The template that we use is

Contact: <salesFirst> <salesLast>, <salesContact>

and it will create output similar to the following:

```
Contact: Sas Jacobs, sas@aip.net.au
```

The second object, `priceFormat`, creates a Number formatter that formats to two decimal places.

```
{cls: NumberFormatter, settings: {precision:"2"}}
```

In the second block of modified code, we call the `createBinding` function five times to create each of the bindings. As the bindings come from different locations in the results of the XMLConnector, we pass this to the function along with the target component instance and, optionally, a formatter object.

Each of the `location` parameters uses an XPath statement to find a point within the XML tree. For example, reading the path /FeaturedProduct/product/description from right to left describes the <description> element within the <product> element within the root node <FeaturedProduct>.

The only surprise here is the choice of /FeaturedProduct/product within the contact binding. We need to choose the parent node of the child nodes that we'll refer to in the Compose String template. The <salesFirst>, <salesLast>, and <salesContact> nodes all appear within the <product> node in the XML document.

The complete FeaturedProduct class follows. I've added comments to describe each block of code.

```
import mx.controls.TextArea;
import mx.controls.Label;
import mx.data.binding.*;
import mx.data.formatters.*;
import mx.data.components.XMLConnector;

class FeaturedProduct {
  //private properties
  private var __parentContainer_mc:MovieClip;
  private var __productContainer_mc:MovieClip;
  private var __product_txt:TextArea;
  private var __item_lbl:Label;
  private var __description_lbl:Label;
  private var __contact_lbl:Label;
  private var __price_lbl:Label;
  private var __XMLContent:XMLConnector;

  // constructor
  function FeaturedProduct(parent_mc:MovieClip) {
    __parentContainer_mc = parent_mc;
    __productContainer_mc = __parentContainer_mc.createEmptyMovieClip
      ("product_mc", parent_mc.getNextHighestDepth());
  }
```

```actionscript
//public methods
public function init(width:Number, height: Number, xPos:Number,
➡   yPos:Number):Void {
    var compPlacer:Number = yPos + height;

    // create components
    __product_txt = createComponent(TextArea, "product_txt",
➡     {wordWrap: true});
    __item_lbl = createComponent(Label, "item_lbl");
    __description_lbl = createComponent(Label, "description_lbl");
    __contact_lbl = createComponent(Label, "contact_lbl");
    __price_lbl = createComponent(Label, "price_lbl");

    //size components
    __product_txt.setSize(width, height);
    __item_lbl.setSize(width, 20);
    __description_lbl.setSize(width, 20);
    __contact_lbl.setSize(width, 20);
    __price_lbl.setSize(50, 20);

    //place components on the stage
    __product_txt.move(xPos, yPos);
    __item_lbl.move(xPos, compPlacer);
    __description_lbl.move(xPos, compPlacer+20);
    __contact_lbl.move(xPos, compPlacer+40);
    __price_lbl.move(xPos, compPlacer+60);
}

public function loadProduct(XMLFileName:String):Void {
    if (XMLFileName.length > 0) {
        //create XML object
        __XMLContent = new XMLConnector();
        __XMLContent.URL = XMLFileName;
        __XMLContent.direction = "receive";
        __XMLContent.ignoreWhite = true;
        __XMLContent.multipleSimultaneousAllowed = true;
        __XMLContent.suppressInvalidCalls = true;

        //create formatter objects
        var contactFormat:Object = {cls: ComposeString, settings:
➡         {template:"Contact: <salesFirst> <salesLast>, <salesContact>"}};
        var priceFormat:Object = {cls: NumberFormatter, settings:
➡         {precision:"2"}};

        //create bindings
        createBinding("/FeaturedProduct", __product_txt);
        createBinding("/FeaturedProduct/product/productName",
➡         __item_lbl);
        createBinding("/FeaturedProduct/product/description",
➡         __description_lbl);
```

```
        createBinding("/FeaturedProduct/product", __contact_lbl,
➡        contactFormat);
        createBinding("/FeaturedProduct/product/price", __price_lbl,
➡        priceFormat);

        __XMLContent.trigger();
      }
    }

    //private methods
    private function createComponent(compType:Object, instanceName:
➡   String, initObj:Object) {
      return __productContainer_mc.createClassObject(compType,
➡      instanceName, __productContainer_mc.getNextHighestDepth(), initObj)
    }

    private function createBinding(loc:String, desComp:Object, format::
➡   Object):Void{
      var src:Object = {component: __XMLContent, property: "results",
➡      location:loc, event: "result"};
      var des:Object = {component: desComp, property: "text"};
      new Binding(src, des, format);
    }
  }
}
```

Switch to the Flash file and add a Label component to the Library. This is necessary as we'll be adding this component dynamically using the createClassObject method. Test the movie and the logger will display something similar to the image shown in Figure 18-3.

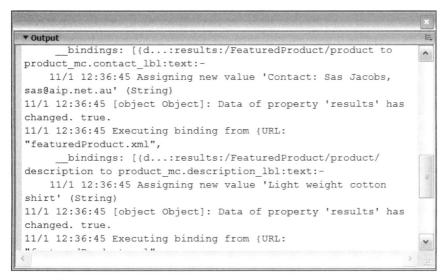

Figure 18-3. Logger output from the multiple binding example

This time, you can see that we've accessed the data using different locations within the results property. The preceding image shows the value of Contact: Sas Jacobs, sas@aip.net.au in the contact_lbl component, created by applying the Compose String formatter.

If you close the Output panel, you should see something similar to the image shown in Figure 18-4. You can find the completed Flash and class files in the resource folder 18-2, in the code download.

Figure 18-4. The output resulting from the binding including formatters

In this example, we used two of the built-in formatters to change the display of data during the binding process. The Compose String formatter created a string of contact information from a template, while the Number formatter displayed the price to two decimal places.

If you need to specify a different or more complicated type of formatting, you'll need to write your own custom formatter. Custom formatters extend the CustomFormatter class, which provides format and unformat methods. You can use these methods to transform and remove transformation from data values.

Understanding custom formatters

Custom formatters are classes that extend the CustomFormatter class. They must contain two functions—format and unformat, as follows:

```
class MyFormat extends mx.data.binding.CustomFormatter {
  function format(rawData:rawType):returnType {
    //do some formatting
    return returnValue;
  }
```

```
function unformat(processedData:processedType):returnType {
    //do some unformatting
    return returnValue;
  }
}
```

To use a custom formatter, you'll have to include it within a binding, similar to the way that you used the built-in formatters. You need to specify the class as well as the settings. For custom formatters, the settings include the classname and classname_class.

```
{cls:mx.data.formatters.Custom, settings:{classname: "MyFormat",
➥classname_class: MyFormat}})
```

Let's modify the previous example to include a custom formatter that adds a currency symbol to the price and rounds up to the nearest whole number.

Create a new ActionScript file called CurrencyFormat.as and save it in the same location as the FeaturedProduct.as file. Add the following code to the file:

```
class CurrencyFormat extends mx.data.binding.CustomFormatter {
  public function format(rawData:Number):String{
    var returnValue:String;
    returnValue = "$" + Math.ceil(rawData);
    return returnValue;
  }
  Public function unformat(processedData:String):Number{
    var returnValue:Number;
    returnValue = Number(processedData.substring(1));
    return returnValue;
  }
}
```

The class file contains two methods—format and unformat. These methods convert and unconvert the data between a number and string. In addition, the format method rounds up to the nearest whole number. Obviously, the unformat method can't retrieve the original number with cents, so it removes the currency symbol and displays the numeric section of the rounded number.

Switch to the FeaturedProduct.as file and change the priceFormat object as shown:

```
var priceFormat:Object = {cls: Custom, settings: {classname:
➥"CurrencyFormat", classname_class: CurrencyFormat}};
```

The line uses the Custom formatter and specifies the CurrencyFormat class for the formatting.

18

Test the Flash file, and you should see something similar to the screen shot shown in Figure 18-5. The price label now displays the value $26 instead of 25.70 as in the previous example.

You can find the files used in this example in the resource folder 18-3.

Figure 18-5. The result of applying a custom formatter to the price field

In this case, the custom formatter rounded the price upwards to the nearest whole number and added a dollar sign. As with all formatters, the transformation took place before the data from the source component was bound to the target component.

You can also include validators that allow you to test bound properties against specified criteria. Normally, you add validators to check user content entered into UI components, but you can also validate external data after it's loaded. In this section, I'll examine validators in more detail and show you how to include them within bindings using the featured product XML document. I'll also introduce you to some of the features in the Component Inspector panel so you can see alternatives to scripted binding.

Including validators

Validators are available to any property that is the destination of a binding. They allow Flash to check the content of a component to make sure that it meets validation criteria. You normally apply validators through the Schema tab of the Component Inspector panel because they relate to the schema properties specified for the component. Flash Professional includes several built-in validators, depending on the datatype of the item. You can also specify a custom validator using an ActionScript class.

When you work with visual bindings, the Schema tab of the Component Inspector specifies the bindable component properties. This tab also lists the datatype of each of the bindable properties and allows you to change these where necessary.

When using UI components, the schema is predefined by the component. In the case of an XMLConnector or WebServiceConnector component, you can import a schema from an external XML document or WSDL file. When using the DataSet component, you would normally define the schema yourself.

Flash recognizes the following datatypes: Array, Attribute, Boolean, Custom, DataProvider, Date, DeltaPacket, Integer, Number, Object, PhoneNumber, RecordSet, SocialSecurity, String, XML, and ZipCode.

You can use validation for the Custom, Integer, Number, String, and XML datatypes. For String datatypes, validation consists of specifying a minimum and maximum length for the string. Validation of the numeric types Integer and Number involves specifying the minimum and maximum values. If you set the datatype to custom, you can work with custom validators.

Validation occurs after executing the binding. Flash generates an event to show the outcome of the validation. In the case of a successful validation, Flash generates the valid event. Where the validation fails, the invalid event is generated. You can write ActionScript that deals with these two events.

We'll start by adding a built-in validator to visual bindings. We'll check that data from an external XML document matches our criteria and display a message in a TextArea component.

Working with built-in validators

In this example, we'll use an XMLConnector component to include data from an external XML document within a Flash movie. This time, we'll use the Component Inspector to apply the settings and add built-in validators. We'll use the same XML document that we used in the previous examples.

Start by creating a new Flash file and save it as featuredProductVisual.fla to distinguish it from your earlier Flash document. Save it in the same folder as the file featuredProduct.xml.

Drag an XMLConnector component to the left of the stage and give it the instance name product_xc. Data components have no visual appearance so it doesn't matter where you place the component.

18

Display the Component Inspector panel and enter the settings shown in Figure 18-6 in the Parameters tab. These settings load the `featuredProduct.xml` document into the product_xc component.

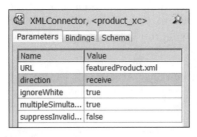

Figure 18-6.
Settings for the XMLConnector component

We'll import a schema from the external XML document. This will allow us to work with the data from the XML document more easily.

Switch to the Schema tab of the Component Inspector and select the results property. Click the import schema button (the one with the arrow), at the right of the panel. Navigate to the file `featuredProduct.xml` and click Open. Figure 18-7 shows the populated Schema tab.

Figure 18-7.
The Schema tab after importing a schema

You can see the elements of the XML file within the Schema tab. Note that the FeaturedProduct and product elements are objects, while the other elements are either strings or numbers.

We'll display the product name, cost, and e-mail address in TextInput components. We'll add built-in validators to the name and cost fields. A little later, we'll create a custom validator for the e-mail address.

Drag three TextInput components to the stage and name them name_txt, price_txt, and email_txt, respectively. Drag a TextArea component to the right of the TextInput components and name it msg_txt. We'll use this to display validation messages, so change the width to 200 and the height to 100.

Click the XMLConnector component and display the Bindings tab of the Component Inspector. Click the plus sign to add a new binding and select the productName property as shown in the Figure 18-8. Click OK.

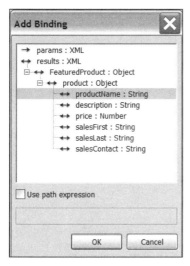

Figure 18-8.
The Add Binding dialog box

In the settings for the Binding, change the direction to out and click the right side of the bound to setting to bring up the Bound To dialog box. Select the name_txt component and bind to the text property as shown in Figure 18-9. The text property is the only available bindable property for the TextInput component.

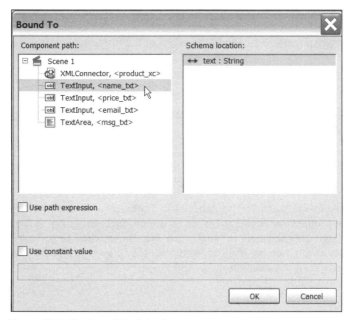

Figure 18-9. The Bound To dialog box

You have created a one-way binding from the productName element to the text property of the name_txt component. Repeat the process to bind the price element to the price_txt component and the salesContact element to email_txt.

Before we can check if the binding has worked, we'll need to trigger the XMLConnector component. Add a new layer to the Flash file called actions and add the following code to trigger the component:

```
product_xc.trigger();
```

The XMLConnector will trigger as soon as the movie runs. Test the file and you should see the TextInput components populated from the XMLConnector component as shown in Figure 18-10.

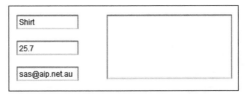

Figure 18-10. The TextInput components displaying bound data from the XMLConnector component

Earlier in the chapter, we scripted formatters. As an alternative, we'll add one visually so you can see the process. Select the name_txt component on the stage and click the text property in the Bindings tab of the Component Inspector. Choose a Compose String formatter and enter Product: <.> in the formatter options section. This will display the word Product before the name from the XML file. Notice that we've used <.> to refer to the current XML node.

Test the file again. Figure 18-11 shows the effect of the formatter.

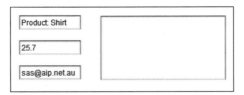

Figure 18-11. The TextInput component with a Compose String formatter

We'll add built-in validators to the two of the TextInput components to check for the length of the product name and the price of the product. I'm going to require that the name be at least 20 characters in length and that the product price is greater than 5. Although they might not be realistic examples, they'll give you some idea about the process of using built-in validation.

Select the name_txt component on the stage and display the Schema tab in the Component Inspector. Select the text property and click in the validation options setting to bring up the String Validation Settings dialog box as shown in Figure 18-12. Enter a value of 20 to specify that the name has to be at least 20 characters long.

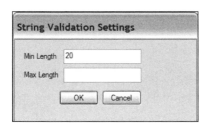

Figure 18-12.
The String Validation Settings dialog box

Select the price_txt component and change the datatype in the Schema tab to Number. Enter a minimum value of 5 in the Number Validation Settings dialog box.

We'll create a class to deal with the validation of the two TextInput components. The class will need to deal with valid and invalid events raised by component after the binding process. The user will be able to specify the validation error message to display.

Create a new ActionScript file and save it as Validator.as in the same folder as the Flash file. Start by importing the classes that we'll need.

```
import mx.controls.TextInput;
import mx.controls.TextArea;
import mx.utils.Delegate;
```

We'll be referring to the TextInput and TextArea components, so we'll import the classes so we can avoid using the fully qualified names. We'll need the Delegate class to respond to events in the correct scope.

Create the class and constructor as well as the functions that respond to the events. Add the following code to the ActionScript file:

```
class Validator {
  private var __msg:String;
  private var __displayComp:TextArea;

  function Validator (compToValidate:TextInput, msg:String,
➥  compToDisplay:TextArea){
    __msg = msg;
    __displayComp = compToDisplay;
    compToValidate.addEventListener("valid", Delegate.create(
➥    this, dataIsValid));
    compToValidate.addEventListener("invalid", Delegate.create(
➥    this, dataIsInvalid));
  }
```

```
    private function dataIsValid(evt:Object):Void {
      __displayComp.text += "Data in " + evt.target._name + " is
➥    valid\n";
    }
    private function dataIsInvalid(evt:Object):Void {
      __displayComp.text += "Data in " + evt.target._name + " is
➥    invalid. " + __msg;
    }
}
```

We start by declaring the class and two private variables. The __msg variable will store the user message relating to the validation error, while __displayComp refers to the component that will display the error message.

The constructor takes three parameters: the component that is to be validated (compToValidate), the error message to display in the case of invalid data (msg), and the component in which to display the error message (compToDisplay).

The constructor function assigns values to the private variables and then adds event listeners to the component being validated. It uses the Delegate class so that the event is called in the scope of the class.

Finally, the class declares two private functions that respond to the valid and invalid events—dataIsValid and dataIsInvalid. In real life, you may not want to respond to valid data, but it's included here as an illustration.

Switch back to the Flash file and add the following lines of code underneath the trigger method:

```
var nameValidator:Validator= new Validator(name_txt, "The name is
➥not long enough", msg_txt);
var priceValidator:Validator= new Validator(price_txt, "Price must be
➥at least 5", msg_txt);
```

The lines create two Validator objects to validate the TextInput components. Each object has its own error message and displays the results of the validation in the msg_txt component. Test the file and you should see something similar to the screenshot shown in Figure 18-13.

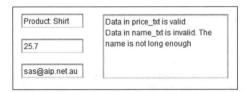

Figure 18-13. The movie after validating the XML content

You can find the files used in this exercise in the resource folder 18-4.

We'll extend the example to create a custom validator. In the next example, we'll check that the e-mail address is valid.

Working with a custom validator

Custom validators allow you to specify your own validation for components so that you can capture errors in data. This is likely to be particularly useful where you need to check changes made by users. You can catch errors in the entry before sending data to external pages for processing. However, in this example, we'll use a custom validator to validate the e-mail address within the XML document.

In order to use a custom validator, you need to set the datatype of the item that you wish to check to Custom. You can then specify the name of a class file to use for the validation. The class file must extend the CustomValidator class and include a method called validate.

Let's work through an example so you can see how this might work. We'll use the files from the previous exercise and add validation for the e-mail address TextInput. You can also use the files from the resource folder 18-4.

Select the email_txt component and display the Schema tab in the Component Inspector. Change the datatype setting to Custom and enter EmailValidator in the validation options setting. This tells Flash to use the class EmailValidator to validate the email_txt component. Now we'll need to create this class.

Create a new ActionScript file called EmailValidator.as and save it in the same folder as the Flash file. Start by importing the binding classes.

```
import mx.data.binding.*;
```

Our class will use a very simplistic check for the e-mail address—checking whether there is an @ sign and at least one dot. This is not terribly robust, but it illustrates custom validation.

Enter the following code in the class file:

```
class EmailValidator extends CustomValidator {
  public function validate(emailAddress:String) {
    var isValid:Boolean = true;
    var atPos:Number = emailAddress.indexOf("@");
    if (atPos == -1) {
      isValid = false;
    }
    var dotPos:Number = emailAddress.indexOf(".");
    if (dotPos == -1) {
      isValid = false;
    }
```

18

413

```
        if (!isValid) {
          this.validationError ("Email address doesn't contain either an
➡          @ sign or .");
          return;
        }
      }
    }
```

The class extends the CustomValidator class. It creates a public method called validate that checks for the existence of an @ sign or a dot. If an error is found, the validation error Email address doesn't contain either an @ sign or . is returned.

We'll modify the Validator class so that we display the error message raised by the validation process rather than our own error message. We'll also stop it from displaying messages for valid elements.

Change the Validator class to the following:

```
import mx.controls.TextInput;
import mx.controls.TextArea;
import mx.utils.Delegate;

class Validator {
  private var __displayComp:TextArea;

  function Validator(compToValidate:TextInput, compToDisplay:
➡  TextArea){
    __displayComp = compToDisplay;
    compToValidate.addEventListener("invalid", Delegate.create(this,
➡    dataIsInvalid));
  }

  private function dataIsInvalid(evt:Object):Void {
    __displayComp.text += "Error in " + evt.target._name + ". ";
    __displayComp.text += evt.messages + "\n";
  }
}
```

We've removed the event listener and function responding to valid data. We've used the messages property of the evt object to refer to messages generated by the validation process. If Flash detects the invalid event, the relevant error message will display, including the validationError from the custom validator.

We'll need to change the method calls within the Flash file and add another call to validate the e-mail address. Change the code in the Flash file as shown:

```
var nameValidator:Validator= new Validator(name_txt, msg_txt);
var priceValidator:Validator= new Validator(price_txt, msg_txt);
var emailValidator:Validator= new Validator (email_txt, msg_txt);
```

Change the e-mail address in the `featuredProduct.xml` file to introduce an error. Test the Flash movie and you should see something similar to the screenshot shown in Figure 18-14.

Figure 18-14. The movie showing error messages

In the previous two examples, we used built-in and custom validators to validate bound data from an external XML file. The examples used visual bindings in the Component Inspector panel. The final example checked the validity of an e-mail address, and you can find the finished files in the resource folder `18-5` with the code download.

Summary

In this chapter, we used data binding to share content between components. We worked through five examples that bound XML content from an XMLConnector component to UI components such as a TextArea, Label, and TextInput. The first three examples used scripted bindings, while the last two used visual bindings through the Component Inspector panel.

When working with scripted bindings, I showed you how to set EndPoints to create a simple binding between components. We used XPath expressions to target specific data within the `results` XML object. I covered the use of formatters to change the display of data, including the built-in Compose Strings and Number formatters. We also used a custom formatter to display a rounded number with a currency sign. Finally, I covered validators, and we used string and numeric built-in validators as well as creating a custom validator for an e-mail address.

This chapter only touches the surface of scripted data binding. Within a single chapter, it's not possible to cover the range of situations that you might encounter. For example, you can work with more complicated bindings that involve arrays of data and that use a DataSet or DataHolder component. Hopefully you've seen enough in this chapter to get you started, and what you've read will encourage you to experiment further.

What's next?

In the next chapter, we'll look at how Flash movies communicate with their container. You may have come across this already when calling JavaScript functions from Flash. If you've tried to use `fscommand`, you'll know how cumbersome this type of communication can be! Flash Player 8 introduces a new type of communication, available through the External API. It offers many advantages and expands the range of communications that are possible to include other languages and applications other than a web browser.

19 COMMUNICATION BETWEEN FLASH AND THE BROWSER

A common requirement for developers is allowing Flash movies to communicate with the hosting web page. Perhaps the Flash movie needs to send values to an HTML form or receive information from a JavaScript function. The Flash movie may need to redirect the browser to a different website or receive authentication information from the hosting page.

There are different ways that developers can achieve this communication, depending on the version of the Flash Player being targeted. For Flash Player 7 and below, developers can use FlashVars or JavaScript to send content into Flash. A Flash movie can also call JavaScript functions with getURL or fscommand, optionally sending variables from Flash into the function. These approaches are available to all developers and, as you'll see shortly, they can be a little cumbersome to use. Flash Player 8 introduces another alternative—the ExternalInterface class, or External API.

The ExternalInterface class allows Flash to communicate with the Flash Player container hosting the movie—usually a web page. It is a static class that provides similar functionality to the ActionScript fscommand or FlashVars. The communication can occur in either direction—from the container to Flash or from Flash back to the container. However, unlike other methods, the calls are synchronous—they can wait for and receive a response. The External API is also a little easier to implement than earlier approaches.

Flash movies aren't limited to browser communication using JavaScript. They can communicate with any container containing Flash Player 8. This means that you can use a language like C#, VB .NET, or Python to communicate with ActionScript. However, as browser communication is likely to be the most common use for developers, we'll focus on ActionScript and JavaScript in this chapter.

The ExternalInterface class requires a browser that supports either ActiveX or the NPRuntime API. You can find out more about this API at www.mozilla.org/projects/plugins/npruntime.html. At the time of writing, the ExternalInterface class can be used with all major web browsers including the following:

- Internet Explorer 5.0 and above for Windows
- Firefox 1.0 and above for both Windows and Macintosh
- Mozilla 1.7.5 and above for both Windows and Macintosh
- Netscape 8 and above for both Windows and Macintosh
- Safari 1.3 and above for Macintosh

Note that you can't use the External API with web pages hosted in Opera, as Opera doesn't support the NPRuntime API. You also need to be aware that Flash Player 8 includes security features that stop you from using the ExternalInterface class unless the container and SWF are both running through a web server.

In this chapter, we'll look at the various ways that Flash can communicate with both Flash Players 7 and 8. We'll start by looking at the different methods for Flash/JavaScript communication with Flash Players earlier than version 8. After that, we'll focus on using the External API for ActionScript/JavaScript communication.

Communication with Flash Player 7 and below

Developers targeting a Flash Player before version 8 can use JavaScript and FlashVars so that an HTML page can send values into a Flash movie. With these methods, communication consists of setting the value of ActionScript variables within the Flash movie. The communication is one way—the Flash movie can't send a response back to the HTML page.

Developers targeting Flash Player 7 and below can also call JavaScript functions from within a Flash movie using the getURL action or the fscommand. The movie can pass an ActionScript variable to a JavaScript function but again, it can't wait for a response from the HTML page. Let's look at the different types of communication for Flash Player 7 and below in more detail.

Sending variables into Flash

FlashVars allows developers to add variables to a Flash movie when it is first loaded, and you can use this approach with Flash Player 6 or later. The variables are added as a parameter in the <object> tag or an attribute in the <embed> tag using variable pairs:

```
<param name=FlashVars value="var1=value1" />
<embed FlashVars="var1=value1" ... />
```

You can achieve the same result by adding variable pairs to the end of the name of the .swf file in either tag:

```
<param name="movie" value="FlashName.swf?var1=value1&var2=value2" />
<embed src=" FlashName.swf?var1=value1&var2=value2" ... />
```

Developers can also use the SetVariable JavaScript method to set variables in Flash:

```
window.document.FlashMovieNameOrID.SetVariable("var1", "value1");
```

JavaScript targets the Flash movie using the ID or name attribute within the <object> or <embed> tag, respectively.

Whichever approach you use, Flash receives the variables from the HTML page when the movie first loads. Bear in mind that it's not possible to determine when the variables become available to Flash. A further drawback is that if the value of the variable changes, the web browser will need to reload the Flash movie.

Calling JavaScript from Flash

Developers can use fscommand and getURL to communicate from the Flash movie back to the HTML page. Of these two methods, the getURL method is probably the more widely supported, and it's certainly simpler to use:

```
getURL("javascript: JSFunction(parameters)");
```

The fscommand action also allows Flash to call a JavaScript function on the HTML page hosting the Flash movie. However, this command is a little harder to implement than the getURL approach. It requires a single, specially named JavaScript function that responds to all fscommand actions from Flash. The JavaScript function can optionally receive parameters from the Flash movie. If the host browser is Internet Explorer, the HTML page has to include a VBScript function as well.

Within Flash, the fscommand action takes two arguments—the name of the command to execute and the parameters to be sent to the JavaScript function:

```
fscommand("CommandToExecute", "Parameters");
```

It's possible for Flash to include multiple fscommand actions, sending different parameters each time. By sending through a command name, the receiving JavaScript function can distinguish between each action.

The JavaScript function is named using the ID (<object> tag) or the name (<embed> tag) of the Flash movie. The suffix _DoFSCommand is added to the function name as shown:

```
<script language ="JavaScript">
function FlashMovieNameOrID_DoFSCommand(command, args) {
  //do something;
}
</SCRIPT>
```

As there can only be a single JavaScript function within the web page, Flash can specify which command to execute:

```
fscommand("Command1", "Parameters1");
fscommand("Command2", "Parameters2");
fscommand("Command3", "Parameters3");
```

The JavaScript function can then act according to the command name:

```
< script language ="JavaScript">
function FlashMovieNameOrID_DoFSCommand (command, args) {
  if(command == "Command1"){
    //do something;
  }
..else if(command == "Command2"){
    //do something else
  }
  else if(command == "Command3"){
    //do something else
  }
}
</SCRIPT>
```

Internet Explorer also requires some VBScript in addition to the JavaScript function. The VBScript subroutine is named in a similar way to the JavaScript function, appending _FSCommand to the name. It then calls the JavaScript function, passing in the arguments from Flash:

```
<script language ="VBScript">
Sub FlashMovieNameOrID_FSCommand(ByVal command, ByVal args)
  call FlashMovieNameOrID_DoFSCommand(command, args)
end sub
</SCRIPT>
```

The only other requirement to enable this communication is that the <embed> tag requires the attribute swLiveConnect to be set to true:

```
<embed swLiveConnect="true"... />
```

As you can see, it's more complicated to use fscommand to call a JavaScript function compared with getURL. Whichever of the two approaches you choose, Flash doesn't receive a response informing it of the outcome of the function call, so it's possible for the communication to fail silently.

An alternative approach is to use the Flash/JavaScript Integration Kit developed by Macromedia.

Using the Flash/JS Integration Kit

Macromedia released the Flash/JavaScript Integration Kit to assist with integration between ActionScript and JavaScript. The Kit makes communication easier by encapsulating the functionality using AS2.0 classes. The Kit allows for the transfer of more complicated datatypes between Flash and JavaScript. These types are Object, Array, String, Number, Date, Boolean, and null. Even though the Kit makes implementation easier than the code shown previously, the Kit uses the same technologies to handle communication, so it suffers from the same limitations.

At the time of writing, the Flash/JavaScript Integration Kit works in the following browsers:

- IE 6.0 for Windows
- Firefox 1.0 for Windows and Macintosh
- Opera 8.0 for Windows and Macintosh
- Safari 1.2.4 and above for Macintosh
- Firefox 1.1 for Linux

You can find out more and download the Kit at http://weblogs.macromedia.com/flashjavascript/. At the time of writing, the zip file was less than 40KB.

19

421

To use the Kit, download the `FlashJavascriptGateway.zip` file from the preceding URL and unpack it anywhere on your computer. You'll need to add `FlashJavascriptGateway\installation\JavaScriptFlashGateway.js` and `FlashJavascriptGateway\installation\JavaScriptFlashGateway.swf` to the folder that contains your Flash movie. You'll also need to copy the `com` folder to the same location.

The JavaScriptProxy class handles the communication within Flash. You can create an instance of the class with the following code:

```
import com.macromedia.javascript.JavaScriptProxy;
var myProxy:JavaScriptProxy = new JavaScriptProxy(FVID, obj);
```

The object requires two arguments—an identifier that will be passed into Flash from JavaScript using FlashVars and a reference to the object receiving calls from JavaScript. If you're working on the main timeline, you can use the keyword `this` or `_level0`.

When we want to call a JavaScript function from within Flash, we can use

```
myProxy.call("JSFunctionName", params);
```

The method specifies the name of the JavaScript function as a string as well as any parameters to be sent to the function.

In the HTML page, we need to include the JavaScriptFlashGateway.js file in the <head> section of the page:

```
<script type="text/javascript" src="JavaScriptFlashGateway.js" />
```

Flash requires a unique identifier for the communication. Creating a JavaScript variable that contains a date time stamp is often a good approach:

```
var FVID = new Date();
```

You also have to create a FlashProxy object. It takes the unique identifier as a parameter as well as the name of the `JavaScriptFlashGateway.swf` file.

```
var myFlashProxy = new FlashProxy(FVID, "JavaScriptFlashGateway.swf");
```

We can then use the call method in JavaScript to call an ActionScript function:

```
myFlashProxy.call("addItem", params);
```

You can use the FlashTag class to generate the <object> and <embed> tags within your HTML page. When you call the constructor function, you'll pass in the name of the `.swf` file, and the width and height of the movie.

```
var myFlash = new FlashTag("sample.swf", 200, 200);
```

You'll also need to use the `setFlashvars` method to pass in the unique identifier you created earlier:

```
myFlash.setFlashvars("FVID =" + FVID);
```

You can then use the write method to write the correct tags to the document.

```
myFlash.write(document);
```

Using the Flash/JavaScript Integration Kit simplifies the process of communication and extends the functionality so that you can pass more complicated variable types between the two languages. However, as mentioned earlier, it still uses the same approach, and you can't create synchronous calls.

If you're targeting a Flash Player prior to version 8, you'll need to use one of the methods listed in this section to allow ActionScript and JavaScript to communicate with each other. However, you can take advantage of the External API if you're targeting Flash Player 8 or above. The advantage here is that you can create synchronous function calls. Let's explore the new approach in more detail.

19

Understanding the ExternalInterface class

The ExternalInterface class is a static class available within the External package that allows you to communicate with the container hosting the Flash Player. Because it's a static class, you don't need to instantiate it first before you can start calling methods. The class has two methods and one property that we'll explore further in the remainder of this chapter.

The ExternalInterface class offers several advantages over other methods of communication with JavaScript:

- The class creates synchronous calls so you can receive an immediate response from the function that is called.

- You can call any JavaScript function from within a Flash movie. When using the fscommand, you can only call a single function.

- There are no limits to the number of arguments that you can send to a JavaScript function. With the fscommand, you must send the command and parameters arguments.

- You can preserve datatypes such as Boolean, Number, and String during function calls.

In order to avoid using the fully qualified name in your code, you can import the ExternalInterface class into your Flash movie using

```
import flash.external.ExternalInterface;
```

You can only use the ExternalInterface class if you're targeting Flash Player 8 and in the majority of cases, you'll probably use this class for JavaScript communication. The web browser that hosts the Flash Player must support either ActiveX or the NPRuntime API, and you can make sure that the class is available for use by checking the available property:

```
ExternalInterface.available;
```

This property returns a Boolean value. If you receive a `false` value, you'll have to use an alternative method of communicating with the container or let the user know that some functionality is unavailable with their current Flash Player.

The ExternalInterface class has two methods, call and addCallback. The addCallback method allows JavaScript to communicate with Flash, while the call method allows Flash to call a JavaScript function. We'll start by looking at the call method, but it's important to be aware of some of the changes to Flash Player 8 security before proceeding.

Understanding Flash Player 8 security

Flash Player 8 implements a new security model that affects the way that JavaScript and ActionScript communicate. The HTML parameter allowScriptAccess determines whether ActionScript can communicate with JavaScript. Be aware that it does not determine the converse—whether the container can communicate with ActionScript.

The allowScriptAccess parameter has three possible values:

- always: Always allow ActionScript to communicate with JavaScript.
- sameDomain: Allow ActionScript to communicate with JavaScript when both the SWF and HTML files come from the same domain.
- never: Don't allow ActionScript to communicate with JavaScript.

You can set this parameter explicitly. In the case of the <object> tag, you can use

```
<param name="allowScriptAccess" value="sameDomain" />
```

The <embed> tag would use

```
<embed allowScriptAccess="sameDomain" ... />
```

If you don't specify this parameter in Flash Player 8, version 8 movies use the value sameDomain. This is a change from earlier version movies, which used the default value always.

Using the call method

The call method allows Flash to call a function in the container, for example, a JavaScript function. You can optionally pass parameters to this function as shown:

```
call(methodName:String, [parameter1:Object, parameter2:Object]);
```

The method returns an object—either the value returned by the container function, or null if the container function is not available. In the case of JavaScript communication, the method looks for a function in the script tag:

```
<script language="JavaScript">
```

If you are using some other type of container for the Flash movie, the call method broadcasts an event named with the methodName parameter to the container for processing.

Let's work through an example to see how Flash can call a JavaScript function. We'll use Flash to enter text and send it through to a JavaScript function. The JavaScript function will display the entered text in an alert and send a response back to Flash. We'll display the response within the Flash movie. It's a fairly abstract example, but hopefully it will demonstrate how the communication works.

Before you start, you'll need to run this example through a web server. I have Internet Information Services (IIS) installed with my Windows XP Professional operating system. You could use this or any other local web server, such as Apache for a Macintosh. You can also upload the files to an external service provider to test them.

19

If you have IIS installed on a PC, you'll need to move your files to a folder within Inetpub ➤ wwwroot on your hard drive before testing them. If you're working externally, use an FTP program to upload the files. You'll need to test the files through a web browser by entering a full http path. When working locally, this is normally http://localhost/folderName/.

I like to work in a folder outside of the web server and then move the files to the web server for testing. I've called my web server folder FOE so the location of the testing files on my computer under IIS is C:\Inetpub\wwwroot\FOE. I'll need to visit http://localhost/FOE/ within my web browser to test the files.

Start by creating a new Flash movie and size it to 250×100 pixels. Add a TextInput and Button component to the Library and save the file as SimpleForm.fla.

Create a new ActionScript file and save it as SimpleForm.as. We'll use this for our new class, SimpleForm. The class will create a user interface with a TextInput and Button component.

Start by adding the following code to the SimpleForm.as file:

```
import flash.external.ExternalInterface;
import mx.controls.TextInput;
import mx.controls.Button;
import mx.utils.Delegate;

class SimpleForm {
  private var __container:MovieClip;
  private var __tiContainer:MovieClip;
  private var __ti:TextInput;
  private var __button:Button;
  private var __enteredText:String;
  private var __response:Object;
}
```

The import statements import the classes that we'll need. This includes the ExternalInterface class as well as the two component classes. I've also imported the Delegate class. I'll use this when registering my event listener so that I can refer to variables in the correct scope.

Importing these classes will save me from having to use their fully qualified names in ActionScript. I've also declared the class SimpleForm and added some private variable declarations.

The __container variable refers to the container movie clip for the form, and this will be passed into the constructor function. The __tiContainer variable refers to the movie clip that holds the UI components. The components that I'll use in the form are stored within the __ti and __button variables. The __enteredText variable references the text property of the TextInput component, while the __response object will contain the JavaScript response.

Add the following class constructor below the variable declarations:

```
function SimpleForm(container:MovieClip) {
  __container = container;
  var TIInitObj:Object = {_x: 20, _y: 20, _width: 200, _height:20};
  var BtnInitObj:Object = {_x: 20, _y:50, label: "Click me!"};
  __tiContainer = __container.createEmptyMovieClip("container_mc",
➥   __container.getNextHighestDepth());
  __ti = __tiContainer.createClassObject(TextInput, "text_txt",
➥   __tiContainer.getNextHighestDepth(),TIInitObj);
  __button = __tiContainer.createClassObject(Button, "click_btn",
➥   __tiContainer.getNextHighestDepth(), BtnInitObj);
  __button.addEventListener("click", Delegate.create(this, sendToJS));
}
```

The class constructor method takes a single parameter, container. This is the movie clip that will hold the form. The first line in the constructor function assigns this value to the private variable __container. The following two lines declare initialization objects for the two components that we'll add to the form. The first, TIInitObj, refers to the TextInput, while BtnInitObj contains the initialization values for the Button component. These objects set the properties for the components when they're created.

The function creates an empty movie clip called container_mc to store the components. The private variable __tiContainer references this movie clip. The code then creates a TextInput and Button component dynamically using the createClassObject method. Note that these components must exist in the Library of the Flash file before we can use the SimpleForm class.

The last line within the function registers an event listener that listens for the click event of the button. We've used the Delegate class so that the function can reference variables in the scope of the SimpleForm class.

To complete the class, we'll need to add the sendToJS function referred to in the last line of the function. Add the following private function before the closing brace:

```
private function sendToJS(evtObj:Object):Void {
  __enteredText = __ti.text;
  if (__enteredText.length > 0 && ExternalInterface.available) {
    __response = ExternalInterface.call("showString", __enteredText);
    __ti.text = String(__response);
  }
}
```

This function creates the call to the JavaScript function. It starts by assigning the text property of the TextInput component to the variable __enteredText. Then, it tests that text has been added and that the ExternalInterface class is available using the available property. Because the External API is a static class, you don't need to instantiate it first.

The ExernalInterface.call method calls the JavaScript function showString, passing the text from the TextInput as a parameter. The JavaScript function returns a response, which is stored in the __response object. Finally, this is cast as a String and displayed within the TextInput component.

Switch back to the SimpleForm.fla file. Rename Layer 1 as actions and add the following code:

```
var theSF:SimpleForm = new SimpleForm(this);
```

This line instantiates a new SimpleForm object, passing the main timeline as a parameter. We won't be able to test this Flash file yet. Instead, we'll need to publish the SWF and HTML pages and add the showString JavaScript function to the HTML page. Once we've finished, we can only test these pages through a web browser, running them through a web server.

Publish a SWF and an HTML page from the Flash file. Open the HTML file and add the following JavaScript function to the <head> section of the page:

```
<script language="JavaScript">
  <!--
  function showString(theString) {
    alert(theString);
    return "Thanks for the text";
  }
  -->
</script>
```

The function showString accepts a parameter called theString. It creates an alert box to display the parameter and returns Thanks for the text.

Close the HTML file. Move the SWF and HTML files to your web server. This may be running locally or at a service provider. As I mentioned earlier, my web server is local so I copied my files to C:\Inetpub\wwwroot\FOE.

427

Open a web browser and enter the URL to the `SimpleForm.html` page. In my case, it's `http://localhost/FOE/SimpleForm.html`. You should see something similar to the screen shot shown in Figure 19-1.

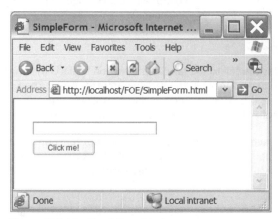

Figure 19-1. The SimpleForm.html page

Enter some text and click the button. You should see a JavaScript alert as shown in Figure 19-2. When you click the OK button in the alert box, the TextInput component should display `Thanks for the text`.

Figure 19-2. The SimpleForm.html page after clicking the Flash movie button

In this example, you saw how the Flash movie could call a JavaScript function and receive a response synchronously. The example was a simple one, but hopefully it illustrated how easy it is to facilitate this type of communication. You can find the files associated with the example in the resource folder 19-1.

The other type of communication that we'll examine in this chapter is where the Flash Player container communicates with the Flash movie. We'll look at how you can call an ActionScript function from within JavaScript using the addCallback method of the External API.

Using the addCallback method

The addCallback method makes a Flash function available to the container. For example, you could use this method so that a JavaScript function in an HTML page can call an ActionScript function. The JavaScript function needs to know the id (in the case of the <object> tag) or name (in the case of the <embed> tag) of the Flash movie.

The addCallback ActionScript method takes the following arguments:

```
addCallback (methodName:String, instance:Object, method:Function);
```

The methodName parameter is the JavaScript reference to the ActionScript function being called. The method argument refers to the ActionScript function that you want to register. Both of these arguments refer to the name of the ActionScript function. However, the first argument is the name that is used by JavaScript when calling the ActionScript function. You don't need to use the same name for both arguments, but you'll probably find it easier to understand your code if you do.

The instance is an object or a movieclip that contains the function. It is equivalent to using the keyword this in the ActionScript function. Most of the time, you'll use this or null for the parameter.

The addCallback method returns a Boolean value indicating whether the callback has succeeded. A return value of false may indicate that there are security restrictions that prevent the callback from executing.

You use the addCallback method in the following way:

```
var result:Boolean = ExternalInterface.addCallback("methodName",
➥ this, method);
```

You can test the value of the result variable and take appropriate action if the addCallback method fails.

Again, you'd probably want to make sure that the External API is available before registering the callback.

```
if (ExternalInterface.available) {
  var result:Boolean = ExternalInterface.addCallback("methodName",
➥   this, method);
}
```

After registering the callback in Flash, you can then call the ActionScript function from within the container for the Flash movie. Most developers will do this using JavaScript on an HTML page.

19

In JavaScript, the first step is to find the id of the Flash movie in the <object> tag or the name from the <embed> tag on the HTML page. The Flash help files recommend that you avoid using the document.getElementById("pluginName") or document.all.pluginName JavaScript methods of accessing the Flash movie id or name because the methods don't work reliably across all web browsers.

To access the id or name correctly, you can use the following JavaScript function. This is taken from the Flash help file:

```
function thisMovie(movieName) {
  var isIE = navigator.appName.indexOf("Microsoft") != -1;
  return (isIE) ? window[movieName] : document[movieName];
  }
```

The code does a browser test and references the Flash movie appropriately using either window[flashMovieName] or document[flashMovieName].

You can use this reference to call the ActionScript function. In the following code, the Flash function with the name functionName is called within the movie whose name or id is flashMovieID. The argument params is sent into the ActionScript function.

```
function callFlash() {
  thisMovie("flashMovieID").functionName(params);
  }
```

Let's work through a simple example where we use JavaScript to play specific frames in a Flash movie. We'll select a frame label from a drop-down list on an HTML page. A TextInput component in Flash will display the frame label, and the playhead will move to that location in the movie.

You can find the resource files within the folder 19-2. I've set up a Flash file called playMe.fla that I'll use for the example. You can also set up your own playMe.fla file. It needs to contain three keyframes labeled start, middle, and end. Each keyframe contains a stop action and some appropriate content. My playMe.fla file is 250×100 in size.

As with the previous example, you'll need to test these files on a web server so you'll either need to create a location on your local web server or upload them to your service provider. This is explained in detail earlier in the chapter.

Start by creating a new ActionScript file and save it as SimpleControl.as. We'll use this to create the SimpleControl class. Add the following ActionScript:

```
import flash.external.ExternalInterface;
import mx.controls.TextInput;

class SimpleControl{
  private var __container:MovieClip;
  private var __TI:TextInput;
```

```
   public function SimpleControl(container:MovieClip) {
     __container = container;
     var __TIInitObj:Object = {_x:20, _y: 20, _width:200, _height:20};
     if (ExternalInterface.available) {
     __TI = __container.createClassObject(TextInput, "in_txt",
➡      __container.getNextHighestDepth(), __TIInitObj);
       ExternalInterface.addCallback("controlMovie", this,
➡        controlMovie);
     }
   }
 }
```

The file starts by importing the classes that we'll need. This includes the ExternalInterface class and the TextInput class. We then declare the SimpleControl class and two private variables. The variable __container references the container movie clip for the TextInput component within the Flash file, whereas the __TI variable refers to the TextInput itself.

The constructor function takes the container movie clip as a parameter. This tells us which timeline we're working on. The function then assigns the argument to the __container variable. The next line declares an initialization object for the TextInput component setting the position and size for the component.

If the External API is available, we create a TextInput component with the createClassObject method, passing in the initialization object. We then add the callback. If we wanted our scripting to be a little more robust, we could assign a Boolean variable and add some error handling. I haven't done that in this case for simplicity.

Notice that I've used the same function name for both the JavaScript call and the ActionScript method in my addCallback method. This isn't a requirement, but it may make my code easier to follow.

The last thing that we need to do is to add the controlMovie function to the class file. This function will receive information from the JavaScript function of the same name. Add the following code before the closing brace in the class file:

```
   public function controlMovie(frameLabel:String):Void {
     __TI.text = frameLabel;
     __container.gotoAndStop(frameLabel);
   }
```

The function receives an argument, frameLabel, from the JavaScript function. It sets this value as the text property for the TextInput component __TI and uses the gotoAndStop action to move the playhead to that frame label in the Flash movie.

Switch to the playMe.fla file. If you've created your own copy of this file, add a TextInput component to the Library. This is necessary so we can add the component dynamically using the createClassObject action.

19

Add a new layer to the file and call it actions. Enter the following code on Frame 1:

```
var theSC:SimpleControl = new SimpleControl(this);
```

This line creates a new SimpleControl object called theSC that references the main timeline.

Publish the Flash file, making sure that you publish both a SWF and an HTML file. You'll need to add some JavaScript and a form to the HTML file. Start by adding the following HTML after the <body> tag:

```
<form name="frmFlash" action="JavaScript:controlMovie();"
method="POST">
  <select name="selFrame">
    <option selected="selected">start</option>
    <option>middle</option>
    <option>end</option>
  </select> 
  <input type="submit" value="Control Flash">
</form>
```

The lines create a form called frmFlash that contains a select box and a button with the label Control Flash. The select box contains the three frame labels from the Flash movie. When the form submits, it calls the JavaScript function controlMovie.

We'll also need to create the relevant JavaScript functions. Add the following lines to the <head> section of the HTML page:

```
<script language="JavaScript">
  <!--
  function thisMovie(movieName) {
    var isIE = navigator.appName.indexOf("Microsoft") != -1;
    return (isIE) ? window[movieName] : document[movieName];
  }

  function controlMovie() {
    var n = document.frmFlash.selFrame.selectedIndex;
    var frameLabel = document.frmFlash.selFrame[n].text;
    thisMovie("playMe").controlMovie(frameLabel);
    }
  -->
</script>
```

The first function, thisMovie, returns the correct reference to the Flash movie, depending on the browser type. As mentioned earlier, this is taken from the Flash help files.

The controlMovie function finds the text associated with the select control and stores it in the variable frameLabel. It then uses the thisMovie function to return the correct reference to the Flash movie called playMe and calls the controlMovie function, passing in the value of the `frameLabel` variable. In other words, when we click the button, the JavaScript function will pass the text from the drop-down box to the TextInput in the Flash file and move the playhead to the appropriate frame. Close the HTML file.

Copy the SWF and HTML files to your web server. My web server is running locally so I copied my files to `C:\Inetpub\wwwroot\FOE`.

Open a web browser and enter the URL to the `playMe.html` page. In my case, it's `http://localhost/FOE/playMe.html`. You should see something similar to the image shown in Figure 19-3.

Figure 19-3. The playMe.html page

Select a different option from the drop-down list and click the `Control Flash` button. You should see the selected frame label appear in the TextInput component and the Flash file move to a different frame as shown in Figure 19-4.

Figure 19-4. The playMe.html page after selecting a different frame label

In this example, we saw how you could call an ActionScript function using JavaScript. We used an HTML select box to control the position of the playhead within a Flash movie. The process involved registering the ActionScript function for a callback and creating the appropriate JavaScript to call this function. The example is a little abstract, but hopefully it demonstrates how you can control Flash with JavaScript. If you want to see a further example of communication, you can find more in the resource folder 19-3.

We've seen two examples of communication between ActionScript and JavaScript. This is likely to be the most common use for the External API. However, it's also possible for ActionScript to communicate with other languages.

ActionScript communication with other languages

In the previous section, we saw how ActionScript can call a JavaScript function. As I mentioned earlier, the External API can also communicate with other languages in applications that host the Flash Player. Although it is beyond the scope of this chapter to explore the area in detail, it's worth mentioning how non-JavaScript communication takes place.

Calling a non-JavaScript method

You may wish to use Flash to communicate with a different type of Flash application, perhaps a desktop application that contains the Flash Player ActiveX control. When you call a non-JavaScript method, the call is captured in a FlashCall event, which sends the event request to the application as an XML string.

The XML string contains the element <invoke> and sets the ActionScript method name as an attribute. It also contains the arguments, sent through in relevant tags:

```
<invoke name="MethodName" returntype="xml">
  <arguments>
    <string>String parameter</string>
    <number>1234</number>
  </arguments>
</invoke>
```

As the preceding arguments are of the string and number types, the XML string contains the tags <string> and <number>.

If you send array datatypes, the XML string contains something similar to the following:

```
<array>
  <property id='0'>
    <string>First</string>
  </property>
  <property id='1'>
    <string>Second</string>
  </property>
</array>
```

Your container application can then call the method referred to in the name attribute and optionally return data to Flash. Any data is returned to Flash in an XML string:

```
<string>This is a sample string being returned</string>
```

The container application needs to call the SetReturnValue method, passing the XML string:

```
flashMovie.SetReturnValue("XML string")
```

Flash blocks until the return value is set or until the event handler finishes executing.

Calling an ActionScript method from an application

Calling an ActionScript method from an application container works in a similar way. First, Flash has to add a callback as shown earlier.

```
addCallback("DesktopFunctionName", this, FlashFunctionName);
```

As previously mentioned, the name of the ActionScript function and the desktop function don't have to be the same, but it may make your code easier to follow if you give them the same names.

Then the container has to call the ActionScript function using the CallFunction method. You can use the same XML structure to pass arguments.

```
<invoke name="FunctionName" returntype="xml">
  <arguments>
    <string>From desktop</string>
  </arguments>
</invoke>
```

When Flash receives the function call, it triggers the Flash function referred to in the callback.

It is beyond the scope of this chapter to explore this topic in detail, but hopefully this section will give you enough information to get started.

Summary

In this chapter, you've seen how a Flash movie can communicate with the Flash Player container. We spent the majority of the chapter looking at ActionScript and JavaScript communication as that is likely to be the focus of most developers' work. We examined how you can call a JavaScript function from within Flash and how you can use JavaScript to access an ActionScript function. You also saw that it's possible for Flash Player 8 to work with other container languages such as C#, VB .NET, and Python.

Within the chapter, we covered several different approaches, according to which Flash Player was being targeted. The bulk of the chapter focused on the External API, which is available to Flash Player 8. One of the key advantages of this approach is the ability to make synchronous function calls. This isn't possible where you're targeting earlier Flash Players.

Hopefully, you'll have seen that the External API offers a more streamlined and functional approach to ActionScript communication with the Flash Player. If you're not able to take advantage of these new features, you may find that using the Flash/JS Integration Kit provides an acceptable alternative.

What's next?

In the next chapter, we'll explore how Flash communicates with data sources across server connections. Specifically, we'll focus on two efficient means of undertaking server communication in Flash: XML and Web Services. Of course, you'll also want to ensure your data exchanges are secure, and the next chapter shows you how.

20 SERVER COMMUNICATION (XML AND WEB SERVICES)

Over the years, Flash has gained respect as a development tool through its support for various methods of loading in external data and communicating with the server. Imagine how limited you'd be developing anything in Flash without the possibility to read in or send out data.

Luckily, the Flash 3 days are well and truly behind us, and we now have numerous ways to communicate with a data source. Two of the most popular and efficient ways to do so are XML and web services, and we'll discuss these in detail in this chapter.

> This chapter provides a valuable summary of using Flash and XML together. However, if this topic really piques your interest, and you want to go deeper into the subject, then friends of ED has another fantastic book available, written by Sas Jacobs (one of the authors of this book), called Foundation XML for Flash (2005, ISBN: 1-59059-543-2).

Understanding XML

In many ways XML, or *eXtensible Markup Language*, defines the web as we know it today. It allows you to store data in a structured way, which is pretty much the Holy Grail for developers, because it enables them to have a representation of the state of an object at any time.

When I first started looking at XML some years ago, I just couldn't figure out what it was all about. I was proficient in developing HTML and assumed that all tags used in an XML document must have some specific purpose and actually "do" something. It wasn't until I understood that the keyword with XML is not "do" but "describe" that I started to see the tremendous power in it. In other words, XML abstracts data one step further: rather than specifying a visual design, it describes the design of your data structure.

XML is a text format that uses tags, or *nodes* as they're called in XML jargon, to define a hierarchical tree structure. One of the rules in writing a valid XML document is that it should start with a single root node, for example, book.

```
<book>
</book>
```

In that root node, you have multiple other nodes that further describe what is contained within the book, like a title and some different chapters.

```
<book>
    <title>Object-Oriented ActionScript for Flash 8</title>
    <chapter>1</chapter>
    <chapter>2</chapter>
</book>
```

If you look at the preceding XML, you can see it describes a book entitled *Object-Oriented ActionScript for Flash 8* that includes a Chapter 1 and Chapter 2. That's nice, but what if we want to include more information about each of those chapters—do we need to keep adding subnodes for each little bit of information, or is there another way to handle this?

```
<book>
  <title>Object-Oriented ActionScript 2.0</title>
  <chapter id="1">
    <title>Introduction to OOP</title>
  </chapter>
  <chapter id="2">
    <title>Programming concepts</title>
  </chapter>
<book>
```

As you can see, XML nodes can also have attributes, such as id in the different chapter nodes. In general, when you have a collection of nodes with the same name, you use an attribute to enable you to filter out the necessary data. Using an id attribute in your nodes has the advantage of allowing easy access data through the XML idMap property, which we'll discuss later on in the section "XML class."

Another important thing to take into consideration is that certain characters are reserved for an internal use by XML, and you either have to escape those by their HTML entity or use a CDATA declaration to bypass the XML parser. Let's look at what those reserved characters are:

ASCII Character	Description	Escape Code
>	Greater than	&gt;
<	Smaller than	&lt;
'	Single quote	&apos;
"	Double quote	&quot;
&	Ampersand	&amp;
%	Percentage	&#37;

So, for example, if you needed to use a string containing an ampersand sign (&) in an attribute for an XML document, you could do it as follows:

```
<example>
  <name value="you &amp; I"></name>
</example>
```

You could use the same approach for a node value, just escaping the reserved character:

```
<example>
  <name>you &amp; I</name>
</example>
```

Or, as mentioned earlier, use a CDATA declaration to tell the XML parser to ignore whatever is contained within it:

```
<example>
  <name><![CDATA[you & I]]></name>
</example>
```

This CDATA declaration starts with `<![CDATA[` and ends with `]]>`, and everything written between those values is free from all laws that govern XML, including reserved characters. What happens when parsing the XML document is that as soon as a CDATA declaration is encountered, the parser just ignores whatever is in there.

Lucky for us, using CDATA not only ignores whatever you use within it, but also treats it as plain text without any syntactical meaning. If, for example, you use some HTML tags inside, it will not parse those tags as XML nodes as you might have expected it to do.

```
<example>
  <name><![CDATA[<strong>bold text</strong>]]></name>
</example>
```

Important to note is that the CDATA declaration is only available for node values, not for use in node attributes. The following example would NOT be parsed as valid XML:

```
<example>
  <name value="<![CDATA[you & I]]>"></name>
</example>
```

XML declarations

Now to finish up, let's talk about XML declarations. Any other tutorial on XML would have covered this first, but because we like to do things our own way (and because Flash doesn't particularly care if you use it or not), let's discuss it now.

Any XML document normally starts with an XML declaration at the very top. That line tells the parser that it is in fact an XML document, what version of the XML format it is using, optionally the character encoding it is using, and whether it is a standalone file or it uses any external **d**ocument **t**ype **d**eclaration (DTD). Document type declarations are somewhat beyond the scope of this chapter, but if you want to read up on them, I can strongly recommend to check out *Foundation XML for Flash* published by friends of ED.

The most basic XML declaration you'll encounter will look something like this:

```
<?xml version="1.0" ?>
```

All that line does is tell the parser it's an XML document that uses XML version 1.0 syntax. If you're using any foreign languages in the XML file, chances are you'd want to save it in Unicode, and you can tell the parser about this by adding the encoding attribute.

```
<?xml version="1.0" encoding="UTF-8" ?>
```

This is the exact same XML declaration as before, only with the character encoding set to UTF-8 for Unicode.

```
<?xml version="1.0" encoding="UTF-8" standalone="yes" ?>
```

Finally, we see the standalone attribute, which determines whether or not an external DTD is associated with the XML. This is completely optional, and if you're just using the XML file as a data source for Flash, its value will always be "yes".

Somewhat surprisingly, the order of the attributes in an XML declaration is fixed; first you have the version attribute, followed by the optional encoding and standalone attributes, respectively.

Now, although ActionScript allows you to retrieve this XML declaration using the xmlDecl property of the XML object, it's not an absolute prerequisite to use it in your file. The parser in Flash doesn't do anything with the information. In general, however, it is always good practice to add that line and make your file a valid XML document, mainly because it will allow compatibility with other technology and allow easy debugging. Most modern browsers will parse XML for you and report any syntax errors you might have made.

Its not really my goal to give you a comprehensive guide on XML in this chapter, but armed with the information covered so far, let's look at the different methods of implementing XML data into Flash projects.

Using XML in Flash

Loading XML into Flash is actually a relatively painless process. Using just a few lines of code, you can load data in and start using it in applications.

The most common ways to get hold of XML data in Flash is using the XMLConnector component or creating an instance of the XML class, both of which we'll discuss in the next few pages.

XMLConnector component

Since Flash MX 2004 (at least in the professional edition), there are a number of useful data connector components that ship with the product. One of these is the XMLConnector component, which is arguably the easiest way to load XML data in your Flash application.

Let's take a closer look at how you actually use this component. For this example, create a new FLA and save it as xmlconnector.fla in a local folder of your choice.

> *You could also download the files for this example from* www.friendsofed.com *and use them instead.*

Obviously, before we are able to load in some XML data, we need an actual XML file. We'll use the example from earlier on—save the code that follows as book.xml in the same folder where the FLA was saved.

```
<book>
  <title>Object-Oriented ActionScript 2.0</title>
  <chapter id="1">
    <title>Introduction to OOP</title>
  </chapter>
  <chapter id="2">
    <title>Programming concepts</title>
  </chapter>
<book>
```

Now we're all set for some component magic! With the FLA open, open up the Components panel (Windows ➤ Components)—you'll find the XMLConnector component in the data folder. Drag this component to the stage of the blank FLA to create an instance of it, as shown in Figure 20-1.

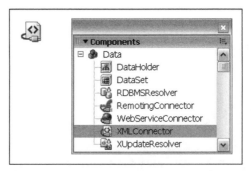

Figure 20-1. XMLConnector component on the stage

Clicking the component instance on stage will likely bring up the Parameter panel, which you see in Figure 20-2. If it doesn't, choose Windows ➤ Properties ➤ Parameters to make the component's Parameters panel appear.

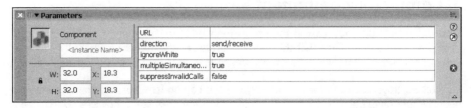

Figure 20-2. Component's Parameters panel

With the Parameters panel open, and the component instance selected, set the instance name as book_xmlconn. Your screen should resemble Figure 20-3.

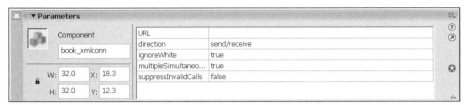

Figure 20-3. Assigning an instance name to the XMLConnector component

Keep the component selected; next we'll specify the URL for the XML file it needs to load. As the XML file is located in the same folder as our FLA, just type book.xml as the URL, as shown in Figure 20-4.

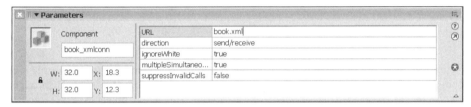

Figure 20-4. Setting the URL parameter for the XMLConnector component

The last thing we need to set is the direction of the XMLConnector—set this to receive because we only want to receive the XML data and not send anything back to the server. For now, you don't need to bother with the other optional component parameters. Next, we'll write a couple of lines of ActionScript code to trigger the XMLConnector component to load the file and output the results.

Create a new layer in the timeline and rename it to actionscript, as shown in Figure 20-5. Click the first frame of that layer in the timeline and open up the Actions panel (Window ➤ Actions).

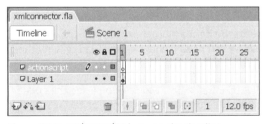

Figure 20-5. actionscript layer on the timeline

With the Actions panel open, select the first frame of the default layer, and enter the following code:

```
import mx.utils.Delegate;

function traceXML(evt:Object):Void {
  trace(evt.target.results);
}

this.book_xmlconn.addEventListener("result",Delegate.create(this,
➡ traceXML));
this.book_xmlconn.trigger();
```

This code we've just written is pretty straightforward. We add an event listener to book_xmlconn (the instance name for the XMLConnector component), which tells it to call the traceXML() function when a result event occurs. Using the mx.utils.Delegate class, we set the scope of the traceXML() function to the container of the XMLConnector component rather than using the component scope. This is particularly useful if this code was used in a class. The result event in the XMLConnector component is invoked when data has successfully been loaded in.

In the traceXML() function, you'll notice that there is one argument called evt (this is a common abbreviation of event). The event listener gets this argument passed through when the result event it subscribed to is triggered. This event object is structured as follows:

- *type*: A string that holds a reference to the event that was triggered, in this case "result"
- *target*: A reference to the instance that broadcasted the event, in this case book_xmlconn

To get hold of the results loaded in, we just need to use the results property on the target that is specified in the event object. The reason why we use evt.target.results in the preceding code snippet rather than book_xmlconn is another one of those best practices: you always want to make sure as little code as possible has any actual hard-coded references to instance names so your application can still be flexible and not require major rewrites when something changes.

So, as you've now seen, the traceXML() function will trace out the XML data that was loaded in. Finally, what we still need to do is call the trigger method on book_xmlconn to have it initiate the load request.

If you now test the FLA (Control ➤ Test Movie), you'll see the code in action and the contents of the book.xml file will appear in the Output panel, as shown in Figure 20-6.

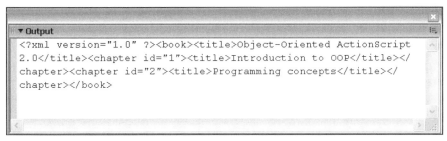

Figure 20-6. Output panel showing contents of XML document

Now that you know how to load XML data in using the XMLConnector component, let's see how to put it to use in your application. One of the most significant advantages of using the XMLConnector component (or data components in general) is it lets you easily use data binding, as discussed in Chapter 17. While it is very powerful, there are occasions where you just want to get a little more control over things and handle the XML data parsing yourself. Of course, Flash allows you to do just that, and we'll discuss how to use the XML object next.

XML class

We've just looked at the easy way to hook up XML in your Flash project, but let's see how to do it without relying on a component to do the dirty work for us. One major advantage of using the XML class rather than the XMLConnector component is that it doesn't have the overhead of using the v2 component framework and results in a smaller file size for the exported SWF.

First we instantiate a new XML instance; you can compare this to dragging an instance of the XMLConnector component on stage.

```
var book_xml:XML = new XML();
```

You now have an instance of the XML class called book_xml. Next, we'll tell this XML instance to load in a file, but before that, there is one other thing we need to take care of. The way an XML document gets parsed in Flash results in Flash considering whitespace in the file to be text nodes. To bypass this problem, we can use the ignoreWhite property and set it to true.

```
this.book_xml.ignoreWhite = true;
```

With that line in place, now we're ready to load in the file using the load method on the book_xml XML class instance.

```
this.book_xml.load("book.xml");
```

This line of code triggers the load request for the XML instance and starts loading in the book.xml file. To capture whatever comes in the XML class requires a number of callback functions. You can consider this an alternative to the event listener system that the XMLConnector component uses. It takes advantage of some specific behavior of ActionScript that allows it to execute a function you dynamically assign to it.

As a little side note, let's look at the following example, CallBack.as, which illustrates the principle of callbacks:

```
class CallBack {

  var onCallBack:function;

  function trigger():Void {
    this.onCallBack();
  }

}

CallBack.fla

var myCallBack:CallBack = new CallBack();
this.myCallBack.onCallBack = function() {
  trace("Please call me back!");
}
this.myCallBack.trigger();
```

You can see from the preceding example that you can just assign any function to the callback property and it will execute that function by simply adding opening and closing parentheses.

Similar to this example, the XML class has three such properties that serve as callbacks:

- onHTTPStatus(): Called if an HTTP error occurs when loading the file (e.g., 404 not found), only available when publishing for Flash Player 8.
- onData(): Called when the data has finished loading, or an error occurred when loading the data from the server—it passes the raw text data.
- onLoad(): Called when the loaded data has finished parsing to an XML object; passes a Boolean value that specifies whether or not it was successful parsing the data to XML.

These three properties allow you to control what happens with the data at any stage during the load process. The callback you'll most commonly use is onLoad() because that happens when the XML class has finished its job and parsed the data to an object you can use in Flash.

```
this.book_xml.onLoad = function(success:Boolean):Void {
  if(success) {
    trace(this);
  } else {
    trace("Error loading XML file");
  }
}
```

Using the onLoad() callback, we now create a function that does exactly the same thing as the traceXML function did in the XMLConnector component example earlier in this chapter: just output the XML data from the file it has loaded in.

The one additional thing we do in this function is use the Boolean that is passed to determine whether the XML file has been parsed successfully. If it wasn't successful, we will instead write an error message to the Output panel, as shown in Figure 20-7.

You can check this works by simply changing the line of code that loads the XML file to some nonexistent file.

```
this.book_xml.load("non-existent.xml");
```

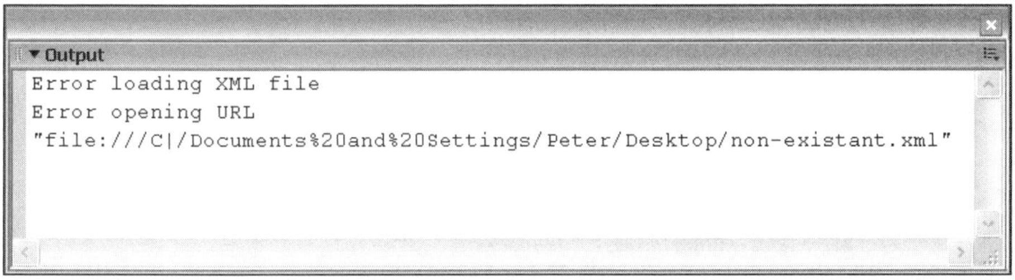

Figure 20-7. Error message in the Output panel

OK, now that we've captured the parsed XML data using onLoad(), we can start the real fun. The XML class has a number of properties that allow you to walk through the XML structure and retrieve any element you need:

- firstChild: Returns a reference to the first child element of the node
- lastChild: Returns a reference to the last child element of the node
- nextSibling: Returns a reference to the next sibling in the parent node
- previousSibling: Returns a reference to the previous sibling in the parent node
- parentNode: Returns a reference to the parent node
- childNodes: Returns an array with references to the child elements of the node
- attributes: Returns an object containing all attributes and corresponding values of the node
- nodeValue: Returns the text value of the node
- nodeName: Returns the name of the node

Let's give these properties a try on our actual XML file and see what they do by using them in an example.

First, let's look at our XML file, book.xml:

```
<?xml version="1.0" ?>
<book>
  <title>Object-Oriented ActionScript 2.0</title>
  <chapter id="1">
```

```
        <title>Introduction to OOP</title>
      </chapter>
      <chapter id="2">
        <title>Programming concepts</title>
      </chapter>
    <book>
```

Next we see the xml-properties.fla file, which uses a number of the XML class properties to get hold of specific data from the XML file that was loaded in and parsed.

```
import mx.utils.Delegate;

var book_xml:XML = new XML();
this.book_xml.ignoreWhite = true;


this.book_xml.onLoad = Delegate.create(this,function(success:Boolean):
➥ Void {
  if(success) {

    trace("root node: "+
    ➥ this.book_xml.firstChild.nodeName);
    // outputs "book"

    trace("first child of root node: "+
    ➥ this.book_xml.firstChild.firstChild.nodeName);
    // outputs "title"

    trace("next sibling of title node: "+
    ➥ this.book_xml.firstChild.firstChild.nextSibling.nodeName);
    // outputs "chapter"

    trace("first chapter id: "+
    ➥ this.book_xml.firstChild.firstChild.nextSibling.
    ➥ attributes["id"]);
      // outputs "1"

  } else {
    trace("Error loading XML file");
  }
});

this.book_xml.load("book.xml");
```

As you can see in this example, it's easy to combine these XML object properties to get hold of the specific information you need out of the XML document. For example, the first statement takes the first child node of the XML data and gets its nodeName. In our XML file, this is the book root node so you'll get the string "book" returned.

The second statement looks for the name of the first child node of the book root node; this returns the string "title". You can see that we just walked down the XML structure.

The other two statements respectively get the node name and the id attribute of the next sibling of the title node. A **sibling** is a node that is on the same level down the structure of the XML file. In our XML file, the title node and chapter nodes are siblings.

In this example, I also used the mx.utils.Delegate class to set the scope for the onLoad callback to its container rather than the XML class instance. We'll do that throughout the chapter as a good practice for callbacks.

Now for something more practical: let's get a list of all chapter titles in our XML document. Create a new FLA document, save it in the same folder where the book.xml file is located, and add the following code to a layer on the timeline:

```
import mx.utils.Delegate;

var book_xml:XML = new XML();
this.book_xml.ignoreWhite = true;
this.book_xml.load("book.xml");

this.book_xml.onLoad = Delegate.create(this,function(success:Boolean):
➥ Void {
  if(success) {

    var title_array:Array = new Array();
    var book_root:Array = this.book_xml.firstChild;
    var book_children:Array = book_root.childNodes;

    for(var i=0; i<book_children.length; i++) {
      if(book_children[i].nodeName == "chapter") {
        var chapter_children:Array = book_children[i].childNodes;
        for(var j=0; j<chapter_children.length; j++) {
          if(chapter_children[j].nodeName == "title") {
            title_array.push(chapter_children[j].firstChild.nodeValue);
            break;
          }
        }
      }
    }

    trace(title_array);

  } else {
    trace("Error loading XML file");
  }
});
```

20

This example looks more complicated than it actually is; in fact, the whole thing could probably be coded in about half as many lines if you hard coded the references to the title child nodes. What makes the bulk of the code here is using the childNodes property to loop through the XML object looking for the correct node.

Looping through the XML document is usually the best approach for doing something like this, as you don't have your code rely on the XML nodes always remaining at the same location in the file.

What the code here does is grab a reference to the child nodes of the root node when the onLoad() function is triggered, and then loop through those looking for nodes called chapter. When it encounters one of those nodes, it grabs a reference to the child nodes of that chapter node and loops through them looking for a title node. Finally, when it finds that title node, it adds the title to the title_array variable we created earlier.

Now that the title_array variable contains the chapter titles from the book.xml file, let's hook them up to a List component. Simply open up the Components panel (Window ➤ Components) and drag an instance of the List component on stage, giving it the instance name chapters_list. Now it's as simple as setting the dataProvider of the List component to reference our title_array where we previously had the trace statement.

```
this.chapters_list.dataProvider = title_array;
```

If you test this movie, you'll see the chapters from the XML document nicely displayed in the List component, as shown in Figure 20-8. However many chapter nodes you add to the XML document later on, they will all be displayed in the component when the data has loaded in.

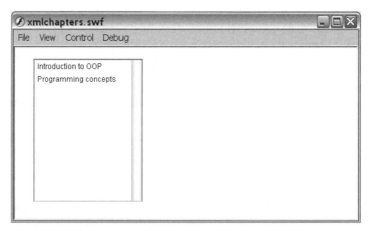

Figure 20-8. List component showing chapter titles from XML file

As an exercise, you might want to create a description node for each chapter in the XML file and update the code to have it display the description for the chapter currently selected in the List component.

Earlier on, I briefly mentioned the XML class having a property called idMap, which was introduced in Flash Player 8. It allows you to access nodes that have an id attribute using array notation, which is incredibly handy. Let's take our book.xml file as an example:

```
<?xml version="1.0" ?>
<book>
  <title>Object-Oriented ActionScript 2.0</title>
  <chapter id="1">
    <title>Introduction to OOP</title>
  </chapter>
  <chapter id="2">
    <title>Programming concepts</title>
  </chapter>
<book>
```

You'll notice that each chapter node has an id attribute with a unique value. Now, after loading in the XML document, you can use the idMap property and reference to that id attribute to get the correct node returned.

```
import mx.utils.Delegate;

var book_xml:XML = new XML();
this.book_xml.ignoreWhite = true;


this.book_xml.onLoad = Delegate.create(this,function(success:Boolean):
➥Void {
  if(success) {

    // output the second chapter node
    trace(this.book_xml.idMap["2"]);

  } else {
    trace("Error loading XML file");
  }
});

this.book_xml.load("book.xml");
```

The example here references the id with value 2, which returns the second chapter node in the XML file. What the idMap feature is incredibly useful for is creating shortcuts when you have complex XML documents. Rather than referencing all the way down the XML tree using the XML class properties, you can just use idMap to immediately get to the nodes you need.

There are more exciting times ahead for using XML in Flash projects; the next version of the Flash Player will reportedly support the E4X standard, which makes XML a native datatype in ActionScript and will allow for much easier data searching and filtering.

20

For now, if you're a Flash developer looking into XML, I can recommend you look at the XPath classes for ActionScript 2.0 created by Neeld Tanksley of XFactorStudio. XPath is a W3C standard for querying XML data sources and will make your life a lot easier when working with complex XML documents. These ActionScript 2.0 classes are available for free under an Apache-style license at www.xfactorstudio.com/ActionScript/AS2/XPath/.

This concludes our look at using XML in Flash projects. If you're planning to work with XML files for your Flash applications across different domains, you will also want to read up on the Flash Player security sandbox later on in this chapter. But first we'll have a look at communicating with web services in Flash 8.

What are web services?

Web services have really been hyped over the last few years as the must-have technology for businesses, and there is definitely some truth in that. A web service allows you to communicate with a remote server (it could technically also be your own), call certain methods on the service, and get results sent back.

To achieve this, web services use a protocol called **S**imple **O**bject **A**ccess **P**rotocol (SOAP), which uses an XML format to send calls back and forward between the different servers. Messages are usually sent over the HTTP or HTTPS protocol on port 80, which means it shouldn't have any problems passing through firewalls. Also, because the communication between servers happens in an XML text format, it is completely cross-platform compatible.

Let's take a closer look at this SOAP protocol and the role it plays in communicating with web services.

Understanding SOAP

As mentioned earlier, SOAP messages are sent in an XML format. The structure of a SOAP message is relatively basic—it consists of an envelope that contains a header and a body. The header part is optional, but could contain information such as authentication for the web service and other information about the service call.

```
<?xml version="1.0" ?>
<Envelope xmlns="http://schemas.xmlsoap.org/soap/envelope/">
  <Body>
    <getEmployeeDetails xmlns="http://www.yourdomain.com/">
      <employeeID>108</employeeID>
    </getEmployeeDetails>
  </Body>
</Envelope>
```

This is about the most basic SOAP call you could imagine—it's just the envelope and the body where it states that a method called getEmployeeDetails() needs to be called, and it passes an argument called employeeID with value 108 to the method.

One thing you'll notice here is that SOAP messages use XML namespaces—we didn't discuss this earlier as Flash doesn't handle those, but they're very important for the SOAP protocol. The XML namespace we use in the envelope node refers to the XML schema for the SOAP protocol, and the namespace we use on the getEmployeeDetails node is there to indicate that part of the XML is not defined in the SOAP schema and refers to the domain where the web service is deployed.

When SOAP has sent across this message, the web service receives it, processes the request by calling the method and passing any arguments that were defined, and then sends back another SOAP message with the results the method returned.

```
<?xml version="1.0" ?>
<Envelope xmlns="http://schemas.xmlsoap.org/soap/envelope/">
  <Body>
    <getEmployeeDetailsResponse
  ➥ xmlns="http://www.yourdomain.com/">
     <getEmployeeDetailsResult>
        <employeeID>108</employeeID>
        <employeeName>John Doe</employeeName>
        <employeeDepartment>Marketing</employeeDepartment>
      </getEmployeeDetailsResult>
    </getEmployeeDetailsResponse>
  </Body>
</Envelope>
```

The result message isn't much more complicated—what simply happened is that the method name we called was used with Response appended to indicate it is a SOAP response. In getEmployeeDetailsResponse there is another node that contains the results, in this case the method name with "Result" appended. Inside getEmployeeDetailsResult() is every property that the method returned after it was called.

Now, of course, something could've gone wrong with our SOAP request. Let's say the getEmployeeDetails() method didn't pass the employeeID parameter. In this case, the web service would send back a SOAP message with information about the fault that occurred.

```
<?xml version="1.0" ?>
<Envelope xmlns="http://schemas.xmlsoap.org/soap/envelope/">
  <Body>
    <Fault>
      <faultcode>Client</faultcode>
      <faultstring>employeeID parameter is missing</faultstring>
    </Fault>
  </Body>
</Envelope>
```

That's pretty neat! If something goes wrong, the SOAP message sends us back the fault code and a description of what went wrong.

These are obviously very basic examples, and SOAP is a complex and extensive topic to discuss, but before you start to worry, bear in mind that you won't need to generate those XML documents yourself or parse the XML from the SOAP messages that get returned yourself. Flash has made this a whole lot easier for us by providing a WebServiceConnector component and access to the WebService class in Flash MX 2004 Professional and Flash Professional 8 for communicating with web services from your Flash application.

Talking to web services

As mentioned earlier, the web services that you consume are generally located on a remote server because XML data is rather verbose and not the most optimized way to connect to local data.

All examples I'll be discussing here use the **M**acromedia **X**ML **N**ews **A**ggregator (MXNA) web service. MXNA is a web-based news aggregator for weblogs that report news on Flash and a variety of other technologies. The MXNA web service offers a whole range of methods, such as retrieving the latest posts in a particular category, lists of all aggregated feeds, most popular postings, etc., which makes it a very interesting web service to experiment with.

If you're interested in trying out some other web services, www.xmethods.net is an interesting site that lists a great number of web services you can use freely.

Now, without further ado, let's look at using the WebServiceConnector component to connect to a web service.

WebServiceConnector component

The WebServiceConnector component is available in the Components panel (Window ➤ Components), listed in the Data category. Like the XMLConnector component, this component allows you to easily connect to a data source (in this case the MXNA web service) and load data into your Flash application.

As always, create a new FLA; save it as webserviceconnector.fla in a local folder. With that FLA open, drag an instance of the WebServiceConnector component to the stage, so your screen resembles Figure 20-9.

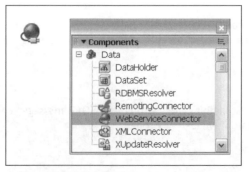

Figure 20-9. WebServiceConnector component on stage

With the component instance selected, open up the component's Parameters panel and give it an instance name of mxna_wsconn, as shown in Figure 20-10.

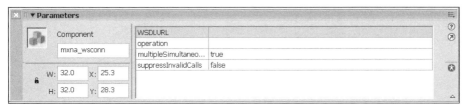

Figure 20-10. Assigning an instance name to the WebServiceConnector component

In the component's Parameters panel, set the WSDLURL parameter to the following URL: http://weblogs.macromedia.com/mxna/webservices/mxna2.cfc?wsdl, as shown below in Figure 20-11.

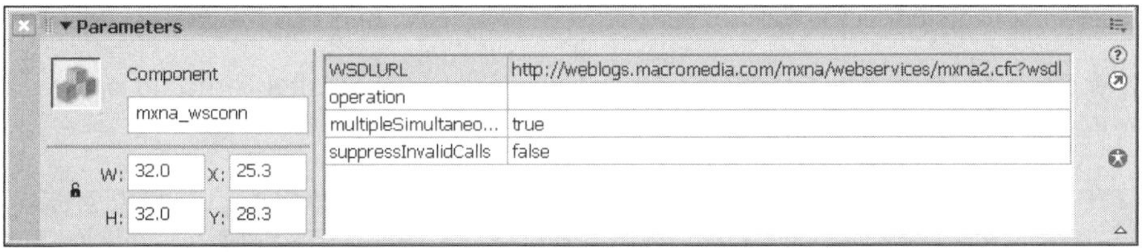

20

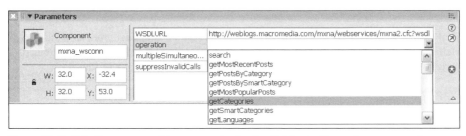

Figure 20-11. Setting the WSDLURL parameter for the WebServiceConnector component

If you now click the down arrow for the operation parameter, you'll notice that Flash has automagically filled that with all available methods for the MXNA web service. For this example, we'll choose the getCategories() method as the operation, as shown in Figure 20-12.

Figure 20-12. Selecting an operation parameter for the WebServiceConnector component

You can leave the other component parameters to their default value. Next, add a new layer to the main timeline of the FLA and rename it actionscript. With Frame 1 of the actionscript layer selected, add the following lines of code to the Actions panel:

```
import mx.utils.Delegate;

onGetCategories = function(evt:Object):Void {
  trace(evt.target.results);
}

this.mxna_wsconn.addEventListener("result",Delegate.create(this,
➥ onGetCategories));
mxna_wsconn.trigger();
```

This code does set up an event listener that calls the onGetCategories() function when it receives the results back from the web service. The onGetCategories() function outputs the results by referencing the target in the event object that gets passed. Finally, we invoke the WebServiceConnector component trigger method to connect to the web service.

If you test this FLA (Control ➤ Test Movie) you'll notice that, after a second or two, a whole lot of objects are traced out to the Output panel, as you see in Figure 20-13.

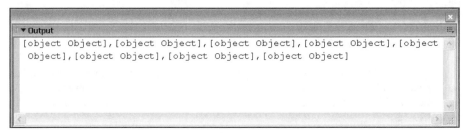

Figure 20-13. Output panel showing results from the web service

That's actually what we'd expect to see; if you look at the documentation for the MXNA web service at the following URL, you'll see that the getCategories() method returns a series of objects, each of which has a categoryID and categoryName property.

http://weblogs.macromedia.com/mxna/webservices/mxna2.html

To get the actual names of the MXNA categories, we change our code to read as follows:

```
import mx.utils.Delegate;

onGetCategories = function(evt:Object):Void {
  var categories:Array = evt.target.results;
  for(var i=0; i<categories.length; i++) {
    trace(categories[i].categoryName);
  }
}
```

```
this.mxna_wsconn.addEventListener("result",Delegate.create(this,
➥ onGetCategories));
this.mxna_wsconn.trigger();
```

Not too difficult, is it? What the code now does is hold the array with results from the web service in a variable called categories, after which we use a for loop to iterate through the array and trace out the categoryName property of each object.

Test this updated code (Control ➤ Test Movie) and the Output panel will now look something like what you see in Figure 20-14.

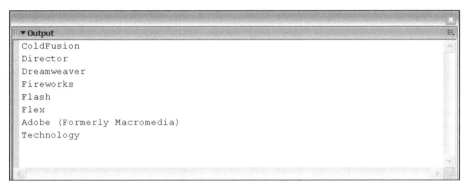

Figure 20-14. Output panel showing category names received from the web service

You've probably guessed what's coming next—yes, we'll hook it up to a List component to display the categories. The easiest way to do this might be to use the data binding feature, but we'll just do it the old-fashioned way for this example.

Drag an instance of the List component to the stage and give it the instance name categories_list, as shown in Figure 20-15.

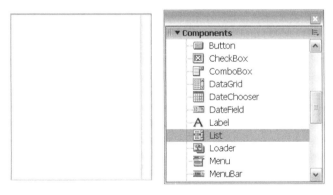

Figure 20-15. List component on stage

459

Now for the actual code to add the web service results to the List component. Change the existing ongetCategories code to read as follows:

```
import mx.utils.Delegate;

onGetCategories = function(evt:Object):Void {
  var categories:Array = evt.target.results;
  for(var i=0; i<categories.length; i++) {
    this.categories_list.addItem(categories[i].categoryName,
    ➥ categories[i].categoryId);
  }
}

this.mxna_wsconn.addEventListener("result",Delegate.create(this,
➥ onGetCategories));
this.mxna_wsconn.trigger();
```

The updated code now uses the addItem() method on the categories_list List component instance to add each of the categories as an item in the List. Additionally we set the categoryId property that the web service passes with each category object on the data field of each of the list items.

If you test this movie (Control ➤ Test Movie), you'll see the List component with all categories that the MXNA web service returned, as shown in Figure 20-16.

Figure 20-16. List component showing categories received from a web service

You might be wondering why we added the categoryId to the data field of each list item. Well, the MXNA web service has another interesting method called getFeedsByCategory() that returns the list of all aggregated weblogs and needs the categoryId as an argument.

Doing this type of project with the WebServiceConnector component shows why it is not always very practical to use. Basically, there are two ways to handle this—either create a new instance of the component on stage or overwrite the component parameters using ActionScript for each call.

For this example, I'll opt to use multiple instances of the WebServiceConnector component, as it separates out the different web service calls more nicely; if you overwrite the component parameters, you'll probably have as much work to do as you'd have using the WebService class.

Drag a second instance of the WebServiceConnector component to the stage and give it the instance name feeds_wsconn, as shown in Figure 20-17.

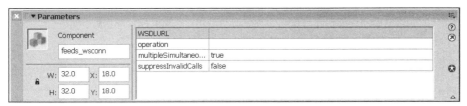

Figure 20-17. Assigning an instance name to the second WebServiceConnector component

Set the WSDLURL component parameter for feeds_wsconn to the same MXNA web service URL, `http://weblogs.macromedia.com/mxna/webservices/mxna2.cfc?wsdl`, and set the operation to getFeedsByCategory(), as shown in Figure 20-18.

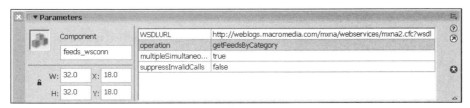

Figure 20-18. Setting the parameters for the second WebServiceConnector component

Drag another instance of the List component to the stage, give it the instance name feeds_list, and resize both instances of the component as needed to accommodate the categories and feed information (see Figure 20-19).

Figure 20-19. Components layed out on stage

Now the only thing left to do is update the code to trigger the web service and pass the categoryId to the getFeedsByCategory() method when the categories_list selection changes.

```
import mx.util.Delegate;

onGetCategories = function(evt:Object):Void {
  var categories:Array = evt.target.results;
  for(var i=0; i<categories.length; i++) {
    this.categories_list.addItem(categories[i].categoryName ,
    ➥ categories[i].categoryId);
  }
}

onGetFeeds = function(evt:Object):Void {
  this.feeds_list.removeAll();
  var feeds:Array = evt.target.results;
  for(var i=0; i<feeds.length; i++) {
    this.feeds_list.addItem(feeds[i].feedName,feeds[i].siteUrl);
  }
}

onCategoryChange = function():Void {
  this.feeds_wsconn.params = [categories_list.selectedItem.data];
  this.feeds_wsconn.trigger();
}

this.mxna_wsconn.addEventListener("result",Delegate.create(this,
➥ this.onGetCategories));
this.feeds_wsconn.addEventListener("result",Delegate.create(this,
➥ onGetFeeds));
this.categories_list.addEventListener("change",Delegate.create(this,
➥ onCategoryChange));

this.mxna_wsconn.trigger();
```

What this code does is first add an additional event listener for the categories_list that listens for a change in the selection. If that happens, the onCategoryChange() function gets invoked, which sets the parameter for the web service call to the data value of the selected value of the currently selected category and triggers the web service.

The feeds_wsconn instance now also has an event listener that listens for the result event, and when that occurs, calls the onGetFeeds() function. The onGetFeeds() function does the work to populate the second List component. It clears all items that might be in there, assigns the result to a feeds array, loops through it, and adds all items to the feeds_list instance with the feedName for the label and the feedUrl as the data value, as you see in Figure 20-20.

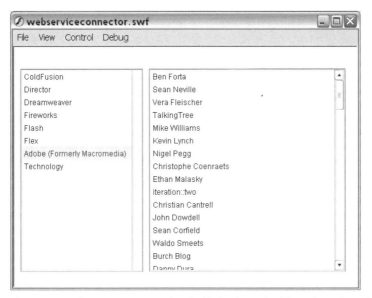

Figure 20-20. List component populated with feeds received from the web service

We'll just add one last thing to our example to complete it, which will allow you to go to the website of the selected feed. Drag an instance of the Button component on stage, give it the instance name feed_btn, and set its label to Visit website.

To point the URL of the selected feed, we need to add the following code to the existing code in the FLA:

```
onButtonClick = function():Void {
  if(this.feeds_list.selectedItem.data != undefined) {
    getURL(this.feeds_list.selectedItem.data,"_blank");
  }
}

this.feed_btn.addEventListener("click",Delegate.create(this,
onButtonClick));
```

This code adds an event listener to the button component for the click event, and when that happens, invokes the onButtonClick() function. The onButtonClick() function checks whether the URL for the selected feed is defined, and if so opens it up in a new browser window (see Figure 20-21).

A great application programmed in around 30 lines of code, using the MXNA web service.

Figure 20-21. Finished web service example running

Next up, we'll look at using the WebService class rather than a data component to connect to web services.

WebService class

Flash 8 has a WebService class that allows you to script your own communication with a web service rather than use the WebServiceConnector component. There are some cases where it is more convenient not to work with component instances and using code is more flexible. One reason, as with the XMLConnector component, is that the components make use of the v2 component framework, which adds significantly to the file size of the exported SWF.

As before, we'll be using the MXNA web service to build an example demonstrating the WebService class. Create yourself a new FLA, and add the following code to a layer on the main timeline. The first thing we'll obviously need to do is create an instance of the class.

```
import mx.services.WebService;
var WS_URL:String =
➥ "http://weblogs.macromedia.com/mxna/
➥ webservices/mxna2.cfc?wsdl";
var mxna_ws:WebService = new WebService(this.WS_URL);
```

This code imports the mx.services.WebService class (which is the complete classpath to the WebService class), and then sets up a string variable called WS_URL that holds the URL for the MXNA web service. Finally, we create a new instance of the WebService class, passing the WS_URL as its target.

The cool thing about the WebService class is that once you have an instance set up, you can call any method as if it was a native method in the WebService instance. For example, we could simply trigger the following methods on the MXNA service as such:

```
this.mxna_ws.getCategories();
this.mxna_ws.getFeedsByCategory(1);
```

There is, however, one caveat: web service calls are asynchronous. Asynchronous calls mean that the Flash Player won't wait for the result of the web service call before executing the next lines of code.

To work around this problem, Flash doesn't actually return results when calling these methods on the web service, but rather returns an instance of the mx.services. PendingCall class. This PendingCall class now handles the web service call and has two callback functions we can use: onResult() and onFault().

```
import mx.services.WebService;
import mx.services.PendingCall;

var WS_URL:String = "
➥ "http://weblogs.macromedia.com/mxna/webservices/ "
➥ mxna2.cfc?wsdl";

var mxna_ws:WebService = new WebService(this.WS_URL);
var categories_pc:PendingCall = this.mxna_ws.getCategories();

this.categories_pc.onResult = function(result_obj:Object):Void {
  trace(result_obj);
}
```

In the preceding code, we call the getCategories() method on the mxna_ws mx.services.WebService class instance we created earlier, which returns an instance of PendingCall to the categories_pc variable. The categories_pc PendingCall instance also has the onResult function defined, which traces out the argument it receives.

Test this movie (Control ➤ Test Movie) and you'll see results shown in Figure 20-22 appear in the Output panel.

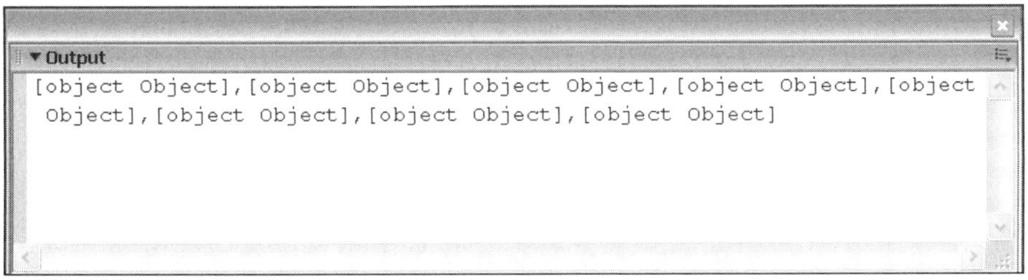

```
▼ Output
[object Object],[object Object],[object Object],[object Object],[object
Object],[object Object],[object Object],[object Object]
```

Figure 20-22. Output panel showing results received from the web service

20

Does this look familiar? The MXNA getCategories() method returns a list of objects that each contain the categoryName and categoryId properties.

Let's double-check by looping through the results and tracing each category name out to the Output panel. Change the code in the FLA to read as follows:

```
import mx.services.WebService;
import mx.services.PendingCall;

var WS_URL:String =
➡ "http://weblogs.macromedia.com/mxna/webservices/
➡ "mxna2.cfc?wsdl";

var mxna_ws:WebService = new WebService(this.WS_URL);
var categories_pc:PendingCall = mxna_ws.getCategories();

this.categories_pc.onResult = function(result_obj:Object):Void {
  var categories:Object = result_obj;
  for(var i=0; i<categories.length; i++) {
    trace(categories[i].categoryName);
  }
}
```

Its always a good idea to make sure you handle any errors should they come up, so we'll go ahead and implement the onFault() callback on the PendingCall instance, so update the code as follows:

```
import mx.services.WebService;
import mx.services.PendingCall;

var WS_URL:String =
➡ "http://weblogs.macromedia.com/mxna/webservices/
➡ mxna2.cfc?wsdl";

var mxna_ws:WebService = new WebService(this.WS_URL);
var categories_pc:PendingCall = mxna_ws.getCategories();

this.categories_pc.onResult = function(result_obj:Object):Void {
  var categories:Object = result_obj;
  for(var i=0; i<categories.length; i++) {
    trace(categories[i].categoryName);
  }
}

this.categories_pc.onFault = function(fault_obj:Object):Void {
  trace("The following error occurred: ");
  trace("Fault code: "+fault_obj.faultcode);
  trace("Fault description: "+fault_obj.faultstring);
}
```

You'll notice that this looks very similar to the onResult() callback; it gets passed an object that contains a faultcode and faultstring property. If you read the introduction to SOAP earlier on in this chapter, those should also be familiar to you.

Now if we only had an error to test that code! It's not too difficult to cause an error—just rename the web service method call to one that doesn't exist.

```
var categories_pc:PendingCall = mxna_ws.getCategorieeeees();
```

Let's try this and keep our fingers crossed that an error gets triggered when we test our movie (Control ➤ Test Movie). You should get a message like the one shown in Figure 20-23.

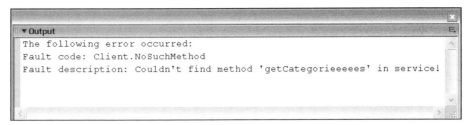

```
▼ Output
The following error occurred:
Fault code: Client.NoSuchMethod
Fault description: Couldn't find method 'getCategorieeeees' in service!
```

Figure 20-23. Output panel showing error message

Yes, we've got ourselves an error! I really like the way these errors are thrown and the amount of information you get. In this case, we get a faultcode with the value Client.NoSuchMethod, which is pretty descriptive in itself, and the faultstring makes it even more obvious: "Couldn't find method 'getCategorieeeees' in service!"

Now that we've covered the basics of the WebService class, we can put it to good use by building our own little MXNA application in Flash. But before we get started on that, I'll show you another great little feature in the Flash IDE that will help you when working with web services.

If you go to Window ➤ Other Panels you'll notice that there is something called the Web Services panel. If you open it up, your screen will look something like Figure 20-24.

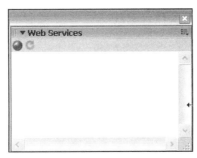

Figure 20-24. Web Services panel

Nothing very impressive yet, but if you click the globe icon, things get more interesting. This opens up a panel where you can add any web service URLs you use, as shown in Figure 20-25. Let's add the MXNA web service by clicking the plus icon and entering the URL http://weblogs.macromedia.com/mxna/webservices/mxna2.cfc?wsdl.

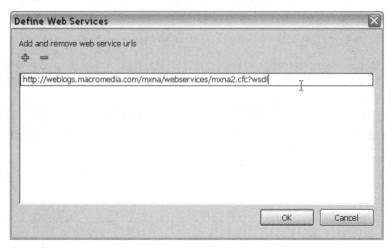

Figure 20-25. Adding a web service to the Web Services panel

Once the URL is added, you'll see that it says it's processing the web service for a second or two, after which you'll see a plus sign next to the web service. If you click that, you'll get a list of all available methods on the MXNA web service, as you see in Figure 20-26.

Figure 20-26. Web Services panel showing available methods for web service

That's nothing—we've seen something similar with the WebServiceConnector component. But this is where the panel gets really useful; if you open up the methods, you'll also get to see the parameters and results for each method and its datatype, as shown in Figure 20-27.

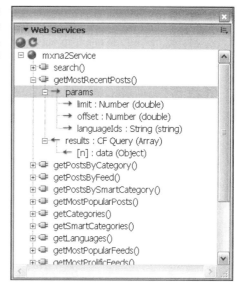

Figure 20-27.
Web Services panel showing params and results for each web service method

Isn't that cool? This panel is really an invaluable tool when using web services in Flash, especially if you don't have detailed documentation on what methods it exposes, the parameters it needs, and what results it sends back.

Enough playing around, let's get back to the business of creating that aggregator application with the MXNA web service. Let's start by creating a new FLA called mxna_aggregator.fla. With that file open, we'll start out by creating the user interface for our application.

Drag an instance of the ComboBox component, two instances of the List component, a Label component, a TextArea component, and a Button component to the stage. Next, resize and position them to look approximately like what you see in Figure 20-28.

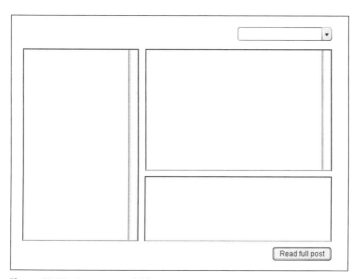

Figure 20-28. Components laid out on stage

The first thing we'll handle is the ComboBox component, which will hold our aggregator categories. Give it the instance name categories_cb. Create a new layer in the main time-line and rename it to actionscript. With the first frame of the actionscript layer selected, open up the Actions panel (Window ➤ Actions) and enter the following code:

```
import mx.services.WebService;
import mx.services.PendingCall;
import mx.utils.Delegate;

var WS_URL:String =
➥ "http://weblogs.macromedia.com/mxna/webservices/
➥ mxna2.cfc?wsdl";
var mxna_ws:WebService = new WebService(this.WS_URL);

var categories_pc:PendingCall = this.mxna_ws.getCategories();

this.categories_pc.onResult = Delegate.create(this,
function(result_obj:Object):Void {
  this.categories_cb.addItem("Select a category");
  var categories:Object = result_obj;
  for(var i=0; i<categories.length; i++) {
    this.categories_cb.addItem(categories[i].categoryName,
    ➥ categories[i].categoryId);
  }
});

this.categories_pc.onFault = function(fault_obj:Object):Void {
  trace("The following error occurred: ");
  trace("Fault code: "+fault_obj.faultcode);
  trace("Fault description: "+fault_obj.faultstring);
}
```

You should almost be able to code this blindly by now if you've followed along with the previous examples. The only changes are to the onResult() function for the categories_pc PendingCall instance.

What we do here is add an item to the ComboBox that tells the user to select a category, after which we loop through the categories we received and add the categoryName property to the label field of the ComboBox component, and the categoryId as its data.

If you test this code (Control ➤ Test Movie) you'll see that it populates the ComboBox component as expected with the initial value "Select a category", followed by the categories we get back from the getCategories() web service call (see Figure 20-29).

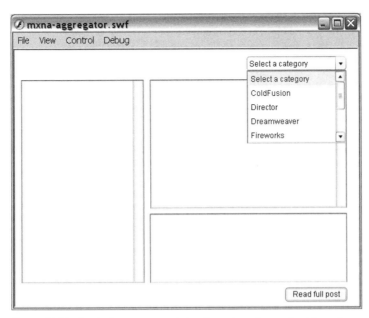

Figure 20-29. ComboBox component showing categories received from the web service

When a category has been selected, we want to do two things—populate the first List component with all feeds that are aggregated in that category, and fill the second List component with the latest posts to that category, including all aggregated feeds.

Start by giving the List component on the left the instance name feeds_list and the other List component posts_list. Next we need to listen for a change event on the categories_cb component to trigger the web service calls. Add the following code under the code you already have:

```
genericFault = function(fault_obj:Object):Void {
  trace("The following error occurred: ");
  trace("Fault code: "+fault_obj.faultcode);
  trace("Fault description: "+fault_obj.faultstring);
}


categories_pc.onFault = Delegate.create(this,genericFault);

this.onCategoryChange = function():Void {
  var catSelected = this.categories_cb.selectedItem.data;
  if(catSelected != undefined) {
    var feeds_pc:PendingCall =
    ➥ this.mxna_ws.getFeedsByCategory(catSelected);
    feeds_pc.onResult = Delegate.create(this,
    function(result_obj:Object):Void {
      this.feeds_list.removeAll();
```

```
        var feeds:Object = result_obj;
        for(var i=0; i<feeds.length; i++) {
          this.feeds_list.addItem(feeds[i].feedName, feeds[i].feedId);
        }
      });
      feeds_pc.onFault = this.genericFault;
    }
  }

  this.categories_cb.addEventListener("change",Delegate.create(this,
➥ onCategoryChange));
```

What we did here was add an event listener for the categories_cb ComboBox component and have it reference the onCategoryChange() function. The onCategoryChange() function then checks whether the selected value in categories_cb is not undefined. If the selected data value is undefined, this would indicate that either the "Select a category" value was selected (which doesn't have a data value) or something went wrong with the web service result and it didn't return a categoryId; in either case the next web service call doesn't need to happen.

If a categoryId is defined in the data field of the selected item in categories_cb, it goes ahead and calls the getFeedsByCategory() method of the MXNA web service, passing the categoryId value as its parameter. The web service call returns a PendingCall instance to our feeds_pc variable, and we use the onResult callback to handle the results that get sent back.

The getFeedsByCategory() method returns a list of objects with a whole lot of information about each feed (feedId, feedName, feedDescription, feedCategories, feedUrl, languageId, lastUpdated, siteName, siteUrl, and siteDescription). We only need feedName and feedId for this example—they are assigned to the label and data field of the feeds_list List component instance, respectively.

To make life easier, I added a genericFault() function, which we can use to catch all PendingCall faults. Since we don't need to handle faults differently for each web service call, this saves us a lot of typing and redundant code. Both instances of the PendingCall class use genericFault() as their callback function onFault().

If you test the code thus far (Control ➤ Test Movie), you'll see that you can now switch between the categories in categories_cb, and it will update the feeds_list accordingly. Now we'll add that second call we wanted to add when the category selection changes.

```
  onCategoryChange = function():Void {
    var catSelected = this.categories_cb.selectedItem.data;
    if(catSelected != undefined) {
      var feeds_pc:PendingCall =
      ➥ this.mxna_ws.getFeedsByCategory(catSelected);
      feeds_pc.onResult = Delegate.create(this,
      function(result_obj:Object):Void {
        var feeds:Object = result_obj;
        for(var i=0; i<feeds.length; i++) {
```

```
        this.feeds_list.addItem(feeds[i].feedName, feeds[i].feedId);
      }
    });
    this.feeds_pc.onFault = this.genericFault;

    var posts_pc:PendingCall =
    ➥ this.mxna_ws.getPostsByCategory(20,0,catSelected,1);
    posts_pc.onResult = Delegate.create(this,
    function(result_obj:Object):Void {
      this.posts_list.removeAll();
      var posts:Object = result_obj;
      for(var i=0; i<posts.length; i++) {
        this.posts_list.addItem(posts[i].postTitle,
      ➥ {postExcerpt:posts[i].postExcerpt,postLink:posts[i].postLink});
      }
    }
    posts_pc.onFault = this.genericFault;

  }
}

this.categories_cb.addEventListener("change",Delegate.create(this,
➥ onCategoryChange));
```

As you can see, we simply add a second web service call in the onCategoryChange() function, which returns a PendingCall instance to our posts_pc variable. Then in the onResult() callback for posts_pc we remove all previous items from the list and loop through the list of objects that the web service returned. For each of these posts, we add the postTitle to the label field of the posts_list List component. There is a slight problem here; we need to have two values for the data field.

An easy way to solve this problem is create an object for the data value, which holds references to all values we need, in this case postExcerpt and postLink. postExcerpt will be displayed in the TextArea component, and postLink provides a link to follow to read the full post when the Button component is clicked.

If you run the code now, you'll see both the feeds_list and posts_list update when a category is selected. Next, we'll make the post excerpt display when a post is selected, give the TextArea component the instance name excerpt_ta, and add the following code:

```
onPostChange = function():Void {
  this.excerpt_ta.text = this.posts_list.selectedItem.data.postExcerpt;
}

this.posts_list.addEventListener("change",Delegate.create(this,
➥ onPostChange));
```

That wasn't too difficult—just add an event listener to posts_list for the change event to have it trigger the onPostChange() function, which sets the text value of the excerpt_ta TextArea component to equal the postExerpt value stored in the selected item in the posts_list data field.

Next we'll add some code to make the button open up the URL of the selected post when clicked. To do this, we need to add an event listener for the click event on the Button component. Give the Button component the instance name postlink_btn, set its label to read "Read full post", and add the following code under the existing code in the main timeline:

```
onButtonClick = function():Void {
  var link:String =  this.posts_list.selectedItem.data.postLink;
  if(link != undefined) {
    getURL(link,"_blank");
  }
}
this.postlink_btn.addEventListener("click",Delegate.create(this,
➦ onButtonClick));
```

If you now test the application (Control ➤ Test Movie) you'll see the excerpt displayed when a post is selected. When the button is clicked, the URL to the full post is launched in a new browser window.

We're almost there; just a few things left to do. When a feed is selected in feeds_list, we want to have posts_list only display posts from that particular feed. To do this, we need to listen for the change event on feeds_list to trigger another call to the MXNA web service.

```
onFeedChange = function():Void {
  var feedSelected = this.feeds_list.selectedItem.data;
  trace(feedSelected);
  if(feedSelected != undefined) {
    var feedposts_pc:PendingCall =
    ➦ this.mxna_ws.getPostsByFeed(20,0,feedSelected);
    ➦ feedposts_pc.onResult = Delegate.create(this,
    function(result_obj:Object):Void {
      this.posts_list.removeAll();
      var posts:Object = result_obj;
      for(var i=0; i<posts.length; i++) {
        this.posts_list.addItem(posts[i].postTitle,
      ➦ {postExcerpt:posts[i].postExcerpt,postLink:posts[i].postLink});
      }
    }
    feedposts_pc.onFault = this.genericFault;
  }
}
this.feeds_list.addEventListener("change",Delegate.create(this,
➦ onFeedChange);
```

This code adds a listener for the change event to feeds_list and has it call the onFeedChange() function. The onFeedChange() function is almost an identical copy of onCategoryChange() with the exception that here we call getPostsByFeed() instead of getPostsByCategory().

The getPostsByFeed() method needs three parameters. The first one defines how many posts you want to have returned. The second parameter allows you to set the post offset; in our case, we want to start at 0 to get the most recent posts. If you want to get paged results, you could use this parameter to get the next batch of posts, starting at a certain offset position. The final parameter is feedId, which we already have stored in the data field of the feeds_list component.

The web service call returns a PendingCall instance that we store in feedposts_pc; when the onResult callback is triggered, we populate the posts_list List component with the values received. Again, as we did in the onCategoryChange() function, we set an object with the postExcerpt and postLink values as the data value of posts_list to have the necessary information stored away in each post item for the excerpt and button to use later on.

There's only one thing left to do now—have the Label component give the user some information about what is happening. As you might have noticed, when using web services, there is always a slight delay between the call and getting information into the Player. If you think about everything that needs to happen behind the scenes, its actually surprisingly fast, but nonetheless something that is best to address.

Here is the full code for the application, including those code changes for the label component, which we'll give an instance name of status_label:

```
import mx.services.WebService;
import mx.services.PendingCall;
import mx.utils.Delegate;

var WS_URL:String =
➡ "http://weblogs.macromedia.com/mxna/webservices/
➡ mxna2.cfc?wsdl";
var mxna_ws:WebService = new WebService(WS_URL);

var categories_pc:PendingCall = mxna_ws.getCategories();

this.status_label.text = "Loading MXNA categories ...";

categories_pc.onResult = function(result_obj:Object):Void {
  this.categories_cb.addItem("Select a category");
  var categories:Object = result_obj;
  for(var i=0; i<categories.length; i++) {
    this.categories_cb.addItem(categories[i].categoryName,
    ➡ categories[i].categoryId);
  }
  this.status_label.text = "";
}

genericFault = function(fault_obj:Object):Void {
  trace("The following error occurred:");
  trace("Fault code: "+fault_obj.faultcode);
  trace("Fault description: "+fault_obj.faultstring);
}
```

```
categories_pc.onFault =  this.genericFault;

onCategoryChange = function():Void {
  var catSelected = this.categories_cb.selectedItem.data;
  if(catSelected != undefined) {
    var feeds_pc:PendingCall =
    ➥ this.mxna_ws.getFeedsByCategory(catSelected);
    this.status_label.text = "Loading "+
    ➥ this.categories_cb.selectedItem.label+" category ...";
    feeds_pc.onResult = Delegate.create(this,
    ➥ function(result_obj:Object):Void {
      this.status_label.text = "Showing "+
      ➥ this.categories_cb.selectedItem.label+" category";
      this.feeds_list.removeAll();
      var feeds:Object = result_obj;
      for(var i=0; i<feeds.length; i++) {
        feeds_list.addItem(feeds[i].feedName, feeds[i].feedId);
      }
    }
    feeds_pc.onFault = this.genericFault;

    var posts_pc:PendingCall =
    ➥ this.mxna_ws.getPostsByCategory(20,0,catSelected,1);
    posts_pc.onResult = Delegate.create(this,
    function(result_obj:Object):Void {
     this.posts_list.removeAll();
     var posts:Object = result_obj;
     for(var i=0; i<posts.length; i++) {
        this.posts_list.addItem(posts[i].postTitle,
      ➥ {postExcerpt:posts[i].postExcerpt,postLink:posts[i].postLink});
     }
    }
    posts_pc.onFault = this.genericFault;

  }
}

onPostChange = function() {
  this.excerpt_ta.text = this.post_list.selectedItem.data.postExcerpt;
}

onButtonClick = function():Void {
  var link:String =  this.post_list.selectedItem.data.postLink;
  if(link != undefined) {
    getURL(link,"_blank");
  }
}
```

```
onFeedChange = function():Void {
  var feedSelected = this.feeds_list.selectedItem.data;
  if(feedSelected != undefined) {
    var feedposts_pc:PendingCall =
    ➥ this.mxna_ws.getPostsByFeed(20,0,feedSelected);
    this.status_label.text = "Loading "+
    ➥ this.feeds_list.selectedItem.label+" posts ...";
    feedposts_pc.onResult = Delegate.create(this,
    ➥ function(result_obj:Object):Void {
      this.status_label.text = "Showing "+
      ➥ this.feeds_list.selectedItem.label+" posts";
      this.posts_list.removeAll();
      var posts:Object = result_obj;
      for(var i=0; i<posts.length; i++) {
        this.posts_list.addItem(posts[i].postTitle,
        ➥ {postExcerpt:posts[i].postExcerpt,postLink:posts[i].postLink});
      }
    });
    feedposts_pc.onFault = this.genericFault;
  }
}

this.feeds_list.addEventListener("change",Delegate.create(this,
➥ onFeedChange));
this.postlink_btn.addEventListener("click",Delegate.create(this,
➥ onButtonClick));
this.posts_lists.addEventListener("change",Delegate.create(this,
➥ onPostChange));
this.categories_cb.addEventListener("change",Delegate.create(this,
➥ onCategoryChange));
```

The few extra lines of code we have added to the final listing utilize the status_label component to display information about what is happening (loading categories, loading posts, etc.). Altogether this entire application is well under 100 lines of code and forms a fully functional Flash aggregator based on the MXNA web service.

Something you might want to try as an exercise is to add functionality to search through posts by using the search method that the MXNA web service implements.

This concludes our look at using web services for your Flash applications. If you'll be using web services across different servers you'll be interested to read the following section on the Flash Player security sandbox, which outlines some of the security measures the Flash Player has implemented to protect data from being loaded in without proper permissions.

20

Flash Player security sandbox

Since the Flash Player 6 release, there has been a movement towards getting security measures in place in what is called the *Flash Player security sandbox.*

This sandbox is defined as the environment wherein your Flash content runs, and any data outside of the sandbox is bound by certain rules. By default, there are no issues with data you load in from the same domain, but as soon as you need to access content from another server, you need to have explicit permissions to do that. This applies to SWF content from a different domain for which you want scripting access, but also for XML files and any other data you want to load into the Flash Player at runtime.

There are a few ways to grant permissions for content to be loaded in, as you'll see now.

System.security.allow.Domain()

The first is for SWF content, for which you can use the System.security.allowDomain() method to set all domains that are granted access.

Let's say we have a file called abc.swf hosted on www.mydomain.com, and a file called xyz.swf hosted on www.myotherdomain.com that contains a doSomething() function. If the file abc.swf loads in the file xyz.swf, by default it has no access to this doSomething() function. To grant permission to abc.swf to load in xyz.swf and call the doSomething() function, xyz.swf needs to have System.security.allowDomain("www.mydomain.com") in place.

Now that isn't too bad, but the downside with this method is that it requires you to recompile your Flash project any time you need to grant another domain access to the SWF.

Cross-domain policy files

The second way to grant permission for your files to be loaded in from a different domain is using a cross-domain policy file. A *cross-domain policy file* is simply an XML file located in the root of the server that hosts the files you want to load in and defines what domains are allowed.

```
<?xml version="1.0"?>
<!DOCTYPE cross-domain-policy SYSTEM
➡ "http://www.macromedia.com/xml/dtds/cross-domain-policy.dtd">
<cross-domain-policy>
    <allow-access-from domain="www.mydomain.com" />
</cross-domain-policy>
```

This XML file would be saved as crossdomain.xml on the domain that hosts the file, in our case http://www.myotherdomain.com/crossdomain.xml. Obviously, XML files and other data formats don't have the option of using a System.security.allowDomain() method, so to use them you will need to use the cross-domain policy file.

When you have a load request to a server other than the one the file is hosted on, the Flash Player checks whether that cross-domain file is present, and if so, whether your domain is granted access to it. If the file is not there, it checks the SWF file for the System.security.allowDomain() settings. If none of these are available, access will be denied.

An important thing to know is that the policy slightly changed between Flash Player 6 and Flash Player 7 and upwards. In Flash Player 6, subdomains were allowed to access all files on the domain, so for example mysite.mydomain.com could load in and access content from yoursite.mydomain.com. Since Flash Player 7 this is no longer the case, and subdomains also need to be explicitly granted permission, which also means that cases like www.mydomain.com and mydomain.com are not allowed to load data from each other.

With that in mind, it might be best to use the following cross-domain policy:

```
<?xml version="1.0"?>
<!DOCTYPE cross-domain-policy SYSTEM
➥ "http://www.macromedia.com/xml/dtds/cross-domain-policy.dtd">
<cross-domain-policy>
    <allow-access-from domain="*.mydomain.com" />
</cross-domain-policy>
```

This example uses the wildcard character to allow all subdomains for mydomain.com to load in and access data from the server. If you want to limit the access to only www.mydomain.com and mydomain.com, the file would look as follows:

```
<?xml version="1.0"?>
<!DOCTYPE cross-domain-policy SYSTEM
➥ "http://www.macromedia.com/xml/dtds/cross-domain-policy.dtd">
<cross-domain-policy>
    <allow-access-from domain="mydomain.com" />
    <allow-access-from domain="www.mydomain.com" />
</cross-domain-policy>
```

If you want to load in data like XML from a remote server and no cross-domain policy is in place, the warning shown in Figure 20-30 will pop up in the Player to notify the user that the site is trying to load in data from a different domain and gives him or her the choice whether or not to allow this.

Figure 20-30.
Flash Player cross-domain warning

Using a server-side proxy script

Finally, there is one other method to "trick" the user to load in the external data, which is by using a server-side script to proxy the file. Let's say there's an XML file on myotherdomain.com you want to load in, but you aren't able to get a cross-domain policy up on that server.

By using a scripting language such as PHP, you can load in that external data, and the Flash Player will consider that to be a local file. For things like a basic XML file, this is easy enough to do:

```php
<?php
  fpassthru($_POST["proxy_url"]);
?>
```

Let's say you save this PHP code as proxy.php on your local server and call proxy.php?proxy_url=http://www.myotherdomain.com/myfile.xml when loading in the XML. Since the Flash Player doesn't know where the script gets its data from, it just loads it in as if it is local data, and no security measures apply.

Now it isn't quite as easy for a web service because it relies on going back and forward with SOAP messages, but it could technically be done as well (providing there is no additional authentication in the web service logic).

You might have been wondering why this didn't cause a problem when we were using the MXNA web service. There are two reasons. The first is that the people running the web service have a cross-domain policy in place and the second is that you were only running the code from within the Flash 8 IDE which, luckily for us, doesn't require the permissions to be in place. Only when you deploy the SWF to a server do these security settings come into play.

These additional security settings can be quite annoying, but all things considered, it's a good thing to have some means to protect your content and have the Flash Player protect itself from loading in any malicious code.

Summary

In this chapter, we looked at two of the most common ways of using external data in your Flash projects. XML and web services are very convenient ways of communicating with a server, each with its own typical use case. Web services are most commonly used for communicating with remote servers because of the overhead of sending and receiving SOAP messages, while XML can be a perfect format for hooking up your Flash application to data from a database or other back-end system. We briefly looked at Flash Player security settings, which you need to take into consideration when deploying your applications and communicating between different domains.

Most applications will rely on connecting up to some sort of external data source, so it's a topic you should get well acquainted with. I'd encourage you to start experimenting with the various available data formats Flash can communicate with and methods of loading it in. One technology we didn't discuss because it's beyond the scope this book is Flash Remoting, which allows for very optimized binary communication between a back end and Flash; this is available both as commercial solutions and as open source implementations such as AMFPHP (www.amfphp.org) for PHP or OpenAMF (www.openamf.org) for Java. Whatever technique or technology you use, be sure to take data security into consideration any time you send sensitive information to or from the server.

What's next?

We've covered so much information in the chapters so far you're probably already feeling dizzy. Sit back and relax with a cup of coffee because in the final chapter, we will put it all together in a complete real-world case study to get you inspired to create your own object-oriented ActionScript applications. A great way to recap everything we've discussed so far!

20

21 CASE STUDY: TIME SHEET APPLICATION

If you're anything like me in that you always have half a dozen different projects going on at the same time, a good application to help keep track of the time you spent on each task is absolutely invaluable. There are numerous great time-tracking desktop and web-based applications available, but I thought it might be good to "eat my own dog food" and build a basic time sheet application in Flash using ActionScript 2.0.

In this chapter, I'll deconstruct the application, and by doing so recap many different topics we've discussed in the last 20 chapters. If you've read through the book sequentially, most of these will be very familiar to you, and the following application will serve as an example of how you might start using object-oriented ActionScript 2.0 in your own projects.

Of course, before we deconstruct the application together, I first need to show you the end product. If you've downloaded the source files from the friends of ED website, open up `timesheet.swf` in the `timesheet` folder to see it in action, or look at Figure 21-1 to get a feel for what the application does.

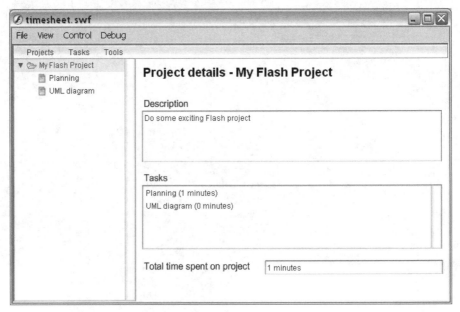

Figure 21-1. Finished time sheet application

Planning the application

Like any project, this application also started with a planning stage. You ask yourself some basic questions that help determine what features will be included and how you'll structure the application.

I've found a good way to do this is to start by writing down keywords that describe what I'm trying to do. For some reason, it seems to work best if this is done with pen and paper. In the case of this time sheet application, I came up with the following:

- Projects
- Tasks
- Time keeping
- Overview

Individually, these keywords don't mean a great deal, but when they're put together, you can see they represent an actual thought process and give you a down-to-basics definition of what you're trying to do with the application. Condensed in a more meaningful form, you could say the application's goal is to create an overview of time spent on your various projects and tasks.

Now you might think that having a few keywords means your application will be relatively basic, but that is not necessarily the case. I would generally recommend not to use too many keywords, as it makes it much more difficult to narrow down the focus to what it actually is you're trying to build. If you find that it is not possible to use all your keywords to clearly describe your application in a single phrase, this is often a sign that it is best to break the application up into different modules; you can then treat each module as if it were a separate application. At a later stage, you would then integrate these various modules into a single working application.

Structuring the application

Once you've got the scope of the application defined, you need to start looking at how you're going to structure it. In the case of the time sheet application, I went back to the original list of keywords and started looking at any relationships between them.

- Application contains projects.
- Projects contain tasks.
- Time can be tracked for tasks.

These relationships between the various elements of an application are incredibly useful to isolate different processes that will need to be handled.

With this basic list of all core functionality we've now got, we can finally start moving from planning to implementing. From now on each of the concepts will be represented by an ActionScript 2.0 class.

I often use a UML class diagram to model classes during the implementation stage of planning of an application. When you look at the class diagram I made for this application (see Figure 21-2), you'll see that this is a prime example of composition. Remember from Chapter 4 the following rule of thumb for recognizing the difference between aggregation and composition:

> *In aggregation, the whole cannot exist without its components, while in a composition, the components cannot exist without the whole.*

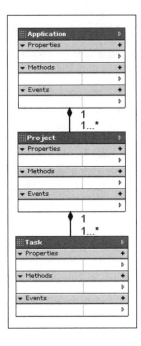

Figure 21-2.
UML class diagram for the time sheet application

This sounds rather philosophical, but it is definitely good to keep this in the back of your mind when you model your application in UML. Using this rule, we can deduce that the time sheet application is an example of composition as, for example, a task cannot exist without a project, while a project can exist without any tasks.

Another thing you'll find on the UML class diagram is the multiplicity notation for each class; from this you can find out how many class instances can be related to one instance of its related class.

Classes that have a one-to-one relationship are usually good candidates for implementing the Singleton design pattern, which enforces this multiplicity relationship by only allowing a single instance of that class to exist in the application scope.

For this project, I chose to implement the MVC pattern (see Figure 21-3) and control the data flow of the application by splitting the logic up into three classes: TimeSheetModel, TimeSheetView, and TimeSheetController.

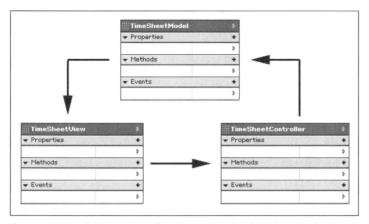

Figure 21-3. Model-View-Controller diagram for the time sheet application

Writing stub code

With all the information we have gathered in the planning stage and when structuring the application, we are now ready to start building some stub code for our ActionScript 2.0 classes. We'll put these classes in the com.friendsofed.timesheet package to avoid any possible conflicts with classes with similar names in the classpath.

Stub code is a good way to start out a project because it gives you a general overview of the complete application structure, and you won't be as tempted to cram all functionality in a single class.

Model-View-Controller classes

The first classes that get built are those that form the MVC pattern: TimeSheetModel, TimeSheetView, and TimeSheetController.

TimeSheetModel class (Model)

The TimeSheetModel class extends the Observer class we discussed in Chapter 12, which provides functionality for adding and removing subscribers and sending notification. By using a separate registerView method to have the View class subscribe to its notification, we have the possibility of adding any number of views to the data model. This is something we don't particularly need for the application as it is set up right now, but it is neverthe-less good to leave it in as such to keep the application structure as flexible as possible.

```
import com.friendsofed.timesheet.Project;
import com.friendsofed.timesheet.Task;

class com.friendsofed.timesheet.TimeSheetModel
extends com.friendsofed.timesheet.Observer {
```

```
private var __projects:Array;
private var __tasks:Array;

function TimeSheetModel() {
}

public function registerView(view:Object):Void {
  super.addSubscriber(view);
}

public function addProject(project_obj:Project):Void {
  super.notifyChanges({operation:"addProject"});
}

public function removeProject(project_name:String):Void {
  super.notifyChanges({operation:"removeProject"});
}

public function addTask(task_obj:Task):Void {
  super.notifyChanges({operation:"addTask"});
}

public function removeTask(project_name:String,
➥ task_obj:Task):Void {
  super.notifyChanges({operation:"removeTask"});
}

public function startTaskTimer(task_obj:Task):Void {
}

public function stopTaskTimer(task_obj:Task):Void {
}

}
```

You'll notice that this stub code already contains all method calls for the TimeSheetModel class to update and retrieve data. The references to Project and Task class instances will be stored in the private __projects and __tasks properties.

Later on in the development process, this class will have some additional helper methods to retrieve and filter out specific project or class instances, but for now this gives us a good idea of what the Model class looks like.

TimeSheetView class (View)

The TimeSheetView class can hold references to both the Model and the Controller class. If any user interaction occurs, the View class passes this on to the Controller, which in turn might trigger the Model to update. If the Model changes, it sends notification to the View class, and the View class can connect to the Model to get the appropriate data.

```
import com.friendsofed.timesheet.TimeSheetModel;
import com.friendsofed.timesheet.TimeSheetController;
import com.friendsofed.timesheet.Project;
import com.friendsofed.timesheet.Task;

class com.friendsofed.timesheet.TimeSheetView {

  private var __model:Object;
  private var __controller:Object;
  private var __scope:MovieClip;

  function TimeSheetView(scope:MovieClip,model:Object,
  ➥ controller:Object) {
    this.__scope = target;
    this.__model = model;
    this.__controller = controller;
    this.__model.registerView(this);
    this.initializeLayout();
  }

  public function initializeLayout() {
    // create the layout elements ...
  }

  public function update() {
    // handle notification from TimeSheetModel
  }

}
```

21

I've strayed from the typical implementation of a View class with this TimeSheetView class. Besides accepting a reference to the Model and Controller, the constructor has a third parameter, which I can use to pass the scope where the interface elements are located. I sometimes prefer this approach rather than having the View class extend MovieClip, because it gives some further abstraction and adds some additional flexibility by allowing you to switch the application scope at runtime. Again, not something we would likely use in this project, but something that is good to consider.

You'll notice that the TimeSheetView constructor takes these three arguments and stores them in private __model, __controller, and __scope properties; it also references the Model to subscribe the View class for notification, and finally calls the initializeLayout() method.

This layout code is not yet implemented in this stub code, but the initializeLayout() method will be used for setting some component instance properties and adding some essential event listeners.

TimeSheetController class (Controller)

The TimeSheetController class holds a reference to the Model and gets calls from the View when any user interaction has occurred. The Controller class connects to the Model when any data needs to be changed. This class acts in many ways as a mediator between the View and the Model.

```
import com.friendsofed.timesheet.TimeSheetModel;
import com.friendsofed.timesheet.Project;
import com.friendsofed.timesheet.Task;

class com.friendsofed.timesheet.TimeSheetController {

  private var __model:Object;

  function TimeSheetController(model:Object) {
    this.__model = model;
  }

  public function addProject(project_name:String,
  ➡ project_description:String):Void {
    var newProject:Project = new Project(project_name,
    ➡ project_description);
    this.__model.addProject(newProject);
  }

  public function removeProject(project_name:String):Void {
    this.__model.removeProject(project_name);
  }

  public function addTask(project_name:String,
  task_name:String, task_description:String):Void {
  ➡ var newTask:Task = new Task(project_name, task_name,
  ➡ task_description);
    this.__model.addTask(newTask);
  }

  public function removeTask(project_name:String,
  ➡ task_obj:Task):Void {
    this.__model.removeTask(project_name,task_obj);
  }

}
```

This TimeSheetController class is very basic if you look at it a bit closer: it forwards method calls directly to the Model except for addProject() and addTask(), where it first creates an instance of the Project or Task class with the arguments it gets passed.

The TimeSheetController constructor just stores the reference to the Model in a private property called __model and is used by the method calls throughout the Controller class later on.

Now that you've seen the stub code for the Model, View, and Controller classes, there are two other important classes for the application that we still need to look at: Project and Task.

Project and Task classes

The Project and Task classes are, for all events and purposes, just value objects that get created and destroyed as needed throughout the application lifespan. Both classes are essentially the same and contain a title and description property and a corresponding method to return them. The Task class, however, has two additional properties: the first, __project, holds a reference to the name of the project that it is part of, and the other one, __timer, keeps hold of the amount of time you've worked on this particular task.

Project class

You can hardly think of a class that is more basic than this—two private properties that hold a title and description. These properties get set by using the arguments that are passed through the constructor method. Finally, we have two methods for retrieving these properties, getTitle() and getDescription().

```
class com.friendsofed.timesheet.Project {

  private var __title:String;
  private var __description:String;

  function Project(title:String,description:String) {
    this.__title = title;
    this.__description = description;
  }

  public function getTitle():String {
    return this.__title;
  }

  public function getDescription():String {
    return this.__description;
  }

}
```

While at this stage it's only supposed to be stub code, this is all there is to the Project class. We won't need to add anything to this later on.

Task class

The Task class isn't much larger than the Project class, and is basically the same, except for the additional __project and __timer properties and corresponding methods.

```
class com.friendsofed.timesheet.Task {

  private var __project:String;
  private var __title:String;
  private var __description:String;
  private var __timer:Number;

  function Task(project_name:String,task_name:String,
➥ task_description:String) {
    this.__project = project_name;
    this.__title = task_name;
    this.__description = task_description;
    this.__timer = 0;
  }

  public function getProject():String {
    return this.__project;
  }

  public function getTitle():String {
    return this.__title;
  }

  public function getDescription():String {
    return this.__description;
  }

  public function setTaskTimer(time:Number):Void {
    this.__timer = time;
  }

  public function getTaskTimer():Number {
    return this.__timer;
  }

}
```

This Task class will have some minor additions later on for keeping track of the current status of the task, but apart from that this class is also ready for use in the application.

Bringing it all together

Now, at least for me, it was surprisingly easy to get to this stage. We did some application planning and structuring and have stub code in place, which we can use to start building the application on.

The one thing that we don't yet have is an actual FLA to bring it all together in. For larger scale applications, I usually opt to attach and position components at runtime, because this technique gives you some additional control over the interface at runtime, and apart from that it just makes you feel like a real hardcore programmer. The downside is that it can make your code rather lengthy and convoluted if not handled with care.

In this case, I chose to just have components positioned on stage and have a number of movie clips to act as panels. The main components I used were a Tree component for displaying the projects and tasks, and a MenuBar component, which gets initialized in the TimeSheetView class to act as the means of navigating the application.

Now for the most important few lines of the entire application, without which nothing would ever happen. On the first frame of the actionscript layer, I added the following code:

```
import com.friendsofed.timesheet.TimeSheetModel;
import com.friendsofed.timesheet.TimeSheetView;
import com.friendsofed.timesheet.TimeSheetController;

var timesheetModel:TimeSheetModel = new TimeSheetModel();
var timesheetController:TimeSheetController =
➥ new TimeSheetController(timesheetModel);
var timesheetView:TimeSheetView =
➥ new TimeSheetView(this,timesheetModel,timesheetController);
```

These lines of code simply initialize the MVC classes of the application. The first three lines are basic import statements for the classes, and after that the TimeSheetModel instance gets created. Next, the TimeSheetController instance is created and passed the newly created instance of the TimeSheetModel class. Finally, an instance of the TimeSheetView is added and passed the scope for the components, the TimeSheetModel and TimeSheetController instances. That's not too complicated, is it?

With everything set up, let's walk through the different pieces of functionality in the application and how they were implemented in the final code.

Initializing the layout

As briefly shown earlier, the TimeSheetView class has an `initializeLayout()` method that does some essential initialization of interface elements.

21

493

TimeSheetView class

```
private function initializeLayout():Void {

    // set panel movie clips to invisible
    this.__scope.addProject_mc._visible = false;
    this.__scope.removeProject_mc._visible = false;
    this.__scope.addTask_mc._visible = false;
    this.__scope.removeTask_mc._visible = false;

    // create Project menu items in MenuBar component
    this.project_menu = this.__scope.nav_menubar.
    addMenu("Projects");
    this.project_menu.addItem({label:"Add project", operation:"add"});
    this.project_menu.addItem({label:"Remove project",
    operation:"remove"});
    this.project_menu.addEventListener("change",
➥ Delegate.create(this,onProjectMenuChange));

    // create Task menu items in MenuBar component
    this.task_menu = this.__scope.nav_menubar. addMenu("Tasks");
    this.task_menu.addItem({label:"Add task", operation:"add"});
    this.task_menu.addItem({label:"Remove task", operation:"remove"});
    this.task_menu.addEventListener("change",
➥  Delegate.create(this,onTaskMenuChange));

    // create Tools menu items in MenuBar component
    this.tools_menu = this.__scope.nav_menubar. addMenu("Tools");
    this.tools_menu.addItem({label:"Import data", operation:"import"});
    this.tools_menu.addItem({label:"Export data", operation:"export"});

      // Add event listeners to MenuBar component menu items
      this.tools_menu.addEventListener("change",
      Delegate.create(this,onToolsMenuChange));
    this.__scope.project_tree.addEventListener
➥  ("change",Delegate.create(this,onProjectChange));
➥ this.__scope.addProject_mc.add_btn.addEventListener
➥  ("click",Delegate.create(this,onAddProject));
➥ this.__scope.removeProject_mc.remove_btn.addEventListener
➥  ("click",Delegate.create(this,onRemoveProject));
    this.__scope.addTask_mc.add_btn.addEventListener
➥  ("click",Delegate.create(this,onAddTask));
      this.__scope.removeTask_mc.remove_btn.addEventListener
      ("click",Delegate.create(this,onRemoveTask));

    // create a Delegate function for the task timer
    this.__onTimerDelegate = Delegate.create(this,onTimer);

}
```

Wow, that's quite a bit of code. You probably weren't expecting that when I said that I chose to have the components on stage rather than attach them with code. Its nothing too daunting though; the first few lines of code set the _visible property of some movie clip. The addProject_mc, removeProject_mc, addTask_mc, and removeTask_mc movie clips are panels that are used to add or remove projects and tasks.

It's a bit unconventional to put those all on stage rather than attach them, but it saves a bit of a headache when you're dealing with v2 components, as I'll explain later on.

The next blocks of code deal with the MenuBar component where we add a Project, Task, and Tools menu. Each of these items in the MenuBar get their own corresponding menu items and an event listener that gets triggered when a menu item is clicked.

The last line of code in the initializeLayout() method creates a Delegate function for the onTimer() method. This onTimer() method is used when a task gets triggered to start recording time. As with each of the menu item event listeners, it uses the Delegate class to get the scope of the function to refer to the TimeSheetView class scope.

Adding a project

21

When an item in the Project menu is clicked in the MenuBar component, it broadcasts a change event that gets picked up by the onProjectMenuChange() method. This method then determines what item in the Project menu was clicked, which in this case is either Add project or Remove project.

Based on that, the code sets the visibility of either the addProject_mc or removeProject_mc movie clip on stage. If the user opts to add a project, the panel will look as shown in Figure 21-4.

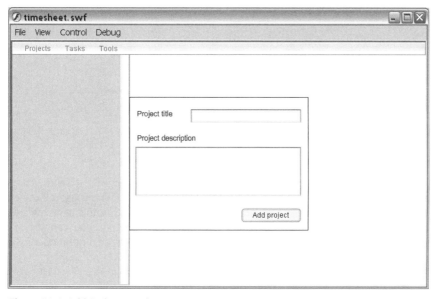

Figure 21-4. Add Project panel

Let's take a closer look to see how the onProjectMenuChange() method handles this.

TimeSheetView class

```
private function onProjectMenuChange(evt:Object):Void {
  switch(evt.menuItem.operation) {

    // when "Add project" was clicked
    case "add":
      this.interfaceEnabled(false);
      this.__scope.addProject_mc._visible = true;
    break;

    // when "Remove project" was clicked
    case "remove":
      var projectList:Array = this.__controller.getProjects();

      // check if there are projects to remove
        if(projectList.length > 0) {

          this.interfaceEnabled(false);
          this.__scope.removeProject_mc._visible = true;
          this.__scope.removeProject_mc.project_cb.removeAll();

          for(var i=0; i<projectList.length; i++) {
          this.__scope.removeProject_mc.project_cb.addItem
          ➥ (projectList[i].getTitle());
          }

        } else {

          Alert.show("There are no projects to remove",
          ➥ "Remove project",Alert.OK);

        }
      break;

    }
  }
```

When the change event gets dispatched to onProjectMenuChange(), it sends an event object with it. This event object contains some information about who triggered the event to broadcast as well as some other data in relation to the event. In this case, I added an operation property to each menu item that describes its task. As you can see in the initializeLayout() method, the Add project menu item has an operation of "add" assigned to it while the Remove project menu item has "remove".

By doing a simple switch statement on the operation property that gets sent along with the event object, the code can now determine whether the user wants to add or remove a project.

You saw what gets displayed when a user chooses to add a project, and from the code you can see that it isn't too exciting. All it does is set the _visible property of the addProject_mc movie clip and call a method named interfaceEnabled() that disables the Tree and MenuBar components so you can't interact with these components as long as the panel is visible.

Now, the Remove Project panel is slightly more interesting. Here I add an additional check to see whether there are actually any projects that can be removed. There's no sense in bringing up the panel if there isn't a project the user can delete.

The way this is handled is by going through the TimeSheetController class as a mediator and getting hold of all projects that are stored in the TimeSheetModel class instance. If the array that gets returned has a length that is higher than zero, there obviously are projects stored in the model that can be deleted; otherwise we'll display an alert box that notifies the user that no projects are available, as shown in Figure 21-5.

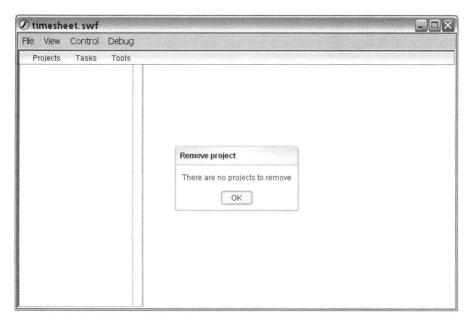

Figure 21-5. Alert box when no projects are available

This alert box is an instance of the Alert component, which we have in the Library panel, that gets called by using the static show() method.

If there are projects available, removeProject_mc will get its _visible property turned on, and you'll be able to select a project instance that you want to delete, as shown in Figure 21-6.

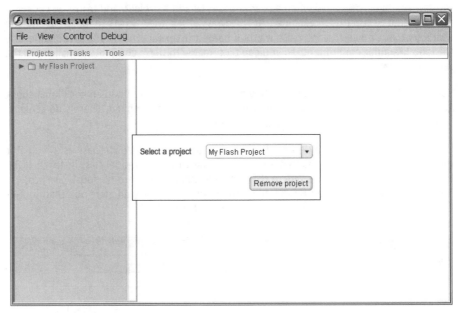

Figure 21-6. Remove Project panel

Displaying projects

All projects that get added to the application are displayed in the Tree component as branches. When the user has added a new project using the addProject_mc movie clip, it gets forwarded to the addProject() method in the TimeSheetController class, which creates a Project instance out of it and passes it on to TimeSheetModel for storage.

Once TimeSheetModel has added this new Project instance, it will broadcast a notification message, which gets picked up by the update() method in the TimeSheetView class.

Since all notifications are handled through this update() method, we need to determine exactly what the notification pertains to. This is done by looking at the data that gets sent along with the notification. In this case, the TimeSheetModel sends an operation property with its notification that has either the value addProject or removeProject.

Both these event notifications will be handled in the same way: when they are received by the update() method, it calls a method in the TimeSheetView class named buildProjectTree(). This method then gets hold of all projects stored in TimeSheetModel by going through the TimeSheetController class and adds those to the Tree component (see Figure 21-7).

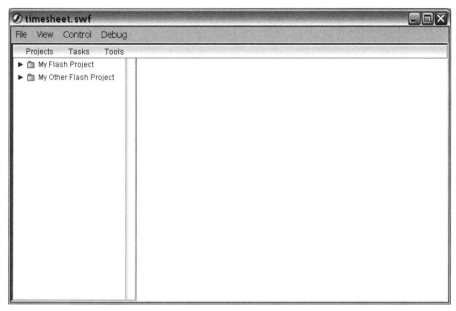

Figure 21-7. Projects listed in the Tree component

If you expect to have a high number of items in the Tree component or items will change very often, rebuilding it every time an item gets added or removed wouldn't be the way to go. But having said that, it's always important to be pragmatic in the way you structure your application, and this approach fits in best with what we are trying to accomplish.

TimeSheetController class

```
public function addProject(project_name:String,
project_description:String):Void {
  var project = new Project(project_name,
  project_description);
  this.__model.addProject(project);
}
```

TimeSheetModel class

```
public function addProject(project_obj:Project) {
  this.__projects.push(project_obj);
  super.notifyChanges({operation:"addProject"});
}
```

TimeSheetView class

```
public function update(evt:Object):Void {

  switch(evt.operation) {
    case "addProject":
      this.buildProjectTree();
    break;
    case "removeProject":
      this.buildProjectTree();
    break;
    case "addTask":
      this.buildProjectTree();
    break;
    case "removeTask":
      this.buildProjectTree();
    break;
  }

}
```

Now the switch statement isn't particularly necessary in the update function as it stands, but it's useful to have this in place in case you ever want to add a specific method call to only one type of event.

TimeSheetView class

```
private function buildProjectTree() {

  // clear all items from the Tree component
    this.__scope.project_tree.removeAll();

  // get array of all projects
  var projectList:Array = this.__controller.getProjects();

  // get array of all tasks
  var taskList:Array = this.__controller.getTasks();

  // loop through all projects
  for(var i=0; i<projectList.length; i++) {

    // add each project title to the Tree component
    var node:XMLNode = this.__scope.project_tree.
    addTreeNode(projectList[i].getTitle());
```

```
        // make each project a branch in the Tree component
        this.__scope.project_tree.setIsBranch(node,true);

        // loop through all tasks
        for(var j=0; j<taskList.length; j++) {

            // if task belongs to the project
            if(taskList[j].getProject() ==
        ➥ node.attributes.label) {

                // get the project branch
                var branch:XMLNode =
            ➥ this.__scope.project_tree.getTreeNodeAt(i);

                // add task to the project
                branch.addTreeNode(taskList[j].getTitle());

                // open the project branch to show task
                this.__scope.project_tree.setIsOpen(branch,true);
            }
        }

    }

    // show the project information panel
    this.__scope.infoPanel_mc.gotoAndStop(1);

}
```

What you might have gathered from looking at the code and I didn't mention before is that buildProjectTree() also loops through all Task instances and adds those to the corresponding Project instance in the Tree component.

The final statement in the buildProjectTree() method tells the infoPanel_mc movie clip on stage to display Frame 1, which is an empty frame. This infoPanel_mc movie clip is used to display information about the selected project or task in the Tree component. When the Tree component is rebuilt, we also reset the movie clip to an empty frame to make sure it doesn't still display information about a project that has already been removed.

Adding a task

The way adding and removing tasks is handled will look familiar to you, as it's exactly the same way for projects. Instead of onProjectMenuChange(), the MenuBar component will broadcast a change event to onTaskMenuChange() when an item from the Task menu is selected.

What happens next is that the onTaskMenuChange() method determines whether the user intends to add or remove a task. If a task needs to be added, the addTask_mc movie clip's _visible property is set to true (see Figure 21-8); when a task needs to be removed, the removeTask_mc movie clip's _visible property is set to true.

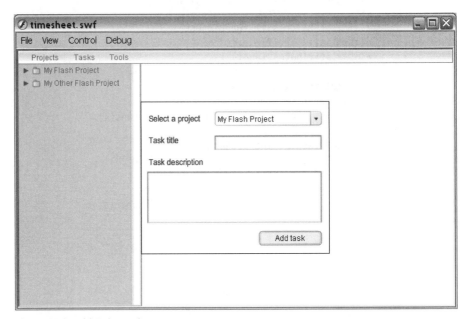

Figure 21-8. Add Task panel

As with a project, when the user chooses to delete a task, the code first checks whether there are any tasks stored in the TimeSheetModel, and if not alerts the user of this instead of displaying the panel. Additionally, it checks that there are in fact any projects defined, as a task can't be added without having a project for it to belong to.

TimeSheetView class

```
private function onTaskMenuChange(evt:Object):Void {

  switch(evt.menuItem.operation) {

    // if "Add task" was clicked
    case "add":

      // get list of all projects
      var projectList:Array =
      ➥ this.__controller.getProjects();
```

```
// if there are projects
if(projectList.length > 0) {

  this.interfaceEnabled(false);
  this.__scope.addTask_mc._visible = true;

  this.__scope.addTask_mc.project_cb.removeAll();

  // loop through projects
  for(var i=0; i<projectList.length; i++) {

    // add projects to combo box in panel
    this.__scope.addTask_mc.project_cb.addItem
    (projectList[i].getTitle());

  }

} else {

  // warn user that no projects are available
  Alert.show("There are no projects to add a
  ➥ task to","Add task",Alert.OK);

}

break;

// if "Remove task" was clicked
case "remove":

  // get list of all tasks
  var taskList:Array = this.__controller.getTasks();

  // if there are tasks available
  if(taskList.length > 0) {

    // get list of projects
    var projectList:Array =
    ➥ this.__controller.getProjects();

    this.interfaceEnabled(false);
    this.__scope.removeTask_mc._visible = true;

    this.__scope.removeTask_mc.project_cb.
    ➥ removeAll();
   this.__scope.removeTask_mc.task_cb.removeAll();
```

```
                              // loop through projects
                              for(var i=0; i<projectList.length; i++) {

                                    // get tasks for specific project
                                    var projectTasks:Array = this.__controller.
                                    ➥ getTasksByProject(projectList[i].getTitle());

                                    // if there are tasks for the project
                                    if(projectTasks.length > 0) {

                                          // add task to ComboBox component
                                          this.__scope.removeTask_mc.project_cb.
                                          ➥ addItem(projectList[i].getTitle());

                                    }

                              }

                                    // add event listener to project ComboBox
                                    this.__scope.removeTask_mc.project_cb.
                                    ➥ addEventListener("change",
                                    ➥ Delegate.create(this,removeTask));

                                    // call removeTask to initialize task ComboBox
                                    this.removeTask();

                        } else {

                              // if no tasks are available warn user
                              Alert.show("There are no tasks to remove",
                              ➥ "Remove task",Alert.OK);

                        }

                        break;

                  }
            }
```

When the user chooses to remove a task and the code finds that there is at least one task available, it will show the panel presented in Figure 21-9.

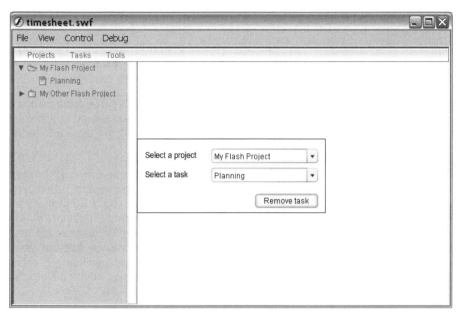

Figure 21-9. Remove Task panel

What is special about this panel is that it uses two ComboBox components, and the one displaying the list of tasks is context-sensitive to the project that is selected in the other component. To achieve this, an event listener was added that listens for change events on the project combo box. If the selected item in the project combo box is changed, the getTasksByProject() method gets called on the controller, which queries the TimeSheetModel for all Task instances related to a specific project. In this way, the task combo box always gets filled with the tasks corresponding with the selected project.

When a task gets added or removed, this happens via the TimeSheetController again, which passes the arguments along to TimeSheetModel, which in turn updates its data and broadcasts a notification to the TimeSheetView class. This completes the circle, and we're back at the update() method in the TimeSheetView class, which calls buildProjectTree() to update the Tree component.

OK, we've covered a great deal of ground now. You've seen how the layout is initialized, how the code handles the adding and removing of Projects and Task class instances, and how the view gets updated when this happens. What we will look at next is how to get information from Project and Task instances and present it to the user.

Project and task details

To present information about the currently selected project or task in the Tree component, a movie clip with the instance name infoPanel_mc is located on the stage. This movie clip has a number of frames representing its different states.

In the initializeLayout() method of the TimeSheetView class, the Tree component was assigned an event listener called onProjectChange(). This method detects whether the selected node in the Tree component is a project or a task and has the infoPanel_mc movie clip display the correct state.

Next, we've got a good example of what I was talking about at the beginning of the chapter when I said attaching components is a bit of a pain. When v2 components get rendered to the screen, they need a one-frame waiting period before everything is initialized and you can start using them. The same thing happens here, and there are a number of ways around it. What I used in this case was a simple onEnterFrame function; because this function gets triggered every frame, it is the most straightforward way to wait one frame before setting the component properties. When the onEnterFrame function gets called, one frame has passed, and we can set reset it to null. One other way around the problem is using an undocumented feature in Flash 8 called setTimeout().

The setTimeout() method is identical to what you probably already know as setInterval(), which calls a given function at a certain interval. There is one major difference between these two methods: setTimeout() only calls the function once. This is a very useful thing to have; in the past when you wanted to have a function called only once at an interval, you needed to store a reference to the interval and use clearInterval() in the function that gets called to make sure it doesn't repeat. Not only is setTimeout() an undocumented feature, the compiler won't let you use it without complaining. The way around this problem is to use the _global scope to call it or use array notation, i.e., this["setTimeout"]().

If you're extending the mx.core.UIObject class, which is most likely what you will do when developing v2 components, there is also a method called doLater that does about the same thing as we do with the onEnterFrame method. The onEnterFrame and doLater methods use a frame-based approach, while setTimeout() and setInterval() use a timed interval. Given that we only need to wait one frame, the first two are probably better suited for this situation.

Using the onEnterFrame workaround, I have either the showProjectDetails() or showTaskDetails() method called in the TimeSheetView class. These methods handle populating the components in infoPanel_mc with the necessary data, for projects this is the project title, description, list of all tasks, and the corresponding time for each task along with a total amount of time spent on all tasks related to the project. The showTaskDetails() method just shows the title, description, and total amount of time spent working on that particular task.

TimeSheetView class

```
private function onProjectChange(evt:Object):Void {

    // if the selected node is a project
    if(this.__scope.project_tree.getIsBranch
    ➥ (this.__scope.project_tree.selectedNode)) {

        // show the project information
        ➥ this.__scope.infoPanel_mc.gotoAndStop(2);

        // call showProjectsDetails method after 1 frame
        this.__scope.onEnterFrame = Delegate.create(this,function() {
          this.showProjectDetails();
          this.__scope.onEnterFrame = null;
        });

    } else {

        // show the task information
        this.__scope.infoPanel_mc.gotoAndStop(3);

        // call showTaskDetails method after 1 frame
        this.__scope.onEnterFrame = Delegate.create(this,function() {
          this.showTaskDetails();
          this.__scope.onEnterFrame = null;
        });

    }

}


private function showProjectDetails() {

// show project title
this.__scope.infoPanel_mc.title_txt.text =
➥ "Project details - "+this.__scope.project_tree.
➥ selectedNode.attributes.label;

// show project description
this.__scope.infoPanel_mc.description_txt.text =
➥ this.__controller.getProjectByName(this.__scope.
➥ project_tree.selectedNode.attributes.label).
➥ GetDescription();
```

```actionscript
    this.__scope.infoPanel_mc.task_list.removeAll();

    // get list of all project tasks
    var projectTasks:Array = this.__controller.
      ➥ getTasksByProject(this.__scope.project_tree.
      ➥ selectedNode.attributes.label);

    // keep track of the total time spent on the project
    var totalProjectTime:Number = 0;

    // loop through project tasks list
    for(var i=0; i<projectTasks.length; i++) {

      // add task to List component with timer value
      this.__scope.infoPanel_mc.task_list.addItem
      ➥ (projectTasks[i].getTitle()+
      ➥ " ("+TimerUtils.format(projectTasks[i].
      ➥ getTaskTimer())+")");

      // add task timer to total time spent on project
      totalProjectTime += projectTasks[i].getTaskTimer();

    }

    // format the timer into hours and minutes
    this.__scope.infoPanel_mc.total_txt.text =
    ➥ TimerUtils.format(totalProjectTime);

  }


  private function showTaskDetails() {

    // get task object
    var taskDetails:Task = this.__controller.getTaskByName
    ➥ (this.__scope.project_tree.selectedNode.parentNode.
    ➥ attributes.label,this.__scope.project_tree.selectedNode.
    ➥ attributes.label);

    // if task is currently running a timer
    if(taskDetails.getIsActive()) {

      // set the timer button label to "Stop timer"
      this.__scope.infoPanel_mc.timer_btn.label =
      ➥ "Stop timer";

    } else {
```

```
      // set the timer button label to "Start timer"
      this.__scope.infoPanel_mc.timer_btn.label =
   ➡ "Start timer";

   }

   // remove the event listener to avoid duplicate calls
   this.__scope.infoPanel_mc.timer_btn.removeEventListener
➡ ("click",this.__onTimerDelegate);

   // set title for task details
   this.__scope.infoPanel_mc.title_txt.text =
➡ "Task details - "+this.__scope.project_tree.selectedNode.
➡ attributes.label;

   // show task description
   this.__scope.infoPanel_mc.description_txt.text =
➡ taskDetails.getDescription();

   // show current formatted timer value for task
   this.__scope.infoPanel_mc.total_txt.text =
➡ TimerUtils.format(taskDetails.getTaskTimer());

   // add click event listener to timer button
   this.__scope.infoPanel_mc.timer_btn.addEventListener
➡ ("click",this.__onTimerDelegate);

}
```

In the showProjectDetails() and showTaskDetails() methods, you'll notice a few references to TimerUtils.format(). This TimerUtils is a little static helper class that at this time only contains one method called format(). The format() method takes the timer value from the Task instance (which is in seconds) as an argument and converts it to hours and minutes.

TimerUtils class

```
class com.friendsofed.timesheet.TimerUtils {

  static function format(timer:Number) {

    // divide time in seconds by 3600 for hours
    var hours:Number = Math.floor(timer/3600);
    var hours_msg:String = "hours";

    // if hours is equal to one make singular
    if(hours == 1) {
      hours_msg = "hour";
```

```
    }
    // divide remaining time by 60 for minutes
    var minutes:Number = Math.floor((timer/60)-(hours*60));
    var minutes_msg:String = "minutes";

    // if minutes is equal to one make singular
    if(minutes == 1) {
      minutes_msg = "minute";
    }

    // if time is an hour or more
    if(hours > 0) {

      // return string with hour and minutes
      return hours+" "+hours_msg+", "+minutes+" "+minutes_msg;

    } else {
      // return string with minutes
      return minutes+" "+minutes_msg;
    }

  }

}
```

One of the last things we still need to cover is how timers are handled for tasks; if you've looked closely at the Task class, you might already have figured it out by now.

Running a task timer

The time sheet application assumes that you can do only one task at a time and as such supports only one task timer running at a time. If you start a timer on a task while a timer is still running on a different task, that old timer will be stopped.

In TimeSheetModel, a private property called __activeTask keeps track of the Task instance that is currently being tracked, and the __taskStartTime property holds a time-stamp when the task started running a timer. When the timer is stopped, what happens is that the current timestamp gets subtracted by __tastStartTime to determine how long it had been running. This value in seconds is then added on to the __timer value of the active Task class instance.

Using the getTaskTimer() method on the Task instance, we can get hold of the total amount of time this task has been running, and the TimerUtils class discussed earlier can then assist in converting that into a more useful format than seconds.

TimeSheetModel class

```
public function startTaskTimer(task_obj:Task):Void {

  // if there is already a timer running
  if(this._activeTask != null) {

    // stop that timer
    this.stopTaskTimer(this._activeTask);

    // set the task to inactive
    this._activeTask.setIsActive(false);

  }

  // set the new task as active
  this._activeTask = task_obj;

  // get a starting timestamp for the timer
  this._taskStartTime = getTimer();

}


public function stopTaskTimer(task_obj:Task):Void {

  // add the timer value in seconds to the task instance
  task_obj.setTaskTimer(task_obj.getTaskTimer()+
  ➡ ((getTimer()-this._taskStartTime)/1000));

  // set the task as inactive
  task.setIsActive(false);

  // erase the starting timestamp
  this._taskStartTime = null;

  // erase the active task reference
  this._activeTask = null;

}
```

These two methods on TimeSheetModel get invoked when the timer button on the task information movie clip is clicked, again using the TimeSheetController class to proxy the call.

21

Persisting time sheet data

At this point, we've got the project running perfectly, adding and removing projects and tasks and keeping track of the time spent on each task. There's only one practical concern with using the application: there is no way to persist data between sessions. This would mean that every time you want to keep track of your projects and tasks, you need to add them again, and you've lost the timer values for all your tasks.

Luckily, this was anticipated when I built the application, and this involves an import and export feature that you can find in the Tools menu of the MenuBar component. What the export feature does is create an XML structure containing all your projects, tasks, and current timer settings, which you can then copy and save to a file. The import feature allows you to paste in that XML document and restore your project, task, and timer settings to continue where you left off. When an item from the Tools menu gets clicked, it broadcasts an event to the onToolsChange() method, which determines whether import or export was selected. Based on this, the function shows the correct form in the infoPanel_mc movie clip.

TimeSheetView class

```
private function onToolsMenuChange(evt:Object) {

  // check whether user clicked import or export
  switch(evt.menuItem.operation) {

    // if import was clicked
    case "import":

    // show the import panel
    this.__scope.infoPanel_mc.gotoAndStop(4);

    // trigger the importXML method after 1 frame
    this.__scope.onEnterFrame = Delegate.create(this,function() {
    this.importXML();
    this.__scope.onEnterFrame = null;
    });

    break;

    // if export was clicked
    case "export":

      // show the export panel
      this.__scope.infoPanel_mc.gotoAndStop(5);

      // trigger the writeXML method after 1 frame
```

```
            this.__scope.onEnterFrame = Delegate.create(this,function() {
              this.writeXML();
              this.__scope.onEnterFrame = null;
            });

        break;

    }

}
```

What you would typically do is call the TimeSheetController class to have it handle the writeXML() method, but I opted to handle it in the TimeSheetView itself in this case and not make the round trip to avoid unnecessarily complicating the code.

TimeSheetView class

```
private function writeXML():Void {

  // copy the XML to the clipboard when button clicked
    this.__scope.infoPanel_mc.copy_btn.
    ➡ addEventListener("click",Delegate.create(this,function() {
        System.setClipboard(this.__scope.
        ➡ infoPanel_mc.xml_txt.text);
  }));

  // get list of projects
  var projectList:Array = this.__controller.getProjects();
  // get list of tasks
  var taskList:Array = this.__controller.getTasks();

  // start writing XML to TextArea component
  this.__scope.infoPanel_mc.xml_txt.text =
  ➡ "<?xml version=\"1.0\" ?>\n";

  this.__scope.infoPanel_mc.xml_txt.text += "<timesheet>\n";

  // loop through projects
  for(var i=0; i<projectList.length; i++) {

    this.__scope.infoPanel_mc.xml_txt.text +=
    ➡ "  <project>\n";
      this.__scope.infoPanel_mc.xml_txt.text +=
      ➡ "    <title>";
      this.__scope.infoPanel_mc.xml_txt.text +=
      ➡ "<![CDATA["+projectList[i].getTitle()+"]]>";
    this.__scope.infoPanel_mc.xml_txt.text +=
    ➡ "</title>\n";
```

```actionscript
      this.__scope.infoPanel_mc.xml_txt.text +=
➥ "   <description>";
      this.__scope.infoPanel_mc.xml_txt.text +=
➥ "<![CDATA["+projectList[i].getDescription()+"]]>";
      this.__scope.infoPanel_mc.xml_txt.text +=
➥ "</description>\n";

      // loop through tasks
      for(var j=0; j<taskList.length; j++) {

        if(taskList[j].getProject() ==

        projectList[i].getTitle()) {

          this.__scope.infoPanel_mc.xml_txt.text +=
➥ "     <task>\n";
          this.__scope.infoPanel_mc.xml_txt.text +=
➥ "       <title>";
          this.__scope.infoPanel_mc.xml_txt.text +=
➥ "<![CDATA["+taskList[j].getTitle()+"]]>";
          this.__scope.infoPanel_mc.xml_txt.text +=
➥ "</title>\n";
            this.__scope.infoPanel_mc.xml_txt.text +=
➥ "      <description>";
          this.__scope.infoPanel_mc.xml_txt.text +=
➥ "<![CDATA["+taskList[j].getDescription()+"]]>";
          this.__scope.infoPanel_mc.xml_txt.text +=
➥ "</description>\n";
          this.__scope.infoPanel_mc.xml_txt.text +=
➥ "       <timer>";
          this.__scope.infoPanel_mc.xml_txt.text +=
➥ "<![CDATA["+taskList[j].getTaskTimer()+"]]>";
          this.__scope.infoPanel_mc.xml_txt.text +=
➥ "</timer>\n";
          this.__scope.infoPanel_mc.xml_txt.text +=
➥ "     </task>\n";

        }

      }

      this.__scope.infoPanel_mc.xml_txt.text +=
➥ "   </project>\n";

    }

    this.__scope.infoPanel_mc.xml_txt.text += "</timesheet>";
  }
```

The writeXML() method is rather lengthy, but this is mainly because I split it up into multiple lines for readability. What the method does is very basic: it gets an array of all projects and tasks and loops through them, building an XML structure that you can then copy to the clipboard and paste into a file for importing again later on.

The XML document that gets exported looks something like this:

```
<?xml version="1.0" ?>
<timesheet>
  <project>
    <title><![CDATA[My Flash Project]]></title>
    <description><![CDATA[Build a cool Flash application]]>
    </description>
    <task>
      <title><![CDATA[Planning]]></title>
      <description>
        <![CDATA[Plan out the application]]>
      </description>
      <timer><![CDATA[60]]></timer>
    </task>
  </project>
</timesheet>
```

This XML structure shows a project with a title node value of "My Flash Application" that has one task called with a title node value of "Planning"; both the project and task have a description, and the task has a timer value of 60, which means the user has already spent one minute working on that task. By adding this export feature, users can now export a schedule of projects and tasks, save it to a file, and load it back in at a later stage.

The importXML() method takes the XML data that the user has pasted in, parses that as XML, and walks through it, updating the TimeSheetModel class.

TimeSheetView class

```
private function importXML():Void {

// when the import button is clicked
this.__scope.infoPanel_mc.import_btn.
➥ addEventListener("click", Delegate.create(this,
➥ function() {

  // clear the model projects and tasks
  this.__controller.resetModel();

  // parse the XML data in the TextArea component
    var xml_data:XML = new XML(this.__scope.
    ➥ infoPanel_mc.xml_txt.text);
```

```
// loop through XML nodes
for(var i=0; i<xml_data.childNodes[1].childNodes.length;
➡ i++) {

  var project_node:XMLNode = xml_data.childNodes[1].
  ➡ childNodes[i];

  // if a project node is encountered
  if(project_node.nodeName == "project") {

    var tasks:Array = new Array();

    // loop through project nodes
    for(var j=0; j<project_node.childNodes.length;
    ➡ j++) {

      if(project_node.childNodes[j].nodeName == "title") {
      var project_title:String = project_node.
      childNodes[j].firstChild.nodeValue;
     }

      if(project_node.childNodes[j].nodeName ==
      ➡ "description") {

        var project_description:String =
        ➡ project_node.childNodes[j].firstChild.
        ➡ nodeValue;

      }

      if(project_node.childNodes[j].nodeName ==
      ➡ "task") {

        var  task_nodes:XMLNode = project_node.
        ➡ childNodes[j];

        for(var k=0; k<task_nodes.childNodes.
        ➡ length; k++) {
          if(task_nodes.childNodes[k].nodeName == "title") {
              var task_title = task_nodes.childNodes[k].
              ➡ firstChild.nodeValue;
          }
          if(task_nodes.childNodes[k].nodeName
          ➡ =="description") {
            var task_description = task_nodes.
            childNodes[k].firstChild.nodeValue;
          }
          if(task_nodes.childNodes[k].nodeName == "timer") {
```

```
              var task_timer = task_nodes.
              childNodes[k].firstChild.nodeValue;
            }
          }
          tasks.push({title:task_title,
              description:task_description,
          ➥ timer:task_timer});
        }
      }

      // add the project
      this.__controller.addProject(project_title,
      ➥ project_description);

      // loop through tasks
      for(var i=0; i<tasks.length; i++) {

        // add the task
        var task:Task = this.__controller.addTask
        ➥ (project_title,tasks[i].title,tasks[i].
        ➥ description);
        task.setTaskTimer(Number(tasks[i].timer));

      }

    }
  }
}));
}
```

Summary

That's it—with the import and export features in place, the application is ready for use! This time sheet project gives you a good idea of what typical Flash applications could look like and how to handle them.

There is definitely room for improvement. In particular, the TimeSheetView class is a bottleneck right now; you could rework the code to have the class attach movie clips at runtime that are associated with separate view classes for projects, tasks, etc., and as such delegate some of the work.

Another thing you might want to try is hooking the application up to a backend. Right now it is designed to run standalone either as a desktop or web application, but it would be relatively easy to set up some server-side scripts that take the XML format the application writes out and store it in a database.

Conclusion

This book has aimed to bring together a whole spectrum of topics relating to object-oriented programming with ActionScript 2.0. From discussing the concepts of object-oriented design, to best practices, project planning, frameworks, and data binding, down to complete example applications (such as the one found in this chapter), I've covered invaluable information for you to get started with developing object-oriented ActionScript 2.0 projects.

I've given you an idea of the tools that are available for you to use; I strongly encourage that, after reading this book, you get started on building your own object-oriented Flash/ActionScript applications, and experiment, experiment, experiment, to find what works best for you.

INDEX

Symbols

< smaller than 441
> greater than 441
" double quote 441
% percentage 441
& ampersand 441
' single quote 441
(*) wildcard character
    import statement 67
.as files 66
.swf files
    commenting, ignored in 68

A

abstraction 99
acceptance tests 61
ActionScript
    built-in formatters 396
    calling a JavaScript function 424–427, 429, 431–432, 434
    communication with other languages 434
        calling ActionScript from an application 435
        calling non-JavaScript method 434–435
    creating simple binding 386
        creating EndPoints 386–387
        creating the binding 388
        example 389–395
        specifying a location 387–388
        using execute method 388
    specifying location of data 387
    using formatters 395
    validators 407
        built-in validators 407–408, 410–413
        custom validators 413–415
ActionScript 2.0
    classes compared to prototypes 104
    compared to version 1.0 20
        classes compared to prototypes 21–25
        declaring variables 20–21
        public and private scope 25–27
    strong typing 27–29
    trouble spots 29–30
ActionScript classes
    .as files 66
    anonymous functions 113
    constructors 106
    implementing 116
        Mover class 116
    methods 112
    packages 66
    static properties 109
    syntax 104

ActionScript Settings dialog box
    adding custom classpath location 22
__activeTask property
    TimeSheetModel class 510
Activity UML diagram 41
Add Binding dialog box 409
addCallback method
    ExternalInterface class 424, 429–433
addEventListener method
    IEventDispatcher interface 210, 212
    List component 182
    UIObject class 287, 315
addListener method
    StyleFormat class 265
addProject method
    TimeSheetController class 490, 498
addSound method
    SoundManager class 274
addStyle method
    StyleManager class 267
addTask method
    TimeSheetController class 490
aggregation
    compared to composition 486
    relationships 44
Alert component 497
all.pluginName
    document object 430
allowScriptAccess parameter
    values 424
_alpha property
    MovieClip class 249
always value
    allowScriptAccess parameter 424
animation and effects 334
    preparation 334
        Animator class 335–336
    transitioning views 360
        BlurTransition class 371, 373–374
        ColorTransition class 369–370
        DissolveTransition class 376, 380
        FadeTransition 363–364
        NoiseTransition class 374–376
        testing transitions 365–367, 369
        Transition class 361–363
        WaterTransition class 376, 380
    tweening properties and events 336
        easer 341–343
        enhancing Tweener 347–349, 351, 354
        motion blur 357–360
        Mover class 354–357
        testing Tweener 344–346
        Tweener class 336–339, 341

Animator class
   dispatchEvent method 335
   importing into Tweener class 337
anonymous functions 113
applyBlur method
   BlurTransition class 373
array of strings
   specifying location of data 387
arrays, description 14
assignSounds method
   soundManager class 329
association relationship 43
attachGraphics method
   InterfaceTest class 319
   SimpleButton class 284, 321, 323
   UIBlock class 283, 293, 302–304
   UIObject class 344
attachGraphics property
   UIBlock class 294
attachMethods method
   SimpleButton class 321
attachMovie method
   MovieClip class 247, 289–290
attachSound method
   SoundManager class 274
attributes, nodes 441
attributes property
   XML class 449
available property
   ExternalInterface class 423

B

base class 122
beginFill method
   MovieClip class 247
beginGradientFill method
   MovieClip class 247, 326
best practices
   commenting 68
   external ActionScript 66
   naming conventions 70
      classess 71
      constants 71
      functions 71
      methods 72
      packages 72
      properties 72
      variables 70
   programming styles 73
Binding class
   execute method 388
   mx.data, description 385
   mx.data.binding package 385

Bindings tab
   Component Inspector 410
BitmapData object
   noise method 374–375
   perlinNoise method 376
   pixelDissolve method 376
Block class
   diagramming 283
Block graphic symbol
   changeState function 307
   creating 304
__blockGraphic property
   SimpleButton class 284
   UIBlock class 283, 293, 304
__blockHolder class 344
blur property
   Mover class 359
BlurFilter class
   importing 357–360
BlurTransition class
   creating 371, 373–374
Boolean formatter 396
   using 396
bottom property
   UIObject class 254, 281
Bouncer class
   applying interface to 150–153
   inheritance 126–128
   testing inheritance 124–125
Bound To dialog box 410
Broadcaster class
   Animator class inherits from 335
   base class for MediaController 204
   creating 210–213
   dispatchEvent method 335
   implementing IEventDispatcher interface 281
browser communication with Flash
   ActionScript communication with other languages 434
      calling ActionScript from an application 435
      calling non-JavaScript method 434–435
   ExternalInterface class 423–424
      addCallback method 429–433
      call method 424–428
      Flash Player 8 security 424
   Flash 7 and below 419
      calling JavaScript from Flash 419–421
      sending variables into Flash 419
      using Flash/JS integration kit 421–422
   introduction 418
buildProjectTree method
   TimeSheetView class 498, 501
Button component 463, 469
Button UI component
   base classes 255

C

Call method
  ExternalInterface class 424–428
callbacks
  good practice for 451
CallFunction method 435
calling functions 15
callTween method
  Tweener class 347, 350
case sensitivity
  ActionScript 2.0 trouble spot 29
case studies
  OOP Media Player 202–239
  time sheet application 484–520
CDATA declarations 442
changeState function
  Block graphic symbol 307
changeState method
  UIBlock class 301
  UIObject class 315
changeState property
  UIBlock class 294
childNodes property
  XML class 449, 452
__children array
  UIObject class 291
__Class array
  UIObject class 310
class hierarchy 122
class keyword 105, 148, 207
Class UML diagram 41
classes
  anonymous functions 113
  as architect's blueprint 146
  building in ActionScript 2.0 22
  constructors 106
  description 16
  implementing
    Mover class 116
    multiple interfaces 152–153
  methods 112
  naming conventions 71
  OOP introduction 3
  static properties 109
  syntax 104
classes property
  UIObject class 310
clear method
  MovieClip class 247
clearInterval method
  IntervalManager class 208, 339
clip property
  Transition class 362

code, definition 12
Collaboration UML diagram 41
ColorTransition class
  creating 369–370
ComboBase class
  extends UIComponent class 255
ComboBox component 182, 469
  base classes 255
commenting
  benchmarks 70
  classes, and 69
  ignored in .swf files 68
  reasons for use 68
communication between browser and Flash. See browser
    communication with Flash
compilation, definition 12
Component Inspector
  Bindings tab 410
  Schema tab 407–408, 411, 413
  setting parameters 316
component property
  EndPoint class 386
Component UML diagram 41
ComponentMixins class
  description 385
  mx.data.binding package 385
components
  interrelationships and interactions between 384
    data binding 384–395
    including validators 406–415
    using formatters 395–406
Compose String formatter 396
  simple example 400
  using 396
composition
  compared to aggregation 486
  composition relationship 44
Concurrent Versions System. See CVS
conditionals, description 16
connect method
  NetConnection class 225
__connection_nc property
  VideoPlayer controller 223
constants, naming conventions 71
constructors 106
__controller property
  TimeSheetView class 489
controlMovie function 432
createChild method
  View class 256
createClassObject method
  InterfaceTest class 319
  UIObject class 253, 290, 319

createEmptyMovieClip method
  MovieClip class 247, 281, 291
createEmptyObject method
  UIObject class 281, 291
createGradientBox method
  Matrix class 326
createObject method
  UIBlock class 293
  UIObject class 253, 281, 290
createSound method
  MediaController class 217
  SWFPlayer class 234
createStyles method
  InterfaceTest class 319, 327
createTextField method
  MovieClip class 247
Cubic class
  easing class 342
  methods 342
_currentframe property
  MovieClip class 249
___currentLoop property
  MediaController class 216
curveTo method
  MovieClip class 247
custom components
  benefits 260
  possible candidates for manager classes 260–261
custom formatters 404–406
CustomFormatter class 396
  custom formatters extend 404
  description 385
  mx.data.binding package 385
CustomValidator class
  description 385
  extending 413
  mx.data.binding package 385
CVS (Concurrent Versions System) 50
  See also TortoiseCVS; MacCVS; WinCVS client
  making changes to files 52
  terminology 51

D

data binding
  creating EndPoints 386–387
  creating simple binding 386
  creating the binding 388
  formatters 395–406
  introduction 384–385
  mx.data.binding package 385–386
  sharing data between components 384
  simple example 389–395
  specifying a location 387–388

  using the execute method 388
  validators 406–415
data flow, planning time sheet application 486
data transfer 40
DataSet component
  schema 407
DataType class
  description 386
  mx.data.binding package 385
Date formatter 396
  using 397
DateChooser component
  extends UIComponent class 255
DateField UI component
  base classes 255
debugging
  strong typing and 20
Decorator pattern 159, 183
  applying pattern 186–188, 190–191
  basic implementation 183–184
  practical implementation 184–186
Delegate class 411, 446
  importing 425
  setting scope for onLoad callback 451
Deployment UML diagram 41
design patterns 158
  implementing 160
    Decorator pattern 183–191
    MVC pattern 191–197
    Observer pattern 160–171
    Singleton pattern 171–183
  understanding 158–159
Design Patterns - Elements of Reusable Object-Oriented
*   Software*
  Gang of Four (GoF) 158
design time, definition 12
destroyChildAt method
  View class 256
destroyObject method
  UIObject class 253
dispatchEvent method
  Animator class 335
  Broadcaster class 219, 335
  IEventDispatcher interface 210, 281
  UIObject class 329
dispatchListener method
  IEventDispatcher interface 213
DissolveTransition class
  creating 376–380
document object
  all.pluginName 430
  getElementById 430
_DoFSCommand suffix
  addinging to function name 420

doLater method
UIObject class 253, 506
draw event
UIObject class 254, 315
drawRect method
Block graphic 316
UIObject class 312
_droptarget property
MovieClip class 250
duplicateMovieClip method
MovieClip class 247
duration property
MP3Player class 239

E

easeFunction function
Transition class 362
easeIn method
Cubic class 342
easeInOut method
Cubic class 342
easeNone method
Linear class 343
easeOut method
Cubic class 342
easing class 342
easing equations
Penner, Robert 341
effects. *See* animation and effects
<embed> tag
generating with FlashTag class 422
name attribute 419–420, 429
sending variables into Flash 419
setting allowScriptAccess parameter 424
swLiveConnect attribute 421
enabled property
MovieClip class 251
UIComponent class 255
UIObject class 282, 288
encapsulation, planning for 35
encapsulation example
code 91
event handler 91
hiding internal details of function 93
testing event handler 94
updating ball properties 95
code improvements
functions 97
properties 96
setting up 84
aligning and locking background 87
converting ball into Library symbol 89
creating layers 85

drawing a ball 88
drawing background 87
updating 104
encoding attribute
XML declarations 443
endFill method
MovieClip class 247
EndPoint class
creating 386–387, 392
description 385
event property 388
location property 387, 399
mx.data.binding package 385
endTransform method
Transition class 362
endTransition event
FadeTransition class 364
Transition class 363
endTransition method
TransitionTest class 367
escape codes
reserved characters 441
esolveGraphic method
UIBlock class 304
event dispatching methods
UIObject class 287
event handler, creating 91
event property
EndPoint class 386, 388
execute method
Binding class 388
execution, definition 12
extends keyword 24, 105, 125, 152
external ActionScript 66
ExternalInterface class
addCallback method 429–433
available property 423
call method 424–428
communication between container and Flash 418
Flash Player 8 security 424
requirements and support 418
understanding 423–424

F

FadeTransition class
creating 363–364
firstChild property
XML class 449
Flash communication with browsers. *See* browser
communication with Flash
Flash 8
setTimeout method 506

Flash ActionScript project analysis 39
  Flash files run on client 39
  securing data sent to server 39
Flash Player 7
  communication with browser 418
Flash Player 8
  security model 424
Flash Player security sandbox 478
  cross-domain policy file 478–479
  System.security.allowDomain() method 478
  using a server-side script to proxy the file 480
Flash/JavaScript Integration Kit
  using 421–422
FlashCall event
  communication with other languages 434–435
FlashProxy object
  creating 422
FlashTag class
  generating object and embed tags 422
FlashVars
  communication between browser and Flash 418
FLVs, controlling 222–227
focusEnabled property
  MovieClip class 251
focusIn event
  UIComponent class 256
focusOut event
  UIComponent class 256
_focusrect property
  MovieClip class 250
for-in loop 165
format method
  TimerUtils class 509–510
formatters
  Boolean formatter 396
  built-in formatters 396
  Compose String formatter 396
  custom formatters 404–406
  Date formatter 397
  Number formatter 397
  Rearrange Fields formatter 397
  simple example 398–401, 403–404
  using 395
Foundation XML for Flash
  Jacobs, Sas 440
_framesloaded property
  MovieClip class 250
framework 242
  See also v2framework
  introduction 242, 244–246
  MovieClip class 246–252
  summary 257
  UIComponent class 255–256

UIObject class 253–255
  View class 256–257
fscommand function 418–419
  compared to benefits of using ExternalInterface class 423
_FSCommand suffix
  addinging to function name 421
functions
  calling functions 15
  description 15
  function parameters 15
  naming conventions 71
  narrowing focus with 97
  simple functions compared to complex function 98

G

Gamma, Erich. *See* Gang of Four
Gang of Four (GoF)
  Design Patterns - Elements of Reusable Object-Oriented Software 158
generalization relationship 44
genericFault method
  PendingCall class 472
getBounds method
  MovieClip class 247
getBytesLoaded method
  MovieClip class 247
getBytesTotal method
  MovieClip class 247
getCategories method 466
  MXNA web service 457–458
  WebService class 465
getChild method
  UIObject class 281
getChildAt method
  View class 256
getDepth method
  MovieClip class 247
getDescription method
  Project class 491
getElementById
  document object 430
getEnabled method
  UIObject class 282, 288
getFeedsByCategory method 472
  MXNA web service 460
getFocus method
  UIComponent class 255
getGraphic method
  UIBlock class 304
  UIObject class 321
getInstanceAtDepth method
  MovieClip class 247

getInterval method
  Tweener class 349
getNextHighestDepth method
  MovieClip class 248
getStyle method
  UIObject class 253
getSWFVersion method
  MovieClip class 248
getTasksByProject method
  TimeSheetController class 505
getTaskTimer method
  TimeSheetModel class 510
getTextSnapshot method
  MovieClip class 248
getTitle method
  Project class 491
getTweenID method
  Tweener class 349–350
getURL function 418–419
getURL method
  MovieClip class 248
globalGraphic property
  UIBlock class 304, 306–307
globalToLocal method
  MovieClip class 248
GoF (Gang of Four)
  *Design Patterns - Elements of Reusable Object-Oriented
    Software* 158
gotoAndPlay method
  MovieClip class 248
gotoAndStop method
  MovieClip class 248
GradientBorderRect class
  creating 325–327
__graphic property
  UIBlock class 294, 302
__graphic_mc property
  UIBlock class 293
Gravity class
  implementing empty interface 153–155
  inheritance 129–132

H

halt method
  FadeTransition class 364
  Transition class 363
haltTween method
  Tweener class 337, 350
_height property
  MovieClip class 250
  UIObject class 254, 287
Helm, Richard. *See* Gang of Four

hide event
  UIObject class 254
hitArea property
  MovieClip class 251
hitTest method
  MovieClip class 248

I

IAudible interface
  creating 214
ID attribute
  <object> tag 419–420, 429
IDE, definition 12
idMap property
  XML class 441, 453
IEventDispatcher
  defining 209–213
IEventDispatcher interface
  addEventListener method 281
  implemented by Broadcaster class 204, 281
  implemented by UIObject class 286
if-then-else statement 16
ignoreWhite property
  XML class 447
implements keyword
  adding to Mover class 149
import statements 22
  (*) wildcard character 67
  frames, and 67
  instantiating classes 23
importXML method
  TimeSheetView class 515
inheritance 105, 122
  Bouncer class 126–128
  class hierarchy 122
  Gravity class 129–132
  OOP introduction 8
  planning for 36
  summary 133
  syntax 125–126
  testing 122–125
init method
  MediaController class 217
  UIObject class 286
initController method
  MediaController class 217, 223, 230
__initialHeight property
  UIObject class 287
__initialized property
  UIObject class 302
initializeLayout method
  TimeSheetView class 489, 493, 495–496, 506

__initialWidth property
    UIObject class 287–288
inline comments 69
interface keyword 148
interfaces 146
    implementing 148–155
    overview 146
    sample interface 147
    use-cases 147
InterfaceTest class
    createStyles method 327
    creating 317, 323–324
interrelationships between components 384
    data binding 384–395
    including validators 406–415
    using formatters 395–406
_interval property
    MediaController class 216
__intervalID property
    IntervalManager class 207–208
IntervalManager class
    building 207–209
    clearInterval method 339
    importing into Tweener class 337
    IntervalManager method 338
    manages intervals called by classes 204
IntervalManager method
    IntervalManager class 338
__intervals property
    Tweener class 338
intervalTime property
    Tweener class 338
intrinsic classes 244
    example 245
invalidate method
    UIObject class 253
IPlayable interface
    creating 214
    media controller methods 204
    methods to control playback of SWFPlayer class 234
    startMedia method 225
ispatchEvent method
    UIObject class 287
iteration planning 60

J

Jacobs, Sas
    Foundation XML for Flash 440
Johnson, Ralph. *See* Gang of Four

K

Key object 252
keyDown event
    UIComponent class 256
keyUp event
    UIComponent class 256
keywords
    planning time sheet application 485
    structuring time sheet application 485

L

Label component 469
    extends UIObject class 253
lastChild property
    XML class 449
left property
    UIObject class 254, 281
Library symbols
    converting ball into 89
Linear class
    easeNone method 343
lineStyle method
    MovieClip class 248
lineTo method
    MovieClip class 248
Linkage Properties dialog box 24
List component 459, 469
    addEventListener method 182
__listeners property
    IntervalManager class 207
    SoundManager class 273
    StyleManager class 266
load event
    UIObject class 254
loadMedia method
    MediaController class 219
    SWFPlayer class 234
    VideoPlayer class 225
loadMovie method
    MovieClip class 248
loadSound method
    Sound class 239
    SoundManager class 274
loadVariables method
    MovieClip class 248
localToGlobal method
    MovieClip class 248
location property
    EndPoint class 386–387, 399

_lockroot property
  MovieClip class 250
__loop property
  MediaController class 216, 222
loops, description 16

M

MacCVS 52
Macromedia XML News Aggregator. *See* MXNA
Make New Module dialog box 54
manager classes 260
  building managers 263
    adding style 269–272
    SoundManager class 272–274
    StyleFormat class 263–265
    StyleManager class 266, 268–269
    testing 275–276
  planning the framework 260
    candidates for manager classes 260–261
    diagramming the classes 261
Matrix class
  createGradientBox method 326
Media Player case study
  building 206
    controlling FLVs 222–226, 228
    controlling media 215–222
    controlling SWFs 229–230, 232–236
    IEventDispatcher interface 209–213
    IntervalManager class 207–209
    media interfaces 214
    MP3Player class 238
    SWF view 236, 238
    video view 228–229
  defining interfaces 209
  planning 202
    class structure 204
    interface 203
    MVC model 202
__mediaClip property
  MediaController class 216, 223
MediaController class
  defining common methods and properties for media
      controllers 204
  defining properties 215–216
  initController method 230, 232
  private methods 216–217
  public methods 218–222
__mediaDuration property
  MediaController class 216
__mediaFile property
  MediaController class 216

__mediaHeight property
  VideoPlayer controller 223
__mediaWidth property
  VideoPlayer controller 223
MenuBar component
  extends UIComponent class 255
  navigating application 493
  onProjectMenuChange method 495
  Project menu 495
methods, naming conventions 72
__model property
  TimeSheetController class 491
  TimeSheetView class 489
Model, View, and Controller pattern. *See* MVC patten
modules, planning time sheet application 485
move method
  UIObject class 253, 254
Mover class
  applying interface to 148–150
  blur property 359
  creating 354–357
  implementing 116
  startMoving method 126, 136, 147
  testing inheritance 122–125
moveTo method
  MovieClip class 248
MovieClip class
  accessing 244
  attachMovie method 289–290
  beginGradientFill method 326
  createEmptyMovieClip method 281
  events 251–252
  methods 247–249
  properties 249–251
  UI components derive from 242
  understanding 246
  _x property 281
  _y property 281
MovieClipLoader class
  loading SWFs 232
MP3Player class
  buildling 238
  properties and methods inherited from MediaPlayer 204
multiple values
  storing in arrays 14
MVC pattern 159, 191
  basic implementation 192–193
  planning time sheet application 486
  practical implementation 193–196
  putting it all together 196–197
  TimeSheetController class as controller 490
  TimeSheetModel class as model 487
  TimeSheetView class as view 488
  utilizing for OOP Media Player 202

mx.data.binding package
classes 385–386
MXNA web service 456
getCategories method 457–458, 466
getFeedsByCategory method 460, 472

N

name attribute
<embed> tag 419–420, 429
_name property
MovieClip class 250
naming conventions
classes 71
constants 71
functions 71
methods 72
packages 72
properties 72
variables 70
NetStream class 225
onMetaData method 225
onStatus method 225
pause method 226
seek method 226
never value
allowScriptAccess parameter 424
new keyword 104
nextFrame method
MovieClip class 249
nextSibling property
XML class 449
nodeName property
XML class 449
nodes
attributes 441
understanding XML 440
nodeValue property
XML class 449
noise method
BitmapData object 374–375
NoiseTransition class
creating 374–376
Number formatter
using 397
Number Formatter formatter 396
numChildren property
View class 257
NumericStepper component
extends UIComponent class 255
___numLoops property
MediaController class 216, 222

O

Object class
registerClass method 290
Object Oriented Programming. *See* OOP
<object> tag
generating with FlashTag class 422
ID attribute 419–420, 429
sending variables into Flash 419
setting allowScriptAccess parameter 424
Object UML diagram 41
objects
as houses built from blueprint 146
description 16
OOP introduction 3
specifying location of data 387
Observer class
TimeSheetModel class extends 487
Observer pattern 159–160
basic implementation 160–166
practical implementation 167–169
extending 169–171
utilizing for controller media classes 204
offButton event
SimpleButton class 284
onButtonClick function 463
onButtonRelease handler
SimpleButton class 324
onCategoryChange function 472
onData event
MovieClip class 251
onData property
XML class 448
onDragOut event
MovieClip class 251
onDragOver event
MovieClip class 251
one-to-one relationships
Singleton design pattern 486
onEnterFrame event
MovieClip class 251
onEnterFrame function 233, 360, 506
onFault function
PendingCall class 465–466
onGetCategories() function 458
onHTTPStatus property
XML class 448
onKeyDown event
MovieClip class 252
onKeyUp event
MovieClip class 252
onKillFocus event
MovieClip class 252

onLoad event
  MovieClip class 252
onLoad property
  XML class 448, 452
onLoadInit method
  SWFPlayer class 232
onMetaData method
  NetStream class 225
onMouseDown event
  MovieClip class 252
onMouseMove event
  MovieClip class 252
onMouseUp event
  MovieClip class 252
onPress event
  MovieClip class 252
onProjectChange method
  Tree component 506
onProjectMenuChange method
  TimeSheetView class 495–496
onRelease event
  MovieClip class 252
onReleaseOutside event
  MovieClip class 252
onResult function
  PendingCall class 465
onRollOut event
  MovieClip class 252
onRollOver event
  MovieClip class 252
onSetFocus event
  MovieClip class 252
onStatus method
  NetStream class 225
onTaskMenuChange method
  TimeSheetView class 502
onToolsChange method
  Tools menu 512
onToolsMenuChange method
  TimeSheetView class 512
onUnload event
  MovieClip class 252
OOP (Object-Oriented Programming)
  introduction 2
    classes and objects 3
    inheritance 8
    polymorphism 7
    properties 3
OOP concepts 16
  encapsulation 84
OOP guidelines
  analyzing Flash ActionScript project 39
  planning 34
  UML modeling 40

OOP Media Player. See Media Player
operation property
  TimeSheetModel class 498
__outerSWFHolder_mc property
  SWFPlayer class 230
outputString function 30
__overButton property
  SimpleButton class 284

P

packages 22
  ActionScript classes 66
  naming conventions 72
pair development 61
__pan property
  MediaController class 216
parameters
  for functions 15
_parent property
  MovieClip class 250
parentNode property
  XML class 449
parsing data 40
pause method
  NetStream class 226
__paused property
  MediaController class 216, 219
pauseMedia method
  IPlayable interface 214
  MediaController class 219
  VideoPlayer class 226
PendingCall class 473
  callback functions 465
  genericFault method 472
  onFault function 466
Penner, Robert
  easing equations 341
perlinNoise method
  BitmapData object 376
pixelDissolve method
  BitmapData object 376
planning 34
  encapsulation 35
  importance 34
  inheritance 36
  reusability 35
play method
  MovieClip class 249
__playing property
  MediaController class 216, 219
Point object
  position property 281

polymorphism 136
  basic concept of polymorphism 138–139
  example 136–138
  function names 138
  functional polymorphism at work 139–142
  implementing for application reuse 138
  OOP introduction 7
position property
  MP3Player class 239
  Point object 281
  UIObject class 281
pressButton event
  SimpleButton class 284
___pressedButton property
  SimpleButton class 284
prevFrame method
  MovieClip class 249
previousSibling property
  XML class 449
private scope 25
procedural programming 2
programming approaches 58
  RAD methodology 59
  usability testing 62
  XP methodology 60
programming concepts 12
  building blocks 13–16
  definitions 12
  OOP concepts 16
programming styles 73
  consistency and spacing 74
  grouping 76
ProgressBar component
  extends UIObject class 253
Project class
  introduction 491
Project menu
  MenuBar component 495
___project property
  Task class 491, 492
project workflow 50
  version control 50
___projects property
  TimeSheetModel class 488
properties
  description 17
  enhancing behavior with 96
  naming conventions 72
  OOP introduction 3
property property
  EndPoint class 386
prototype keyword 104
prototype systems 59
prototypes 21

Q

_quality property
  MovieClip class 250

R

RAD (Rapid Application Development)
  as programing approach 59
  steps 59
Rearrange Fields formatter 396
  using 397
redraw method
  UIObject class 253
refactoring 61
registerClass method
  Object class 290
registerForSound method
  SoundManager class 274
registerSound method
  SoundManager class 274
registerView method
  TimeSheetModel class 487
relationships between keywords
  structuring time sheet application 485
release planning 60
remove method
  UIObject class 291
Remove Project panel 497–498
removeChild method
  UIObject class 291
removeEventListener method
  IEventDispatcher interface 210, 212, 281
  UIObject class 287
removeListener method
  StyleFormat class 265
removeMovieClip method
  MovieClip class 249, 291
removeStyle method
  StyleManager class 267
removeTransitionEffects method
  FadeTransition class 364
repository
  maintaining CVS source code 50
  TortoiseCVS and setting up local repository 52
resize event
  UIObject class 254
resolveGraphic method
  SimpleButton class 321
  UIBlock class 304
results property
  target class 446
  XMLConnector class 384, 386–387, 399, 408
reusability, planning for 35

reveal event
UIObject class 254
right property
UIObject class 254, 281
root nodes
understanding XML 440
_rotation property
MovieClip class 250
runtime, definition 12
runTween method
Tweener class 337–339, 343
runTweenCall method
Tweener class 348, 350–351

S

sameDomain value
allowScriptAccess parameter 424
scale properties
UIObject class 281
scaleMedia method
SWFPlayer class 232
__scaleToClip property
SWFPlayer class 230
scaleX property
UIObject class 254
scaleY property
UIObject class 254
Schema tab
Component Inspector 407–408, 411, 413
scope
definition 21
public and private 25
__scope property
TimeSheetView class 489
Secure Socket Layer
data transfer 40
seek method
IPlayable interface 214
MP3Player class 239
NetStream class 226
Sequence UML diagram 41
server communication 440
web services 456
WebService class 464–475, 477
WebServiceConnector component 456, 458–463
XML 443
declarations 442–443
understanding 440–442
XMLConnector component 443–445, 448–453
setEnabled method
SimpleButton class 323
UIObject class 282, 288

setEvents method
SimpleButton class 321–322
setFocus method
UIComponent class 255
setInterval method
compared to setTimeout method 506
IntervalManager class 204, 207–208
setMask method
MovieClip class 249
setPosition function 22, 24
setSize method
UIBlock class 294, 301
UIObject class 253, 281, 288–289, 315
setSkin method
UIObject class 253
setStyle method
UIObject class 253
setTimeout method
undocumented feature in Flash 8 506
setTransform method
ColorTransition class 370
MediaController class 221
SetVariable function
setting variables into Flash 419
showProjectDetails method
TimeSheetView class 506
showTaskDetails method
TimeSheetView class 506
SimpleButton class
assigning style to 327
creating 320–324
diagramming 284
extends UIComponent class 255
SimpleRect skin
creating 315
Singleton design pattern
one-to-one relationships 486
Singleton pattern 159, 171
basic implementation 172–177
building an interface 181–182
practical implementation 177–180
using for global manager class 266
utilizing for IntervalManager class 204
SOAP, introduction 454–456
software reuse
encapsulation, inheritance and polymorphism 138
Sound class
methods 239
__sound property
MediaController class 216
__sounds property
SoundManager class 273
_soundbuftime property
MovieClip class 250

SoundManager class
    as candidate for manager class 261
soundManager class
    assignSounds method 329
SoundManager class
    building 272–274
    instantiating 276
    UML diagram 262
SSL (Secure Socket Layer)
    data transfer 40
standalone attribute
    XML declarations 443
start method
    FadeTransition class 364
    MP3Player class 239
    Transition class 363
startAlpha property
    FadeTransition class 364
startDrag method
    MovieClip class 249
startMedia method
    IPlayable interface 214, 224–225
    VideoPlayer class 226
startMoving method
    Mover class 126, 136, 147
_startOnLoad property
    MediaController class 216
__startOnLoad property
    MediaController class 222
    SWFPlayer class 232
    VideoPlayer class 225
startTrackProgress method
    MediaController class 217
    SWFPlayer class 233
    VideoPlayer class 224
startTransform method
    Transition class 362
__state property
    UIBlock class 294
Statechart UML diagram 41
static properties 109
static property
    UIBlock class 303
stop method
    MovieClip class 249
    MP3Player class 239
stopDrag method
    MovieClip class 249
stopMedia method
    IPlayable interface 214, 224
    VideoPlayer class 226
__stream property
    SWFPlayer class 230

__stream_ns property
    VideoPlayer controller 223
strong typing
    and code hints 27
    debugging and 20
    description 14
style method
    StyleManager class 268
StyleFormat class
    building 263–265
    dynamic 326
    updateStyles method 311
styleFormat property
    Block instance 309
styleFormatName property
    Block instance 310, 312
StyleManager class
    adding StyleFormat to 327
    as candidate for manager class 261
    building 266, 268–269
    styling Block instances 308–312
    UML diagram 262
__styles property
    StyleManager class 266
subclass 122
super keyword 133
swapDepths method
    MovieClip class 249
SWF files
    commenting, ignored in 68
    controlling 229–230, 232–236
SWF view
    buildling 236, 238
__SWFHolder_mc property
    SWFPlayer class 230
SWFPlayer class
    creating 229–230, 232–236
SWFPlayer controller
    properties and methods inherited from MediaPlayer 204
swLiveConnect attribute
    <embed> tag 421

T

tabChildren property
    MovieClip class 251
tabEnabled property
    MovieClip class 251
tabIndex property
    MovieClip class 251
    UIComponent class 255
    View class 257
target class
    results property 446

_target property
    MovieClip class 250
Task class
    additional properties 491
    introduction 492
___tasks property
    TimeSheetModel class 488
___taskStartTime property
    TimeSheetModel class 510
testing transitions 365–367, 369
text property
    TextArea class 384, 386
    TextInput component 409
TextArea class 469
    importing 411
    text property 384, 386
TextInput class
    extends UIComponent class 255
    importing 411, 431
    text property 409
    validating 411
TextSnapshot object 248
this keyword 109
    ActionScript 2.0 trouble spot 30
    introduction 109
time property
    Transition class 362
time sheet application case study 484
    adding a project 495–498
    adding a task 501, 504–505
    building application 493
    displaying projects 498–501
    finished application 484
    initializing the layout 493, 495
    MVC classes 487
        Project class 491
        TimeSheetController class 490–491
        TimeSheetModel class 487
        TimeSheetView class 488–489
    persisting time sheet data 512–513, 515
    planning application 484
    project and task details 506, 509–510
    running a task timer 510–511
    structuring application 485
    Task class 492
    writing stub code 487
___timer property
    Task class 491, 492
TimerUtils class
    format method 509–510
TimeSheetController class 497
    addProject method 498
    creating 493
    getTasksByProject method 505

planning time sheet application 486
    writing 490
TimeSheetModel class 497
    ___activeTask property 510
    creating 493
    getTaskTimer method 510
    operation property 498
    planning time sheet application 486
    ___taskStartTime property 510
    writing 487
TimeSheetView class
    buildProjectTree method 498, 501
    coding 500
    creating 493
    importXML method 515
    initializeLayout method 493, 495–496, 506
    onProjectMenuChange method 495–496
    onTaskMenuChange method 502
    onToolsMenuChange method 512
    planning time sheet application 486
    showProjectDetails method 506
    showTaskDetails method 506
    update method 498, 505
    writeXML method 513, 515
    writing 488–489
Tools menu
    onToolsChange method 512
top property
    UIObject class 254, 281
TortoiseCVS 52
    setting up local repository 52
    version history 57
TortoiseCVS Add dialog box 55
TortoiseCVS Commit dialog box
    Comment field 56
TortoiseCVS History dialog box
    version history 57
TortoiseCVS initialize repository dialog box 54
TortoiseCVS revision graph 58
_totalframes property
    MovieClip class 250
trace statement 107, 110, 163
traceXML() function 446
trackAsMenu property
    MovieClip class 251
trackProgress method
    MediaController class 218
    SWFPlayer class 233
    VideoPlayer controller 224
Transition class
    creating 361–363
transitionImageIn function
    TransitionTest class 366

transitionImageOut function
    TransitionTest class 366
transitioning views 360
    BlurTransition class 371, 373–374
    ColorTransition class 369–370
    DissolveTransition class 376, 380
    FadeTransition class 363–364
    NoiseTransition class 374–376
    testing transitions 365–367, 369
    Transition class 361–363
    WaterTransition class 376, 380
TransitionTest class
    creating 365–367, 369
Tree component
    displaying the projects and tasks 493
    onProjectChange method 506
    projects listed 498
tween method
    Tweener class 337–339, 343
Tweener class
    callTween method 347, 350
    creating 336–339, 341–343
    enhancing 347–349, 351, 354
    getInterval method 349
    getTweenID method 349–350
    haltTween method 350
    __intervals property 338
    intervalTime property 338
    methods 337
    runTween method 338–339, 343
    runTweenCall method 348, 350–351
    testing 344–346
    tween method 338–339, 343
    __tweenID property 349
    tweenTo method 339, 341, 343
__tweenID property
    Tweener class 349
tweenTo method
    Tweener class 337, 339, 341, 343
type property
    Transition class 362
TypedValue class
    description 386
    mx.data.binding package 385

U

UI components
    base classes derived from 242
UI widgets 280
    adding style 308–312
    attaching from scratch 316–317, 319–320
    basic building block 292–294
    building a component 294, 296–298, 300–301, 303

changing state 307–308
creating foundation 285–292
diagramming classes 280
    Block 283
    SimpleButton 284
    UIObject 280–281
events 320–324
pulliing it all together 325–328
skinning a widget 303–304, 306–307
skinning components 313–314, 316
UIBlock class
    changeState method 301
    creating 292, 294, 303–304
    globalGraphic property 307
    setSize method 301
    static property 303
UIComponent class
    events 256
    methods 255
    properties 255
    UI components derive from 242
    understanding 255
UIObject class
    adding new property 300
    assigning StyleFormat instance to 310
    attachGraphics method 344
    __Class array 310
    classes property 310
    createClassObject method 319
    creating 285–292
    declaring properties 286
    diagramming 280–281
    dispatchEvent method 329
    drawRect method 312
    event dispatching methods 287
    events 254
    extending 506
    implements IEventDispatcher interface 286
    initialization methods 286
    __initialized property 302
    methods 253
    properties 254
    restyle event 315
    UI components derive from 242
    understanding 253
    updateStyles method 315
UML class attributes and methods 42
UML class diagram 42
UML class notation 42
UML modeling 40
    aggregation relationship 44
    association relationship 43
    composition relationship 44
    generalization relationship 44

537

overview of different diagrams 41
planning time sheet application 485
reasons for using 41
UML class attributes and methods 42
UML class diagram 42
UML class notation 42
Unified Modeling Language. *See* UML
unit testing 61
unload event
UIObject class 254
unloadMovie method
MovieClip class 249
update method
TimeSheetView class 498, 505
updateStyles
SimpleButton class 323
updateStyles method
StyleFormat class 265, 311
UIObject class 315
_url property
MovieClip class 250
usability testing 62
Use case UML diagram 41
useHandCursor property
MovieClip class 251

V

v2 framework 242
benefits 260
component architecture class hierarchy 244
validators
built-in validators 407–408, 410–413
custom validators 413–415
introduction 406–407
var keyword 21
variable data 14
variables
ActionScript 2.0 trouble spot 30
arrays 13
conditionals 13
declaring 20
definition 13
description 13
functions 13
loops 13
naming conventions 70
variable data 14
version control 50
CVS 50
video view
building 228–229
_videoEnded
VideoPlayer class 226

VideoPlayer controller
creating 222–226, 228
properties and methods inherited from MediaPlayer 204
View class
methods 256
properties 257
UI components derive from 242
understanding 256
_visible property
MovieClip class 250
visible property
UIObject class 254
Vlissides, John. *See* Gang of Four
__volume property
MediaController class 216

W

WaterTransition class
creating 376–380
web services
introduction 454
talking to 456
WebService class 464–475, 477
WebServiceConnector component 456, 458–463
WebService class 464–475, 477
getCategories method 465
importing 464
WebServiceConnector component 456, 458–463
schema 407
WSDLURL parameter 457
_width property
MovieClip class 250
width property
UIObject class 254
WinCVS client 52
writeXML method
TimeSheetView class 513, 515
WSDLURL parameter
WebServiceConnector component 457

X

_x property
MovieClip class 250, 281
x property
UIObject class 254
XML
understanding 440–442
CDATA declarations 442
declarations 442–443
reserved characters 441

using in Flash 443
  XML class 448–453
  XMLConnector component 443–445
XML class
  childNodes property 452
  idMap property 441, 453
  ignoreWhite property 447
  onLoad property 452
  properties 449–453
  properties that srerve as callbacks 448
  using XML in Flash 447–449
  xmlDecl property 443
XMLConnector class
  binding XML data to UI components 384
  results property 384, 386–387, 399, 408
  schema 407
XMLConnector component
  using XML in Flash 443, 445–447
xmlDecl property
  XML class 443
_xmouse property
  MovieClip class 250
XPath expression
  specifying location of data 387
_xscale property
  MovieClip class 250

Y

_y property
  MovieClip class 251, 281
y property
  UIObject class 254
_ymouse property
  MovieClip class 251
_yscale property
  MovieClip class 251

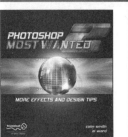

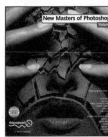